鳥 山 明

Happy New Year! I made my debut as a manga artist on my 23rd New Year, and now, as I write this, I'm facing my 30th. I guess somehow I've "made it" as a manga artist. This is a tough business—if you've got work to do then you are so busy that there's no time to sleep. If you don't have any work, then you don't have anything to do *but* sleep. I don't like to be too busy, but I also don't like to be in a bind, so I try to keep working hard.

—Akira Toriyama, 1986

Artist/writer Akira Toriyama burst onto the manga scene in 1980 with the wildly popular **Dr. Slump**, a science fiction comedy about the adventures of a mad scientist and his android "daughter." In 1984 he created his hit series **Dragon Ball**, which ran until 1995 in Shueisha's best-selling magazine **Weekly Shonen Jump**, and was translated into foreign languages around the world. Since **Dragon Ball**, he has worked on a variety of short series, including **Cowa!**, **Kajika**, **SandLand**, and **Neko Majin**, as well as a children's book, **Toccio the Angel**. He is also known for his work on video games, particularly the **Dragon** ... with his family in Japan.

DRAGON BALL VOL. 2
SHONEN JUMP Manga Edition

STORY AND ART BY
AKIRA TORIYAMA

English Adaptation/Gerard Jones
Translation/Mari Morimoto
Touch-Up Art & Lettering/Wayne Truman
Cover Design/Izumi Evers, Dan Ziegler
Graphics & Design/Sean Lee
Original Editor/Trish Ledoux
Graphic Novel Editor/Jason Thompson

In the original Japanese edition, DRAGON BALL and DRAGON BALL Z
are known collectively as the 42-volume series DRAGON BALL. The
English DRAGON BALL Z was originally volumes 17–42 of the Japanese
DRAGON BALL.

Printed in the U.S.A.

Published by VIZ Media, LLC
P.O. Box 77010
San Francisco, CA 94107

14
First printing, March 2003
Fourteenth printing, April 2017

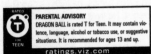

PARENTAL ADVISORY
DRAGON BALL is rated T for Teen. It may contain vio-
lence, language, alcohol or tobacco use, or suggestive
situations. It is recommended for ages 13 and up.

ratings.viz.com

SHONEN JUMP MANGA

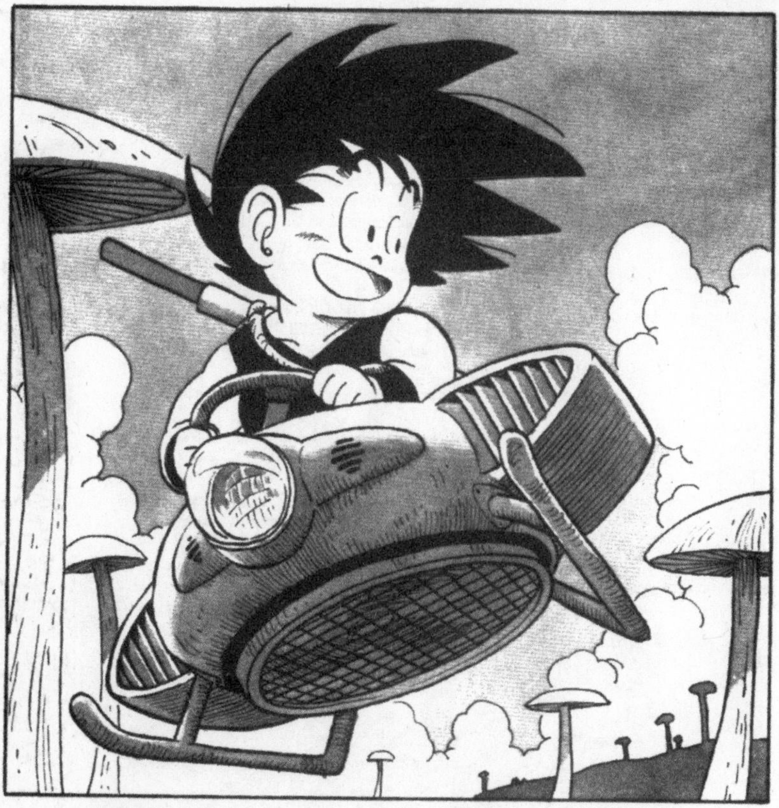

DRAGON BALL

Vol. 2

DB: 2 of 42

STORY AND ART BY

AKIRA TORIYAMA

THE MAIN CHARACTERS

Son Goku
Monkey-tailed young Goku learned kung-fu and inherited the magic *nyoi-bô* staff from his grandfather Gohan. Bulma is the first girl he ever saw.

Yamcha
A martial artist and bandit, Yamcha intends to steal the Dragon Balls from our heroes. His one weakness is that he's scared of girls.

Oolong
Immature, shapeshifting Oolong can change into anything, but only for five minutes at a time. He used to be a villain, but now he has (against his will) joined our heroes.

Pu'ar
Yamcha's shapeshifting friend.

Bulma
A genius inventor, Bulma created the Dragon Radar which detects the location of the Dragon Balls.

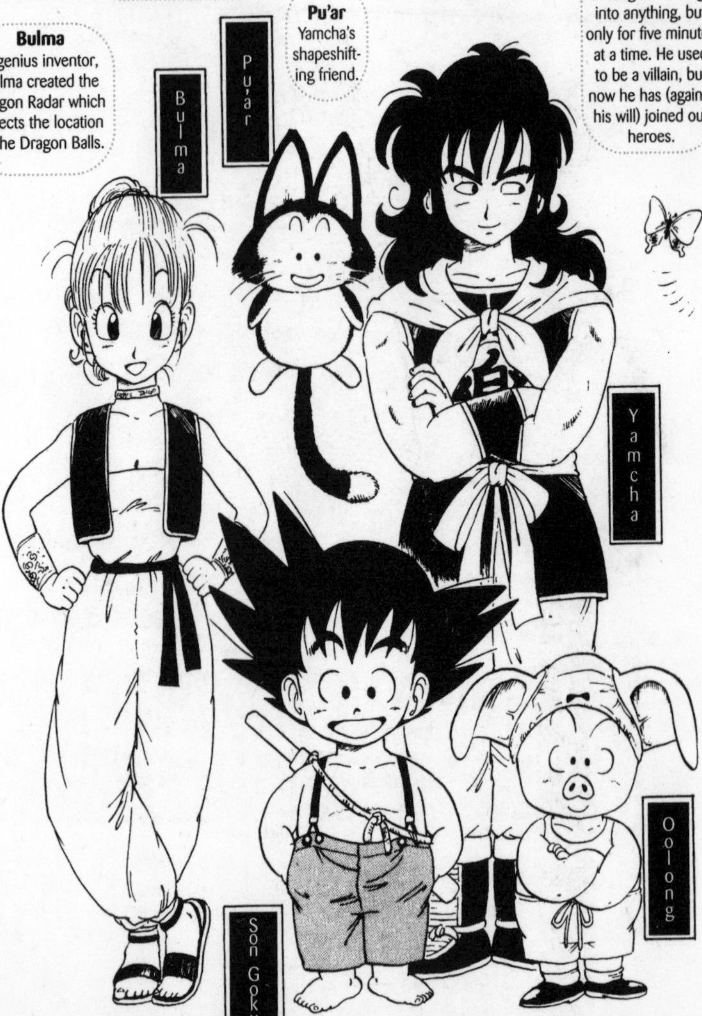
Bulma
Pu'ar
Yamcha
Son Goku
Oolong

Gyû-Maô
The fearsome lord of Fry-Pan Mountain, Gyû-Maô, aka the "Ox King", has been known to deal harshly with trespassers.

Kame-Sen'nin (The "Turtle Hermit")
A mystical dirty old man who gave Goku the *kinto'un*, or flying cloud, and gave Bulma the third Dragon Ball, in return for helping his turtle friend.

Gyû-Maô

Kame-Sen'nin

Chi-Chi

Chi-Chi
A strange girl who Yamcha and Pu'ar ran into. She has a tendency to overreact.

Deep in the mountains lived an innocent boy named Son Goku, until he was found by Bulma, a girl from the city who was searching for the seven magical Dragon Balls. According to legend, when all the Dragon Balls are brought together, Shen Long – the eternal dragon – will appear and grant any one wish. When Bulma saw how strong Goku was, she convinced him to join her on the adventure. Now, they have gathered five of the seven Balls, and along the way, they have met many strange people and things...

DRAGON BALL 2

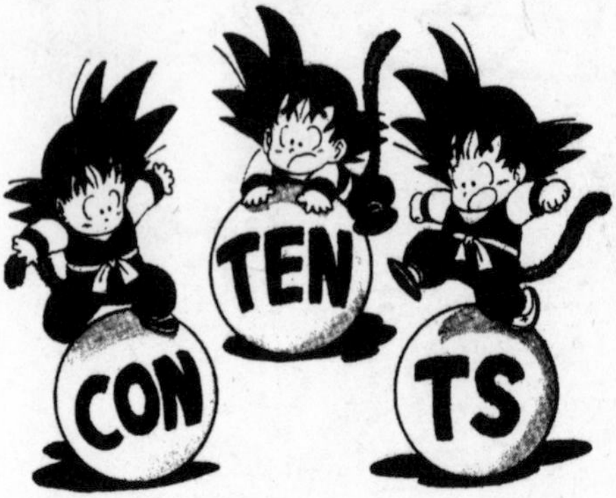
CON
TEN
TS

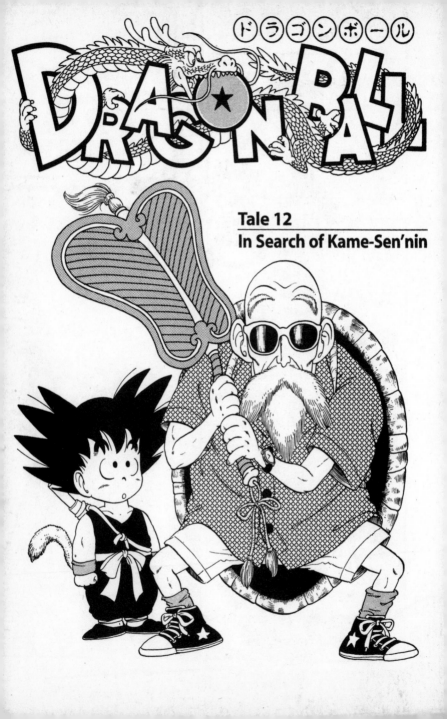

ドラゴンボール

DRAGON BALL

Tale 12
In Search of Kame-Sen'nin

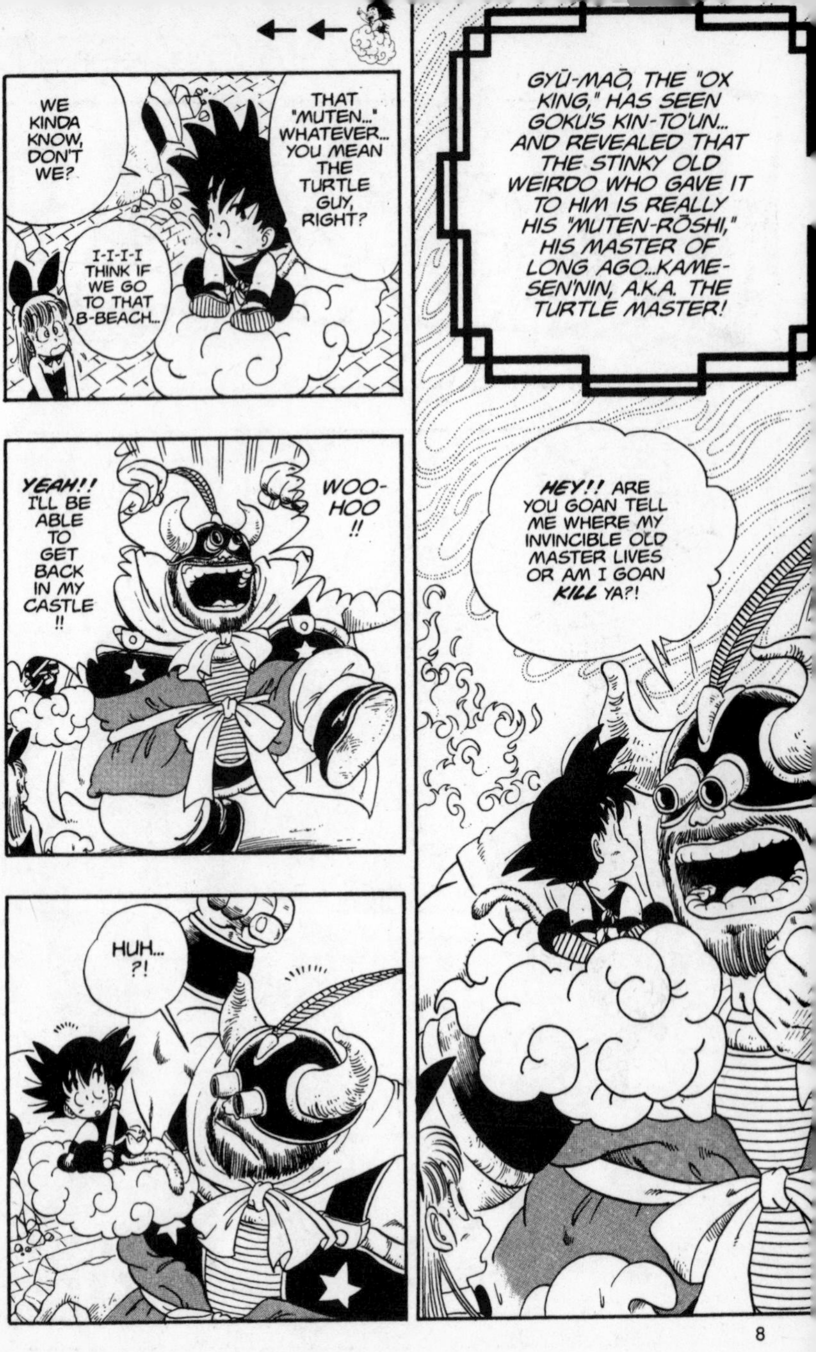
GYŪ-MAŌ, THE "OX KING," HAS SEEN GOKU'S KIN-TO'UN... AND REVEALED THAT THE STINKY OLD WEIRDO WHO GAVE IT TO HIM IS REALLY HIS "MUTEN-RŌSHI," HIS MASTER OF LONG AGO...KAME-SEN'NIN, A.K.A. THE TURTLE MASTER!
HEY!! ARE YOU GOAN TELL ME WHERE MY INVINCIBLE OLD MASTER LIVES OR AM I GOAN KILL YA?!
THAT "MUTEN..." WHATEVER... YOU MEAN THE TURTLE GUY, RIGHT?
WE KINDA KNOW, DON'T WE?
I-I-I-I THINK IF WE GO TO THAT B-BEACH...
WOO-HOO !!
YEAH!! I'LL BE ABLE TO GET BACK IN MY CASTLE !!
HUH... ?!

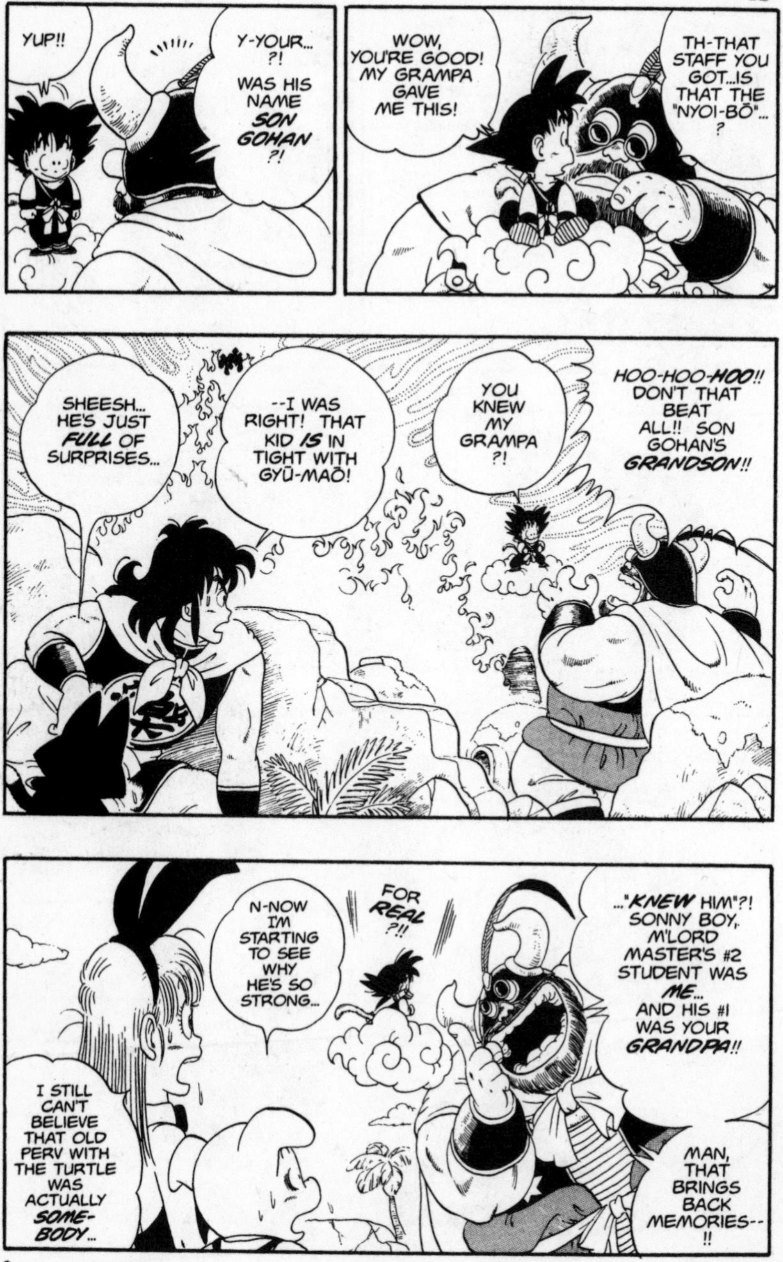
TH-THAT STAFF YOU GOT...IS THAT THE "NYOI-BŌ"... ?
WOW, YOU'RE GOOD! MY GRAMPA GAVE ME THIS!
Y-YOUR... ?! WAS HIS NAME SON GOHAN ?!
YUP!!
HOO-HOO-HOO!! DON'T THAT BEAT ALL!! SON GOHAN'S GRANDSON!!
YOU KNEW MY GRAMPA ?!
--I WAS RIGHT! THAT KID IS IN TIGHT WITH GYŪ-MAŌ!
SHEESH... HE'S JUST FULL OF SURPRISES...
..."KNEW HIM"?! SONNY BOY, M'LORD MASTER'S #2 STUDENT WAS ME... AND HIS #1 WAS YOUR GRANDPA!!
MAN, THAT BRINGS BACK MEMORIES-- !!
FOR REAL ?!!
N-NOW I'M STARTING TO SEE WHY HE'S SO STRONG...
I STILL CAN'T BELIEVE THAT OLD PERV WITH THE TURTLE WAS ACTUALLY SOME-BODY...

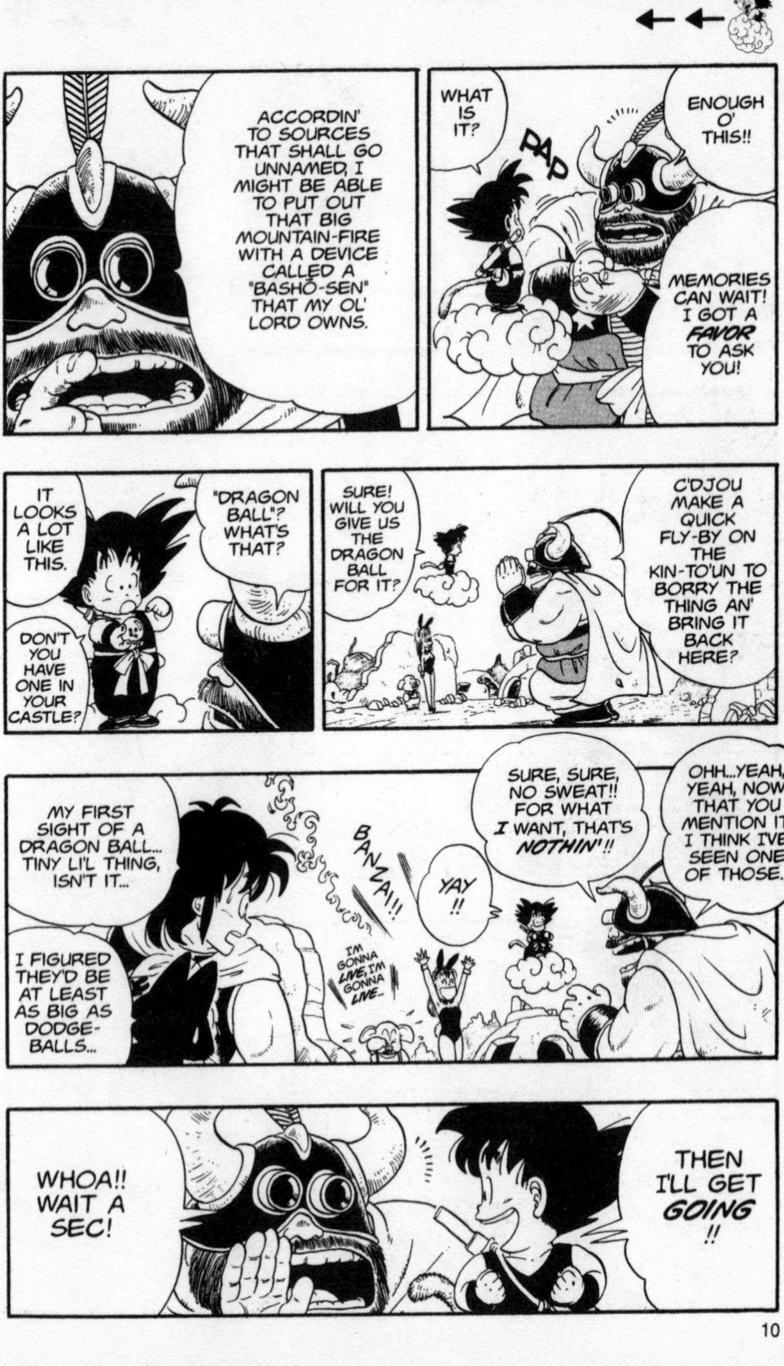
ENOUGH O' THIS!!
PAP
MEMORIES CAN WAIT! I GOT A FAVOR TO ASK YOU!
WHAT IS IT?
ACCORDIN' TO SOURCES THAT SHALL GO UNNAMED, I MIGHT BE ABLE TO PUT OUT THAT BIG MOUNTAIN-FIRE WITH A DEVICE CALLED A "BASHŌ-SEN" THAT MY OL' LORD OWNS.
C'DJOU MAKE A QUICK FLY-BY ON THE KIN-TO'UN TO BORRY THE THING AN' BRING IT BACK HERE?
SURE! WILL YOU GIVE US THE DRAGON BALL FOR IT?
"DRAGON BALL"? WHAT'S THAT?
IT LOOKS A LOT LIKE THIS.
DON'T YOU HAVE ONE IN YOUR CASTLE?
OHH...YEAH, YEAH, NOW THAT YOU MENTION IT, I THINK I'VE SEEN ONE OF THOSE...
SURE, SURE, NO SWEAT!! FOR WHAT I WANT, THAT'S NOTHIN'!!
YAY!!
BANZAI!!
I'M GONNA LIVE, I'M GONNA LIVE...
MY FIRST SIGHT OF A DRAGON BALL... TINY LI'L THING, ISN'T IT...
I FIGURED THEY'D BE AT LEAST AS BIG AS DODGE-BALLS...
THEN I'LL GET GOING!!
WHOA!! WAIT A SEC!

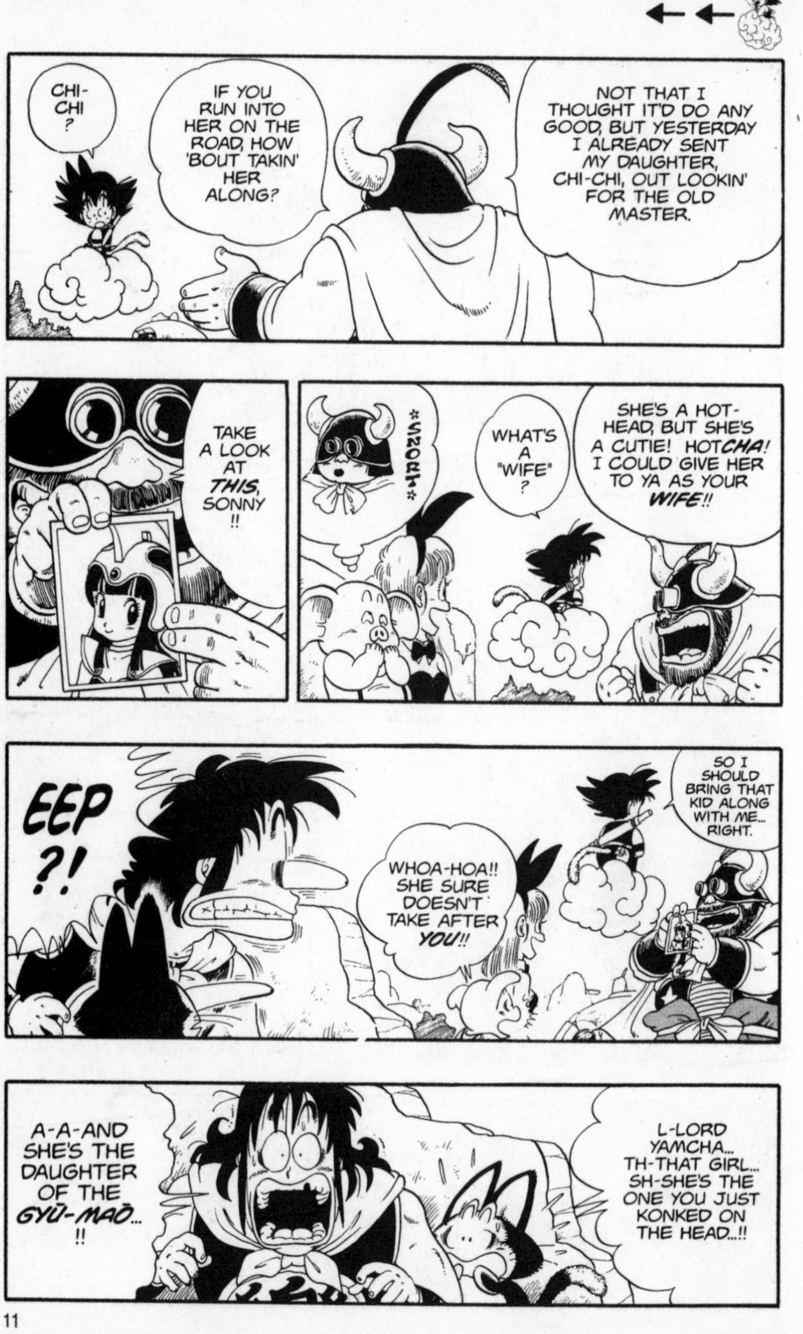
NOT THAT I THOUGHT IT'D DO ANY GOOD, BUT YESTERDAY I ALREADY SENT MY DAUGHTER, CHI-CHI, OUT LOOKIN' FOR THE OLD MASTER.
IF YOU RUN INTO HER ON THE ROAD, HOW 'BOUT TAKIN' HER ALONG?
CHI-CHI?
SHE'S A HOT-HEAD, BUT SHE'S A CUTIE! HOTCHA! I COULD GIVE HER TO YA AS YOUR WIFE!!
WHAT'S A "WIFE"?
SNORK
TAKE A LOOK AT THIS, SONNY!!
SO I SHOULD BRING THAT KID ALONG WITH ME... RIGHT.
WHOA-HOA!! SHE SURE DOESN'T TAKE AFTER YOU!!
EEP ?!
L-LORD YAMCHA... TH-THAT GIRL... SH-SHE'S THE ONE YOU JUST KONKED ON THE HEAD...!!
A-A-AND SHE'S THE DAUGHTER OF THE GYŪ-MAŌ... !!

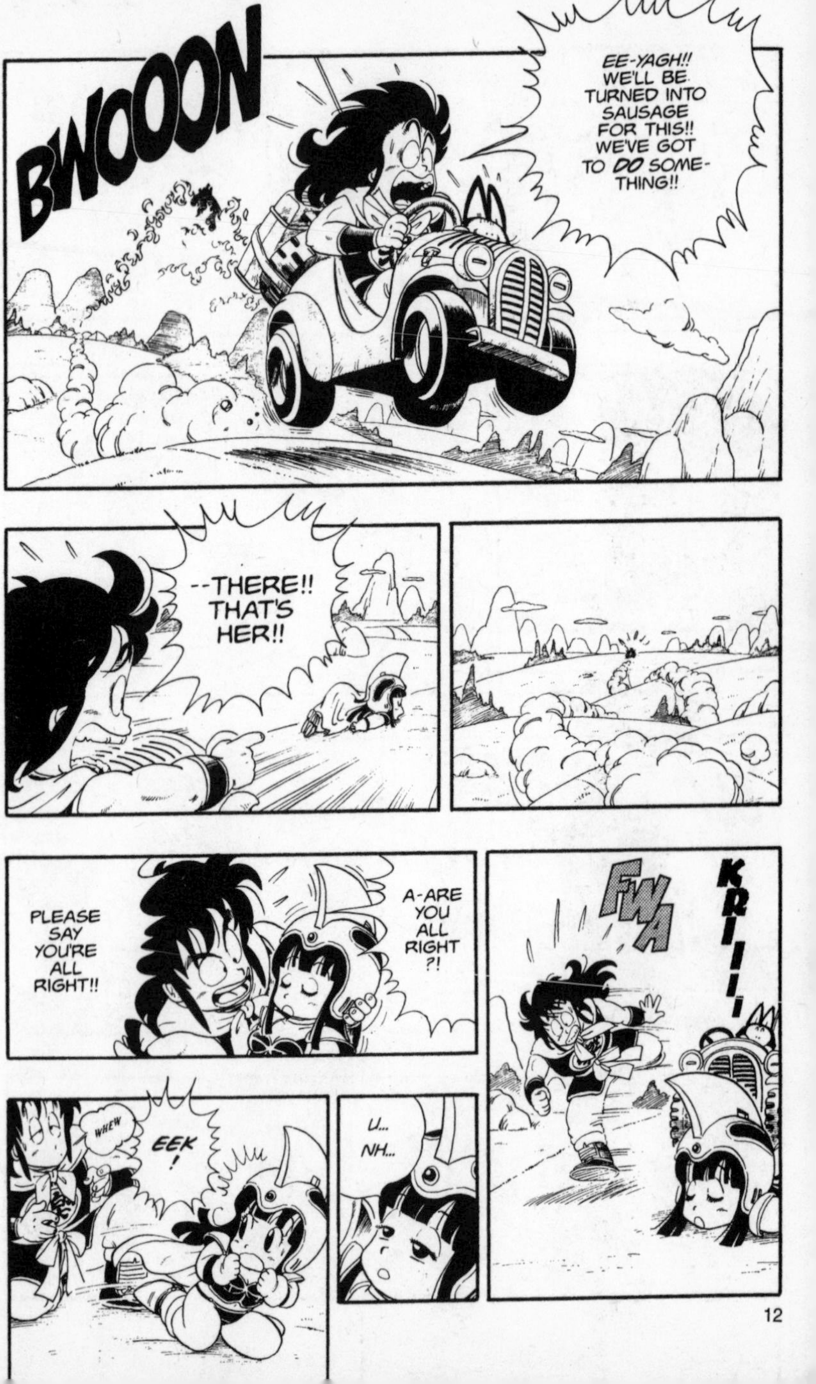
BWOOON
EE-YAGH!! WE'LL BE TURNED INTO SAUSAGE FOR THIS!! WE'VE GOT TO *DO* SOME-THING!!
--THERE!! THAT'S HER!!
FWA
KRIIII
A-ARE YOU ALL RIGHT ?!
PLEASE SAY YOU'RE ALL RIGHT!!
U... NH...
EEK !
WHEW

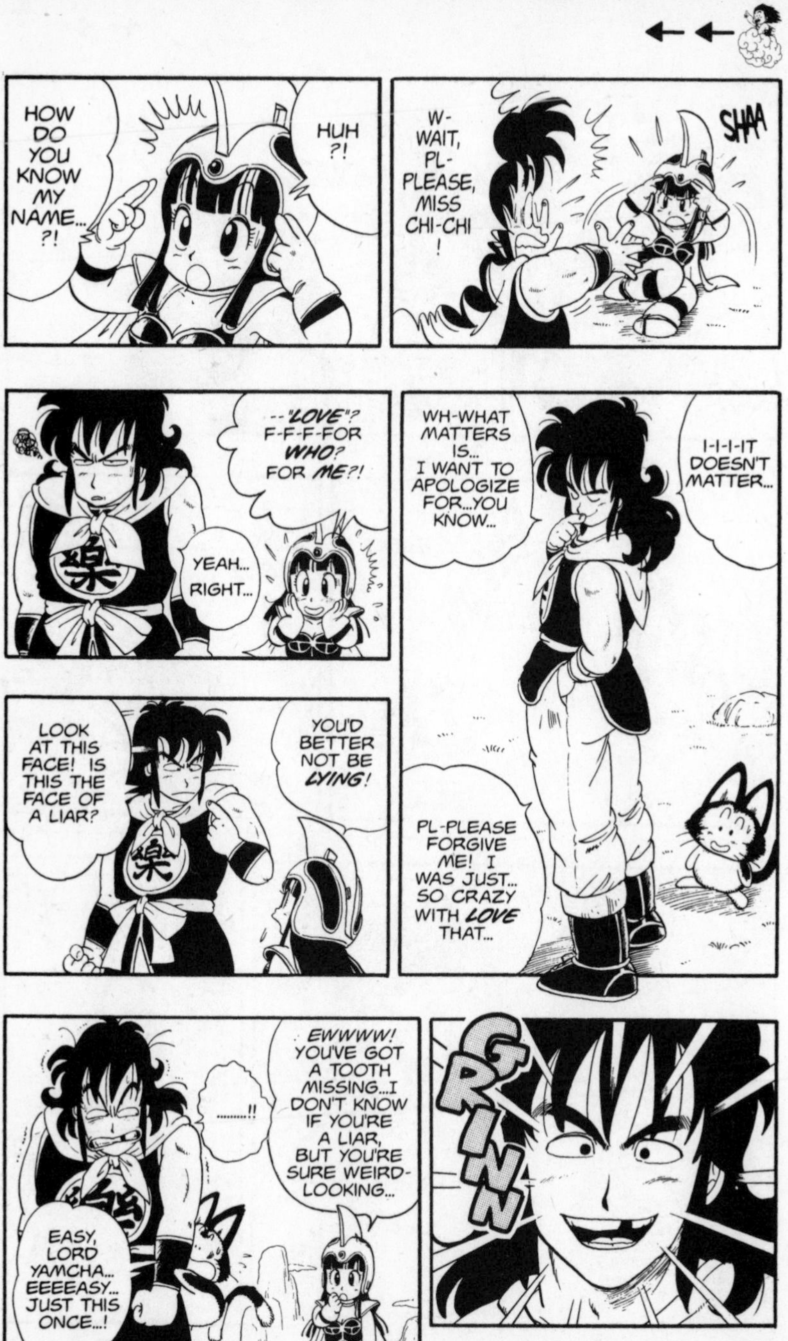

SHAA
W-WAIT, PL-PLEASE, MISS CHI-CHI!
HUH?!
HOW DO YOU KNOW MY NAME...?!
I-I-I-IT DOESN'T MATTER...
WH-WHAT MATTERS IS... I WANT TO APOLOGIZE FOR...YOU KNOW...
PL-PLEASE FORGIVE ME! I WAS JUST... SO CRAZY WITH *LOVE* THAT...
--"*LOVE*"? F-F-F-FOR *WHO*? FOR *ME*?!
YEAH... RIGHT...
YOU'D BETTER NOT BE *LYING*!
LOOK AT THIS FACE! IS THIS THE FACE OF A LIAR?
GRINN
EWWWW! YOU'VE GOT A TOOTH MISSING...I DON'T KNOW IF YOU'RE A LIAR, BUT YOU'RE SURE WEIRD-LOOKING...
.........!!
EASY, LORD YAMCHA... EEEEASY... JUST THIS ONCE...!

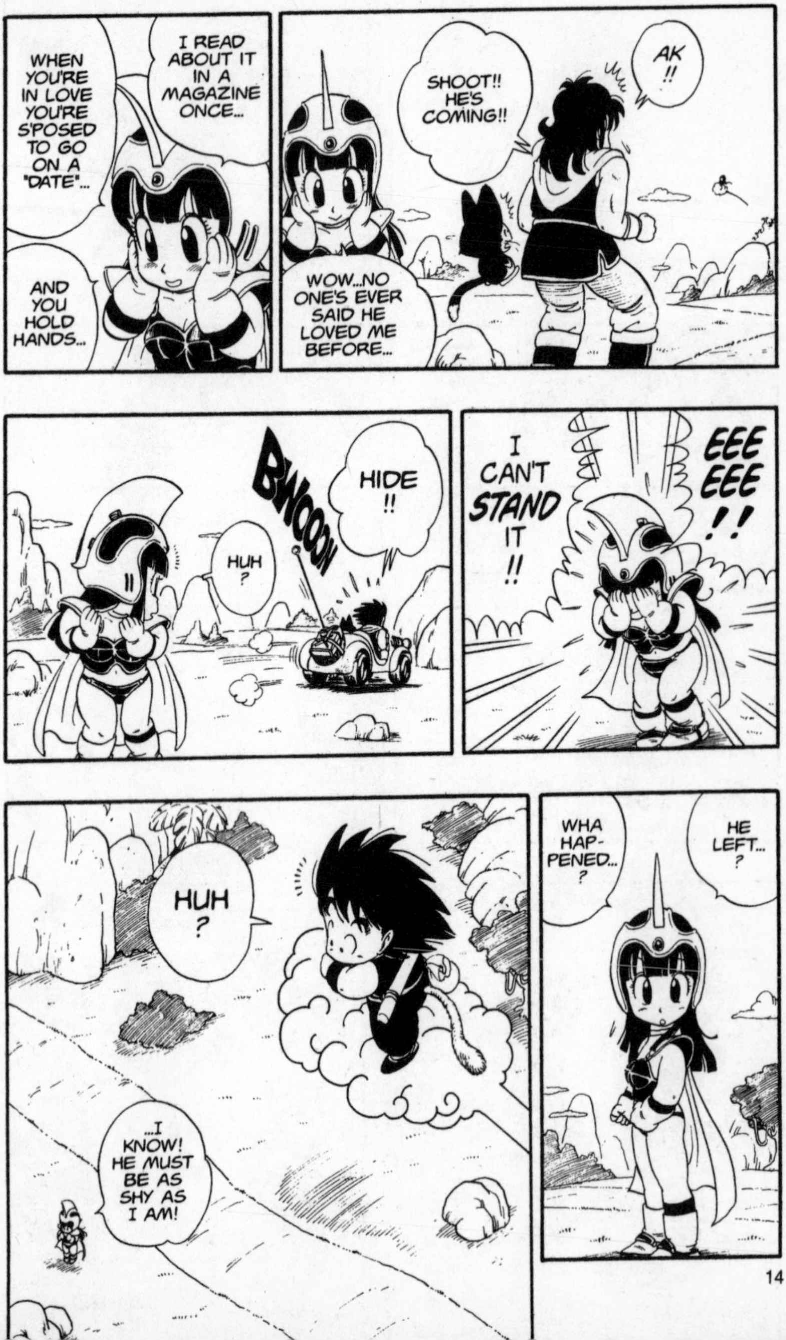
AK !!
SHOOT!! HE'S COMING!!
WOW...NO ONE'S EVER SAID HE LOVED ME BEFORE...
I READ ABOUT IT IN A MAGAZINE ONCE...
WHEN YOU'RE IN LOVE YOU'RE S'POSED TO GO ON A "DATE"...
AND YOU HOLD HANDS...
EEE EEE !!
I CAN'T STAND IT !!
HIDE !!
BWOOOOM
HUH ?
HE LEFT... ?
WHA HAP-PENED... ?
HUH ?
...I KNOW! HE MUST BE AS SHY AS I AM!

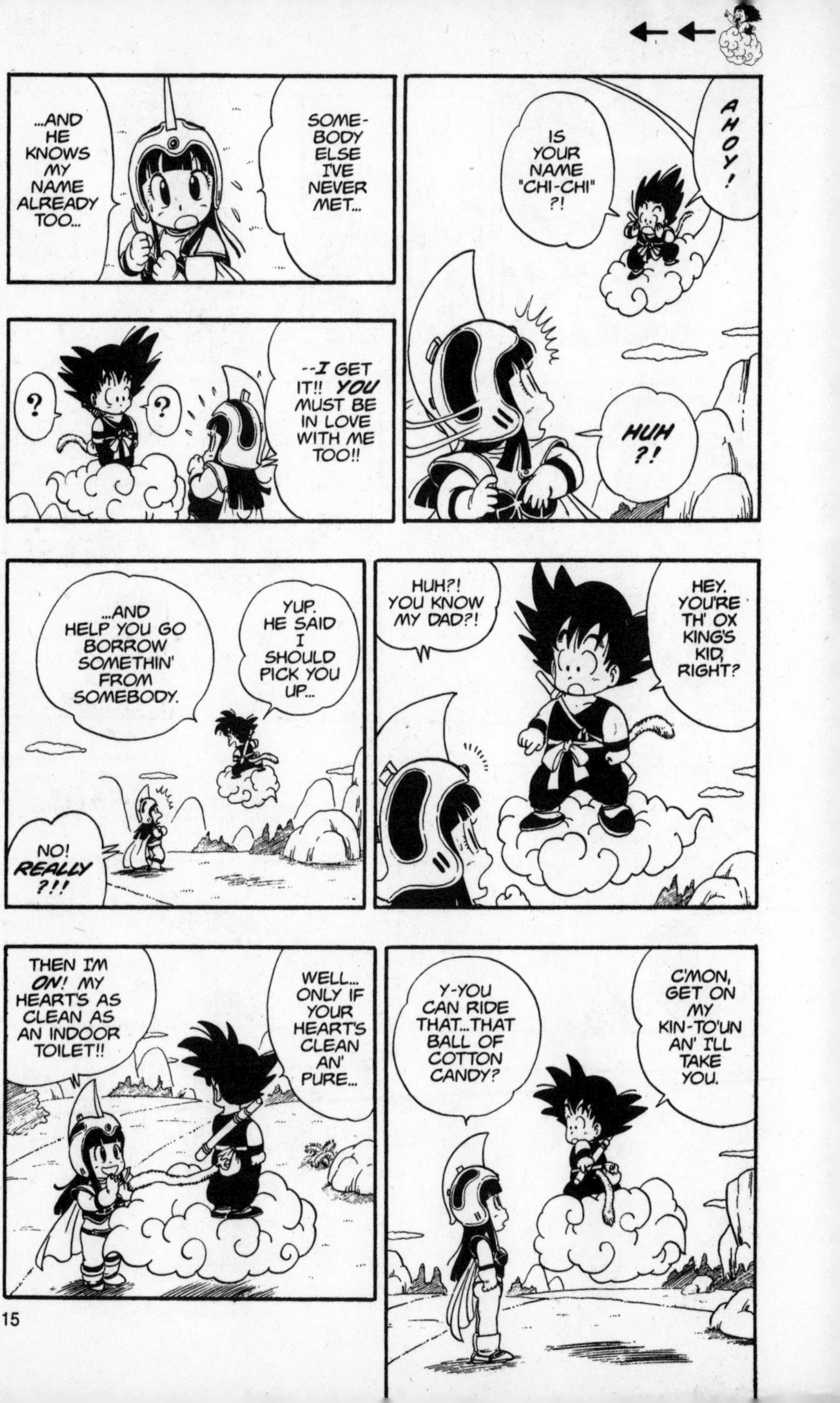
AHOY!
IS YOUR NAME "CHI-CHI" ?!
HUH ?!
SOME-BODY ELSE I'VE NEVER MET...
...AND HE KNOWS MY NAME ALREADY TOO...
--I GET IT!! YOU MUST BE IN LOVE WITH ME TOO!!
?
?
HEY. YOU'RE TH' OX KING'S KID, RIGHT?
HUH?! YOU KNOW MY DAD?!
YUP. HE SAID I SHOULD PICK YOU UP...
...AND HELP YOU GO BORROW SOMETHIN' FROM SOMEBODY.
NO! REALLY ?!!
C'MON, GET ON MY KIN-TO'UN AN' I'LL TAKE YOU.
Y-YOU CAN RIDE THAT...THAT BALL OF COTTON CANDY?
WELL... ONLY IF YOUR HEART'S CLEAN AN' PURE...
THEN I'M ON! MY HEART'S AS CLEAN AS AN INDOOR TOILET!!

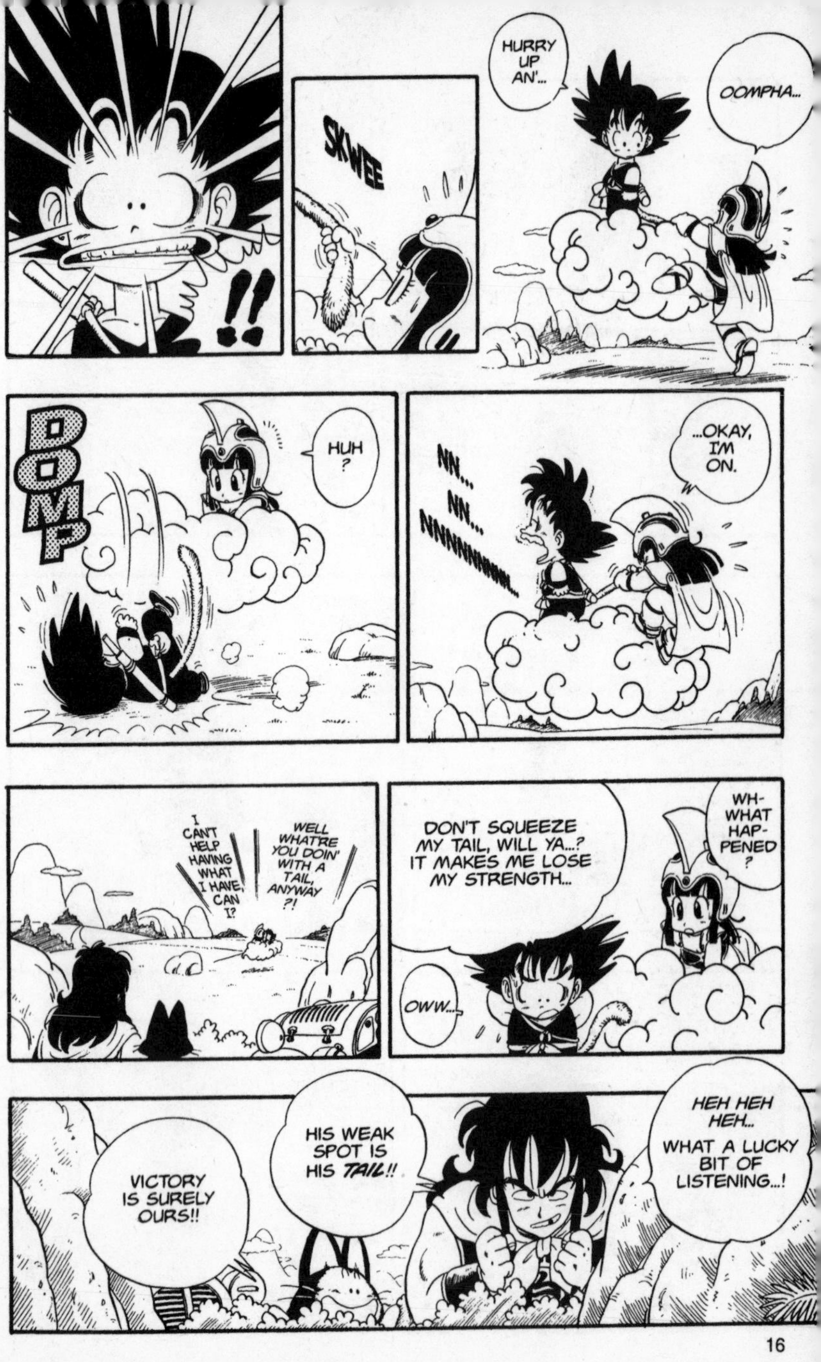
HURRY UP AN'...
OOMPHA...
SKWEE
!!
...OKAY, I'M ON.
NN... NN... NNNNNNNN...
HUH?
DOMP
WH-WHAT HAP-PENED?
DON'T SQUEEZE MY TAIL, WILL YA...? IT MAKES ME LOSE MY STRENGTH...
OWW...
WELL WHAT'RE YOU DOIN' WITH A TAIL, ANYWAY?!
I CAN'T HELP HAVING WHAT I HAVE, CAN I?
HEH HEH HEH... WHAT A LUCKY BIT OF LISTENING...!
HIS WEAK SPOT IS HIS TAIL!!
VICTORY IS SURELY OURS!!

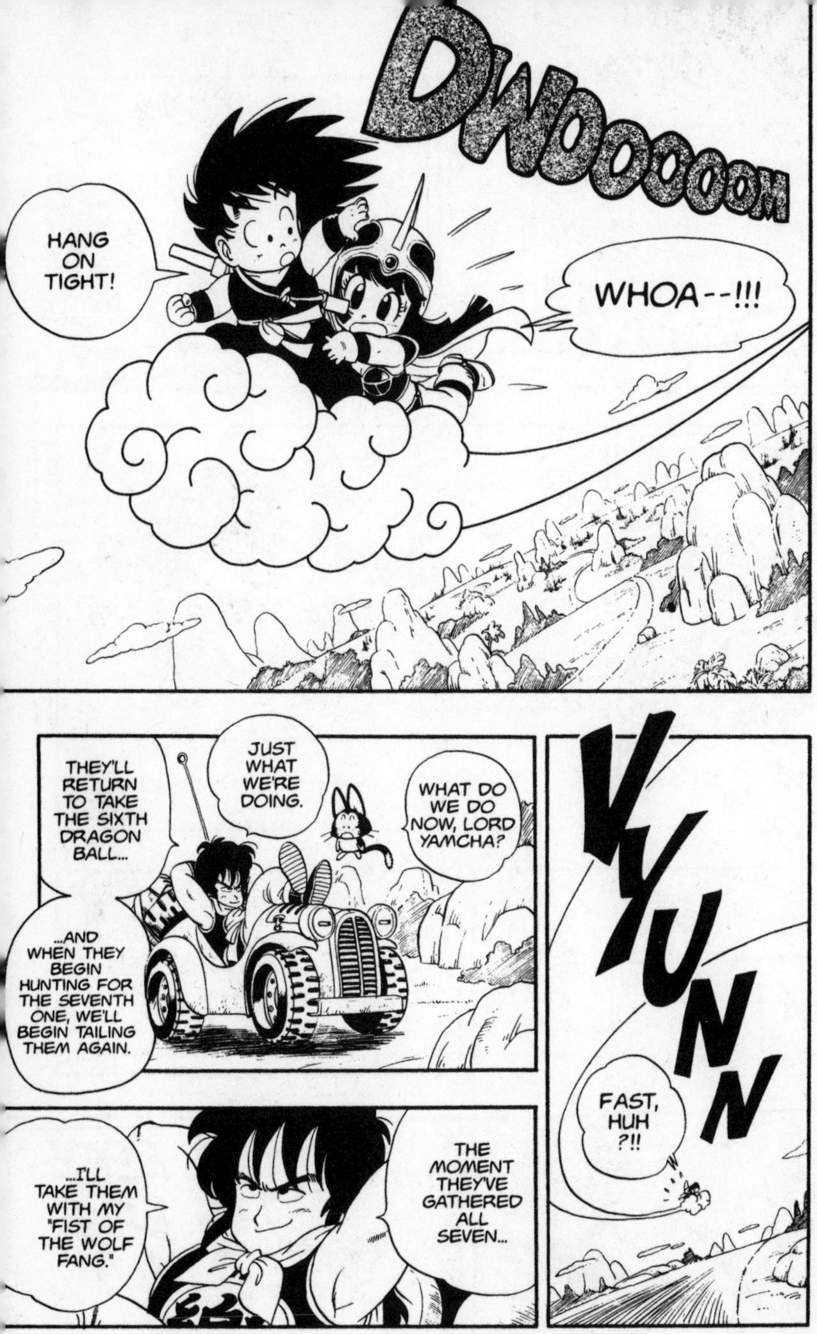
DWOOOOOOOM
WHOA--!!!
HANG ON TIGHT!
VYUNN
FAST, HUH ?!!
WHAT DO WE DO NOW, LORD YAMCHA?
JUST WHAT WE'RE DOING.
THEY'LL RETURN TO TAKE THE SIXTH DRAGON BALL...
...AND WHEN THEY BEGIN HUNTING FOR THE SEVENTH ONE, WE'LL BEGIN TAILING THEM AGAIN.
THE MOMENT THEY'VE GATHERED ALL SEVEN...
...I'LL TAKE THEM WITH MY "FIST OF THE WOLF FANG."

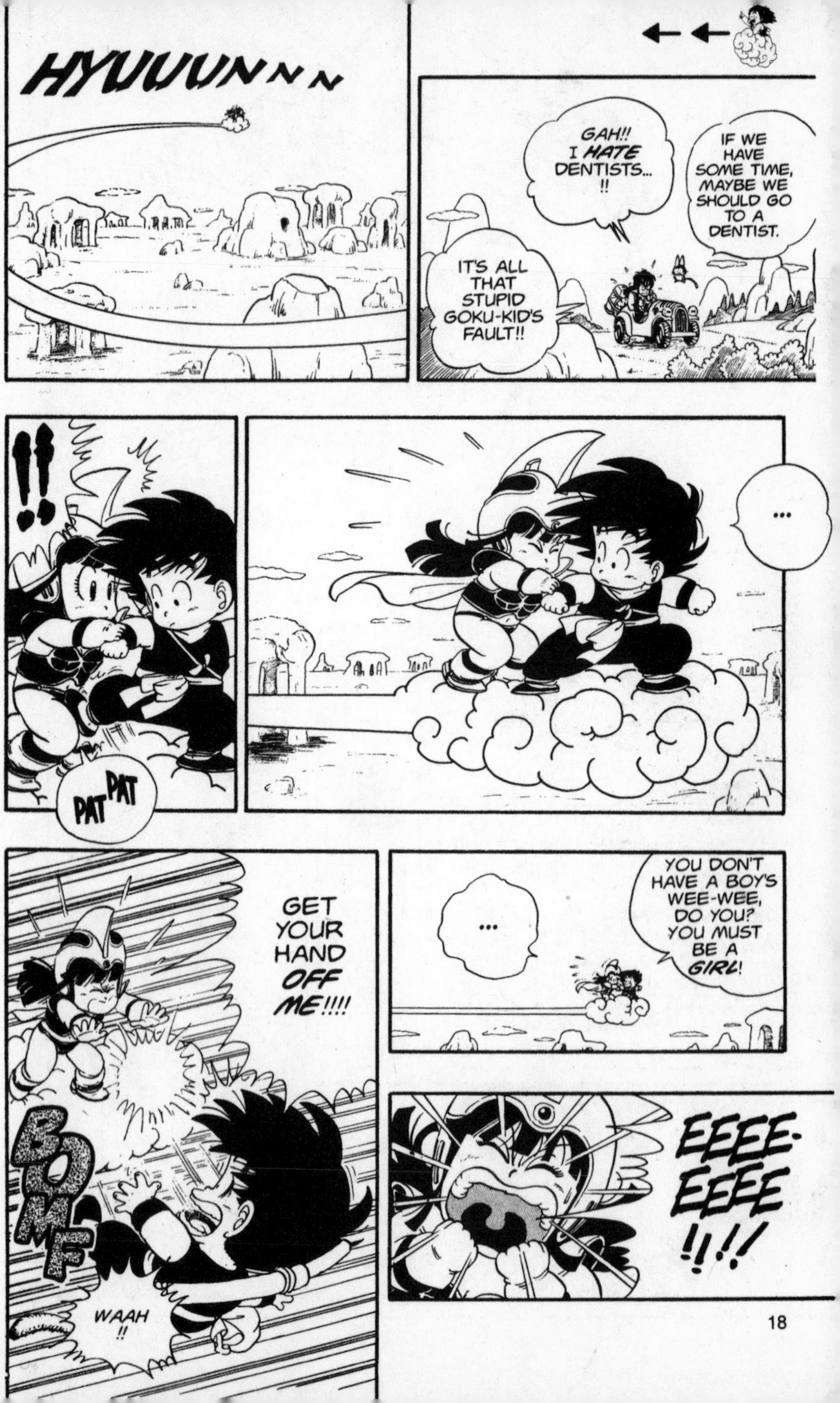
IF WE HAVE SOME TIME, MAYBE WE SHOULD GO TO A DENTIST.
GAH!! I HATE DENTISTS... !!
IT'S ALL THAT STUPID GOKU-KID'S FAULT!!
HYUUUUNNNN
...
!!
PAT PAT
YOU DON'T HAVE A BOY'S WEE-WEE, DO YOU? YOU MUST BE A GIRL!
...
EEEE-EEEE!!!!
GET YOUR HAND OFF ME!!!!
BOMF
WAAH!!

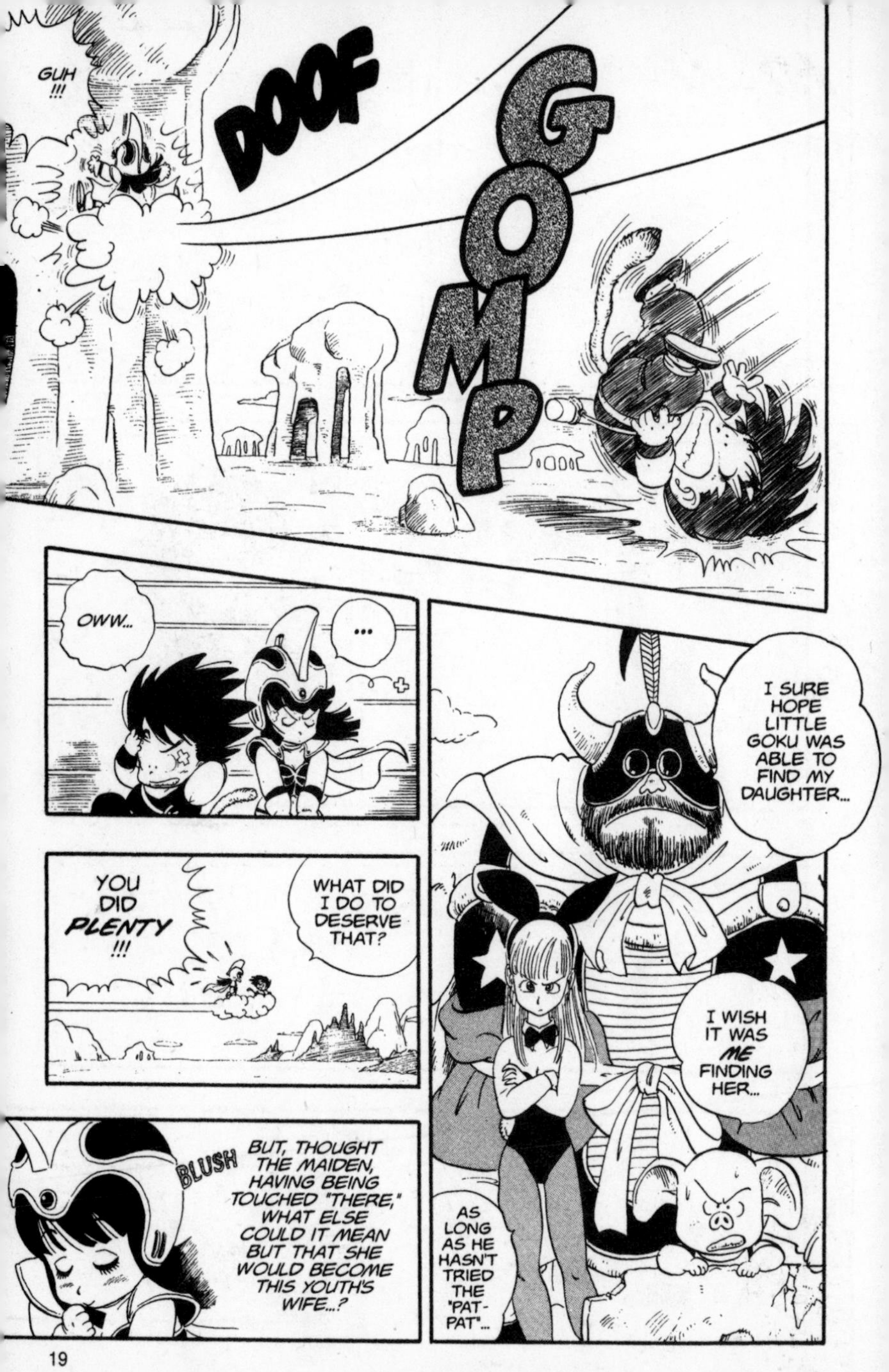
GOMP
DOOF
GUH !!!
I SURE HOPE LITTLE GOKU WAS ABLE TO FIND MY DAUGHTER...
I WISH IT WAS *ME* FINDING HER...
AS LONG AS HE HASN'T TRIED THE "PAT-PAT"...
...
OWW...
WHAT DID I DO TO DESERVE THAT?
YOU DID *PLENTY* !!!
BLUSH
BUT, THOUGHT THE MAIDEN, HAVING BEING TOUCHED "THERE," WHAT ELSE COULD IT MEAN BUT THAT SHE WOULD BECOME THIS YOUTH'S WIFE...?

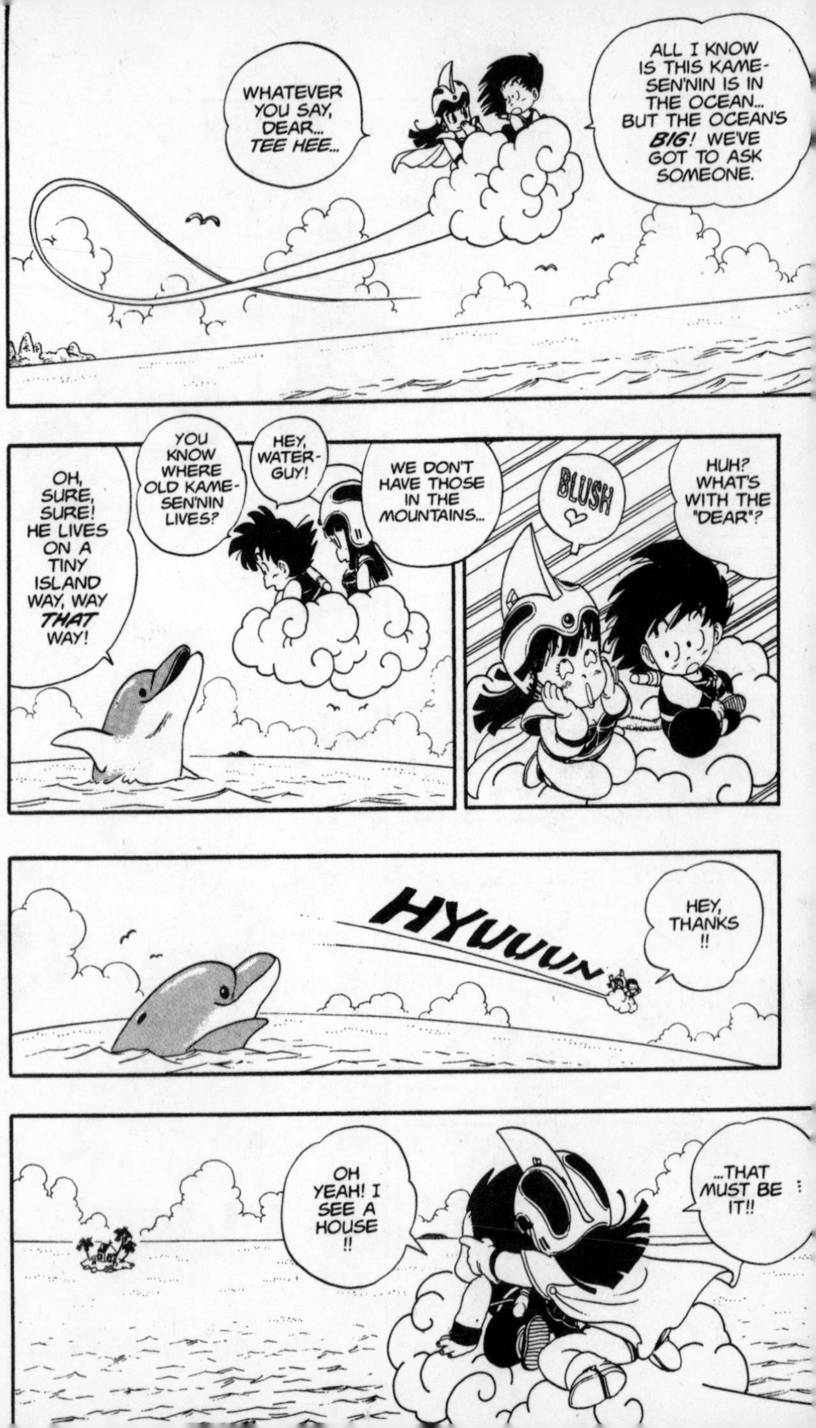
ALL I KNOW IS THIS KAME-SEN'NIN IS IN THE OCEAN... BUT THE OCEAN'S *BIG!* WE'VE GOT TO ASK SOMEONE.
WHATEVER YOU SAY, DEAR... *TEE HEE...*
HUH? WHAT'S WITH THE "DEAR"?
BLUSH
WE DON'T HAVE THOSE IN THE MOUNTAINS...
HEY, WATER-GUY!
YOU KNOW WHERE OLD KAME-SEN'NIN LIVES?
OH, SURE, SURE! HE LIVES ON A TINY ISLAND WAY, WAY *THAT* WAY!
HEY, THANKS !!
HYUUUUN
...THAT MUST BE IT!!
OH YEAH! I SEE A HOUSE !!

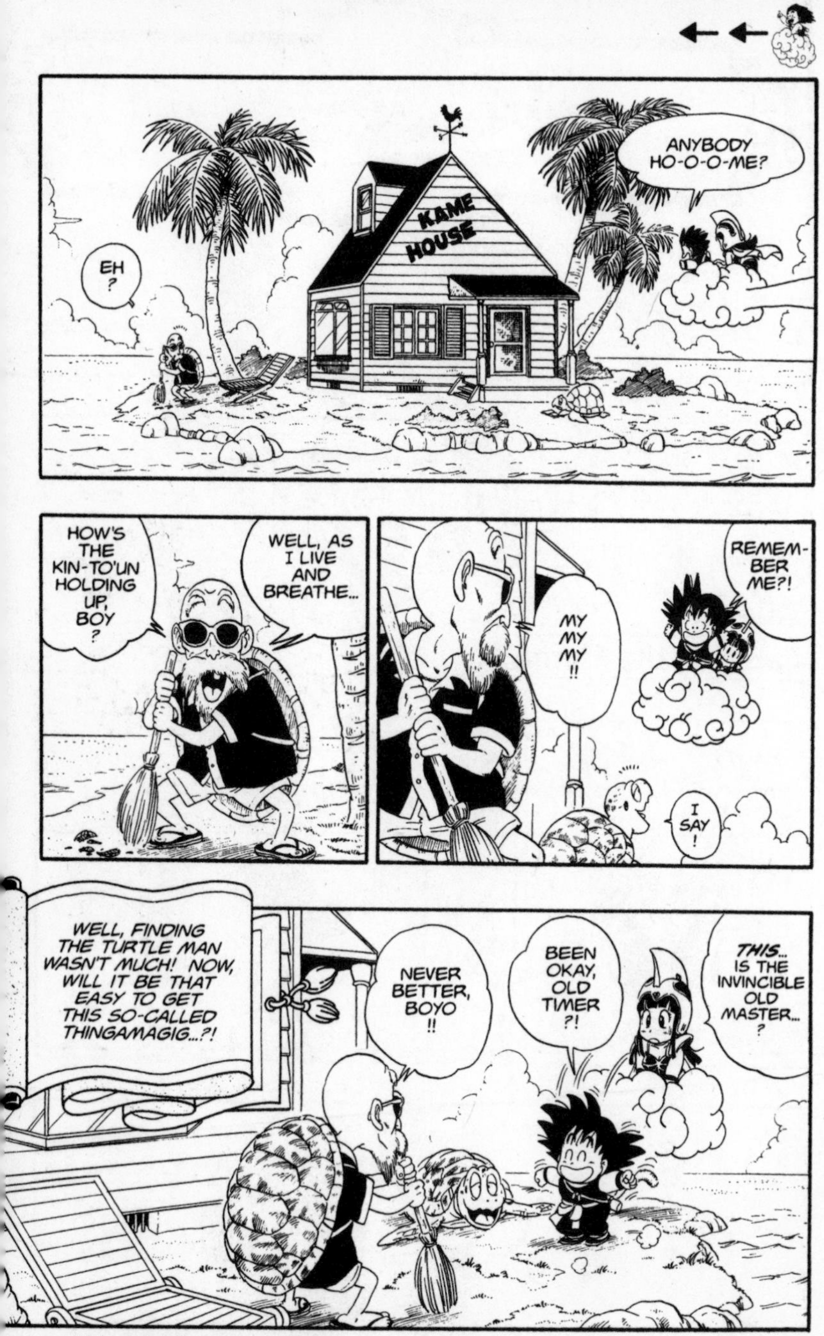
ANYBODY HO-O-O-ME?
KAME HOUSE
EH?
REMEM-BER ME?!
MY MY MY!!
I SAY!
WELL, AS I LIVE AND BREATHE...
HOW'S THE KIN-TO'UN HOLDING UP, BOY?
THIS... IS THE INVINCIBLE OLD MASTER...?
BEEN OKAY, OLD TIMER?!
NEVER BETTER, BOYO!!
WELL, FINDING THE TURTLE MAN WASN'T MUCH! NOW, WILL IT BE THAT EASY TO GET THIS SO-CALLED THINGAMAGIG...?!

NEXT: YOUR BIGGEST FAN!

Tale 13
Fanning the Flame

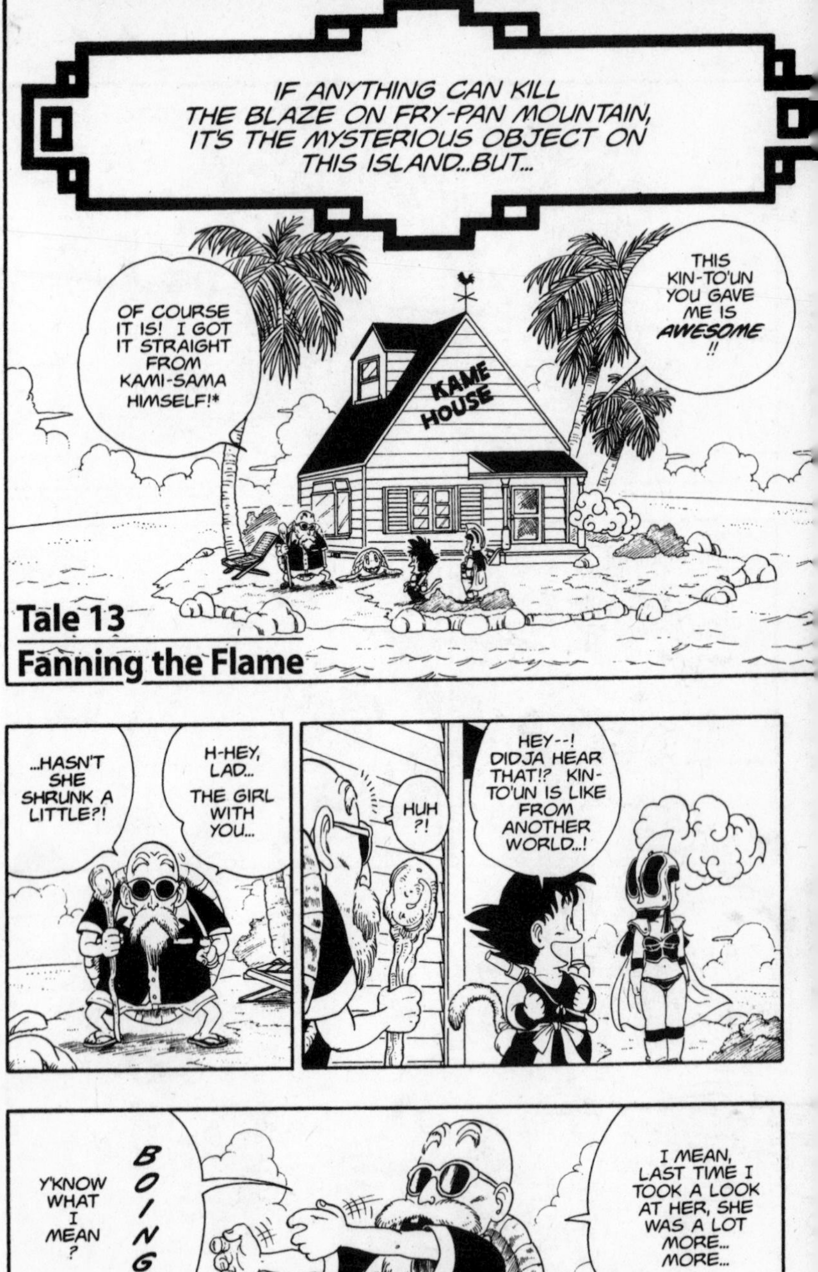

IF ANYTHING CAN KILL THE BLAZE ON FRY-PAN MOUNTAIN, IT'S THE MYSTERIOUS OBJECT ON THIS ISLAND...BUT...
THIS KIN-TO'UN YOU GAVE ME IS AWESOME !!
OF COURSE IT IS! I GOT IT STRAIGHT FROM KAMI-SAMA HIMSELF!*
KAME HOUSE
HEY--! DIDJA HEAR THAT!? KIN-TO'UN IS LIKE FROM ANOTHER WORLD...!
HUH ?!
H-HEY, LAD... THE GIRL WITH YOU...
...HASN'T SHE SHRUNK A LITTLE?!
I MEAN, LAST TIME I TOOK A LOOK AT HER, SHE WAS A LOT MORE... MORE...
BOING!
Y'KNOW WHAT I MEAN ?

*ONE WAY OF SAYING "GOD," TORIYAMA'S "KAMI-SAMA" ISN'T MEANT TO STAND IN FOR A FIRE-AND-BRIMSTONE JEHOVAH, BUT AS AN OTHERWORLDLY POWER OF OBSCURE ORIGIN. --ED.

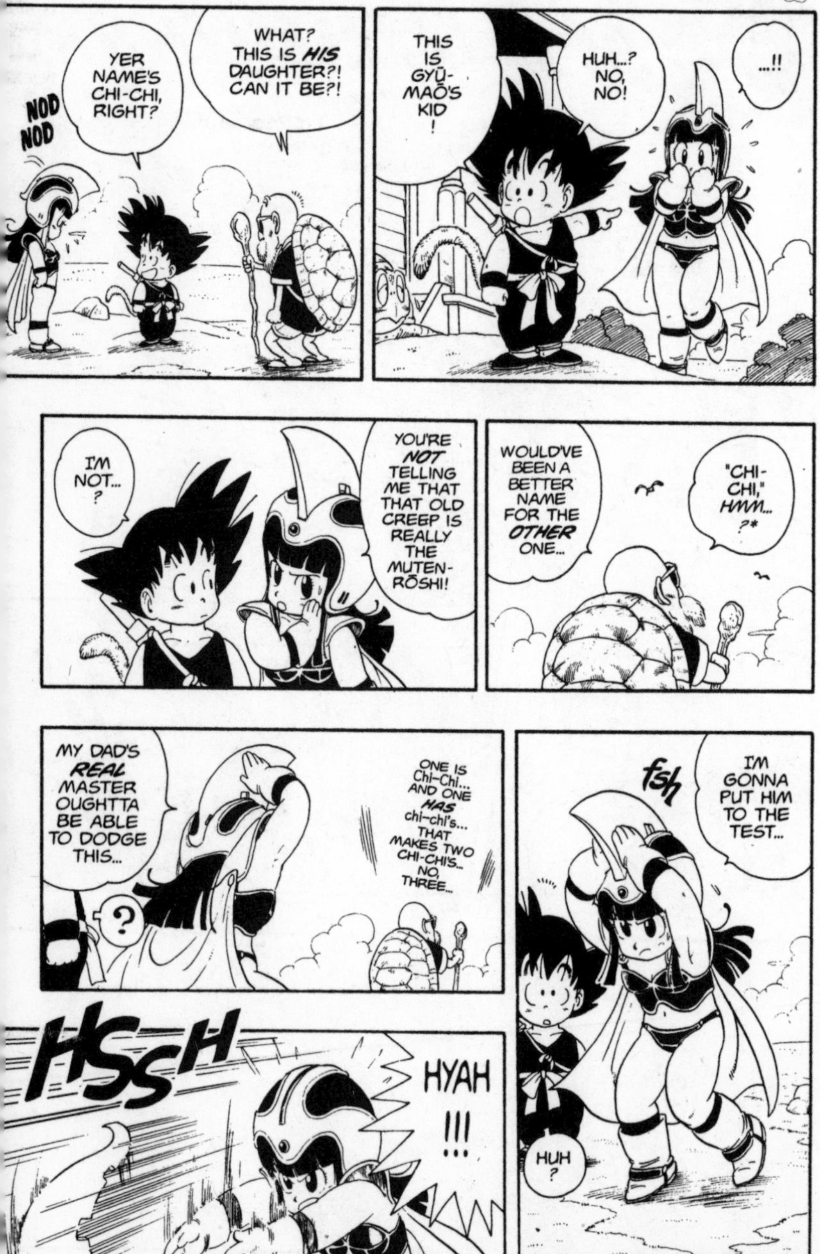
...!!
HUH...? NO, NO!
THIS IS GYŪ-MAŌ'S KID!
WHAT? THIS IS HIS DAUGHTER?! CAN IT BE?!
YER NAME'S CHI-CHI, RIGHT?
NOD NOD
"CHI-CHI," HMM... ?*
WOULD'VE BEEN A BETTER NAME FOR THE OTHER ONE...
YOU'RE NOT TELLING ME THAT THAT OLD CREEP IS REALLY THE MUTEN-RŌSHI!
I'M NOT... ?
fsh
I'M GONNA PUT HIM TO THE TEST...
HUH ?
ONE IS Chi-Chi... AND ONE HAS chi-chi's... THAT MAKES TWO CHI-CHI'S... NO, THREE...
MY DAD'S REAL MASTER OUGHTTA BE ABLE TO DODGE THIS...
?
HYAH !!!
HSSH

*AS YOU MAY BE ABLE TO GUESS FROM KAME-SEN'NIN'S MURMURINGS, "CHI-CHI" IS A JAPANESE BABY-WORD FOR "BREASTS." COMPLICATING IT FURTHER IS THAT IT'S ALSO A WORD FOR "FATHER."

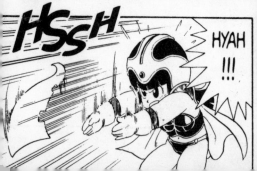

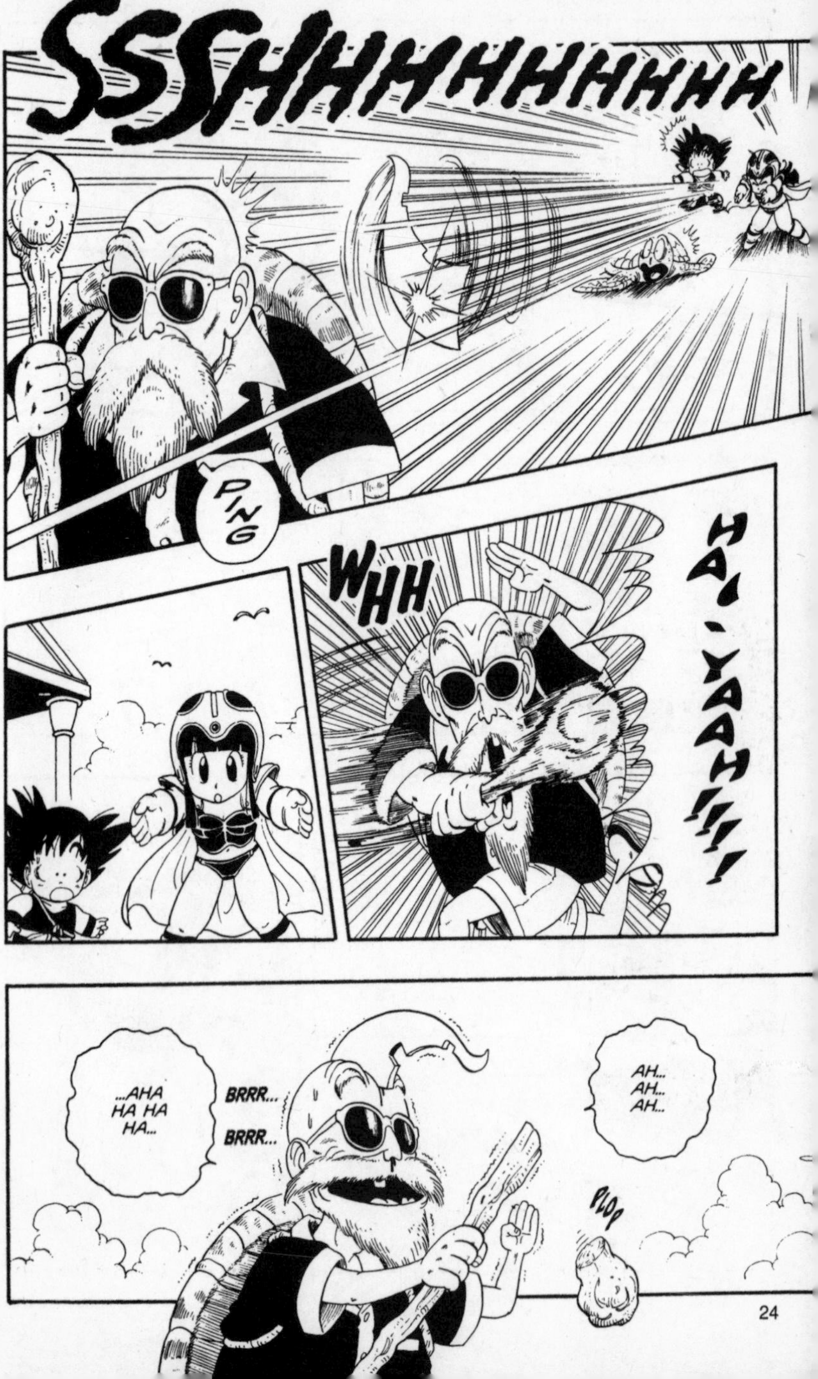
SSHHHHHHHHHHH
PING
WHH
HA!-YAAAH!!!!!
AH... AH... AH...
PLOP
BRRR... BRRR...
...AHA HA HA HA...

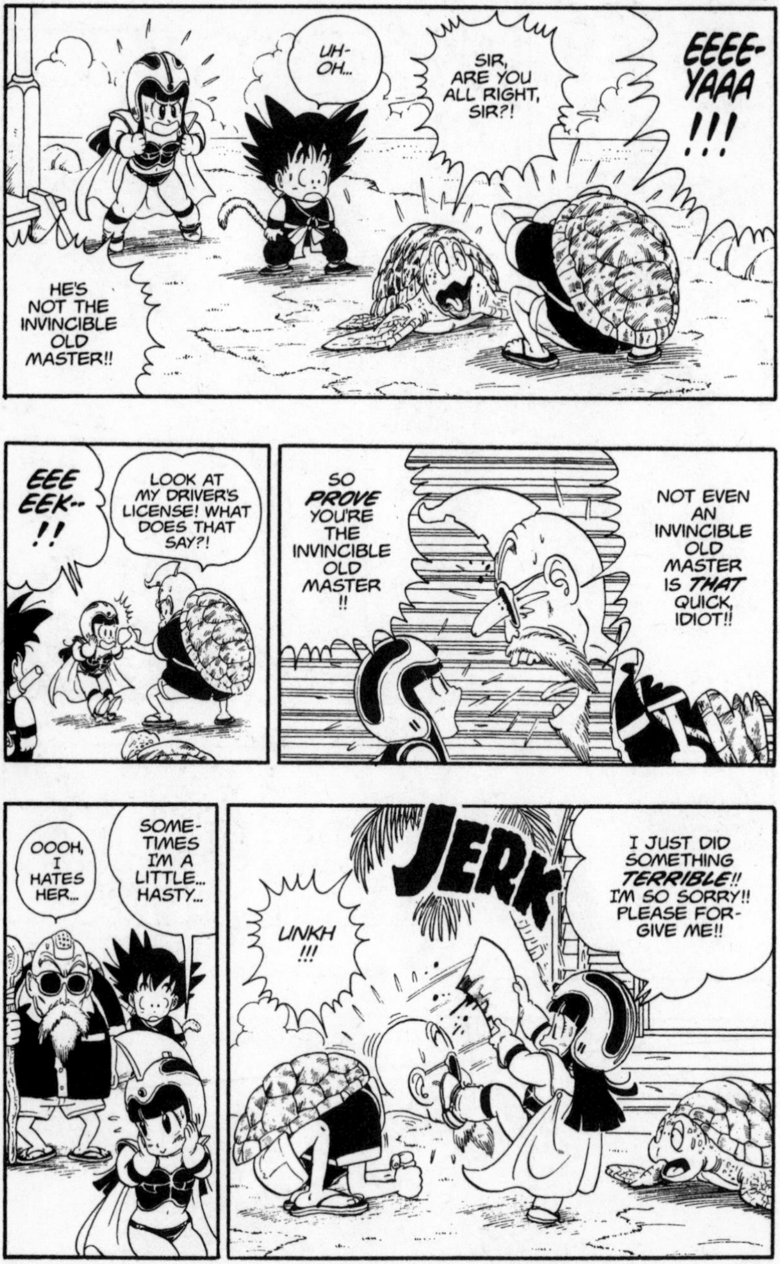
EEEE-YAAA!!!
SIR, ARE YOU ALL RIGHT, SIR?!
UH-OH...
HE'S NOT THE INVINCIBLE OLD MASTER!!
NOT EVEN AN INVINCIBLE OLD MASTER IS *THAT* QUICK, IDIOT!!
SO *PROVE* YOU'RE THE INVINCIBLE OLD MASTER!!
LOOK AT MY DRIVER'S LICENSE! WHAT DOES THAT SAY?!
EEE EEK--!!
I JUST DID SOMETHING *TERRIBLE*!! I'M SO SORRY!! PLEASE FOR-GIVE ME!!
JERK
UNKH!!!
SOME-TIMES I'M A LITTLE... HASTY...
OOOH, I HATES HER...

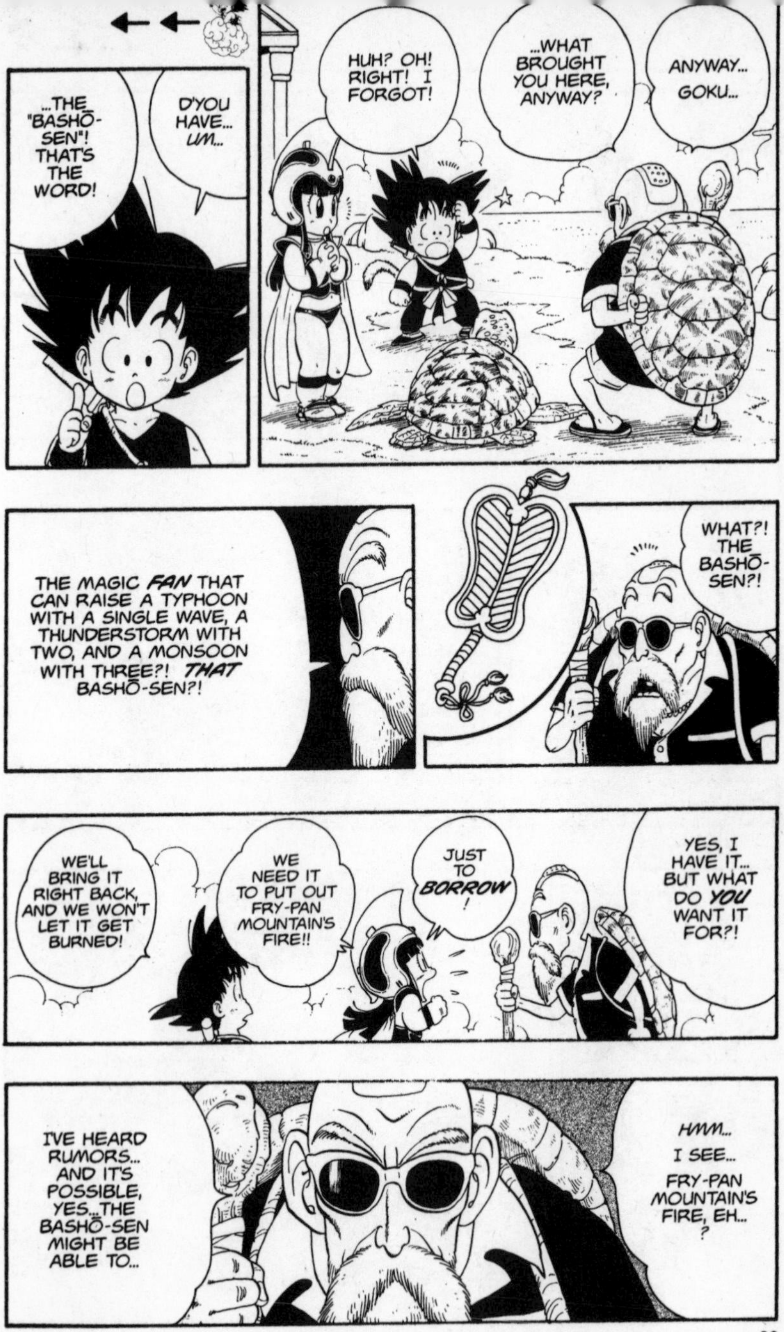
ANYWAY... GOKU...
...WHAT BROUGHT YOU HERE, ANYWAY?
HUH? OH! RIGHT! I FORGOT!
D'YOU HAVE... *UM*...
...THE "BASHŌ-SEN"! THAT'S THE WORD!
WHAT?! THE BASHŌ-SEN?!
THE MAGIC *FAN* THAT CAN RAISE A TYPHOON WITH A SINGLE WAVE, A THUNDERSTORM WITH TWO, AND A MONSOON WITH THREE?! *THAT* BASHŌ-SEN?!
YES, I HAVE IT... BUT WHAT DO *YOU* WANT IT FOR?!
JUST TO ***BORROW***!
WE NEED IT TO PUT OUT FRY-PAN MOUNTAIN'S FIRE!!
WE'LL BRING IT RIGHT BACK, AND WE WON'T LET IT GET BURNED!
HMM... I SEE... FRY-PAN MOUNTAIN'S FIRE, EH...?
I'VE HEARD RUMORS... AND IT'S POSSIBLE, YES... THE BASHŌ-SEN MIGHT BE ABLE TO...

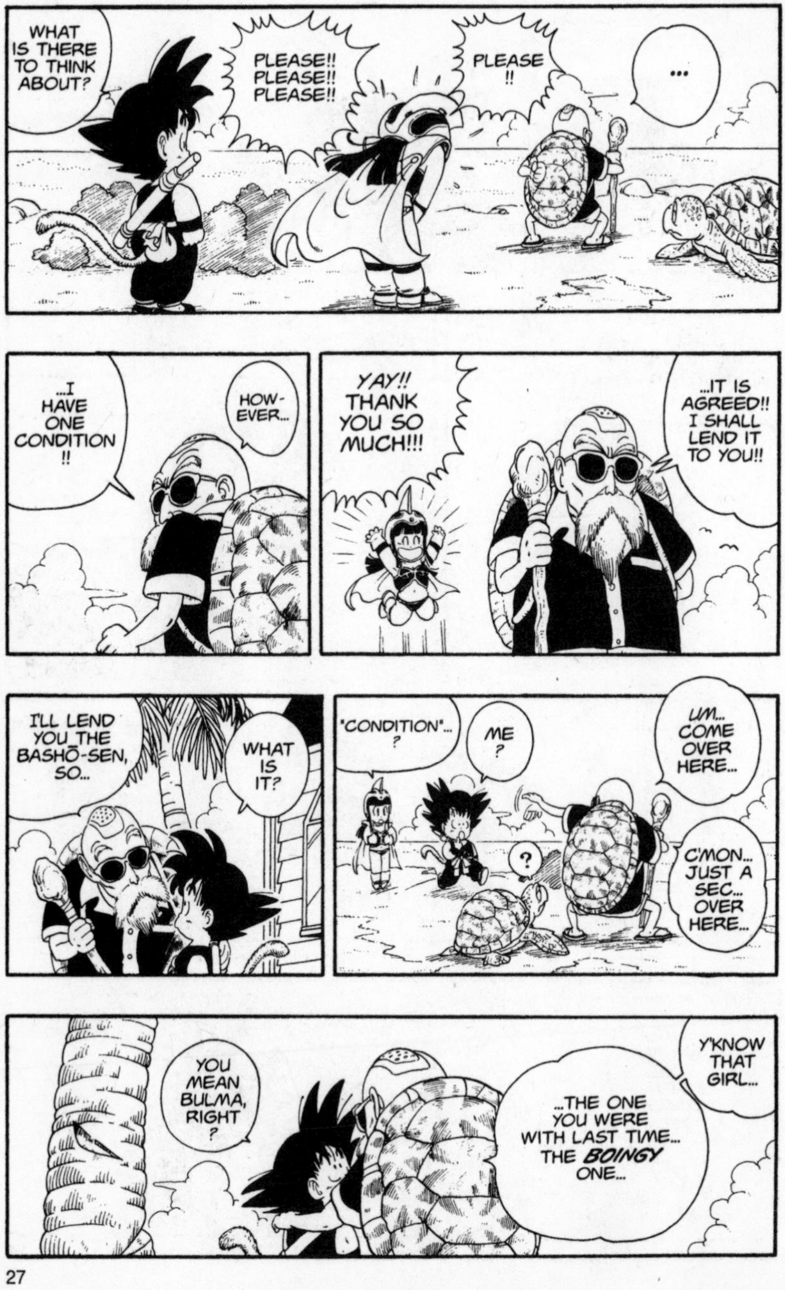
...
PLEASE !!
PLEASE!! PLEASE!! PLEASE!!
WHAT IS THERE TO THINK ABOUT?
...IT IS AGREED!! I SHALL LEND IT TO YOU!!
YAY!! THANK YOU SO MUCH!!!
HOW-EVER...
...I HAVE ONE CONDITION !!
UM... COME OVER HERE...
ME ?
"CONDITION"... ?
C'MON... JUST A SEC... OVER HERE...
?
WHAT IS IT?
I'LL LEND YOU THE BASHŌ-SEN, SO...
Y'KNOW THAT GIRL...
...THE ONE YOU WERE WITH LAST TIME... THE BOINGY ONE...
YOU MEAN BULMA, RIGHT ?

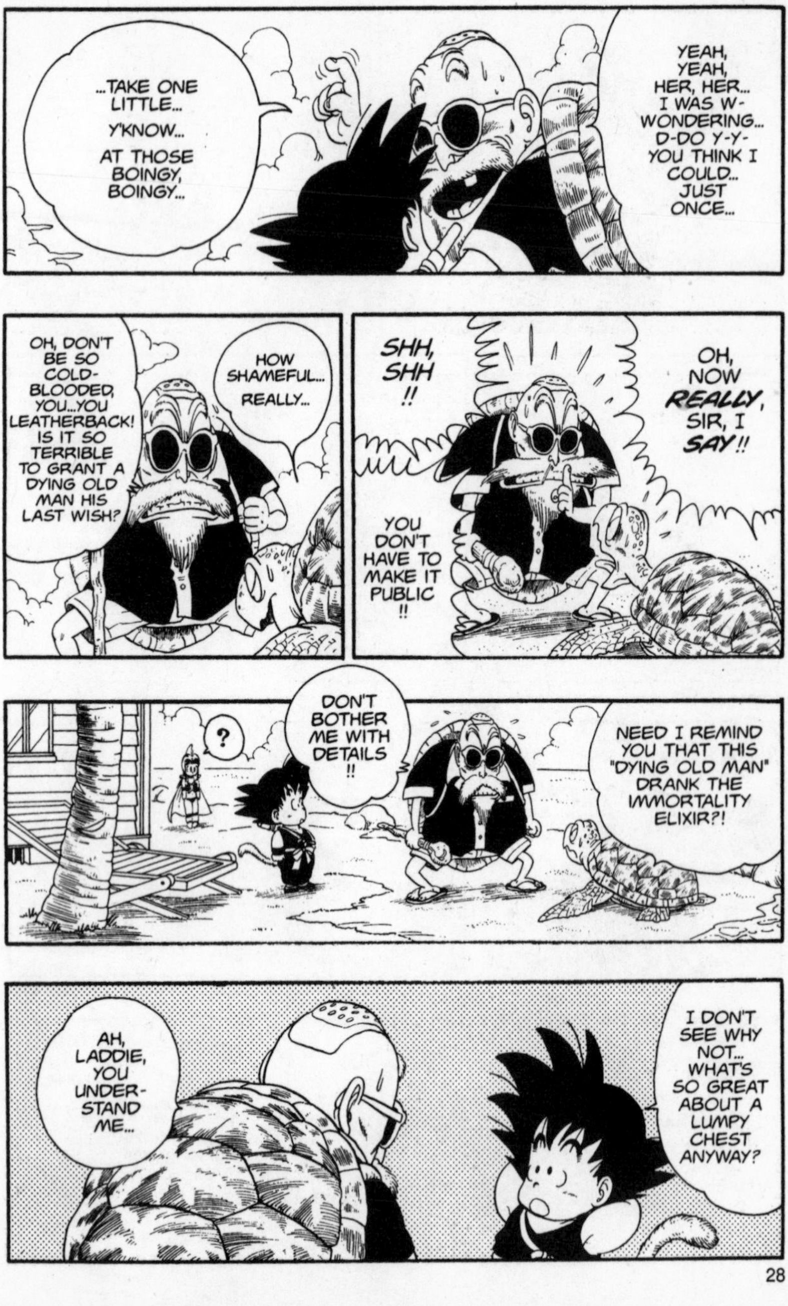
YEAH, YEAH, HER, HER... I WAS W-WONDERING... D-DO Y-Y-YOU THINK I COULD... JUST ONCE...
...TAKE ONE LITTLE...
Y'KNOW...
AT THOSE BOINGY, BOINGY...
OH, NOW *REALLY*, SIR, I *SAY*!!
SHH, SHH!!
YOU DON'T HAVE TO MAKE IT PUBLIC!!
HOW SHAMEFUL... REALLY...
OH, DON'T BE SO COLD-BLOODED, YOU...YOU LEATHERBACK! IS IT SO TERRIBLE TO GRANT A DYING OLD MAN HIS LAST WISH?
NEED I REMIND YOU THAT THIS "DYING OLD MAN" DRANK THE IMMORTALITY ELIXIR?!
DON'T BOTHER ME WITH DETAILS!!
?
I DON'T SEE WHY NOT... WHAT'S SO GREAT ABOUT A LUMPY CHEST ANYWAY?
AH, LADDIE, YOU UNDERSTAND ME...

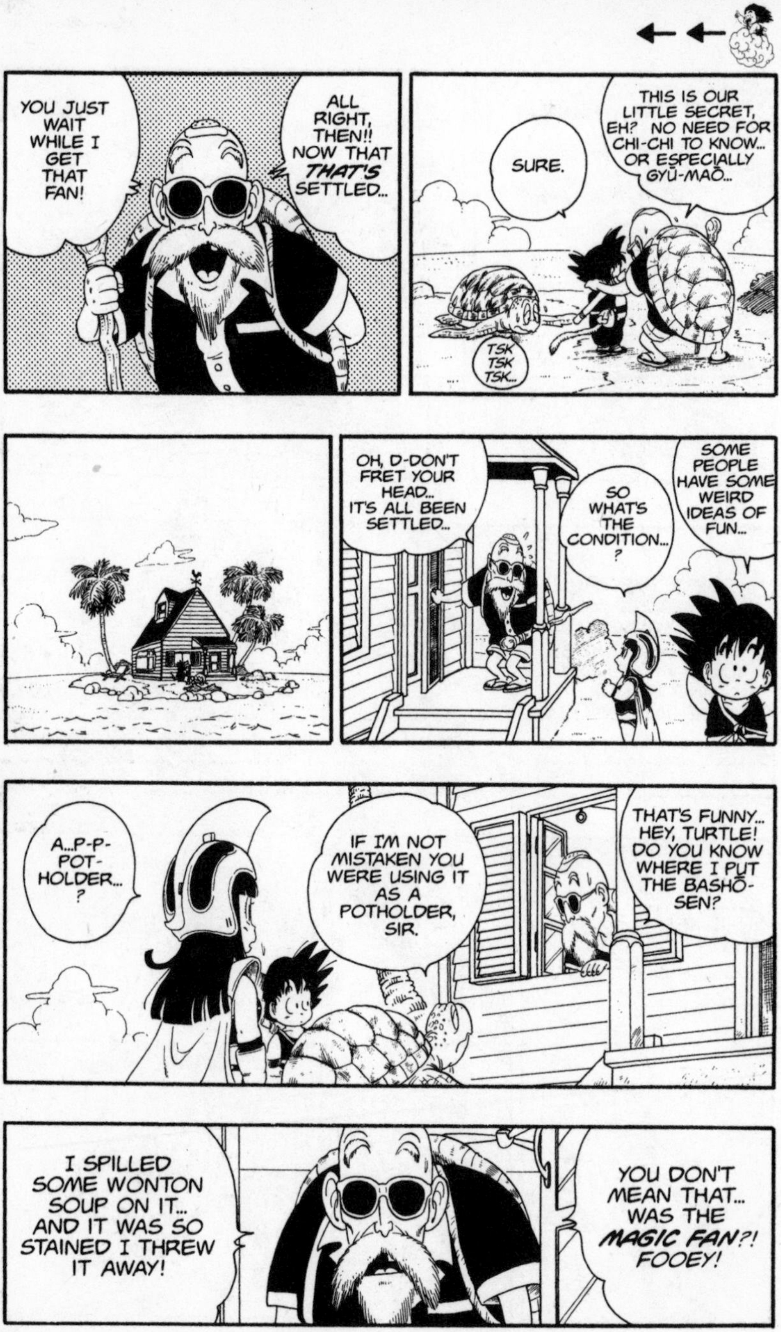
THIS IS OUR LITTLE SECRET, EH? NO NEED FOR CHI-CHI TO KNOW... OR ESPECIALLY GYŪ-MAŌ...
SURE.
TSK TSK TSK...
ALL RIGHT, THEN!! NOW THAT THAT'S SETTLED...
YOU JUST WAIT WHILE I GET THAT FAN!
SOME PEOPLE HAVE SOME WEIRD IDEAS OF FUN...
SO WHAT'S THE CONDITION...?
OH, D-DON'T FRET YOUR HEAD... IT'S ALL BEEN SETTLED...
THAT'S FUNNY... HEY, TURTLE! DO YOU KNOW WHERE I PUT THE BASHŌ-SEN?
IF I'M NOT MISTAKEN YOU WERE USING IT AS A POTHOLDER, SIR.
A...P-P-POT-HOLDER...?
YOU DON'T MEAN THAT... WAS THE MAGIC FAN?! FOOEY!
I SPILLED SOME WONTON SOUP ON IT... AND IT WAS SO STAINED I THREW IT AWAY!

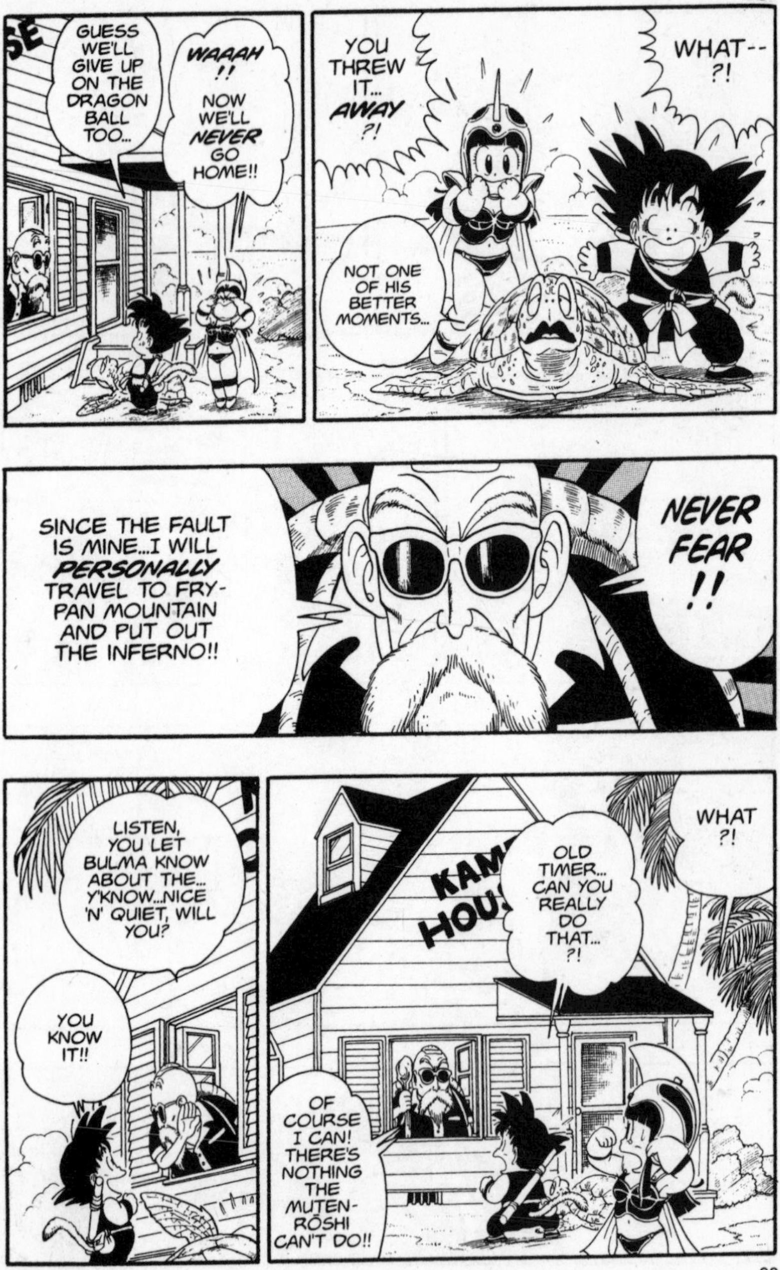
WHAT--?!
YOU THREW IT... AWAY?!
NOT ONE OF HIS BETTER MOMENTS...
WAAAH!! NOW WE'LL NEVER GO HOME!!
GUESS WE'LL GIVE UP ON THE DRAGON BALL TOO...
NEVER FEAR!!
SINCE THE FAULT IS MINE...I WILL PERSONALLY TRAVEL TO FRY-PAN MOUNTAIN AND PUT OUT THE INFERNO!!
WHAT?!
OLD TIMER... CAN YOU REALLY DO THAT...?!
OF COURSE I CAN! THERE'S NOTHING THE MUTEN-RŌSHI CAN'T DO!!
LISTEN, YOU LET BULMA KNOW ABOUT THE... Y'KNOW...NICE 'N' QUIET, WILL YOU?
YOU KNOW IT!!

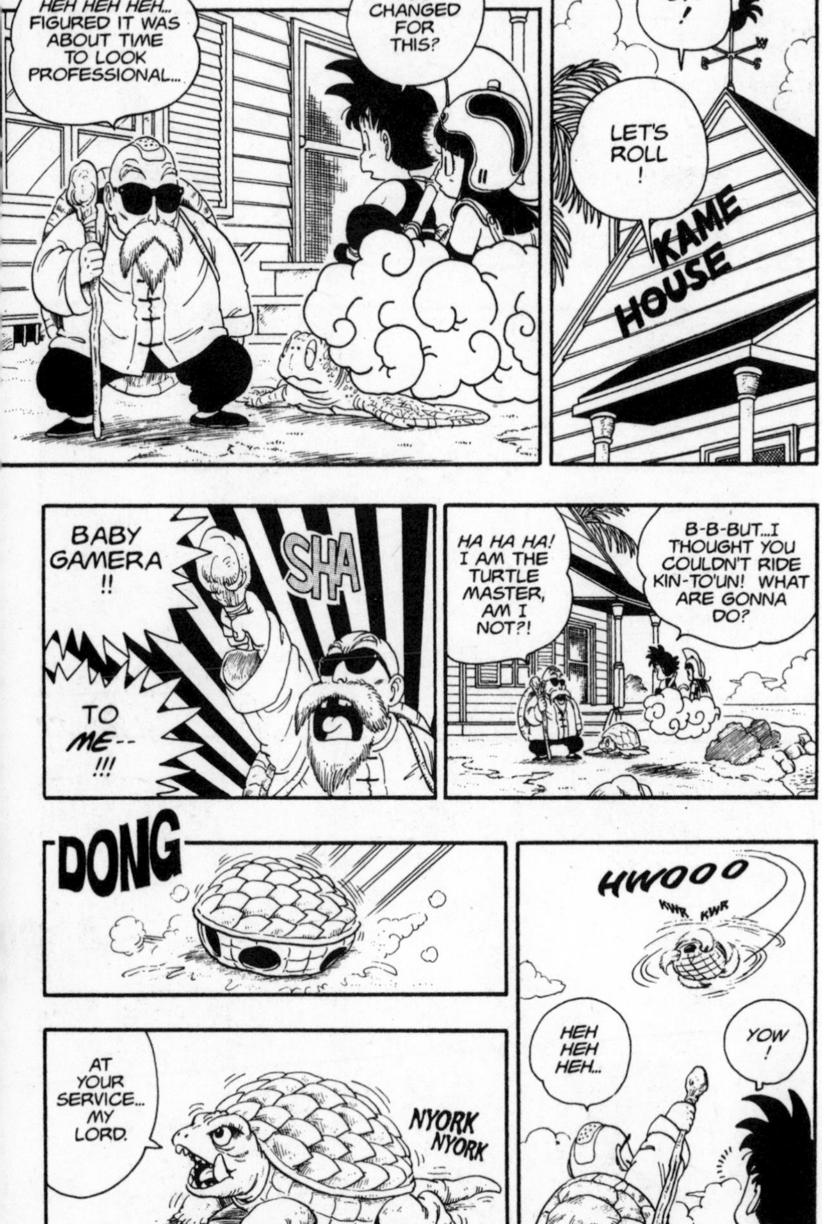
OK!
LET'S ROLL!
KAME HOUSE
YOU CHANGED FOR THIS?
HEH HEH HEH... FIGURED IT WAS ABOUT TIME TO LOOK PROFESSIONAL...
B-B-BUT...I THOUGHT YOU COULDN'T RIDE KIN-TO'UN! WHAT ARE GONNA DO?
HA HA HA! I AM THE TURTLE MASTER, AM I NOT?!
SHA
BABY GAMERA!!
TO ME--!!!
HWOOO
KWR KWR
YOW!
HEH HEH HEH...
DONG
NYORK NYORK
AT YOUR SERVICE... MY LORD.

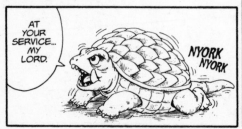

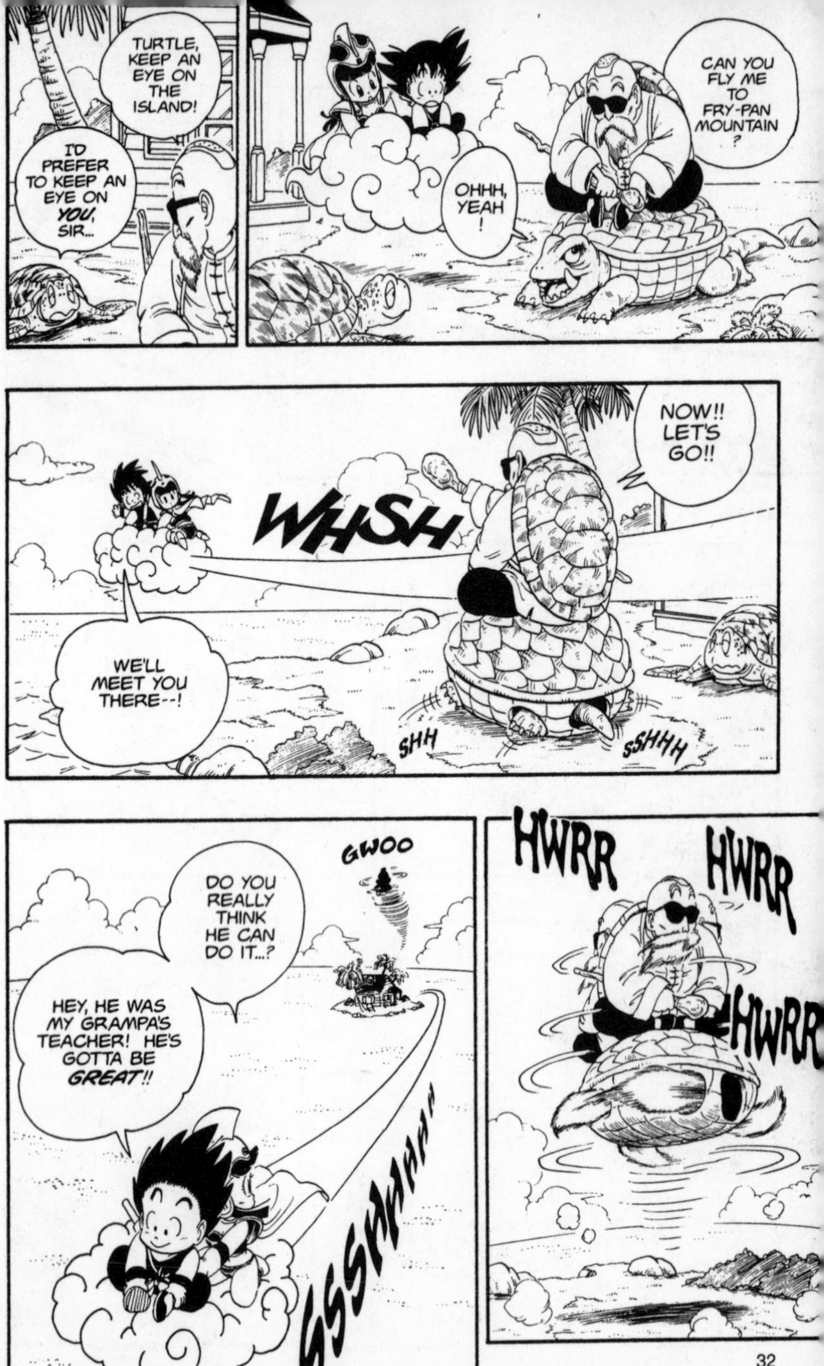
CAN YOU FLY ME TO FRY-PAN MOUNTAIN?
OHHH, YEAH!
TURTLE, KEEP AN EYE ON THE ISLAND!
I'D PREFER TO KEEP AN EYE ON *YOU*, SIR...
NOW!! LET'S GO!!
WHSH
WE'LL MEET YOU THERE--!
SHH
SSHHH
HWRR
HWRR
HWRR
GWOO
DO YOU REALLY THINK HE CAN DO IT...?
HEY, HE WAS MY GRAMPA'S TEACHER! HE'S GOTTA BE ***GREAT***!!
SSSHHHHH

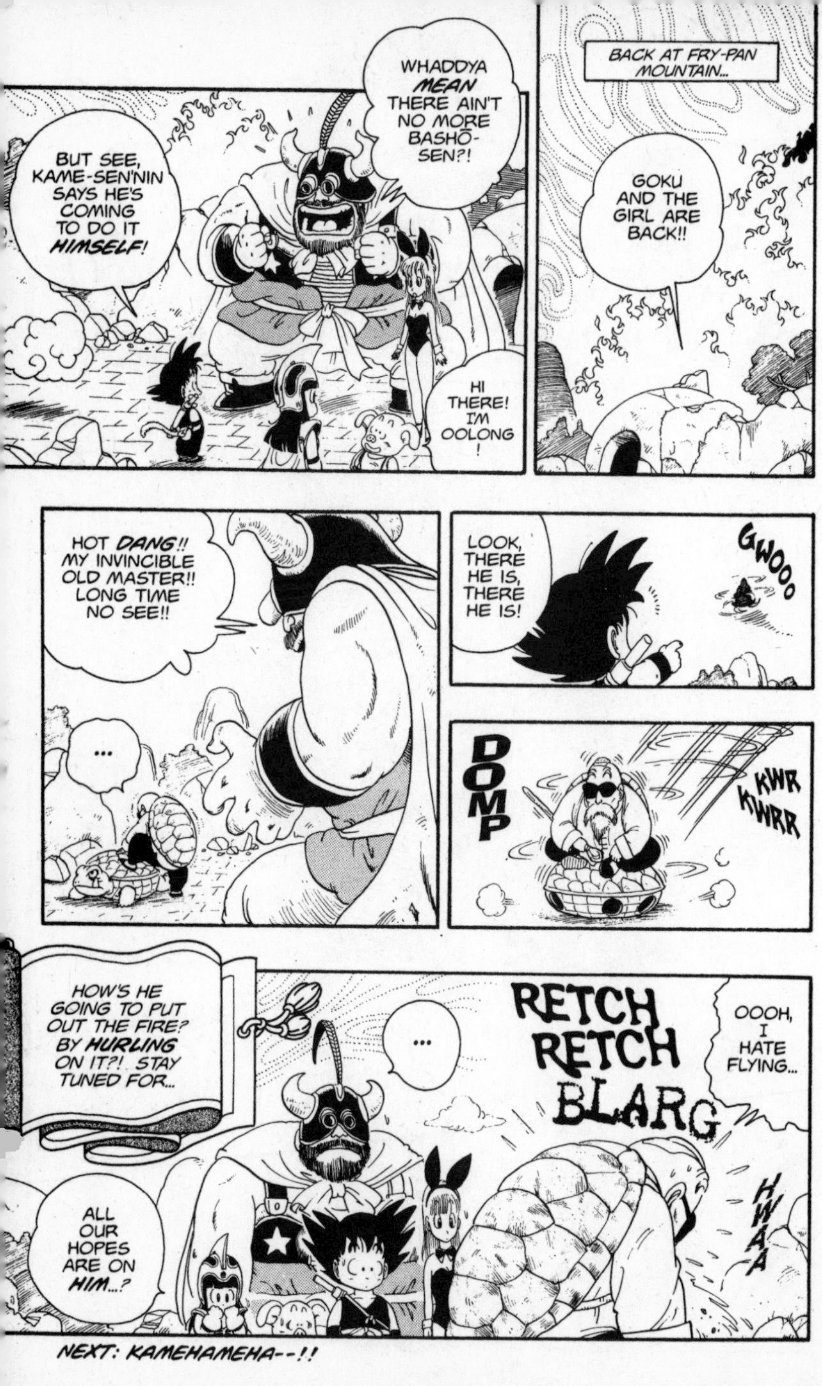
BACK AT FRY-PAN MOUNTAIN...
GOKU AND THE GIRL ARE BACK!!
WHADDYA MEAN THERE AIN'T NO MORE BASHŌ-SEN?!
BUT SEE, KAME-SEN'NIN SAYS HE'S COMING TO DO IT HIMSELF!
HI THERE! I'M OOLONG!
GWOOO
LOOK, THERE HE IS, THERE HE IS!
KWR KWRR
DOMP
HOT DANG!! MY INVINCIBLE OLD MASTER!! LONG TIME NO SEE!!
...
OOOH, I HATE FLYING...
RETCH RETCH BLARG
HWAAA
...
ALL OUR HOPES ARE ON HIM...?
HOW'S HE GOING TO PUT OUT THE FIRE? BY HURLING ON IT?! STAY TUNED FOR...

NEXT: KAMEHAMEHA--!!

ドラゴンボール

DRAGON BALL

Tale 14 Kame Kame Kame Kame Kame Chameleon

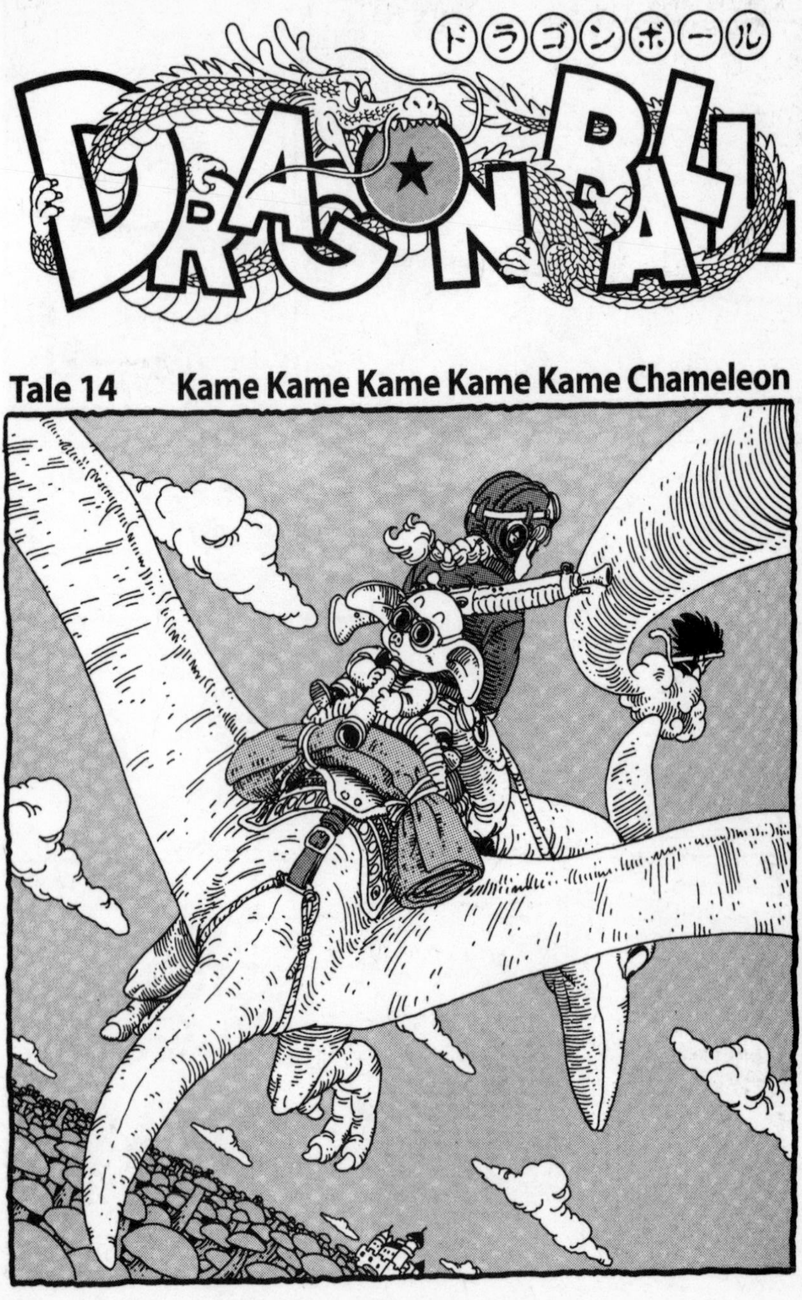

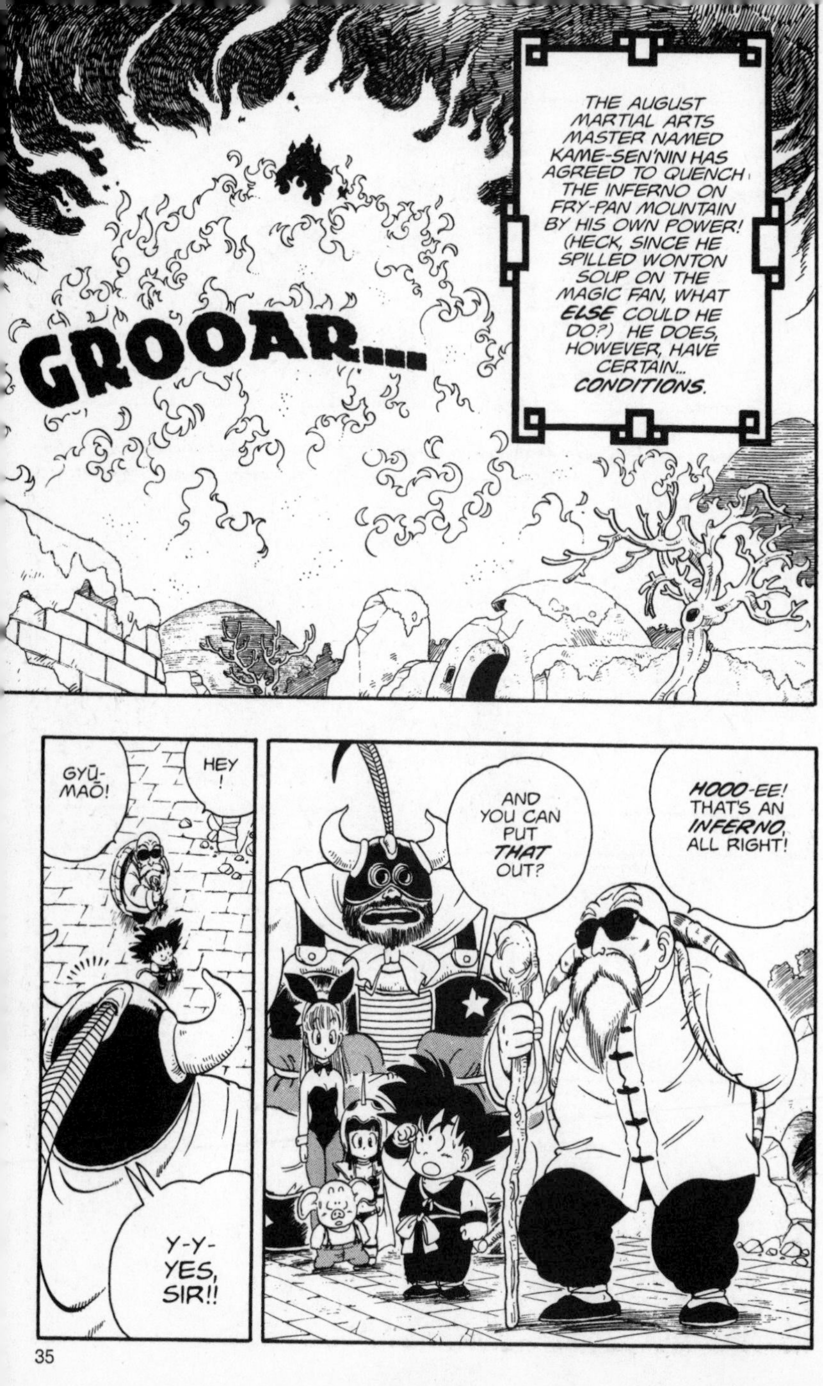
THE AUGUST MARTIAL ARTS MASTER NAMED KAME-SEN'NIN HAS AGREED TO QUENCH THE INFERNO ON FRY-PAN MOUNTAIN BY HIS OWN POWER! (HECK, SINCE HE SPILLED WONTON SOUP ON THE MAGIC FAN, WHAT ELSE COULD HE DO?) HE DOES, HOWEVER, HAVE CERTAIN... CONDITIONS.
GROOAR....
HOOO-EE! THAT'S AN INFERNO, ALL RIGHT!
AND YOU CAN PUT THAT OUT?
HEY!
GYŪ-MAŌ!
Y-Y-YES, SIR!!

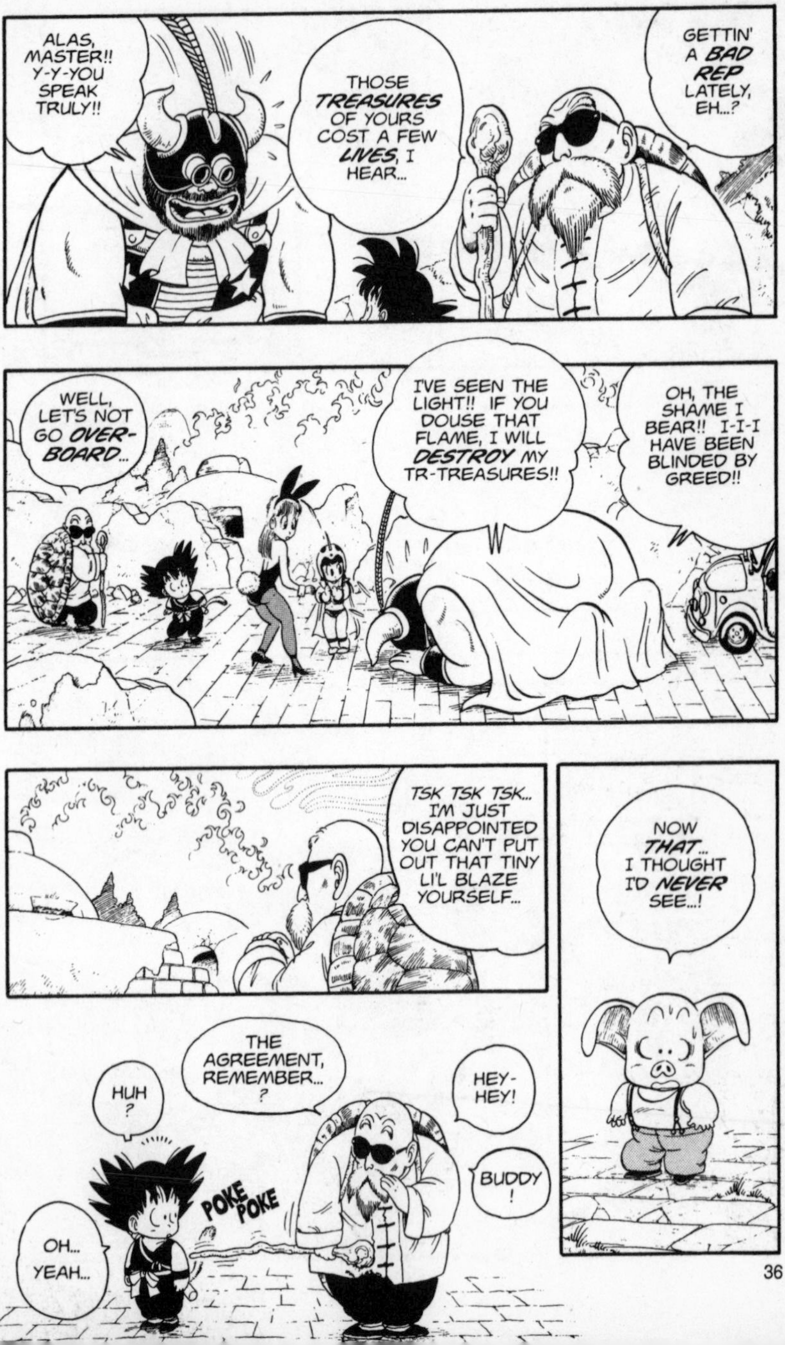
GETTIN' A BAD REP LATELY, EH...?
THOSE TREASURES OF YOURS COST A FEW LIVES, I HEAR...
ALAS, MASTER!! Y-Y-YOU SPEAK TRULY!!
OH, THE SHAME I BEAR!! I-I-I HAVE BEEN BLINDED BY GREED!!
I'VE SEEN THE LIGHT!! IF YOU DOUSE THAT FLAME, I WILL DESTROY MY TR-TREASURES!!
WELL, LET'S NOT GO OVER-BOARD...
NOW THAT... I THOUGHT I'D NEVER SEE...!
TSK TSK TSK... I'M JUST DISAPPOINTED YOU CAN'T PUT OUT THAT TINY LI'L BLAZE YOURSELF...
HEY-HEY!
BUDDY!
THE AGREEMENT, REMEMBER...?
HUH?
POKE POKE
OH... YEAH...

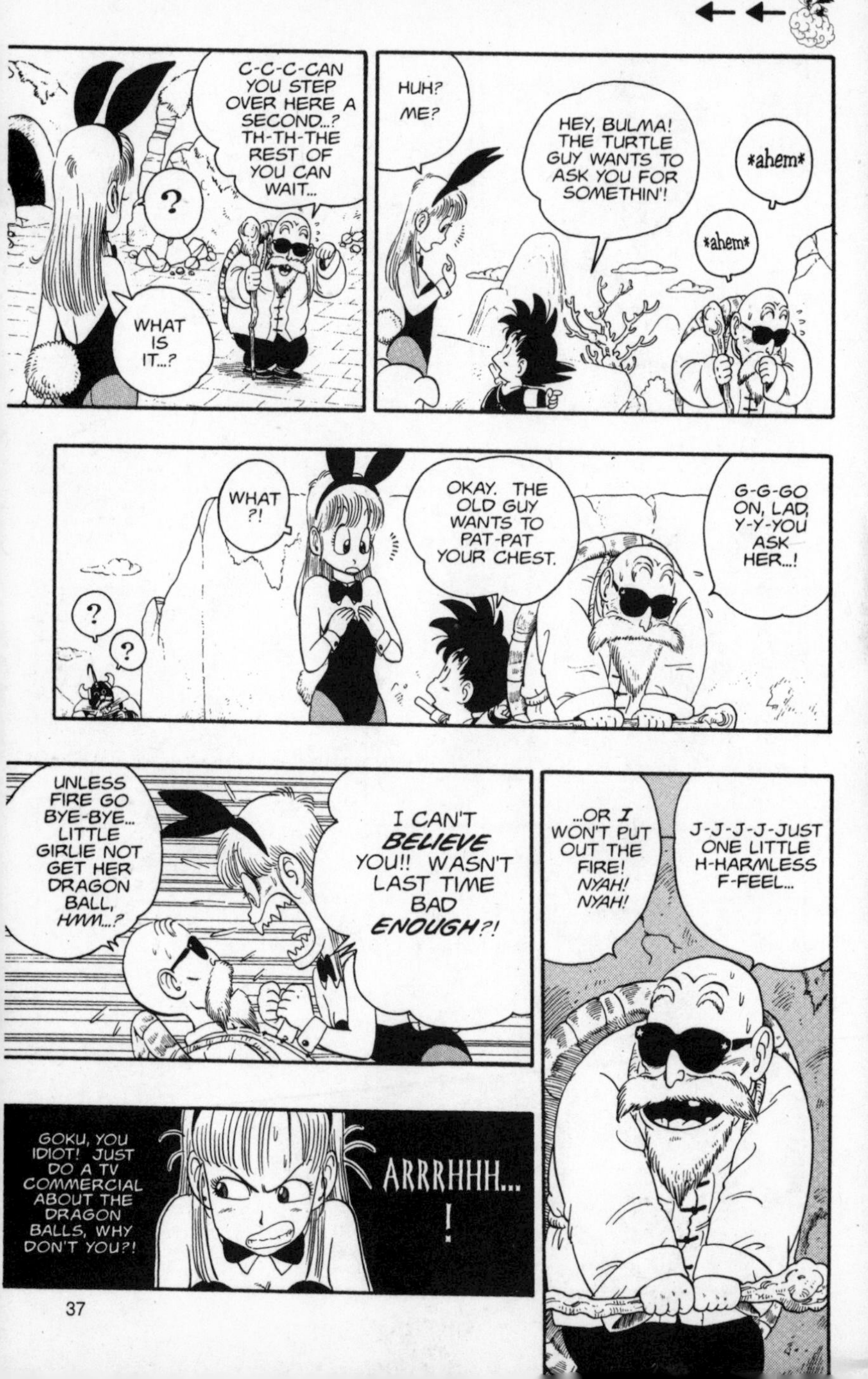
HUH? ME?
HEY, BULMA! THE TURTLE GUY WANTS TO ASK YOU FOR SOMETHIN'!
ahem
ahem
C-C-C-CAN YOU STEP OVER HERE A SECOND...? TH-TH-THE REST OF YOU CAN WAIT...
?
WHAT IS IT...?
G-G-GO ON, LAD, Y-Y-YOU ASK HER...!
OKAY. THE OLD GUY WANTS TO PAT-PAT YOUR CHEST.
WHAT ?!
?
?
J-J-J-J-JUST ONE LITTLE H-HARMLESS F-FEEL...
...OR I WON'T PUT OUT THE FIRE! NYAH! NYAH!
I CAN'T BELIEVE YOU!! WASN'T LAST TIME BAD ENOUGH?!
UNLESS FIRE GO BYE-BYE... LITTLE GIRLIE NOT GET HER DRAGON BALL, HMM...?
ARRRHHH... !
GOKU, YOU IDIOT! JUST DO A TV COMMERCIAL ABOUT THE DRAGON BALLS, WHY DON'T YOU?!

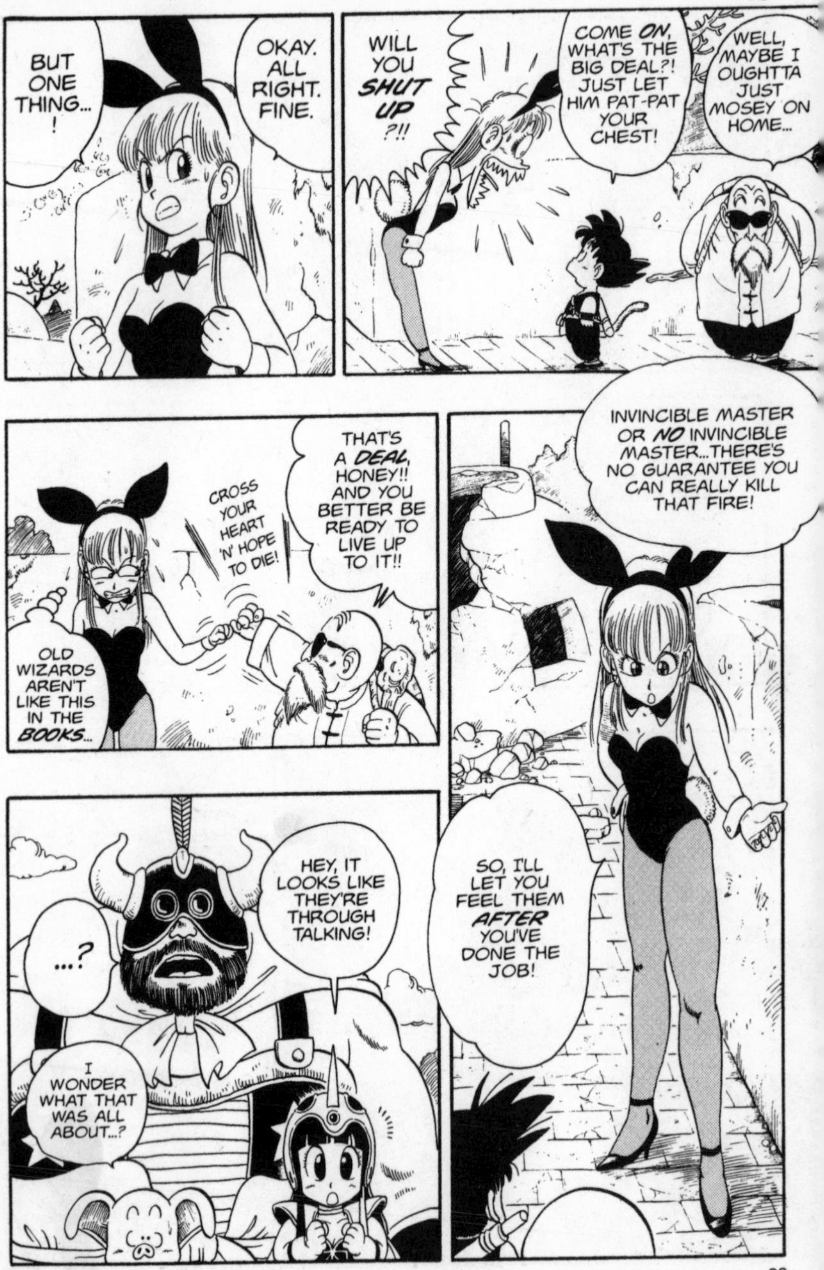
WELL, MAYBE I OUGHTTA JUST MOSEY ON HOME...
COME ON, WHAT'S THE BIG DEAL?! JUST LET HIM PAT-PAT YOUR CHEST!
WILL YOU SHUT UP?!!
OKAY. ALL RIGHT. FINE.
BUT ONE THING...!
INVINCIBLE MASTER OR NO INVINCIBLE MASTER...THERE'S NO GUARANTEE YOU CAN REALLY KILL THAT FIRE!
SO, I'LL LET YOU FEEL THEM AFTER YOU'VE DONE THE JOB!
THAT'S A DEAL, HONEY!! AND YOU BETTER BE READY TO LIVE UP TO IT!!
CROSS YOUR HEART 'N' HOPE TO DIE!
OLD WIZARDS AREN'T LIKE THIS IN THE BOOKS...
HEY, IT LOOKS LIKE THEY'RE THROUGH TALKING!
...?
I WONDER WHAT THAT WAS ALL ABOUT...?

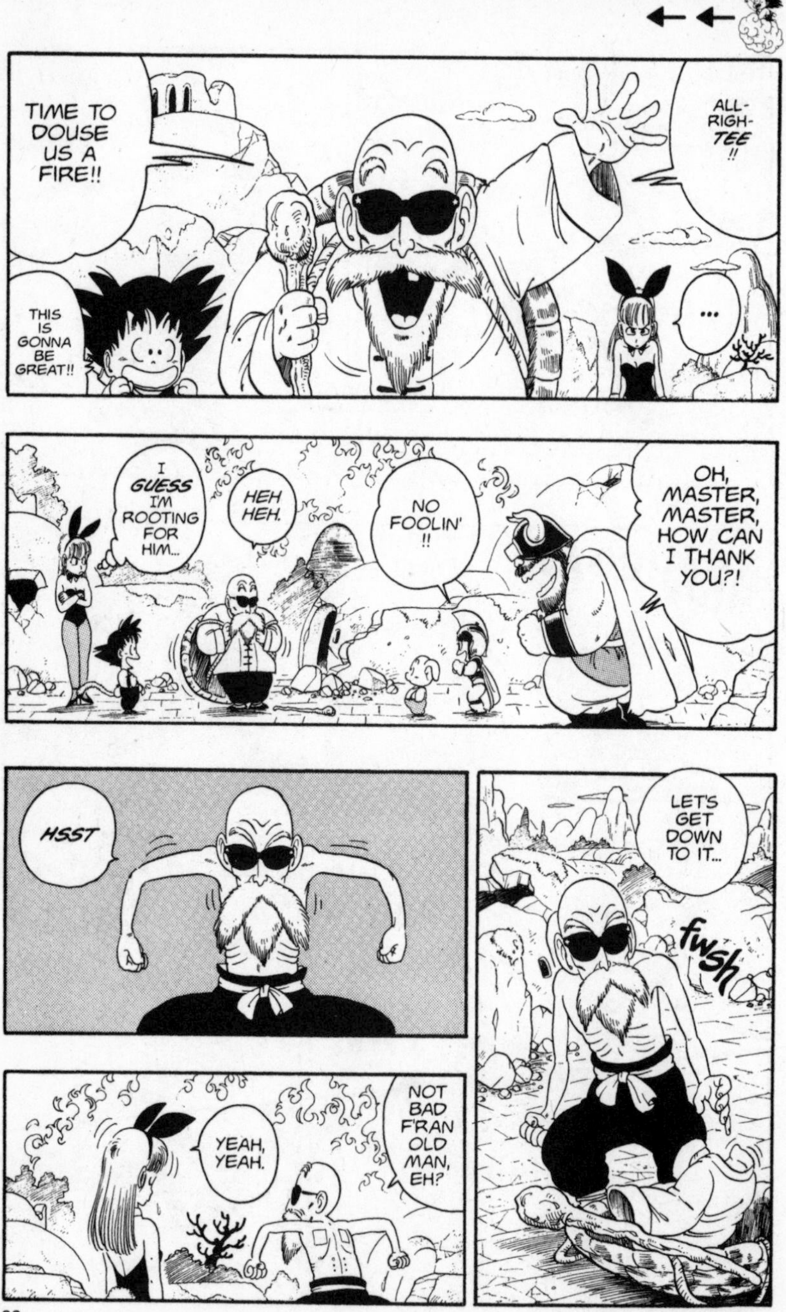
ALL-RIGH-TEE!!
TIME TO DOUSE US A FIRE!!
...
THIS IS GONNA BE GREAT!!
OH, MASTER, MASTER, HOW CAN I THANK YOU?!
NO FOOLIN'!!
HEH HEH.
I GUESS I'M ROOTING FOR HIM...
LET'S GET DOWN TO IT...
fwsh
HSST
NOT BAD F'RAN OLD MAN, EH?
YEAH, YEAH.

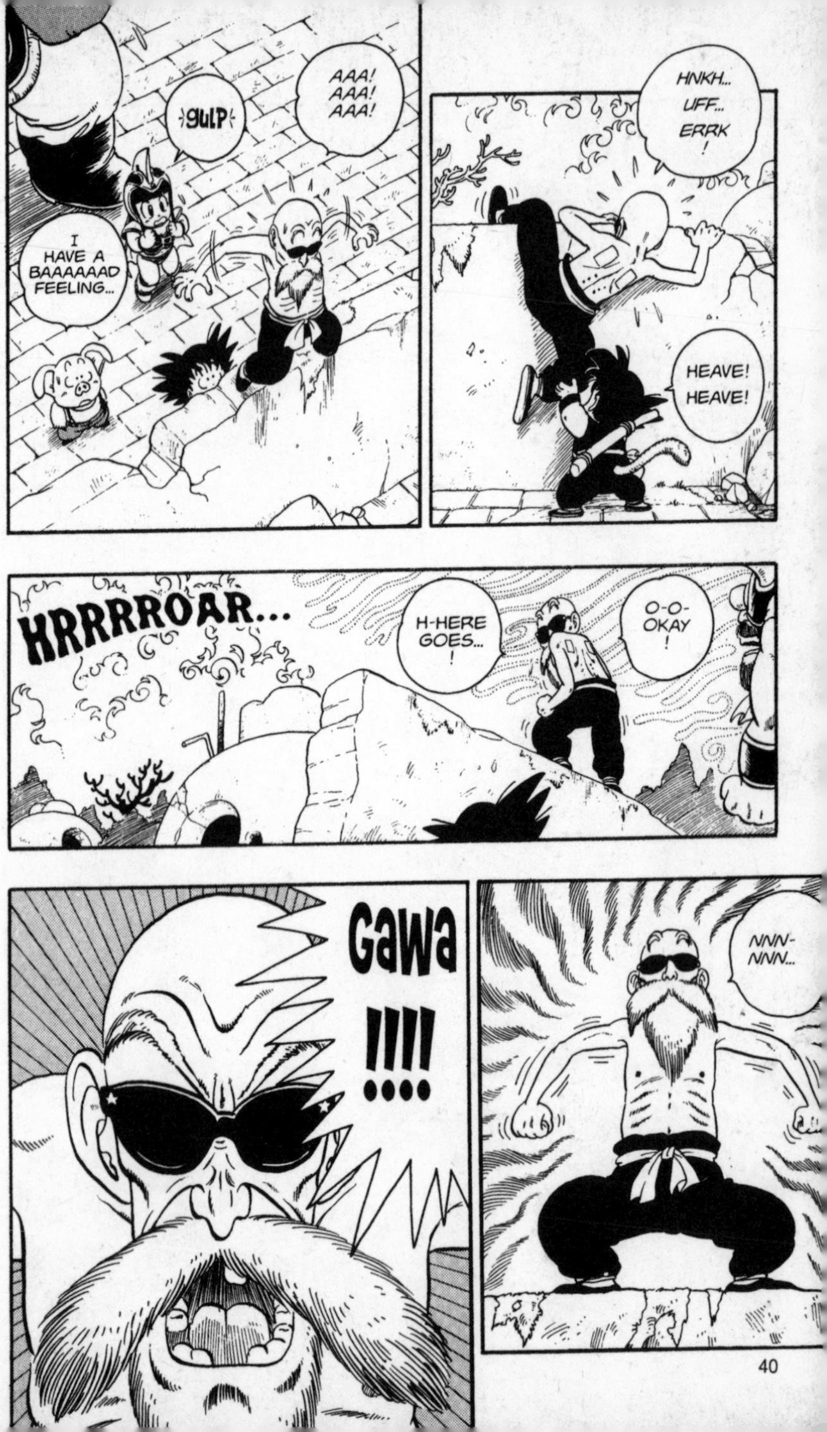
HNKH... UFF... ERRK!
HEAVE! HEAVE!
AAA! AAA! AAA!
gulp
I HAVE A BAAAAAAD FEELING...
O-O-OKAY!
H-HERE GOES...!
HRRRROAR...
NNN-NNN...
Gawa !!!!

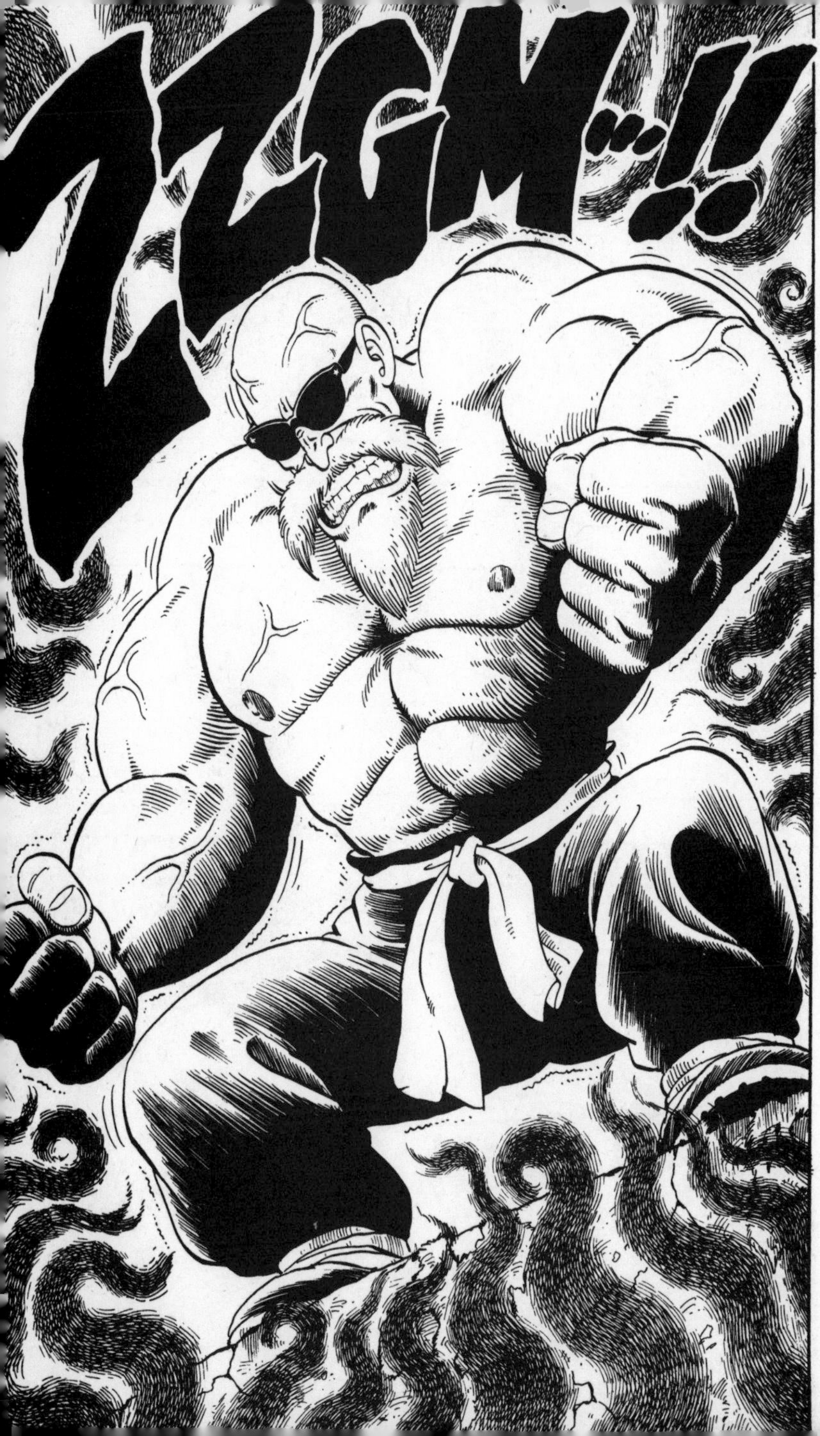
ZZGM..!!

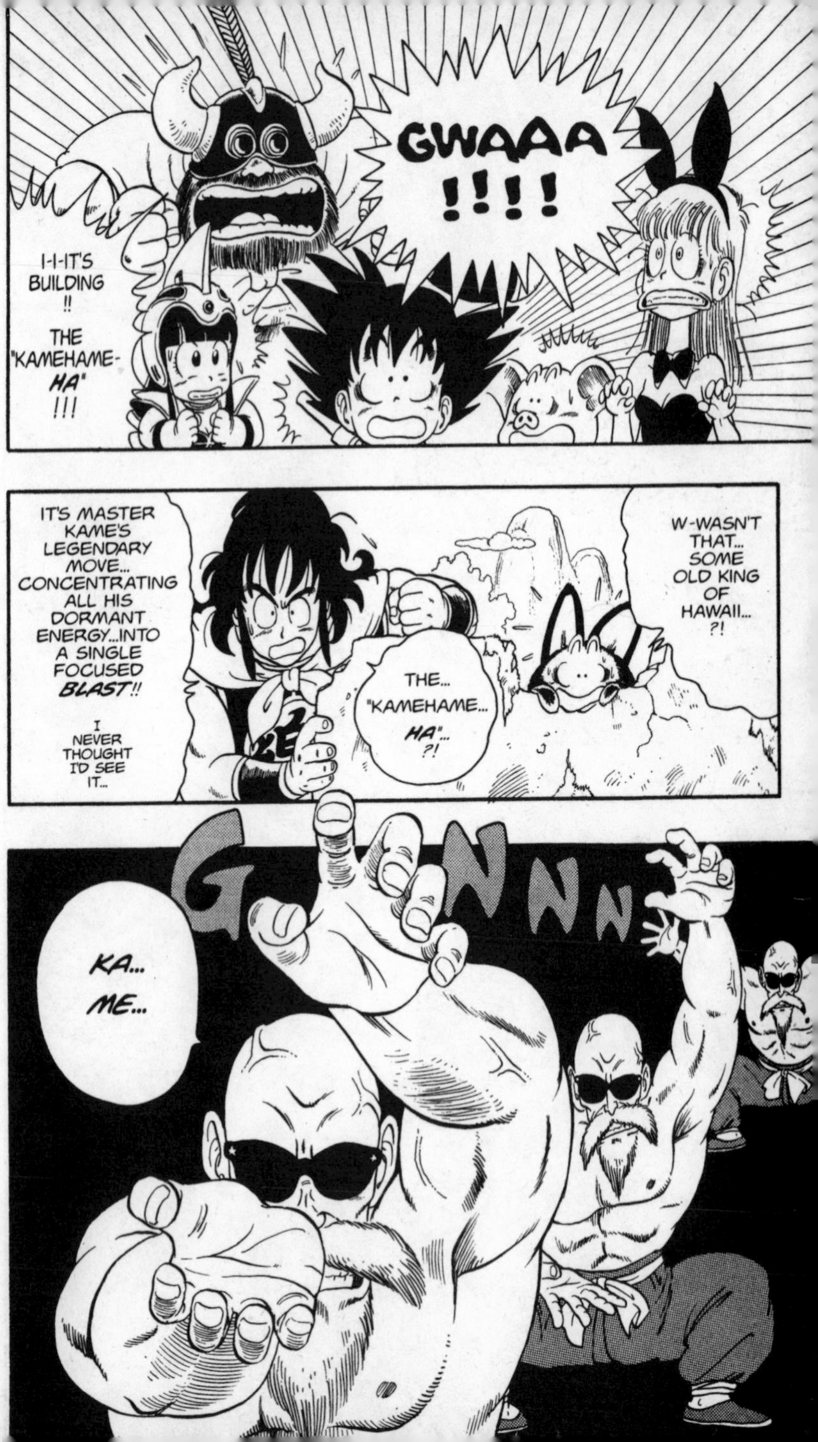
GWAAAA!!!!
I-I-IT'S BUILDING!!
THE "KAMEHAME-HA"!!!
W-WASN'T THAT... SOME OLD KING OF HAWAII...?!
THE... "KAMEHAME... HA"...?!
IT'S MASTER KAME'S LEGENDARY MOVE... CONCENTRATING ALL HIS DORMANT ENERGY...INTO A SINGLE FOCUSED BLAST!!
I NEVER THOUGHT I'D SEE IT...
GNNN
KA... ME...

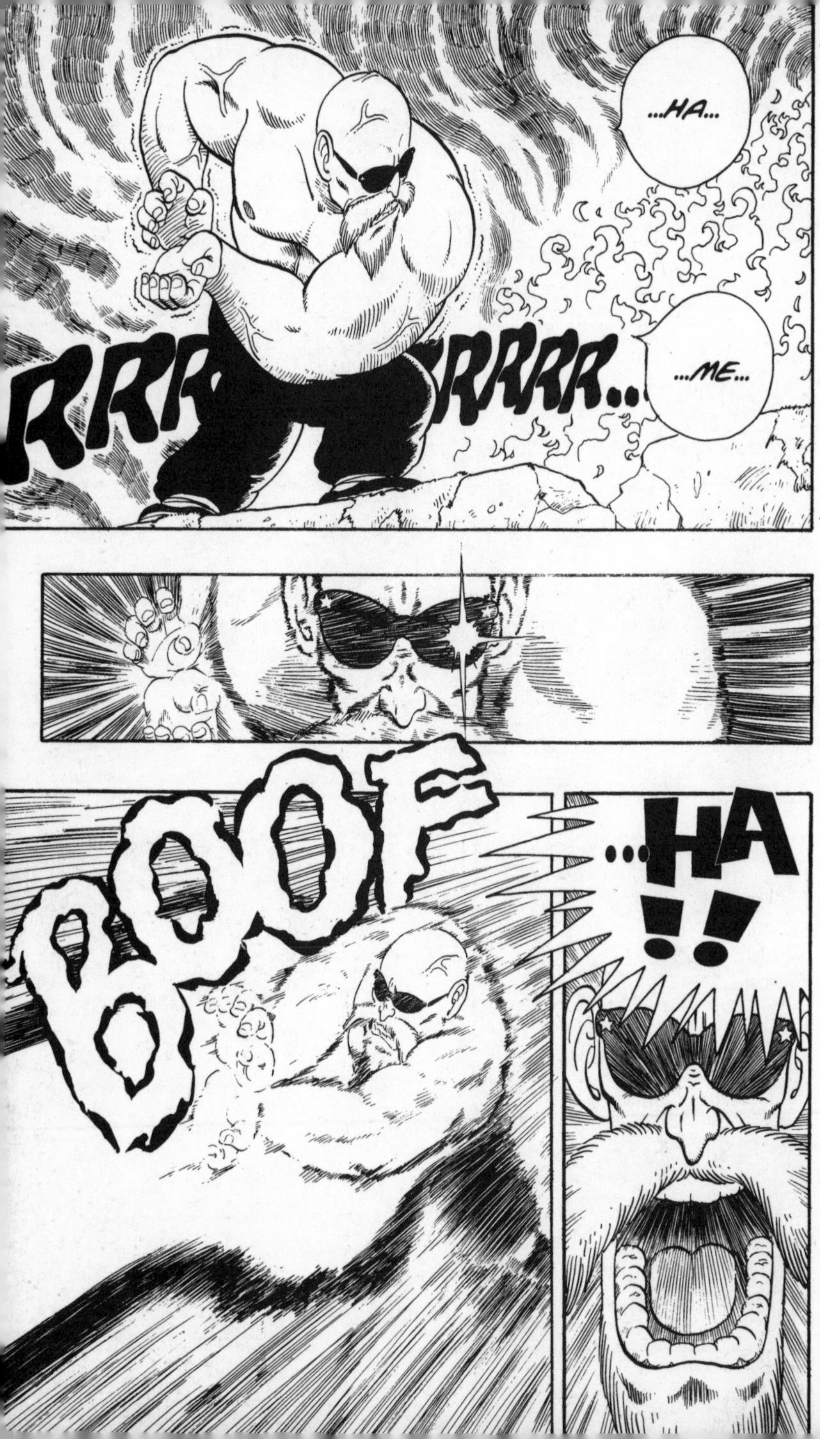
...HA...
...ME...
RRRRRRRRRR...
...HA!!
BOOF

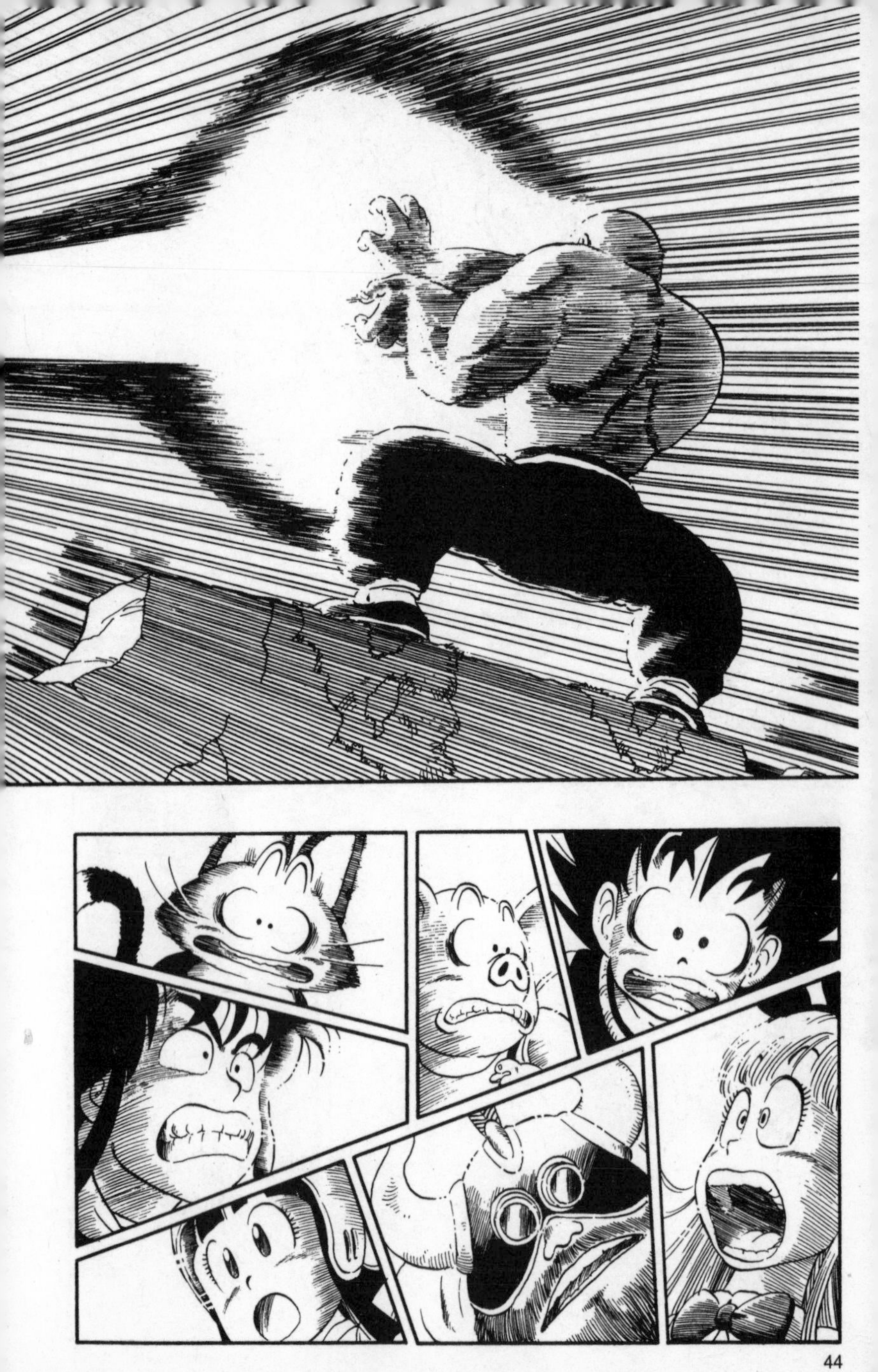

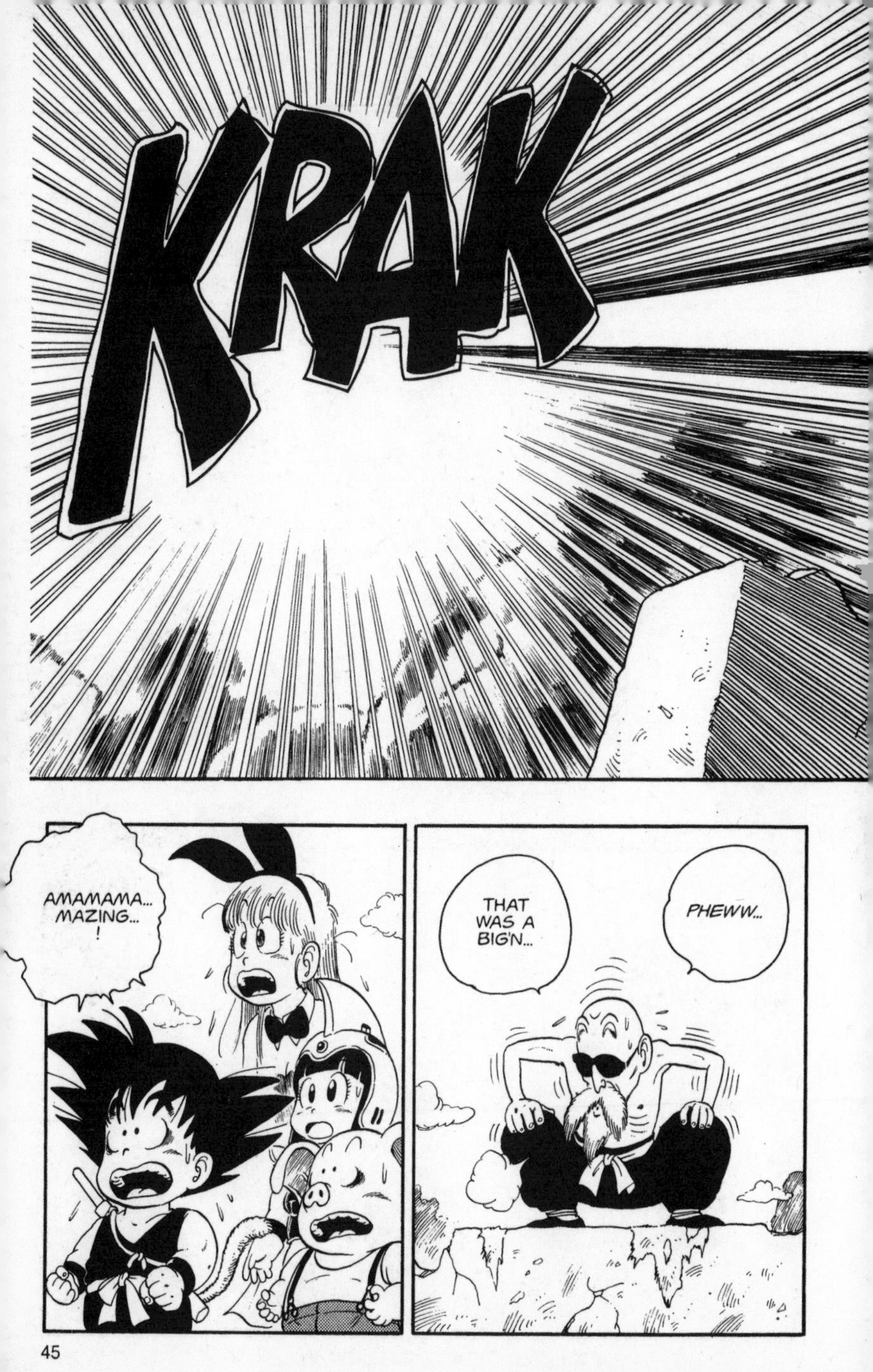
KRAK
PHEWW...
THAT WAS A BIG'N...
AMAMAMA... MAZING... !

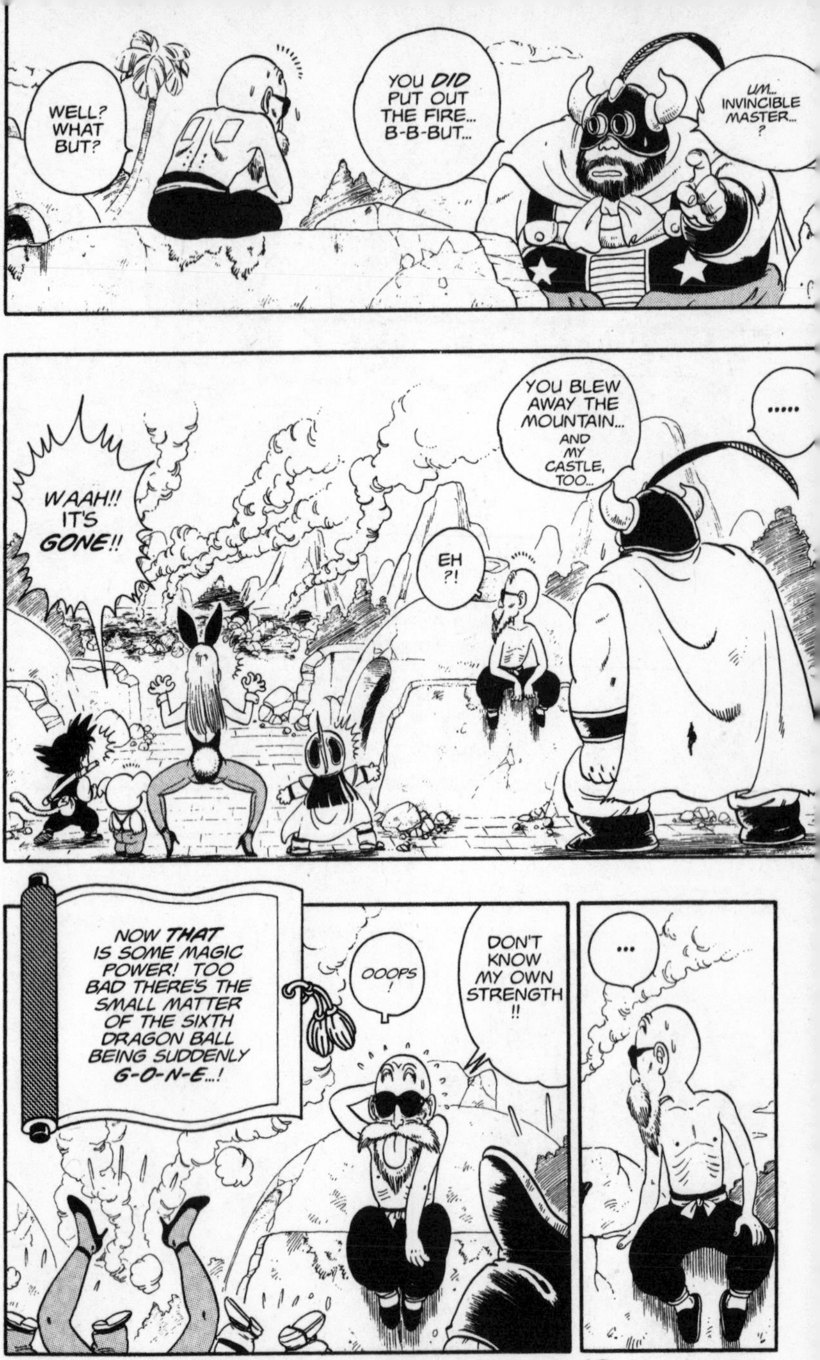
UM... INVINCIBLE MASTER... ?
YOU DID PUT OUT THE FIRE... B-B-BUT...
WELL? WHAT BUT?
......
YOU BLEW AWAY THE MOUNTAIN... AND MY CASTLE, TOO...
EH ?!
WAAH!! IT'S GONE!!
...
DON'T KNOW MY OWN STRENGTH !!
OOOPS !
NOW THAT IS SOME MAGIC POWER! TOO BAD THERE'S THE SMALL MATTER OF THE SIXTH DRAGON BALL BEING SUDDENLY G-O-N-E...!

NEXT: OUT OF ***FRY-PAN... AND*** THE ***FIRE...***

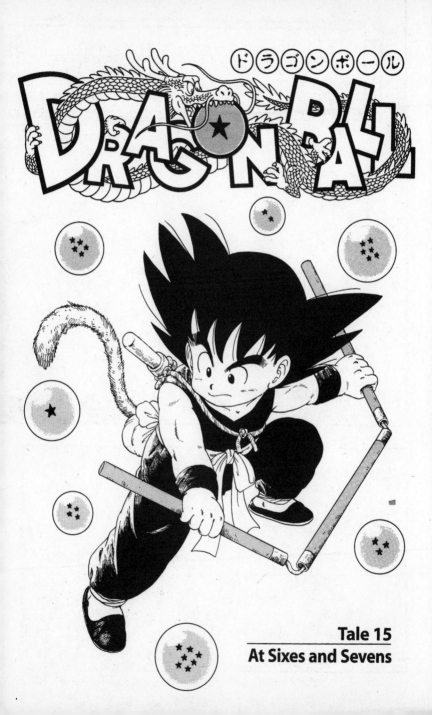

ドラゴンボール

DRAGON BALL

Tale 15
At Sixes and Sevens

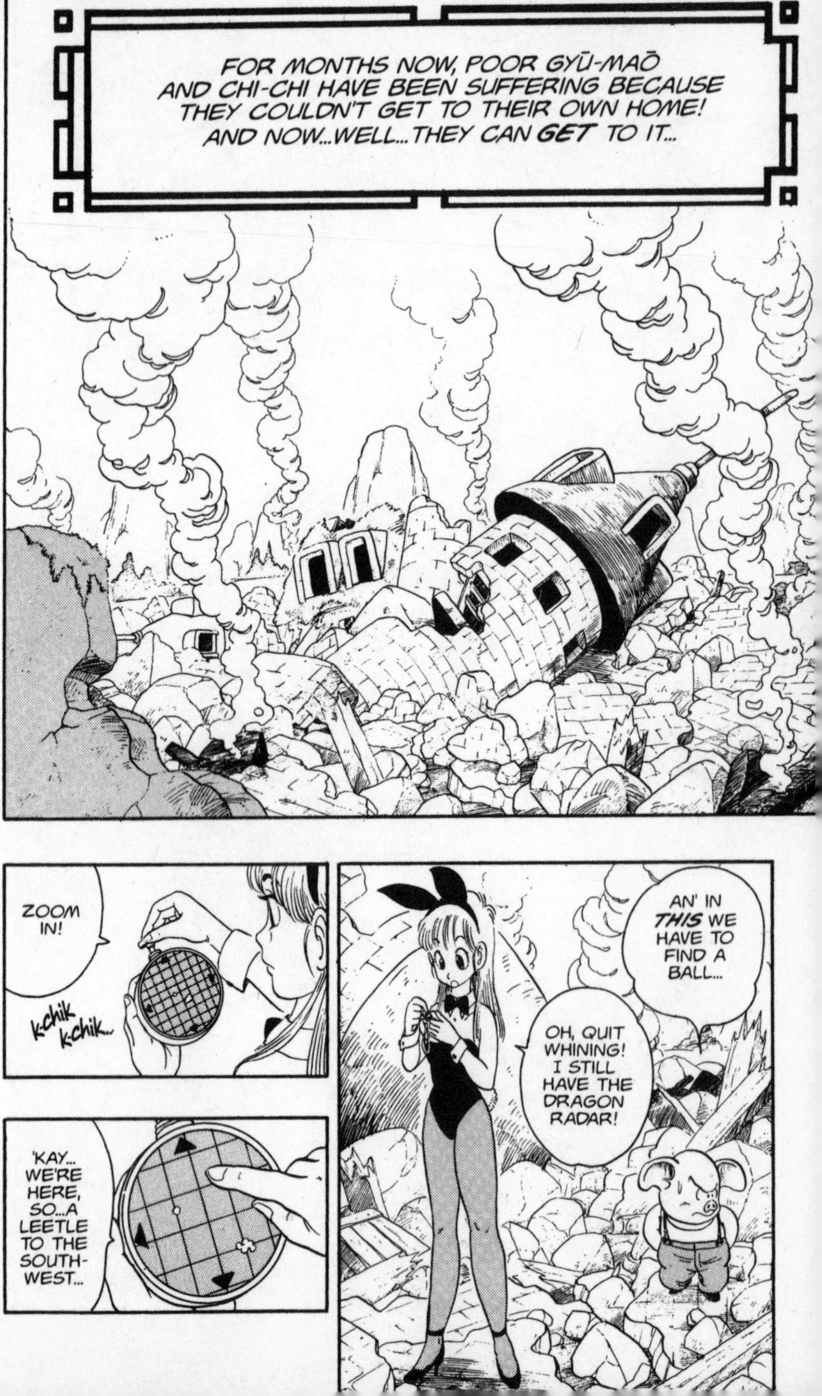
FOR MONTHS NOW, POOR GYŪ-MAŌ AND CHI-CHI HAVE BEEN SUFFERING BECAUSE THEY COULDN'T GET TO THEIR OWN HOME! AND NOW...WELL...THEY CAN **GET** TO IT...
AN' IN **THIS** WE HAVE TO FIND A BALL...
OH, QUIT WHINING! I STILL HAVE THE DRAGON RADAR!
ZOOM IN!
k-chik k-chik...
'KAY... WE'RE HERE, SO...A LEETLE TO THE SOUTH-WEST...

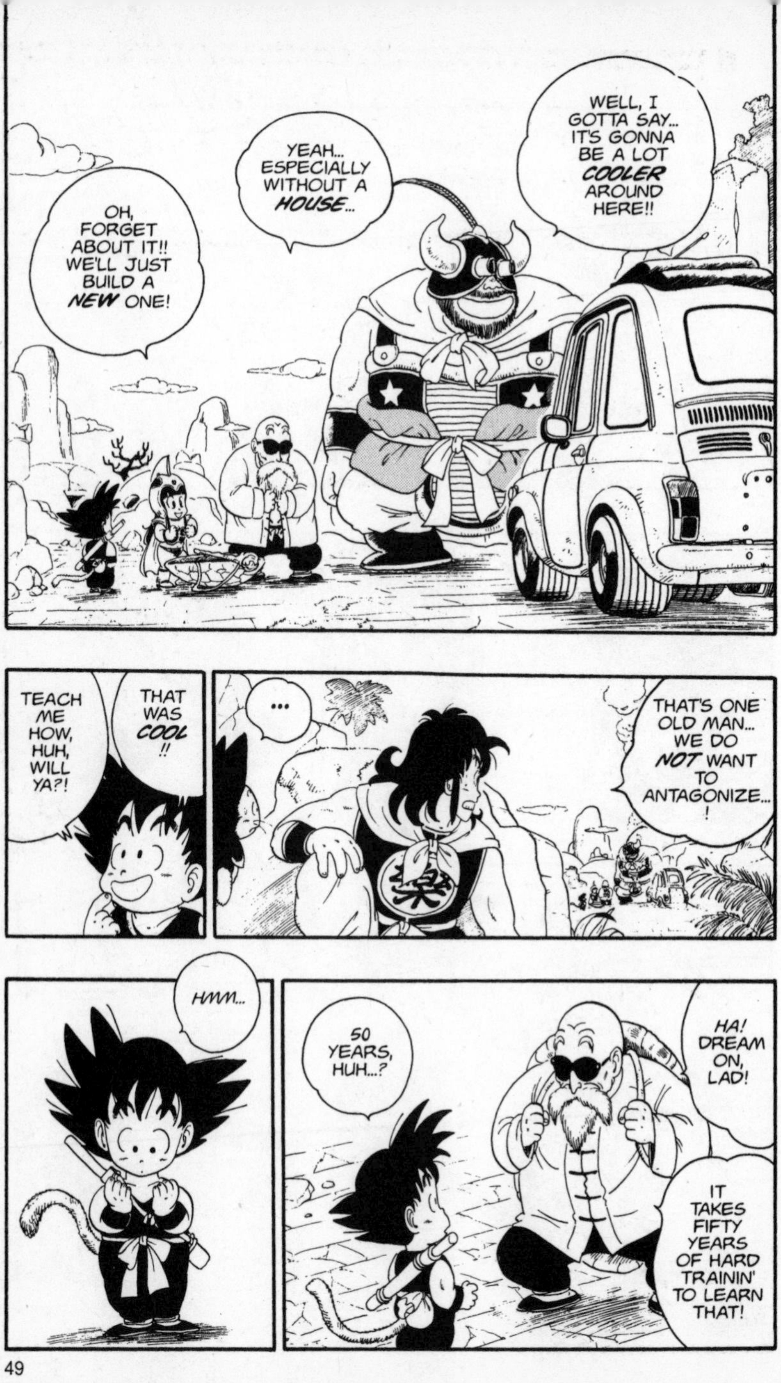
WELL, I GOTTA SAY... IT'S GONNA BE A LOT COOLER AROUND HERE!!
YEAH... ESPECIALLY WITHOUT A HOUSE...
OH, FORGET ABOUT IT!! WE'LL JUST BUILD A NEW ONE!
THAT'S ONE OLD MAN... WE DO NOT WANT TO ANTAGONIZE...!
...
THAT WAS COOL!!
TEACH ME HOW, HUH, WILL YA?!
HA! DREAM ON, LAD!
IT TAKES FIFTY YEARS OF HARD TRAININ' TO LEARN THAT!
50 YEARS, HUH...?
HMM...

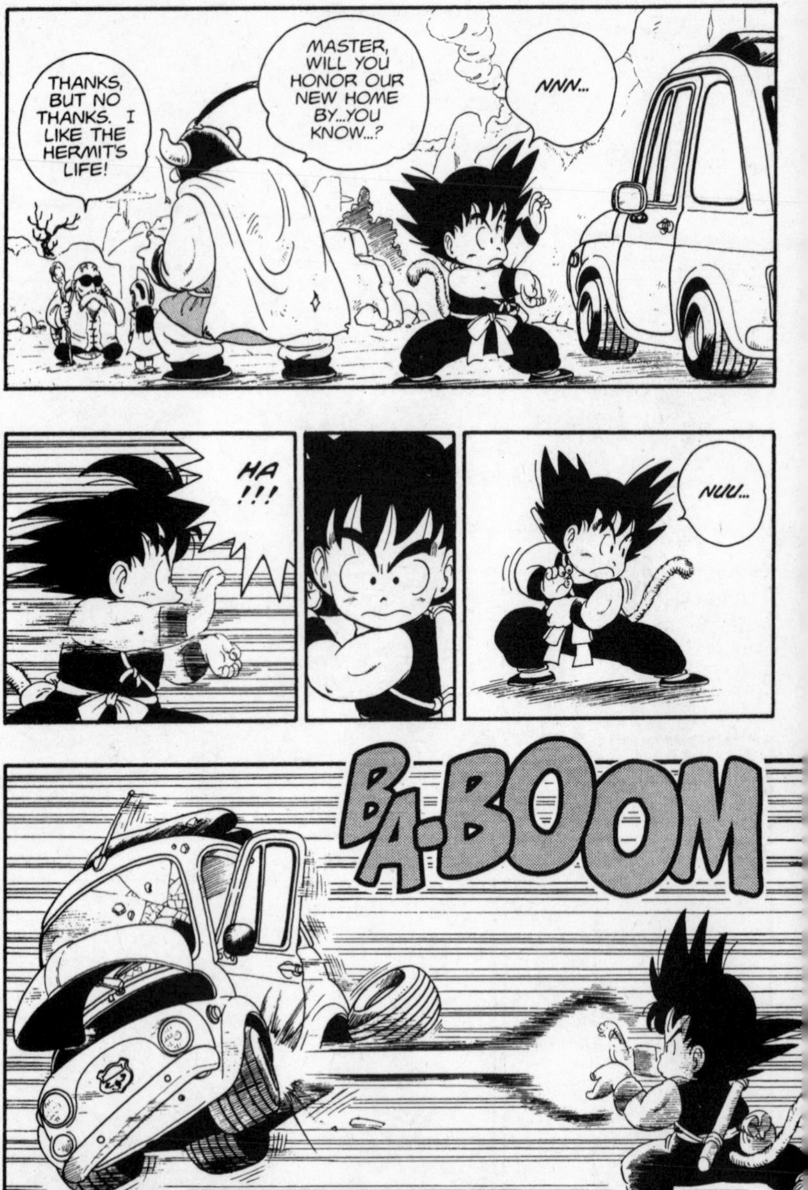
NNN...
MASTER, WILL YOU HONOR OUR NEW HOME BY...YOU KNOW...?
THANKS, BUT NO THANKS. I LIKE THE HERMIT'S LIFE!
NUU...
HA !!!
BA-BOOM

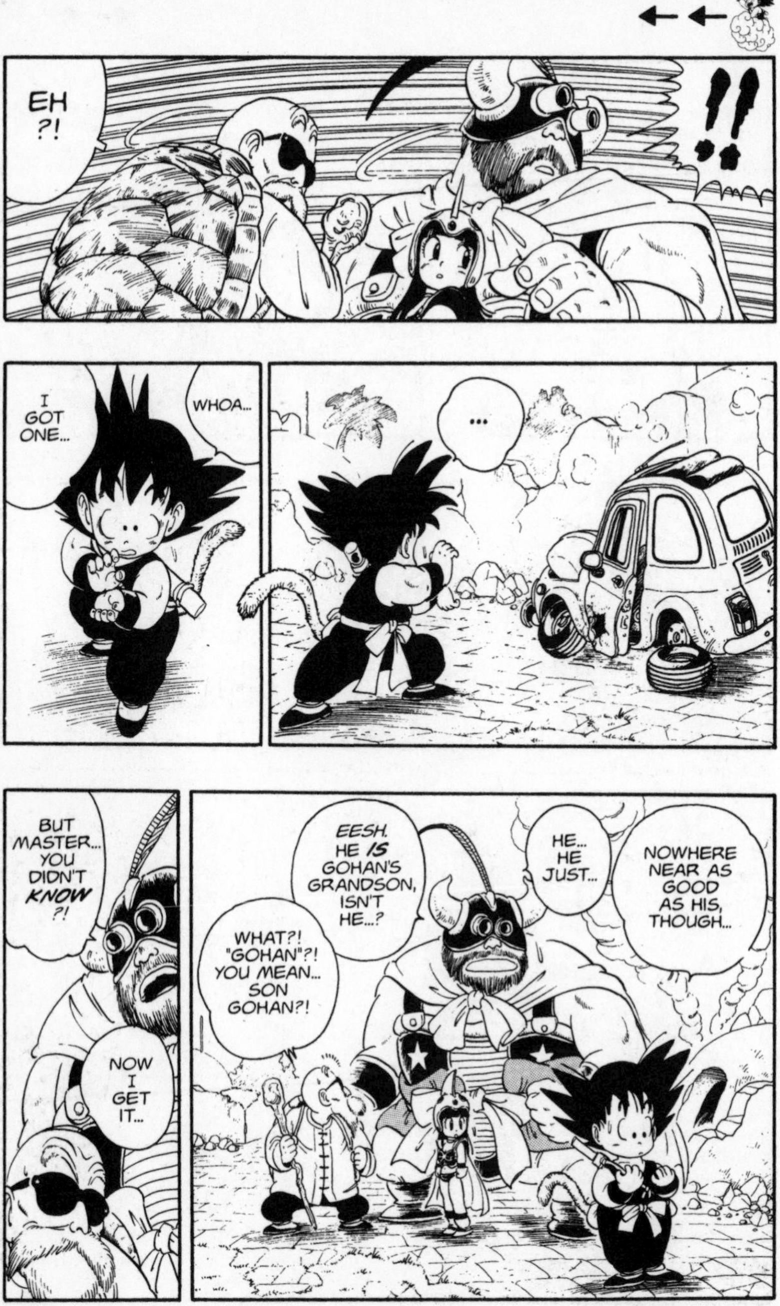

!!
EH ?!
...
WHOA...
I GOT ONE...
NOWHERE NEAR AS GOOD AS HIS, THOUGH...
HE... HE JUST...
EESH. HE *IS* GOHAN'S GRANDSON, ISN'T HE...?
WHAT?! "GOHAN"?! YOU MEAN... SON GOHAN?!
BUT MASTER... YOU DIDN'T *KNOW* ?!
NOW I GET IT...

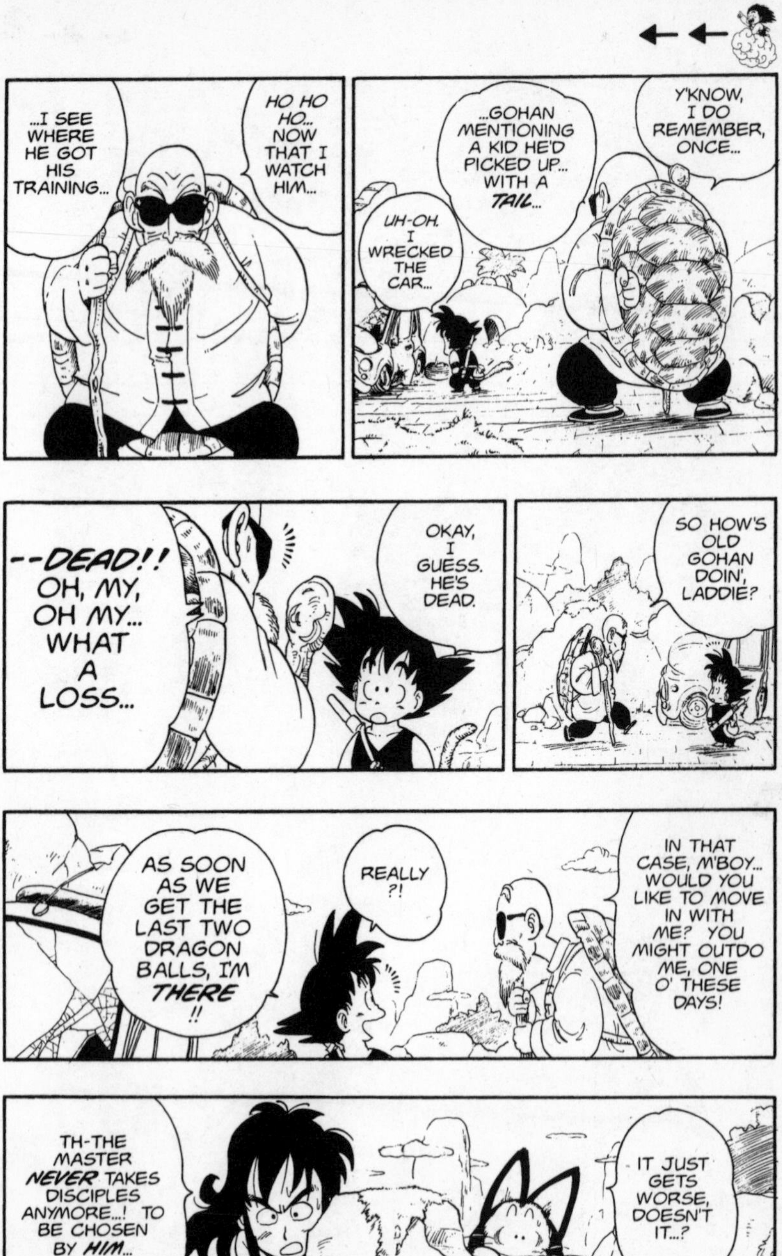
Y'KNOW, I DO REMEMBER, ONCE...
...GOHAN MENTIONING A KID HE'D PICKED UP... WITH A TAIL...
UH-OH. I WRECKED THE CAR...
HO HO HO... NOW THAT I WATCH HIM...
...I SEE WHERE HE GOT HIS TRAINING...
SO HOW'S OLD GOHAN DOIN', LADDIE?
OKAY, I GUESS. HE'S DEAD.
--DEAD!! OH, MY, OH MY... WHAT A LOSS...
IN THAT CASE, M'BOY... WOULD YOU LIKE TO MOVE IN WITH ME? YOU MIGHT OUTDO ME, ONE O' THESE DAYS!
REALLY ?!
AS SOON AS WE GET THE LAST TWO DRAGON BALLS, I'M THERE !!
IT JUST GETS WORSE, DOESN'T IT...?
TH-THE MASTER NEVER TAKES DISCIPLES ANYMORE...! TO BE CHOSEN BY HIM... BRRRR!

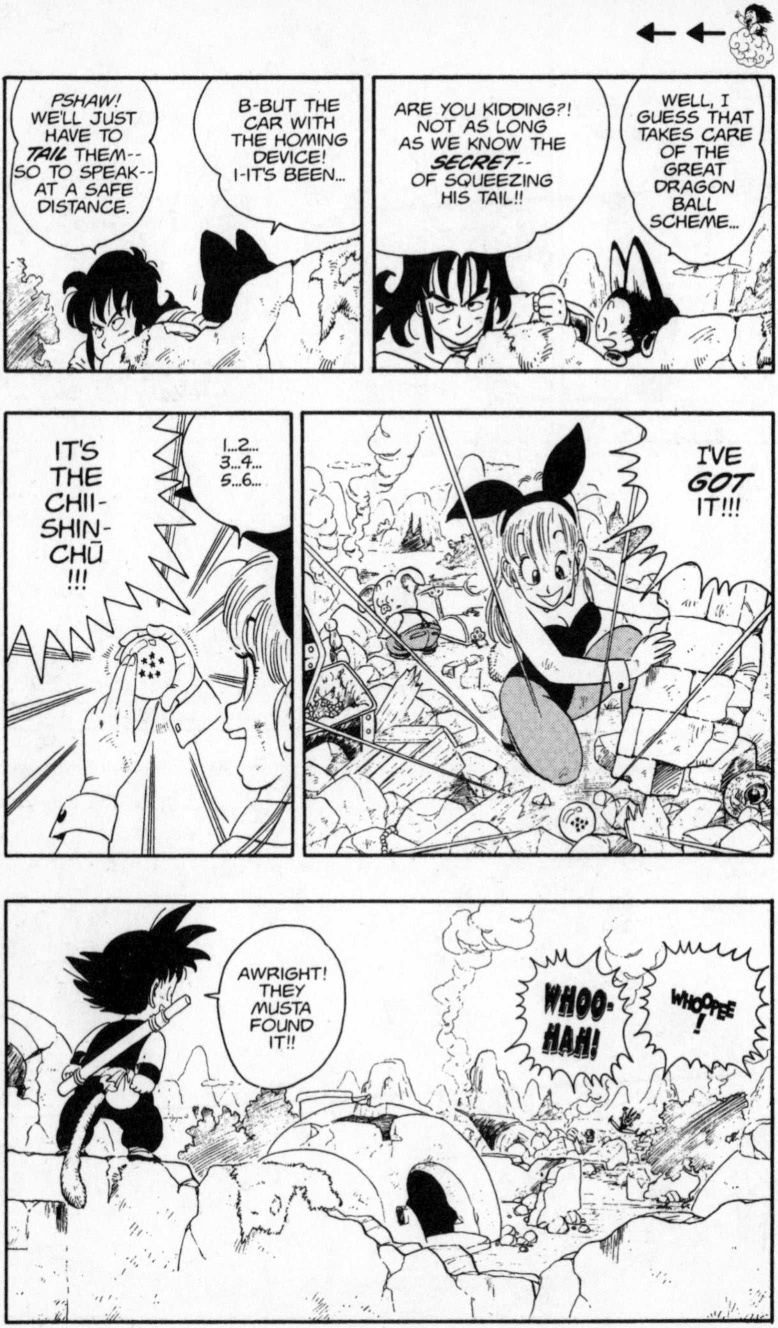
WELL, I GUESS THAT TAKES CARE OF THE GREAT DRAGON BALL SCHEME...
ARE YOU KIDDING?! NOT AS LONG AS WE KNOW THE SECRET-- OF SQUEEZING HIS TAIL!!
B-BUT THE CAR WITH THE HOMING DEVICE! I-IT'S BEEN...
PSHAW! WE'LL JUST HAVE TO TAIL THEM-- SO TO SPEAK-- AT A SAFE DISTANCE.
I'VE GOT IT!!!
1...2... 3...4... 5...6...
IT'S THE CHII-SHIN-CHŪ!!!
WHOOPEE!
WHOO-HAH!
AWRIGHT! THEY MUSTA FOUND IT!!

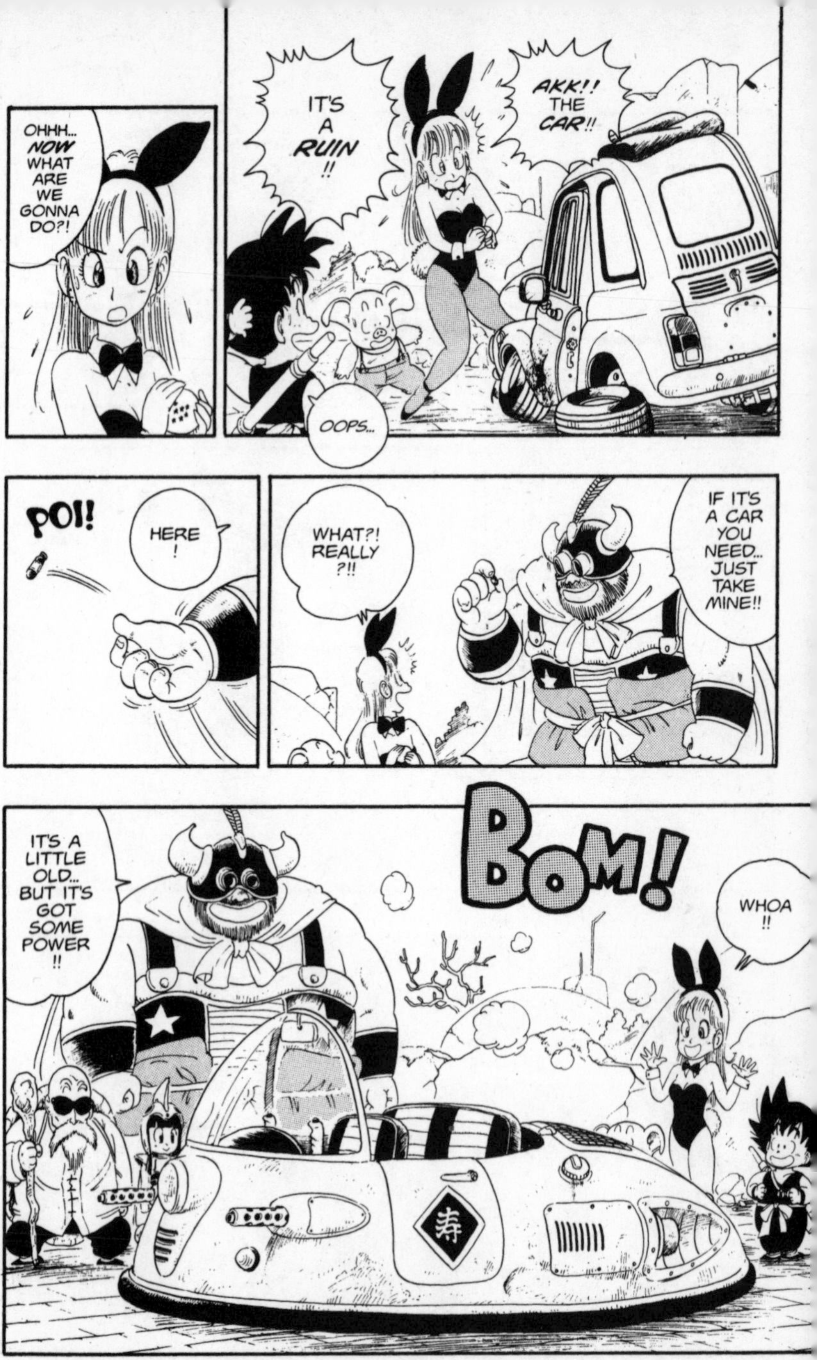
AKK!! THE CAR!!
IT'S A RUIN!!
OOPS...
OHHH... NOW WHAT ARE WE GONNA DO?!
IF IT'S A CAR YOU NEED... JUST TAKE MINE!!
WHAT?! REALLY?!!
POI!
HERE!
BOM!
WHOA!!
IT'S A LITTLE OLD... BUT IT'S GOT SOME POWER!!

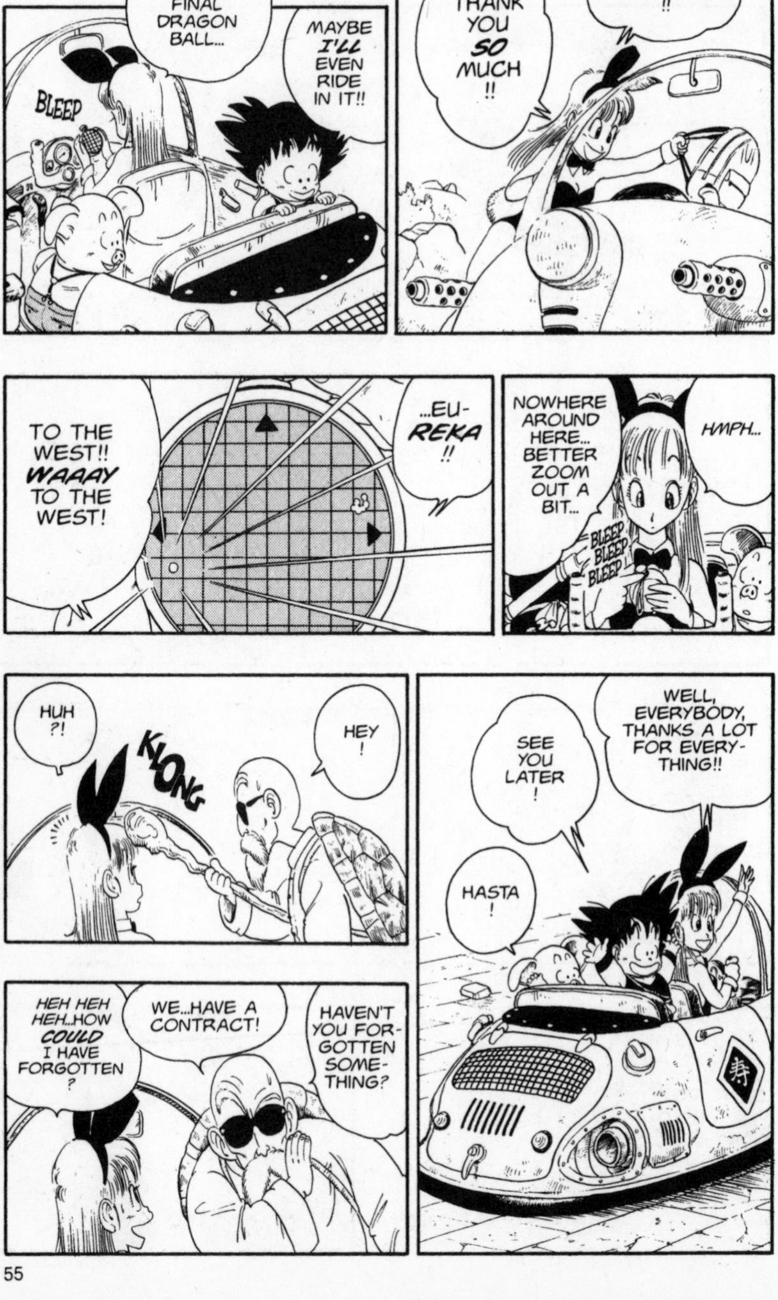
IT'S GORGEOUS!!
THANK YOU SO MUCH!!
MAYBE I'LL EVEN RIDE IN IT!!
NOW... FOR THE FINAL DRAGON BALL...
BLEEP
HMPH...
NOWHERE AROUND HERE... BETTER ZOOM OUT A BIT...
BLEEP BLEEP BLEEP
...EU-REKA!!
TO THE WEST!! WAAAY TO THE WEST!
WELL, EVERYBODY, THANKS A LOT FOR EVERY-THING!!
SEE YOU LATER!
HASTA!
HEY!
KLONG
HUH?!
HAVEN'T YOU FOR-GOTTEN SOME-THING?
WE...HAVE A CONTRACT!
HEH HEH HEH...HOW COULD I HAVE FORGOTTEN?

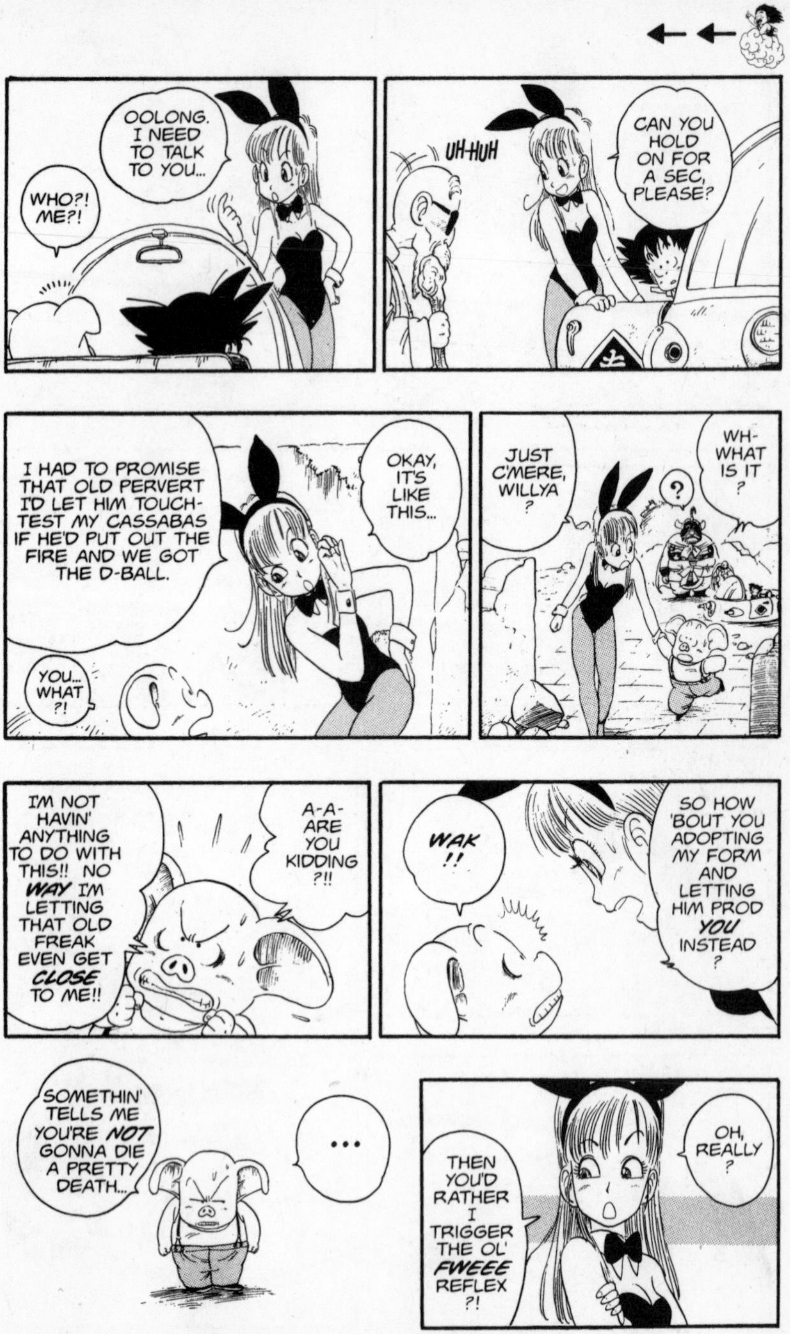
CAN YOU HOLD ON FOR A SEC, PLEASE?
UH-HUH
OOLONG. I NEED TO TALK TO YOU...
WHO?! ME?!
WH-WHAT IS IT?
?
JUST C'MERE, WILLYA?
OKAY, IT'S LIKE THIS...
I HAD TO PROMISE THAT OLD PERVERT I'D LET HIM TOUCH-TEST MY CASSABAS IF HE'D PUT OUT THE FIRE AND WE GOT THE D-BALL.
YOU... WHAT?!
SO HOW 'BOUT YOU ADOPTING MY FORM AND LETTING HIM PROD YOU INSTEAD?
WAK!!
A-A-ARE YOU KIDDING?!!
I'M NOT HAVIN' ANYTHING TO DO WITH THIS!! NO WAY I'M LETTING THAT OLD FREAK EVEN GET CLOSE TO ME!!
OH, REALLY?
THEN YOU'D RATHER I TRIGGER THE OL' FWEEE REFLEX?!
...
SOMETHIN' TELLS ME YOU'RE NOT GONNA DIE A PRETTY DEATH...

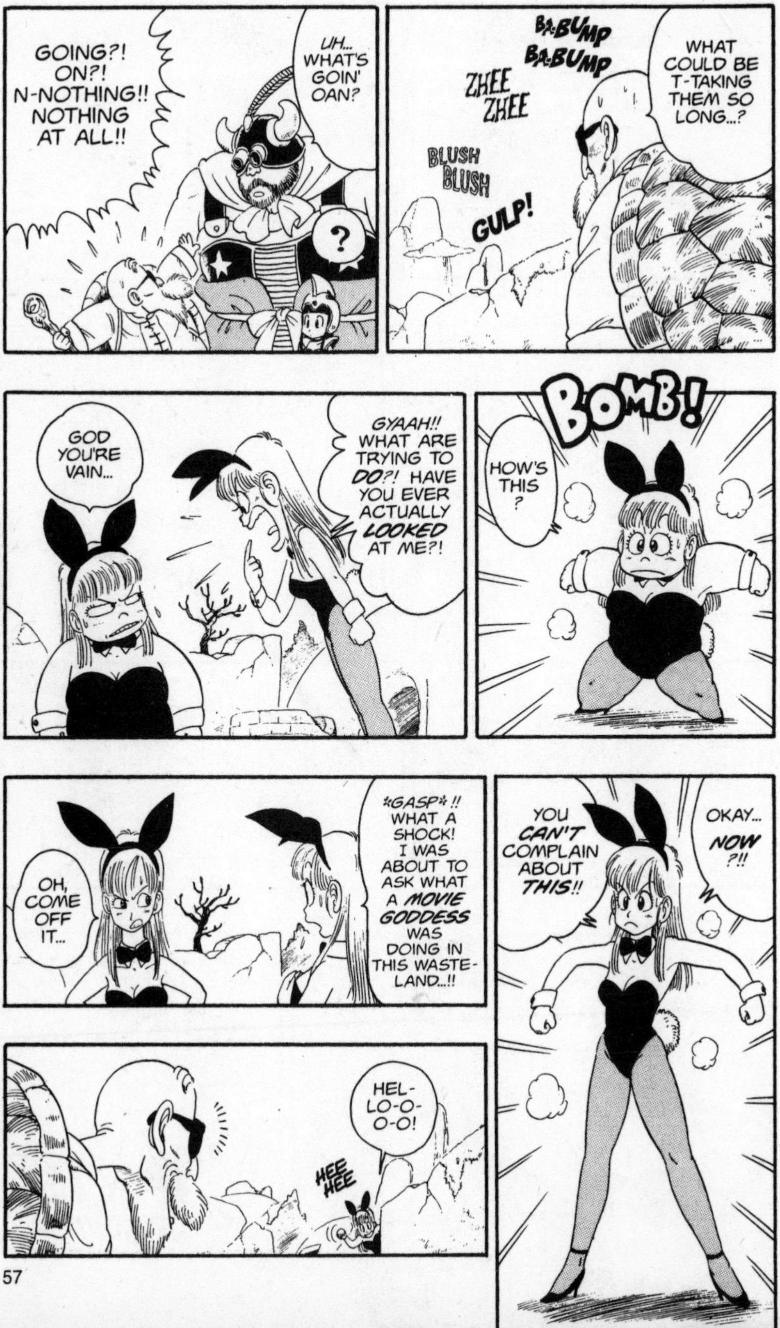
BA-BUMP BA-BUMP
WHAT COULD BE T-TAKING THEM SO LONG...?
ZHEE ZHEE
BLUSH BLUSH
GULP!
UH... WHAT'S GOIN' OAN?
GOING?! ON?! N-NOTHING!! NOTHING AT ALL!!
?
BOMB!
HOW'S THIS?
GYAAH!! WHAT ARE TRYING TO DO?! HAVE YOU EVER ACTUALLY LOOKED AT ME?!
GOD YOU'RE VAIN...
OKAY... NOW?!!
YOU CAN'T COMPLAIN ABOUT THIS!!
GASP !! WHAT A SHOCK! I WAS ABOUT TO ASK WHAT A MOVIE GODDESS WAS DOING IN THIS WASTE-LAND...!!
OH, COME OFF IT...
HEL-LO-O-O-O!
HEE HEE

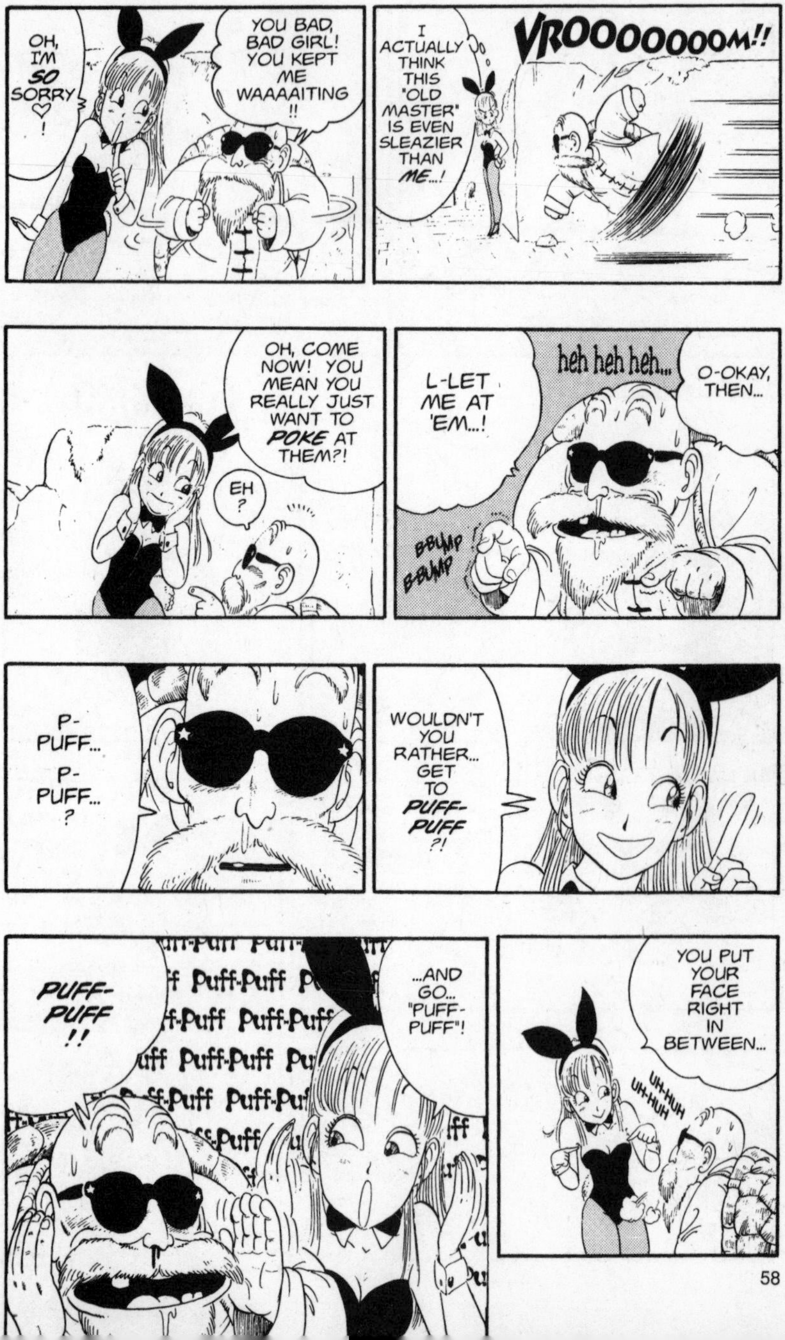
VROOOOOOOM!!
I ACTUALLY THINK THIS "OLD MASTER" IS EVEN SLEAZIER THAN ME...!
YOU BAD, BAD GIRL! YOU KEPT ME WAAAAITING!!
OH, I'M SO SORRY ♡!
O-OKAY, THEN...
heh heh heh...
L-LET ME AT 'EM...!
B-BUMP B-BUMP
OH, COME NOW! YOU MEAN YOU REALLY JUST WANT TO POKE AT THEM?!
EH?
WOULDN'T YOU RATHER... GET TO PUFF-PUFF?!
P-PUFF... P-PUFF...?
YOU PUT YOUR FACE RIGHT IN BETWEEN...
UH-HUH UH-HUH
...AND GO... "PUFF-PUFF"!
PUFF-PUFF!!

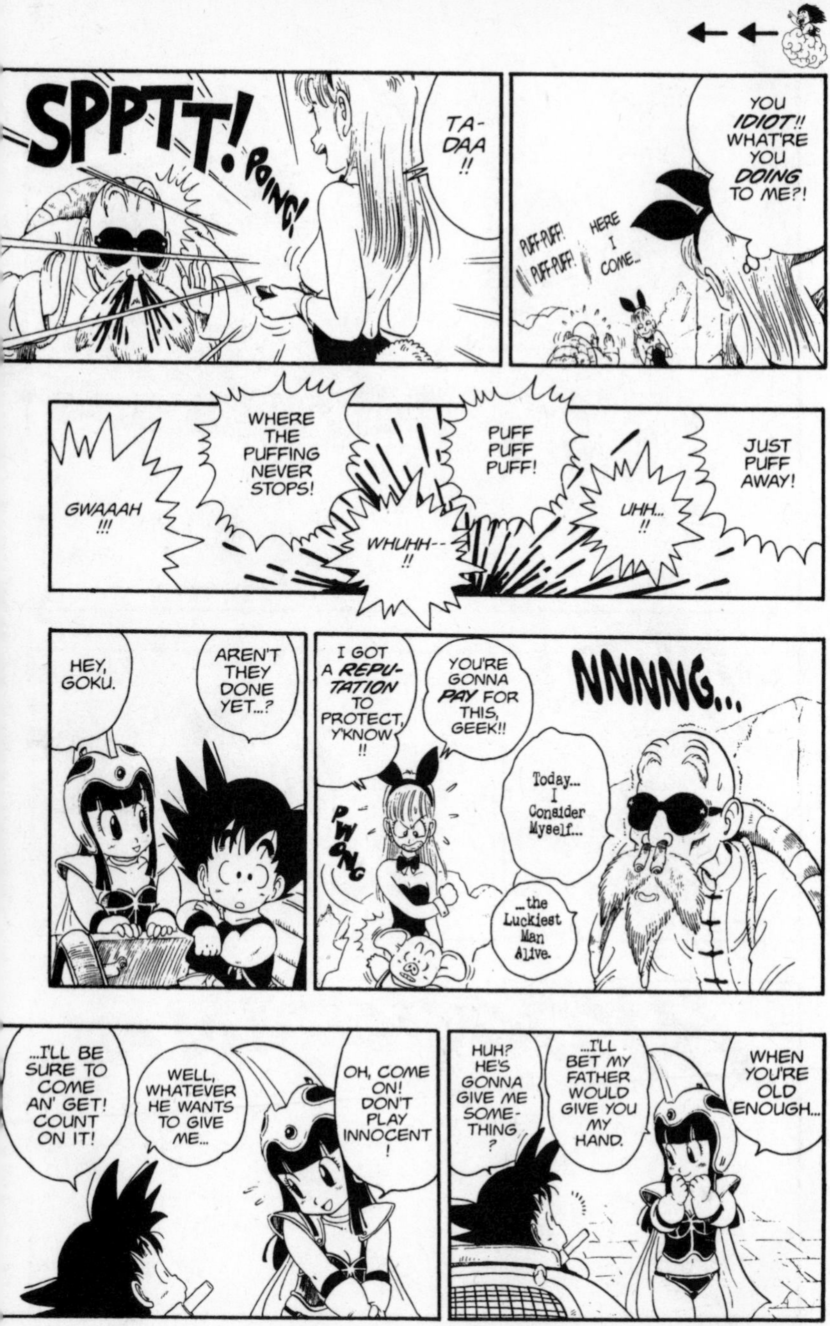
YOU IDIOT!! WHAT'RE YOU DOING TO ME?!
HERE I COME...
PUFF-PUFF! PUFF-PUFF!
TA-DAA!!
SPPTT!
POING!
JUST PUFF AWAY!
UHH...!!
PUFF PUFF PUFF!
WHUHH--!!
WHERE THE PUFFING NEVER STOPS!
GWAAAH!!!
NNNNG...
YOU'RE GONNA PAY FOR THIS, GEEK!!
I GOT A REPUTATION TO PROTECT, Y'KNOW!!
Today... I Consider Myself...
...the Luckiest Man Alive.
PWONG
AREN'T THEY DONE YET...?
HEY, GOKU.
WHEN YOU'RE OLD ENOUGH...
...I'LL BET MY FATHER WOULD GIVE YOU MY HAND.
HUH? HE'S GONNA GIVE ME SOMETHING?
OH, COME ON! DON'T PLAY INNOCENT!
WELL, WHATEVER HE WANTS TO GIVE ME...
...I'LL BE SURE TO COME AN' GET! COUNT ON IT!

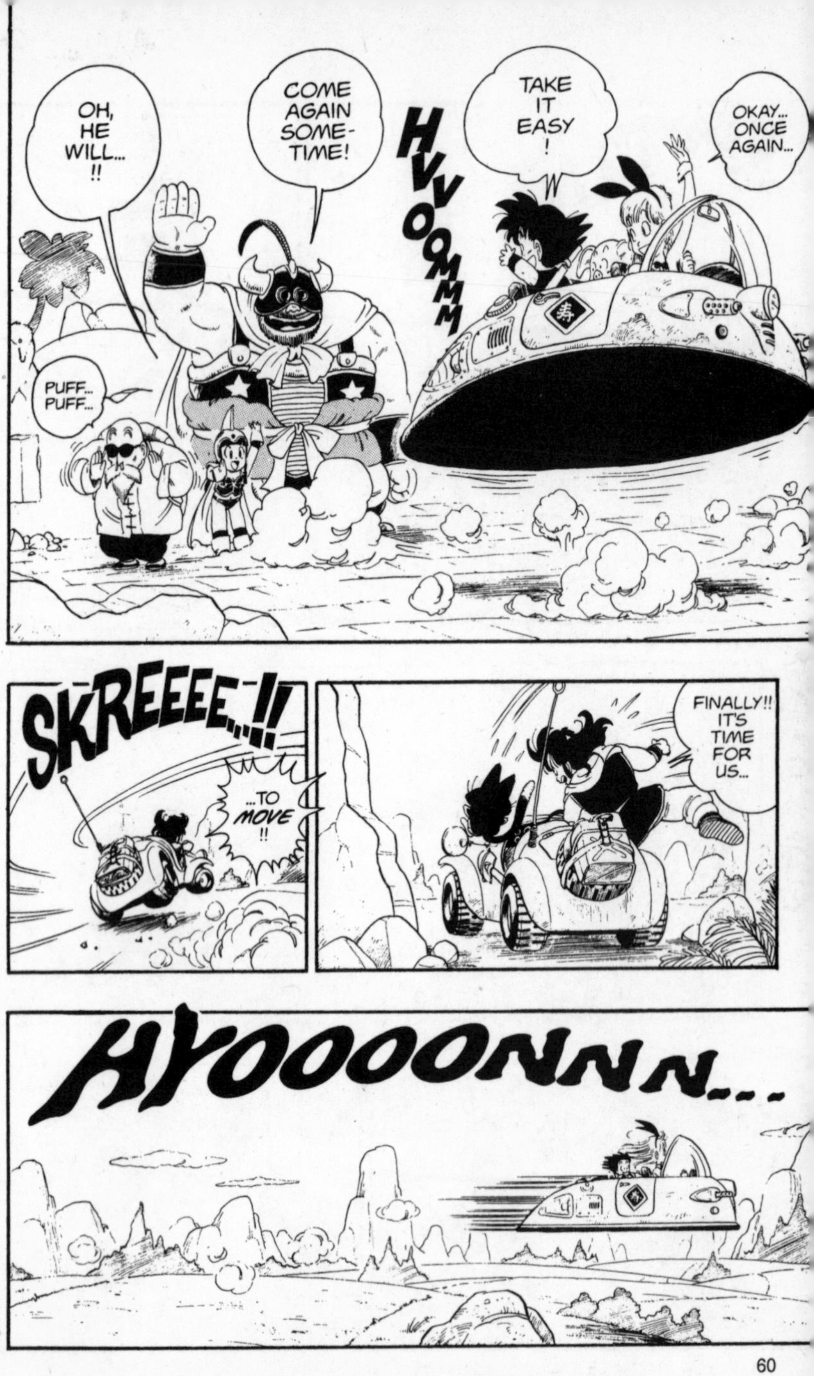
OKAY... ONCE AGAIN...
TAKE IT EASY !
HVVOOMMM
COME AGAIN SOME-TIME!
OH, HE WILL... !!
PUFF.. PUFF...
FINALLY!! IT'S TIME FOR US...
SKREEEE..!!
...TO MOVE !!
HYOOOONNN...

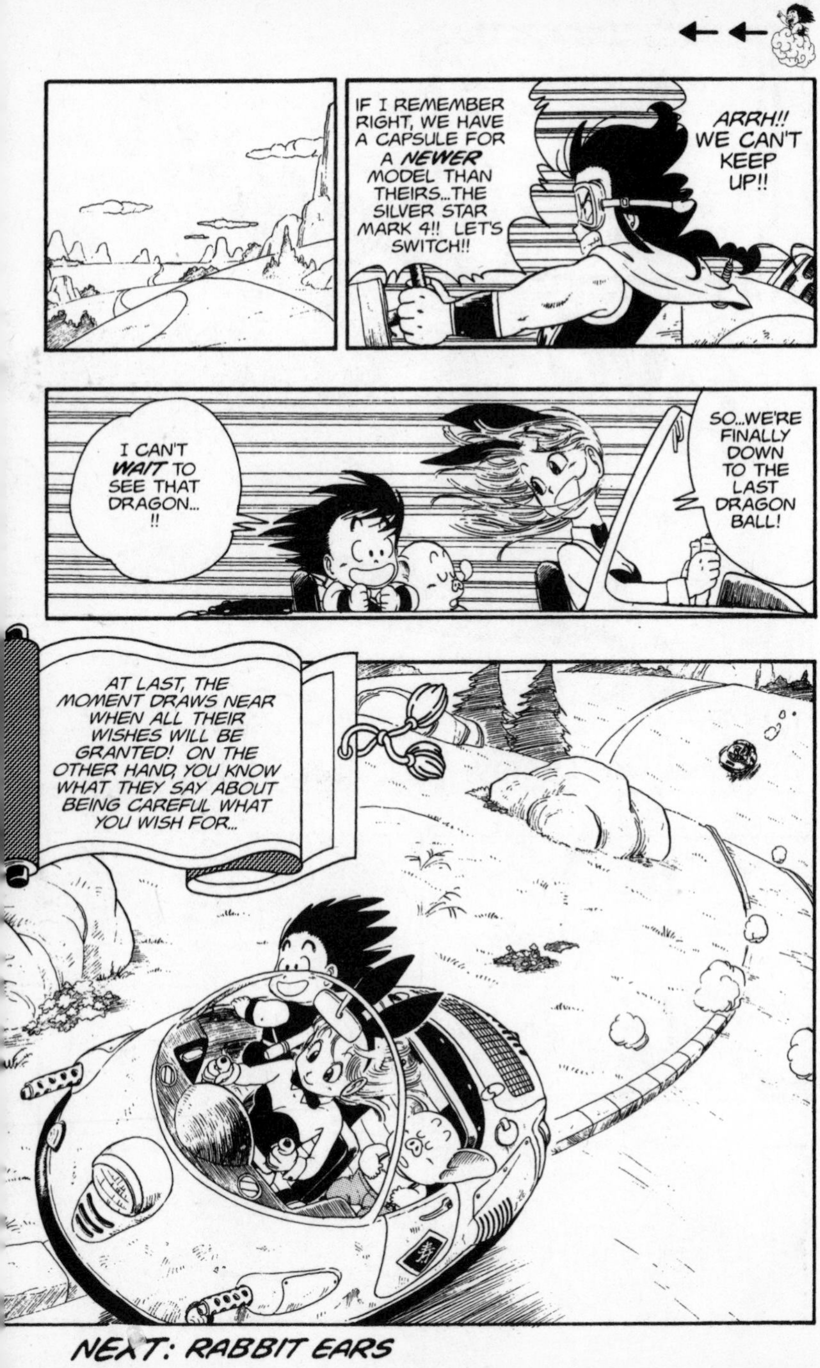
ARRH!! WE CAN'T KEEP UP!!
IF I REMEMBER RIGHT, WE HAVE A CAPSULE FOR A *NEWER* MODEL THAN THEIRS...THE SILVER STAR MARK 4!! LET'S SWITCH!!
SO...WE'RE FINALLY DOWN TO THE LAST DRAGON BALL!
I CAN'T *WAIT* TO SEE THAT DRAGON... !!
AT LAST, THE MOMENT DRAWS NEAR WHEN ALL THEIR WISHES WILL BE GRANTED! ON THE OTHER HAND, YOU KNOW WHAT THEY SAY ABOUT BEING CAREFUL WHAT YOU WISH FOR...

NEXT: RABBIT EARS

Tale 16
One Goal, One Enemy

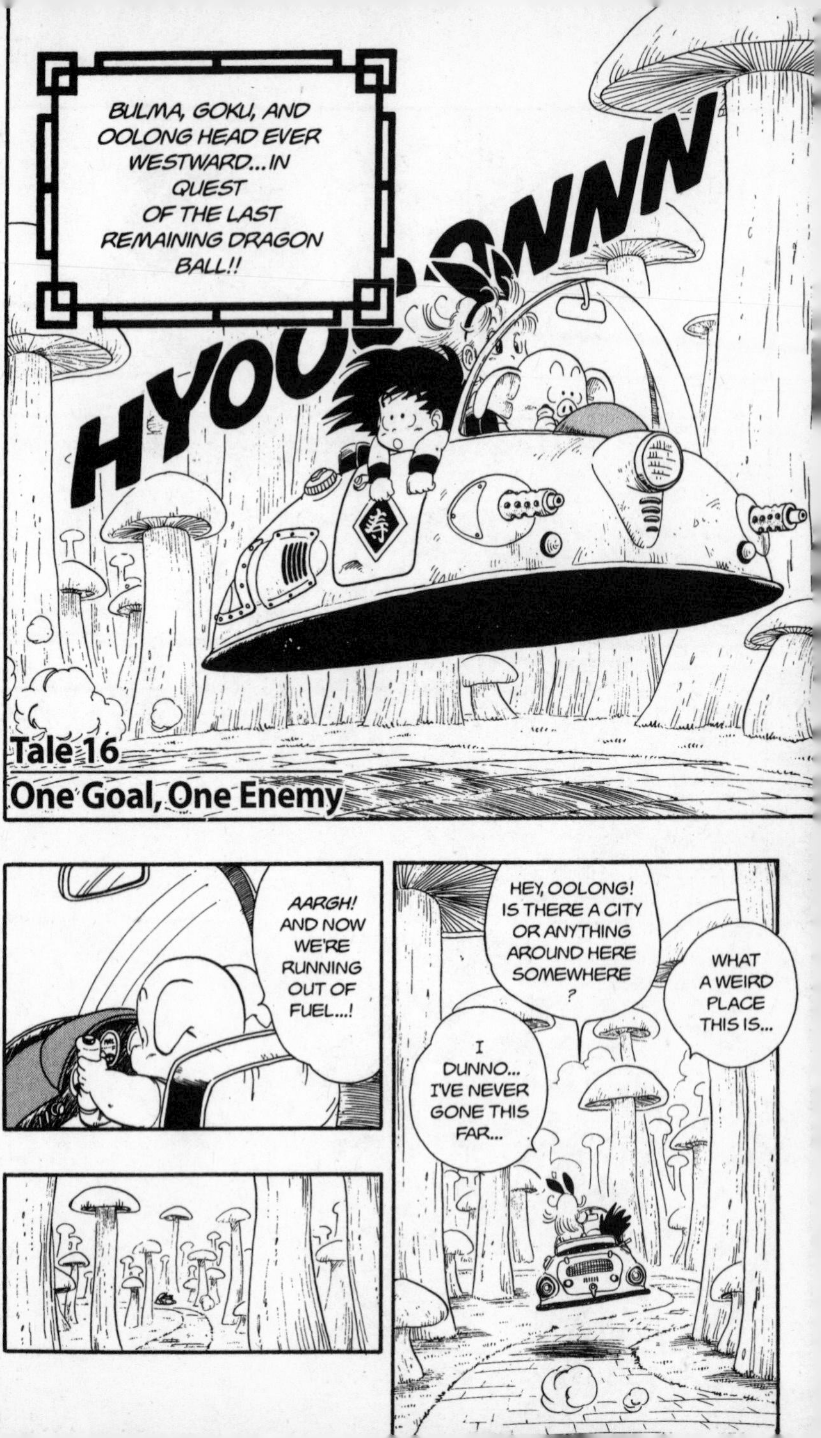
BULMA, GOKU, AND OOLONG HEAD EVER WESTWARD...IN QUEST OF THE LAST REMAINING DRAGON BALL!!
HYOU ONNN
Tale 16
One Goal, One Enemy
WHAT A WEIRD PLACE THIS IS...
HEY, OOLONG! IS THERE A CITY OR ANYTHING AROUND HERE SOMEWHERE?
I DUNNO... I'VE NEVER GONE THIS FAR...
AARGH! AND NOW WE'RE RUNNING OUT OF FUEL...!

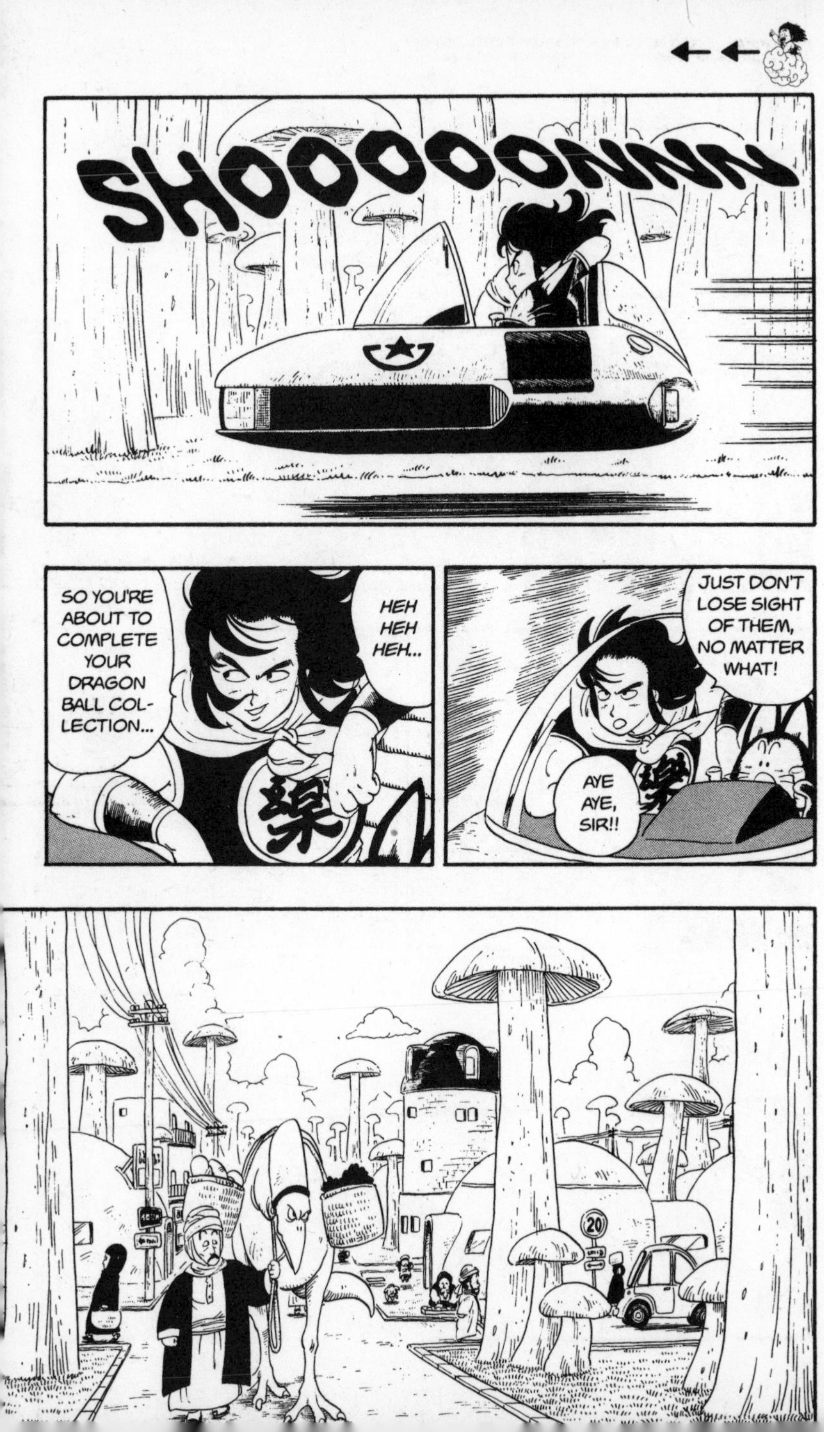
SHOOOONNN
JUST DON'T LOSE SIGHT OF THEM, NO MATTER WHAT!
AYE AYE, SIR!!
HEH HEH HEH...
SO YOU'RE ABOUT TO COMPLETE YOUR DRAGON BALL COL-LECTION...
20

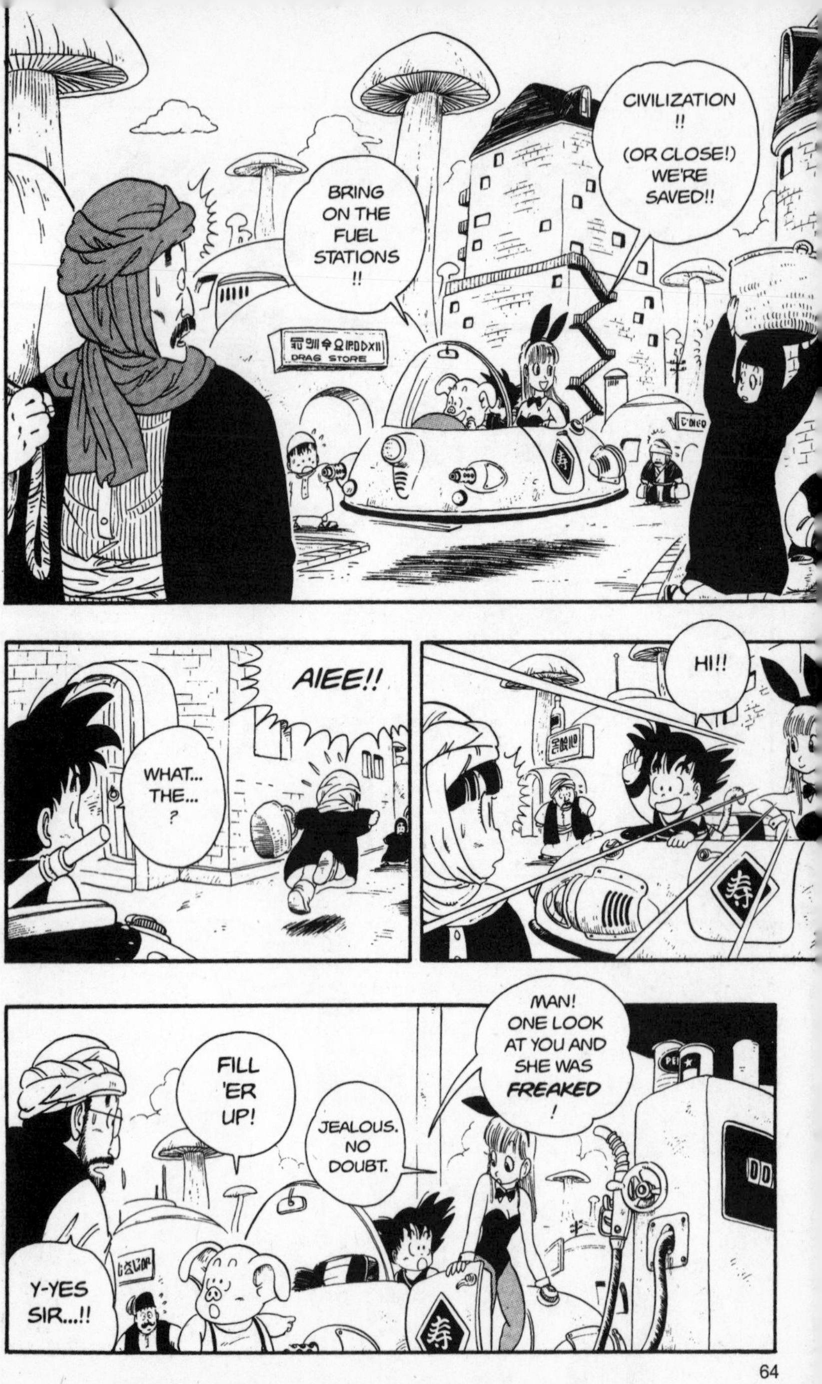
CIVILIZATION !! (OR CLOSE!) WE'RE SAVED!!
BRING ON THE FUEL STATIONS !!
DRAG STORE
HI!!
AIEE!!
WHAT... THE... ?
MAN! ONE LOOK AT YOU AND SHE WAS *FREAKED* !
JEALOUS. NO DOUBT.
FILL 'ER UP!
Y-YES SIR...!!

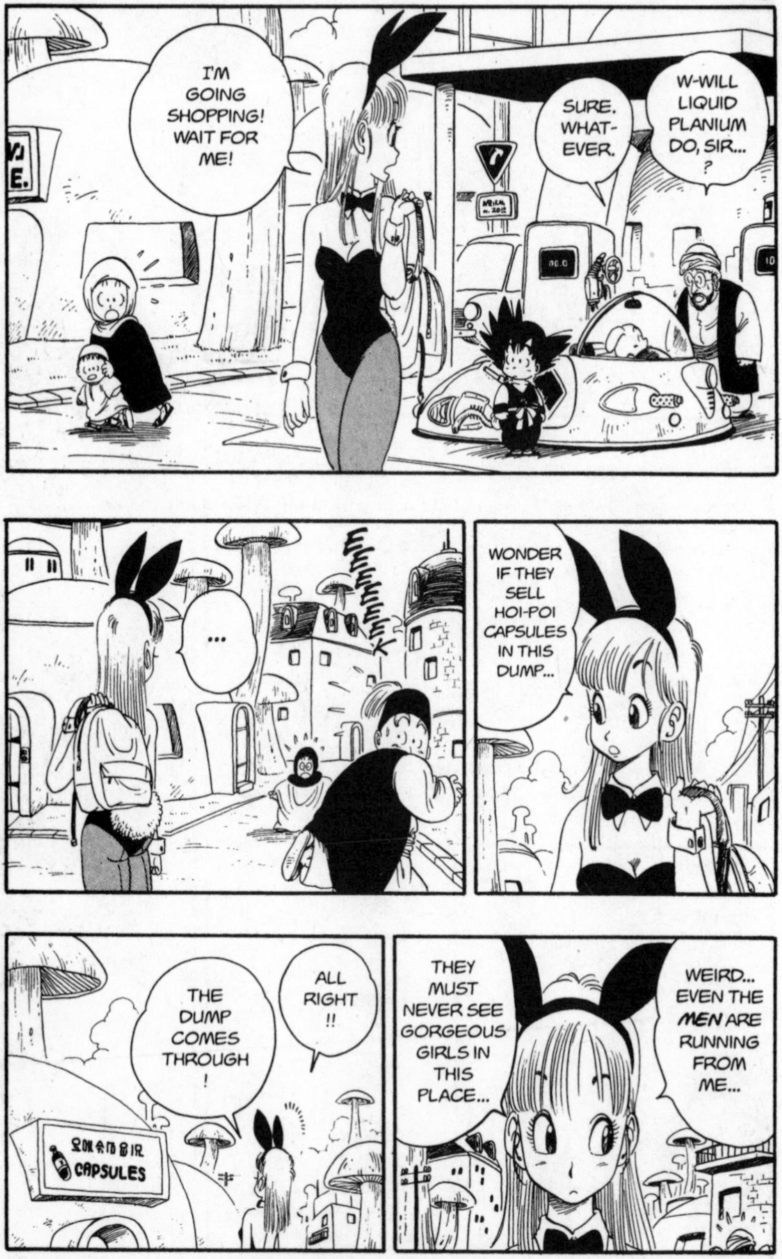
W-WILL LIQUID PLANIUM DO, SIR...?
SURE. WHATEVER.
I'M GOING SHOPPING! WAIT FOR ME!
WONDER IF THEY SELL HOI-POI CAPSULES IN THIS DUMP...
EEEEEEEK
...
WEIRD... EVEN THE MEN ARE RUNNING FROM ME...
THEY MUST NEVER SEE GORGEOUS GIRLS IN THIS PLACE...
ALL RIGHT!!
THE DUMP COMES THROUGH!
CAPSULES

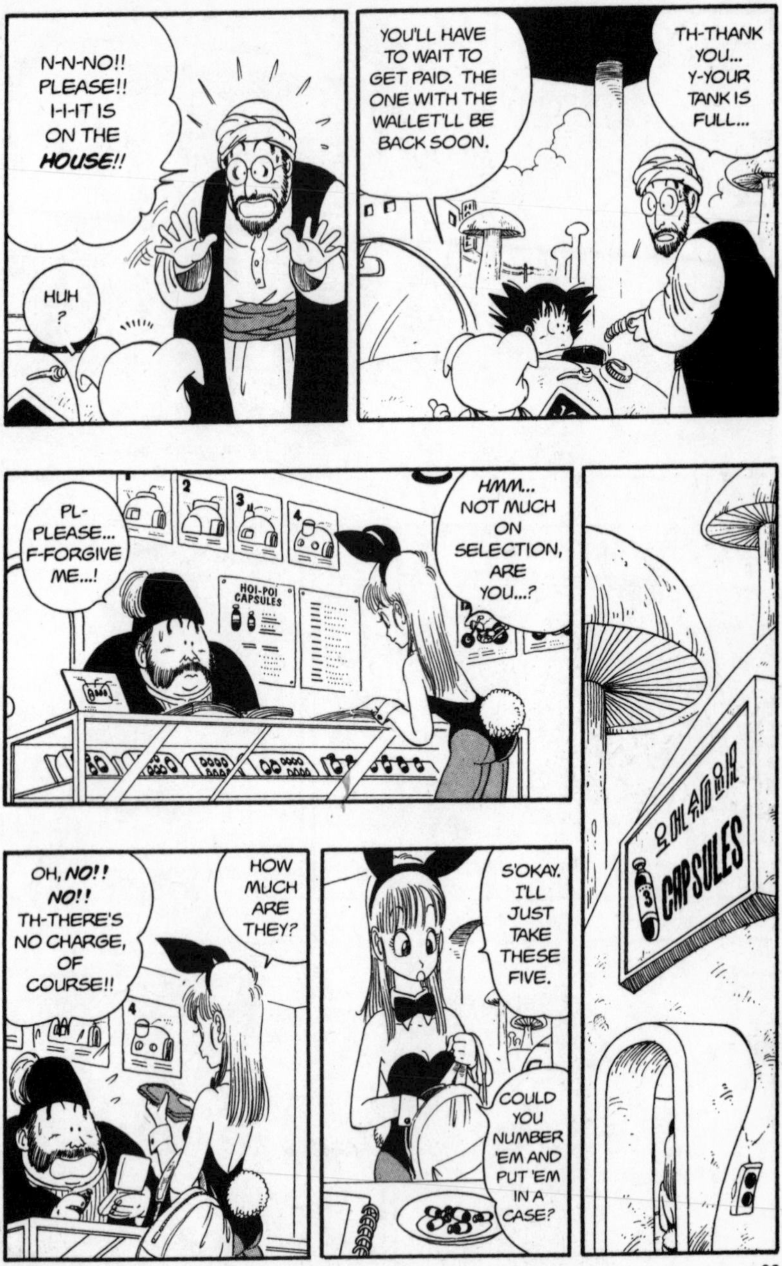
TH-THANK YOU... Y-YOUR TANK IS FULL...
YOU'LL HAVE TO WAIT TO GET PAID. THE ONE WITH THE WALLET'LL BE BACK SOON.
N-N-NO!! PLEASE!! I-I-IT IS ON THE ***HOUSE***!!
HUH?
CAPSULES
HMM... NOT MUCH ON SELECTION, ARE YOU...?
PL-PLEASE... F-FORGIVE ME...!
HOI-POI CAPSULES
S'OKAY. I'LL JUST TAKE THESE FIVE.
COULD YOU NUMBER 'EM AND PUT 'EM IN A CASE?
HOW MUCH ARE THEY?
OH, ***NO!! NO!!*** TH-THERE'S NO CHARGE, OF COURSE!!

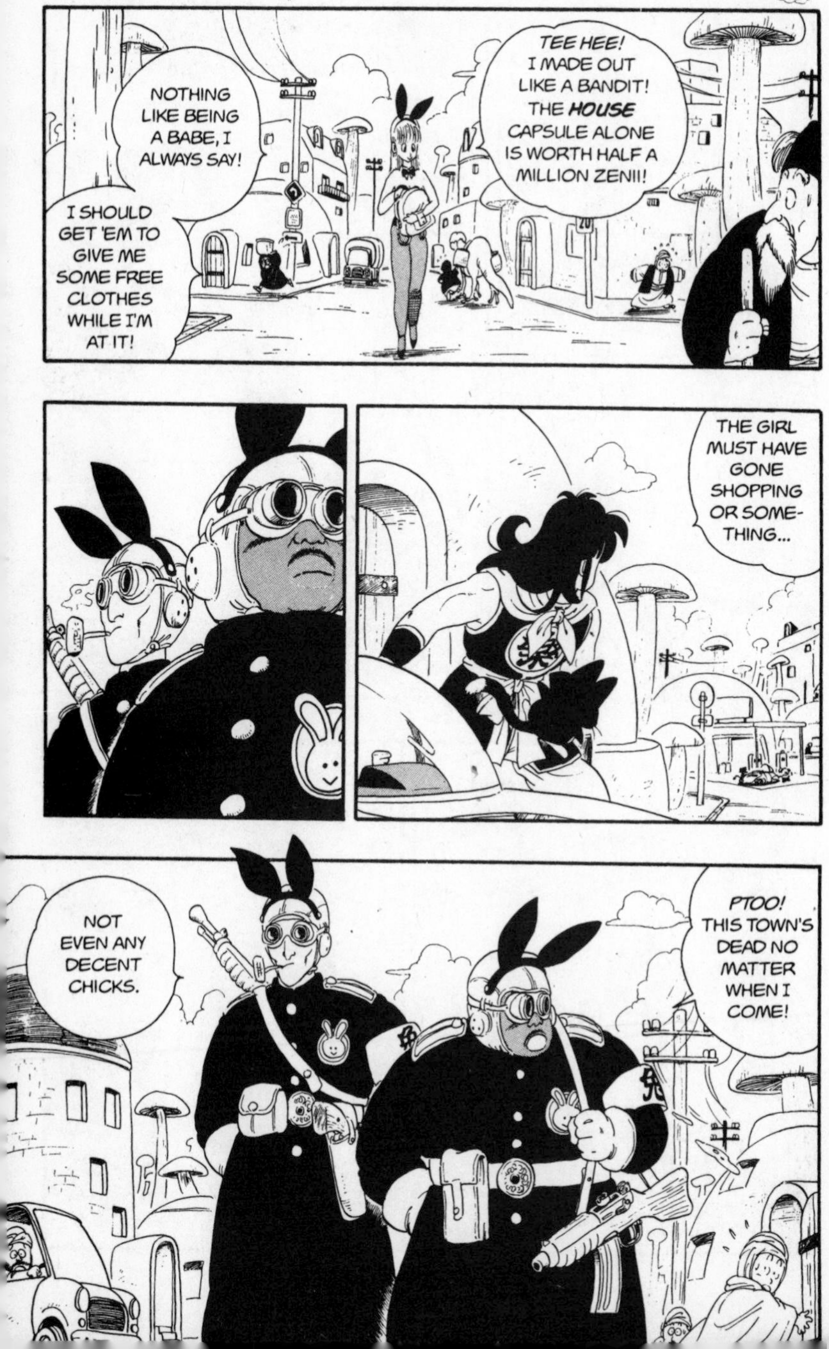
TEE HEE! I MADE OUT LIKE A BANDIT! THE **HOUSE** CAPSULE ALONE IS WORTH HALF A MILLION ZENI!!
NOTHING LIKE BEING A BABE, I ALWAYS SAY!
I SHOULD GET 'EM TO GIVE ME SOME FREE CLOTHES WHILE I'M AT IT!
THE GIRL MUST HAVE GONE SHOPPING OR SOME-THING...
PTOO! THIS TOWN'S DEAD NO MATTER WHEN I COME!
NOT EVEN ANY DECENT CHICKS.

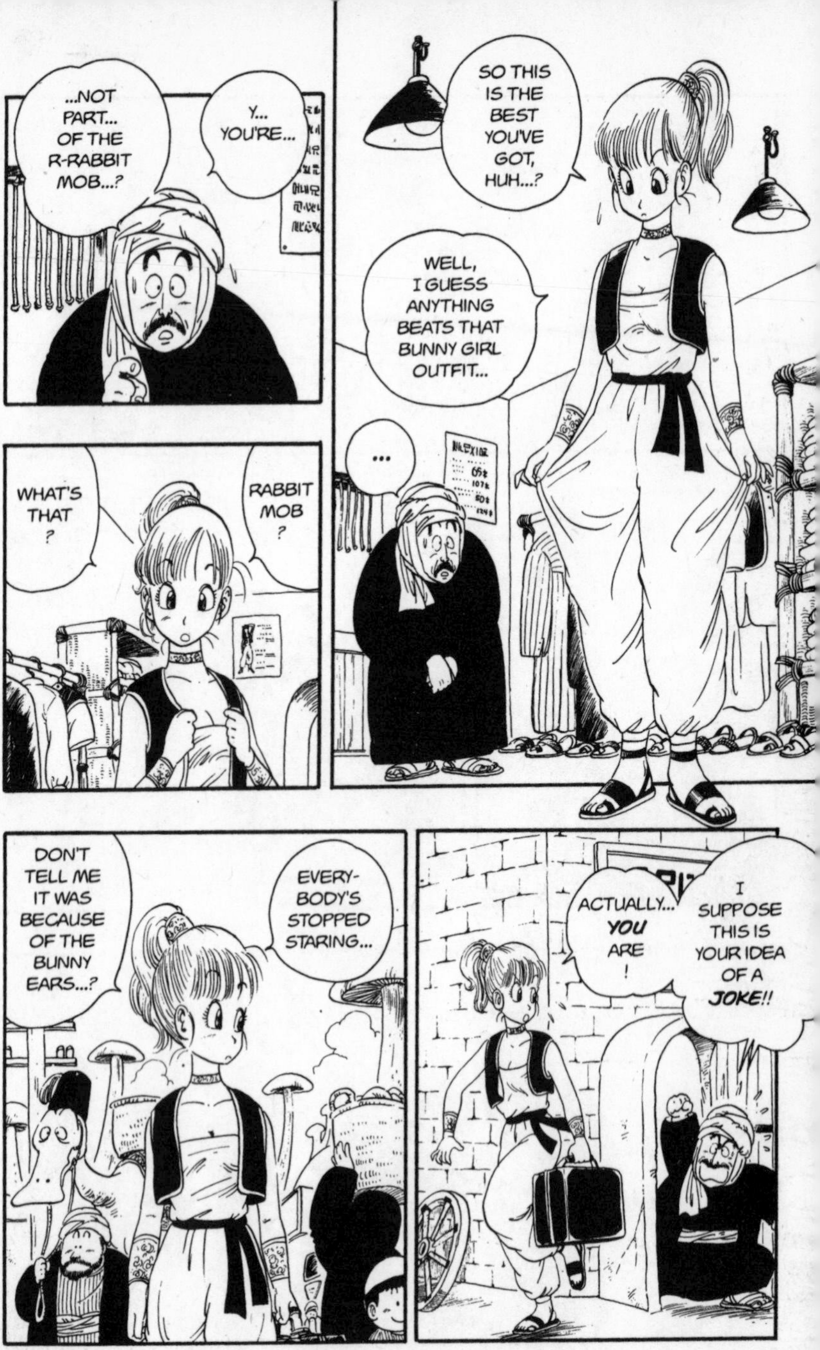
SO THIS IS THE BEST YOU'VE GOT, HUH...?
WELL, I GUESS ANYTHING BEATS THAT BUNNY GIRL OUTFIT...
...
Y... YOU'RE...
...NOT PART... OF THE R-RABBIT MOB...?
RABBIT MOB?
WHAT'S THAT?
I SUPPOSE THIS IS YOUR IDEA OF A **JOKE!!**
ACTUALLY... ***YOU*** ARE!
EVERY-BODY'S STOPPED STARING...
DON'T TELL ME IT WAS BECAUSE OF THE BUNNY EARS...?

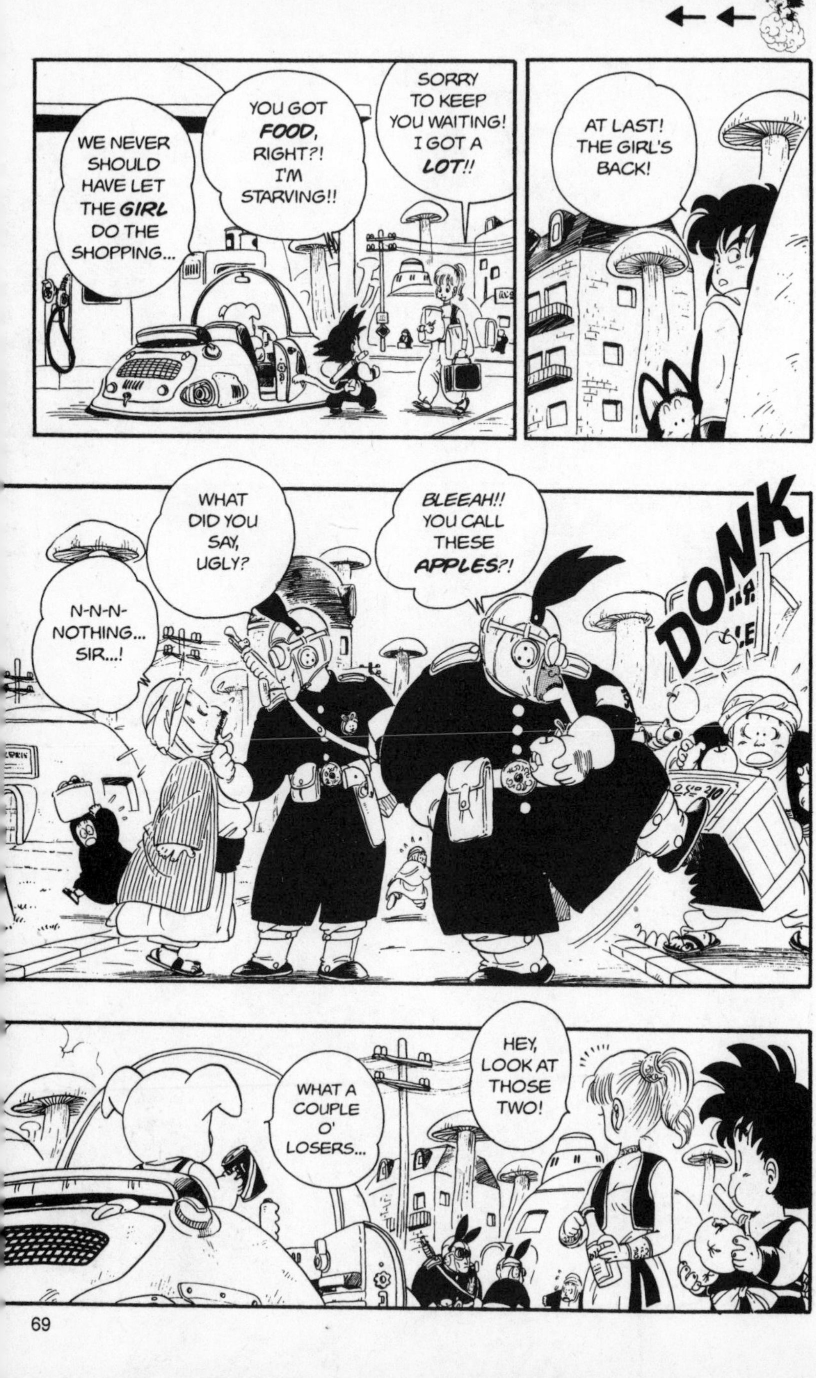
AT LAST! THE GIRL'S BACK!
SORRY TO KEEP YOU WAITING! I GOT A **LOT**!!
YOU GOT **FOOD**, RIGHT?! I'M STARVING!!
WE NEVER SHOULD HAVE LET THE **GIRL** DO THE SHOPPING...
DONK
BLEEAH!! YOU CALL THESE **APPLES**?!
WHAT DID YOU SAY, UGLY?
N-N-N-NOTHING... SIR...!
HEY, LOOK AT THOSE TWO!
WHAT A COUPLE O' LOSERS...

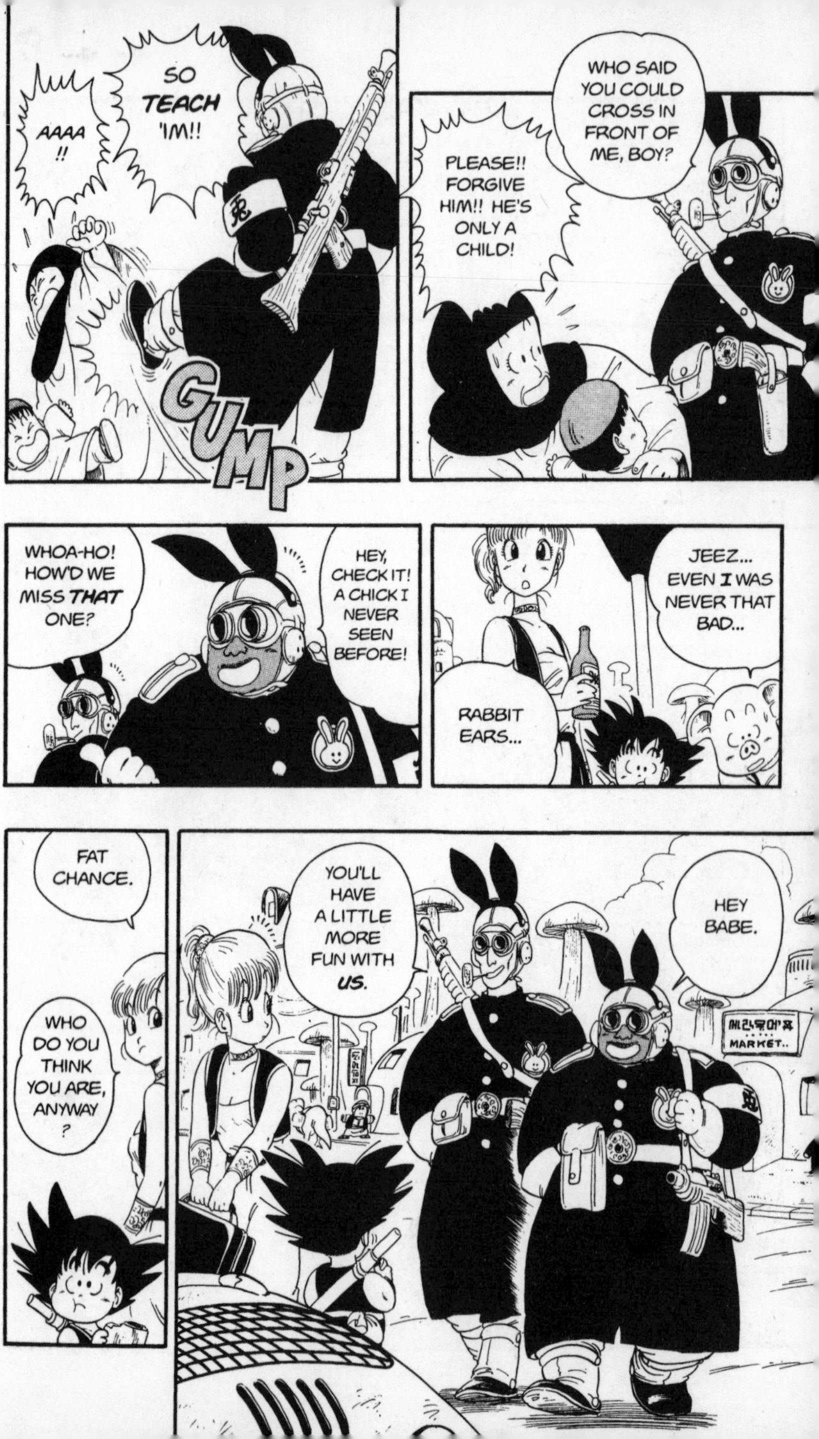
WHO SAID YOU COULD CROSS IN FRONT OF ME, BOY?
PLEASE!! FORGIVE HIM!! HE'S ONLY A CHILD!
SO TEACH 'IM!!
AAAA !!
GUMP
JEEZ... EVEN I WAS NEVER THAT BAD...
RABBIT EARS...
HEY, CHECK IT! A CHICK I NEVER SEEN BEFORE!
WHOA-HO! HOW'D WE MISS THAT ONE?
HEY BABE.
YOU'LL HAVE A LITTLE MORE FUN WITH US.
MARKET..
FAT CHANCE.
WHO DO YOU THINK YOU ARE, ANYWAY ?

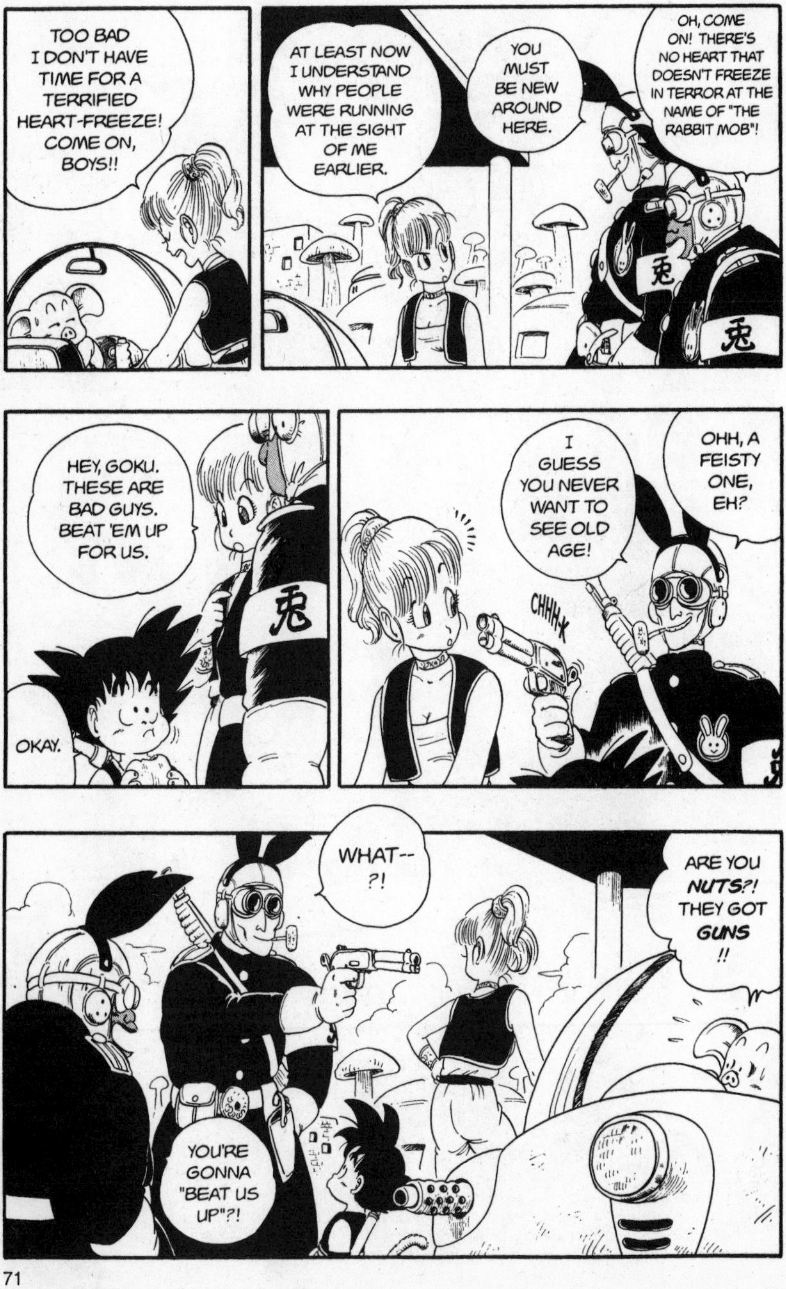
OH, COME ON! THERE'S NO HEART THAT DOESN'T FREEZE IN TERROR AT THE NAME OF "THE RABBIT MOB"!
YOU MUST BE NEW AROUND HERE.
AT LEAST NOW I UNDERSTAND WHY PEOPLE WERE RUNNING AT THE SIGHT OF ME EARLIER.
TOO BAD I DON'T HAVE TIME FOR A TERRIFIED HEART-FREEZE! COME ON, BOYS!!
OHH, A FEISTY ONE, EH?
I GUESS YOU NEVER WANT TO SEE OLD AGE!
CHHH-K
HEY, GOKU. THESE ARE BAD GUYS. BEAT 'EM UP FOR US.
OKAY.
ARE YOU ***NUTS?!*** THEY GOT ***GUNS*** !!
WHAT-- ?!
YOU'RE GONNA "BEAT US UP"?!

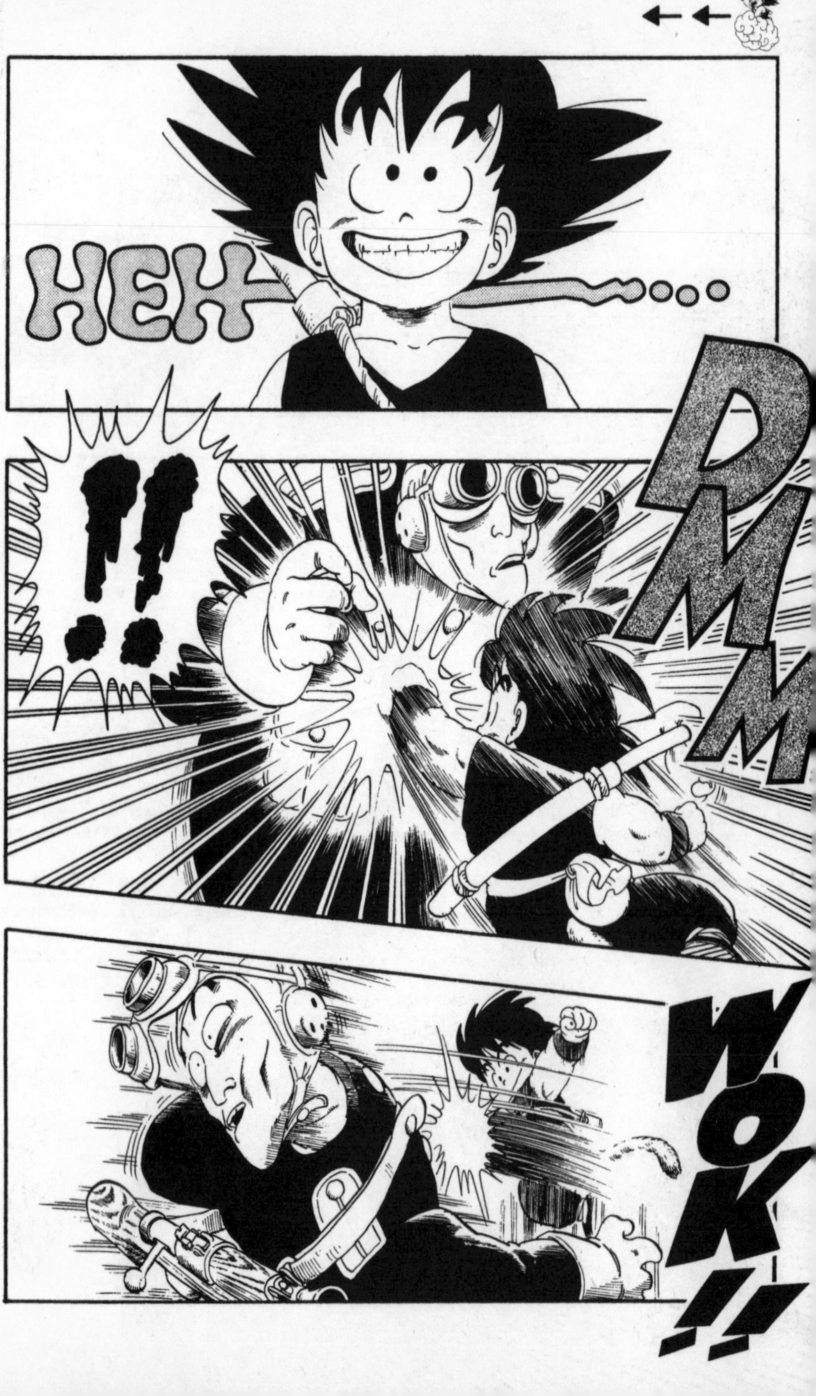
HEH...
DMM
!!
WOK!!

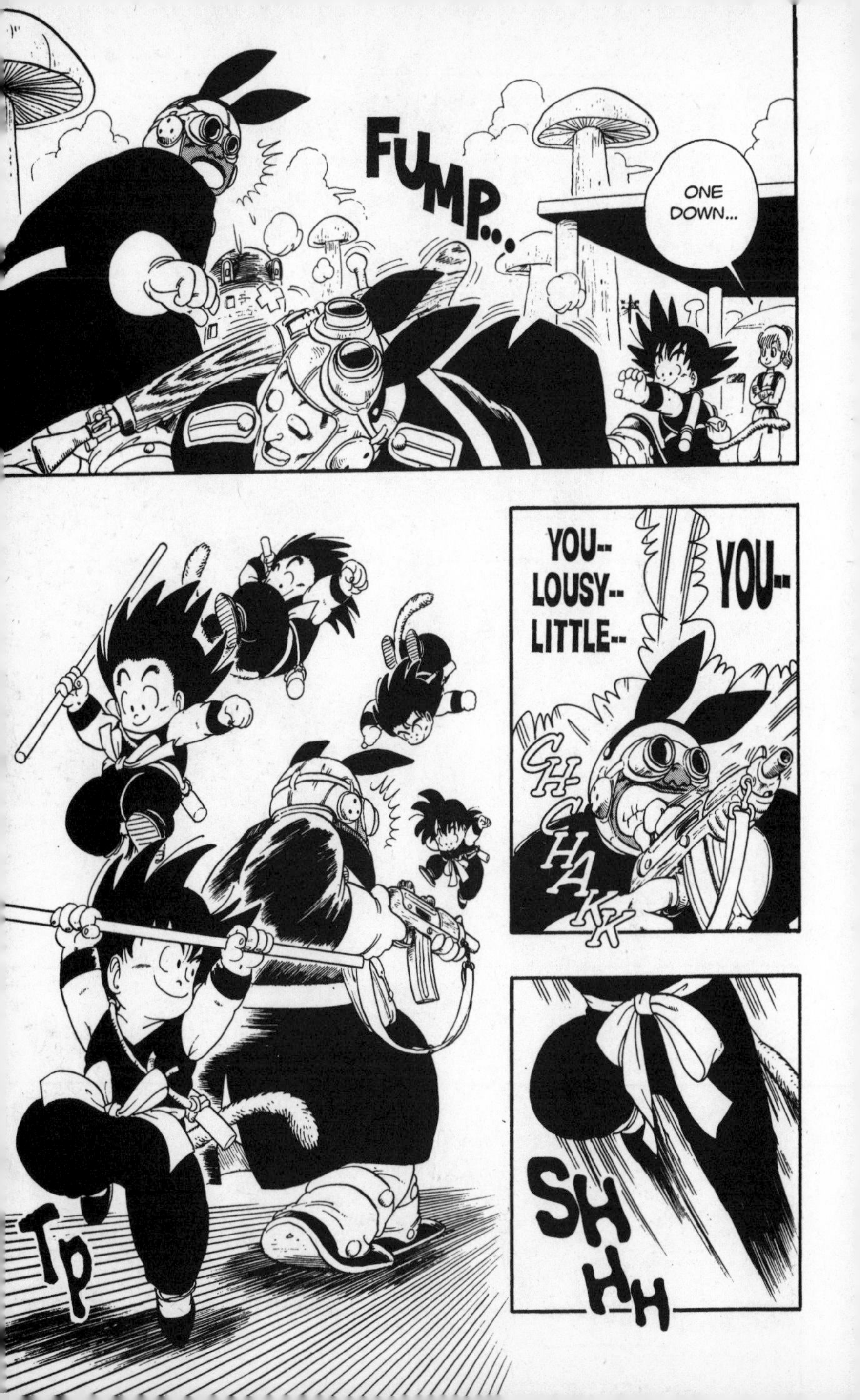
FUMP...
ONE DOWN...
YOU--
YOU-- LOUSY-- LITTLE--
CHCHAKK
SHHHH
Tp

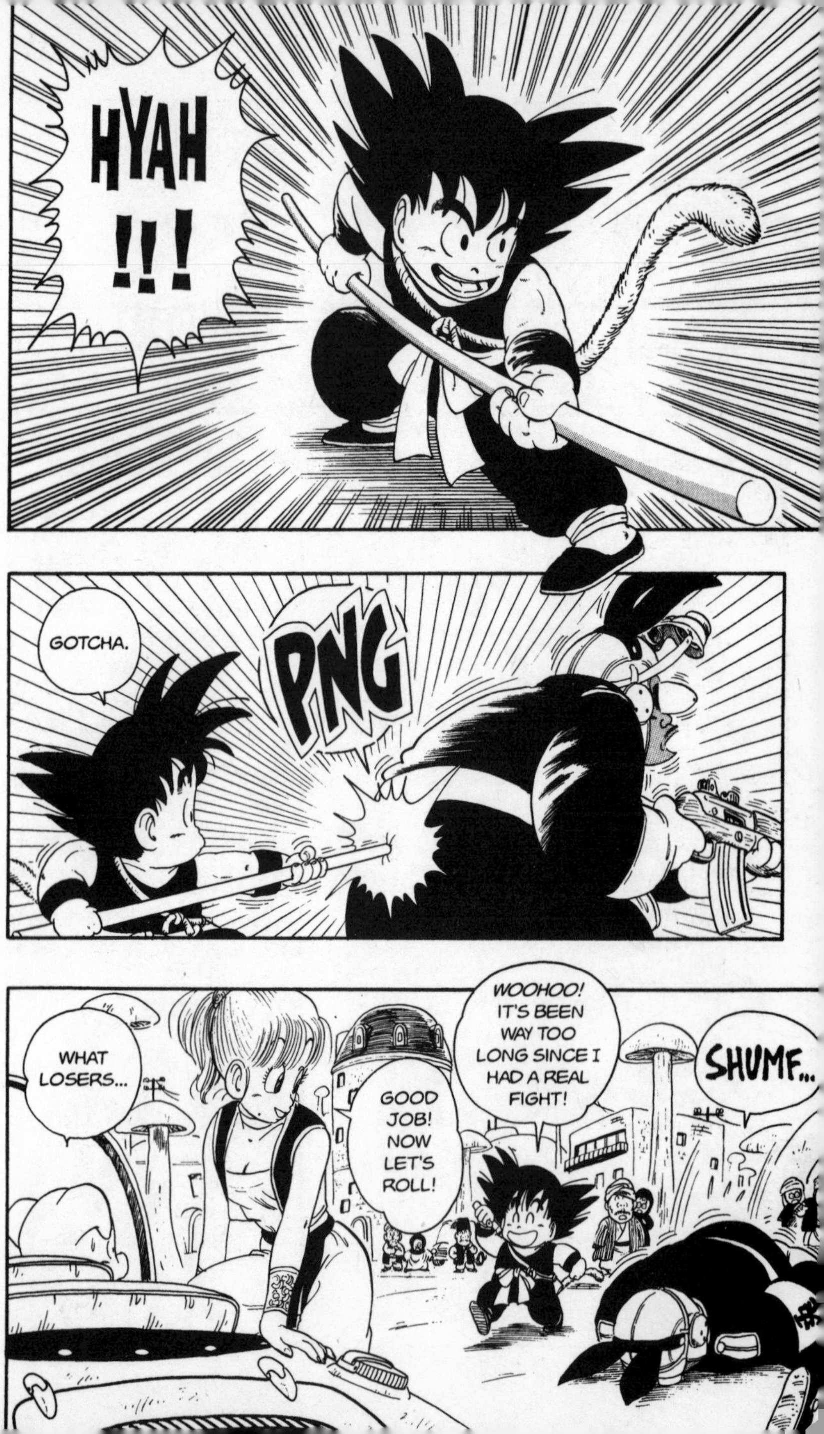
HYAH !!!
PNG
GOTCHA.
SHUMF...
WOOHOO! IT'S BEEN WAY TOO LONG SINCE I HAD A REAL FIGHT!
GOOD JOB! NOW LET'S ROLL!
WHAT LOSERS...

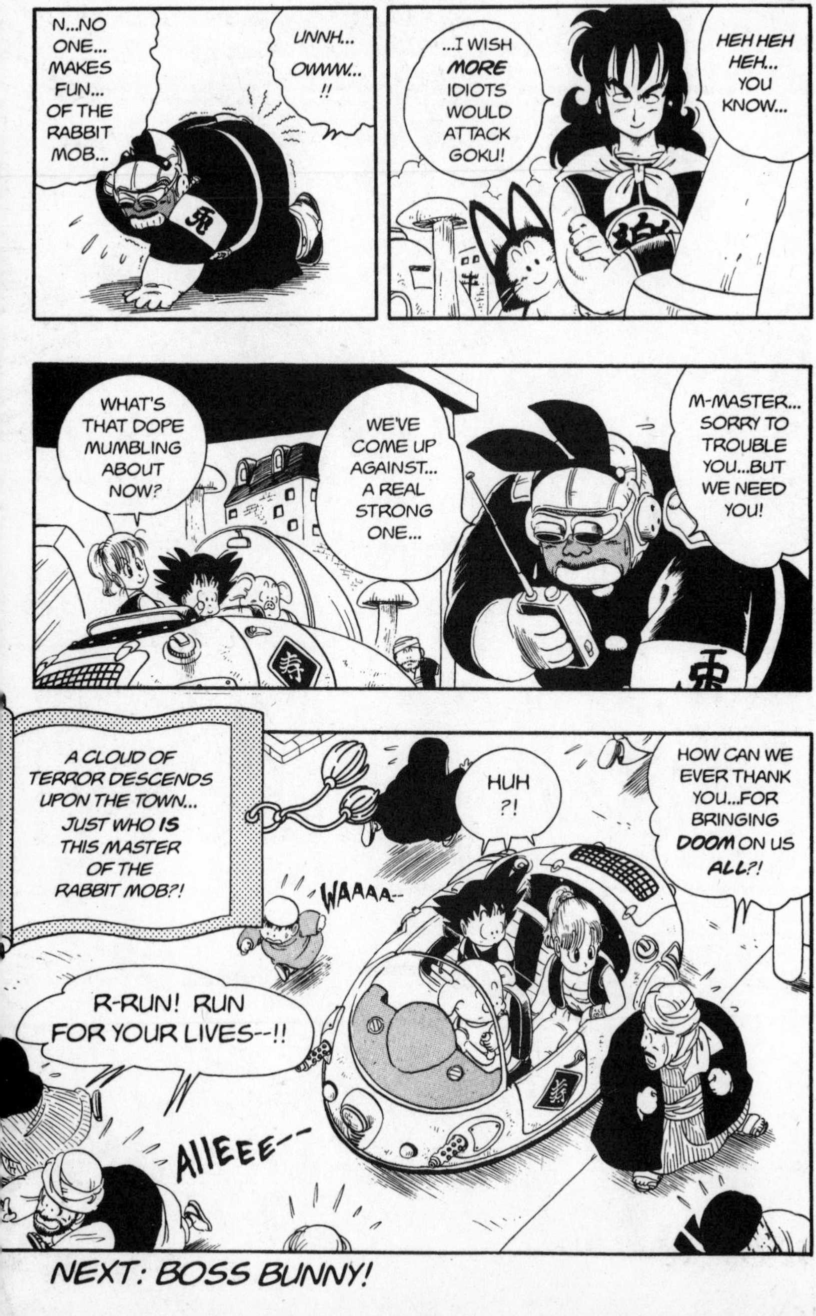
HEH HEH HEH... YOU KNOW...
...I WISH MORE IDIOTS WOULD ATTACK GOKU!
UNNH... OWWW... !!
N...NO ONE... MAKES FUN... OF THE RABBIT MOB...
M-MASTER... SORRY TO TROUBLE YOU...BUT WE NEED YOU!
WE'VE COME UP AGAINST... A REAL STRONG ONE...
WHAT'S THAT DOPE MUMBLING ABOUT NOW?
HOW CAN WE EVER THANK YOU...FOR BRINGING DOOM ON US ALL?!
HUH ?!
WAAAA-
A CLOUD OF TERROR DESCENDS UPON THE TOWN... JUST WHO IS THIS MASTER OF THE RABBIT MOB?!
R-RUN! RUN FOR YOUR LIVES--!!
AIIEEE--

NEXT: BOSS BUNNY!

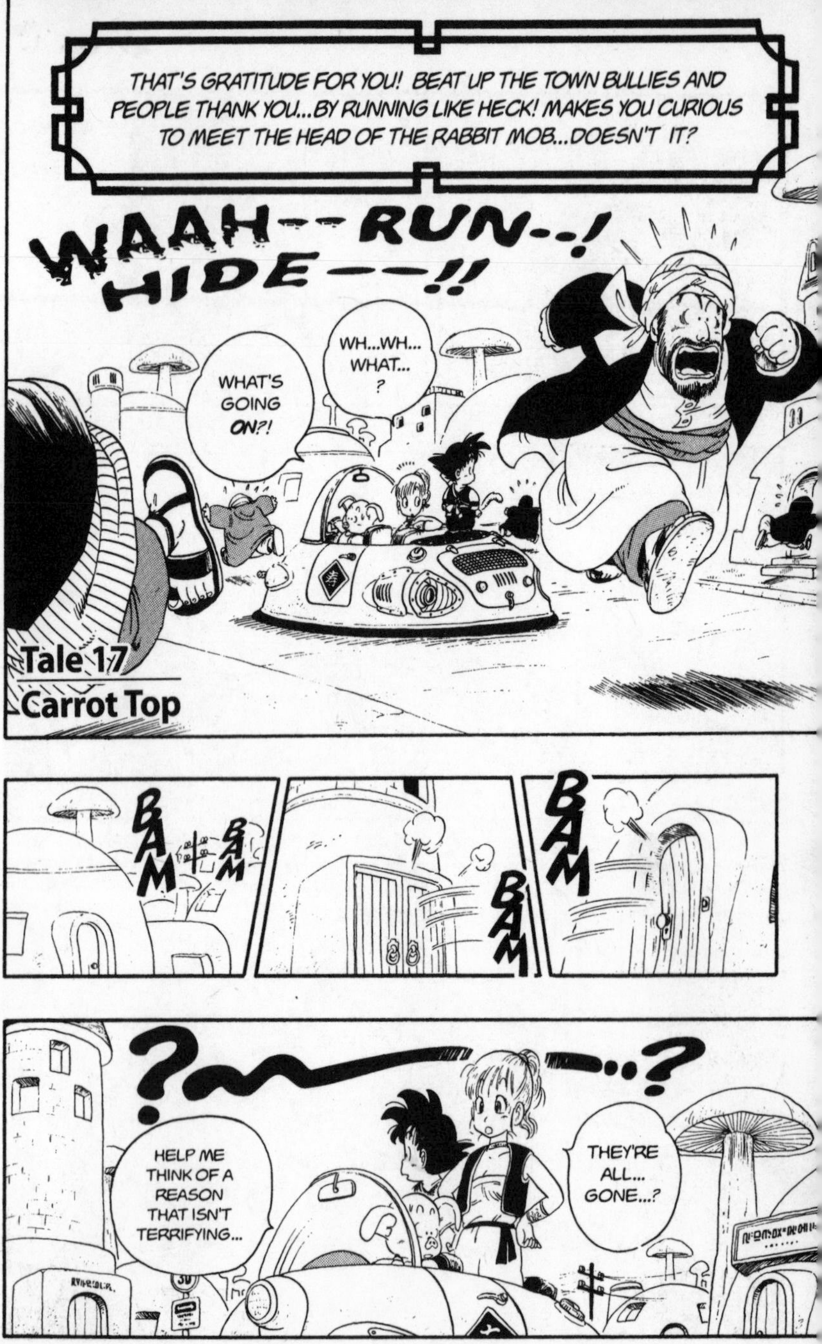
THAT'S GRATITUDE FOR YOU! BEAT UP THE TOWN BULLIES AND PEOPLE THANK YOU...BY RUNNING LIKE HECK! MAKES YOU CURIOUS TO MEET THE HEAD OF THE RABBIT MOB...DOESN'T IT?
WAAH--RUN--! HIDE---!!
WH...WH... WHAT...?
WHAT'S GOING ON?!
Tale 17
Carrot Top
BAM
BAM
BAM
BAM BAM
?~~~--..?
THEY'RE ALL... GONE...?
HELP ME THINK OF A REASON THAT ISN'T TERRIFYING...

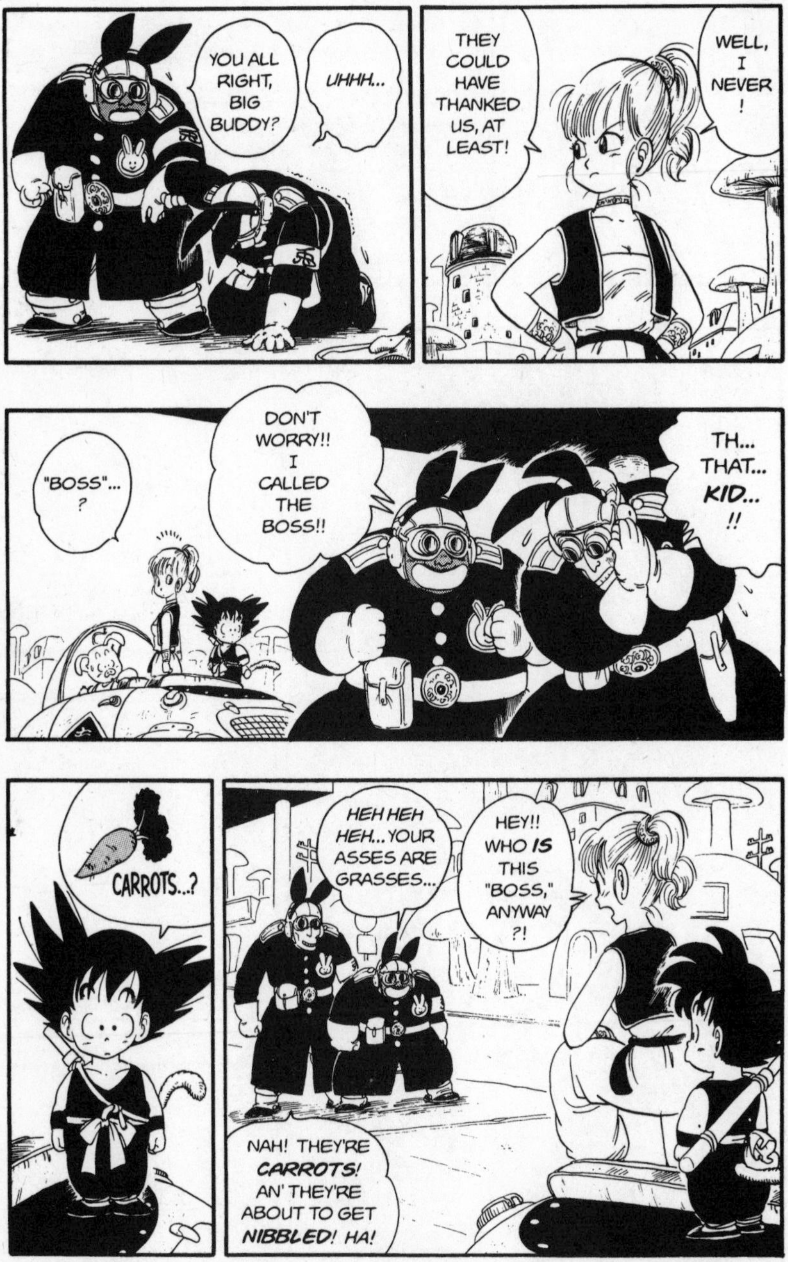
WELL, I NEVER!
THEY COULD HAVE THANKED US, AT LEAST!
UHHH...
YOU ALL RIGHT, BIG BUDDY?
TH... THAT... KID...!!
DON'T WORRY!! I CALLED THE BOSS!!
"BOSS"...?
HEY!! WHO IS THIS "BOSS," ANYWAY?!
HEH HEH HEH... YOUR ASSES ARE GRASSES...
NAH! THEY'RE CARROTS! AN' THEY'RE ABOUT TO GET NIBBLED! HA!
CARROTS...?

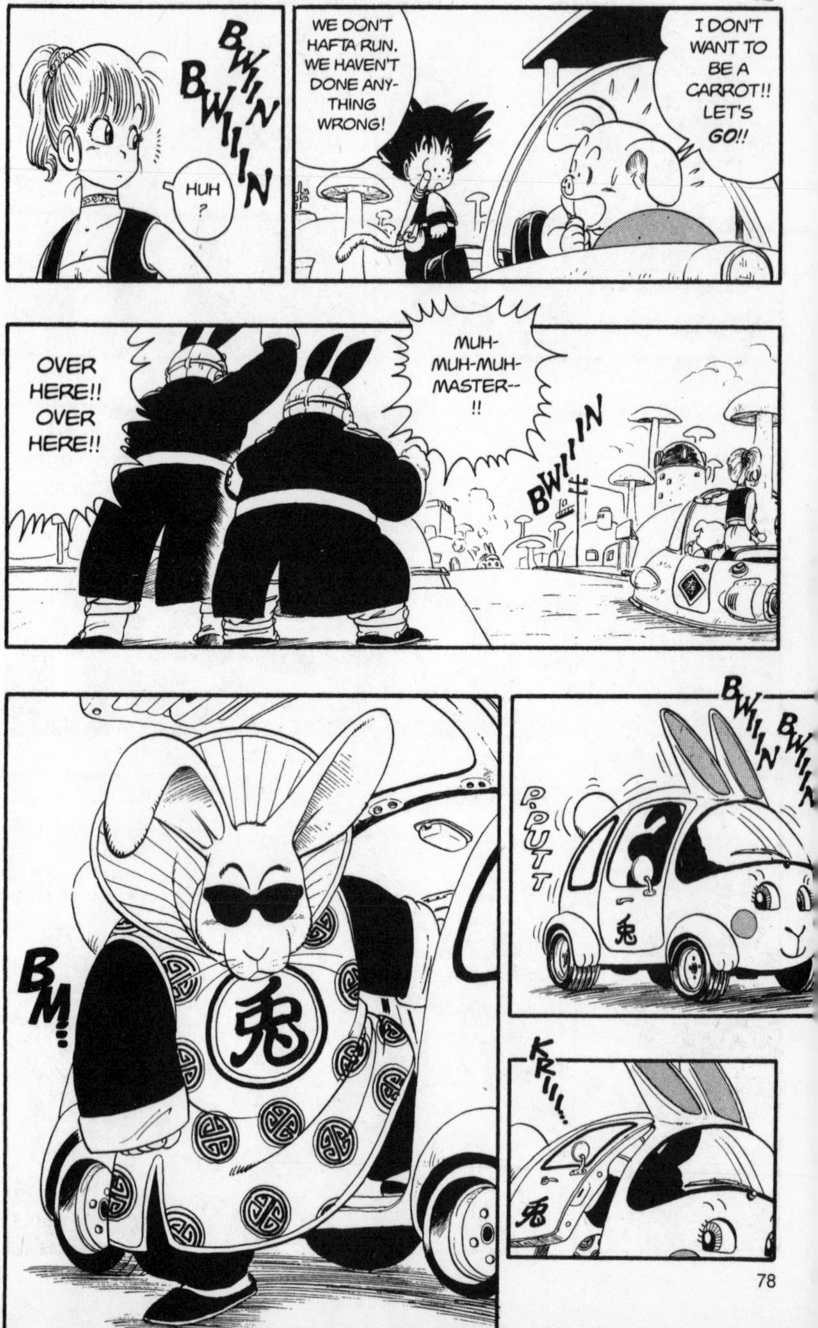

I DON'T WANT TO BE A CARROT!! LET'S GO!!
WE DON'T HAFTA RUN. WE HAVEN'T DONE ANYTHING WRONG!
BWIIN
BWIIIIN
HUH?
BWIIIN
MUH-MUH-MUH-MASTER--!!
OVER HERE!! OVER HERE!!
BWIIIN
BWIII
P.PUTT
KRIIII...
BM!!

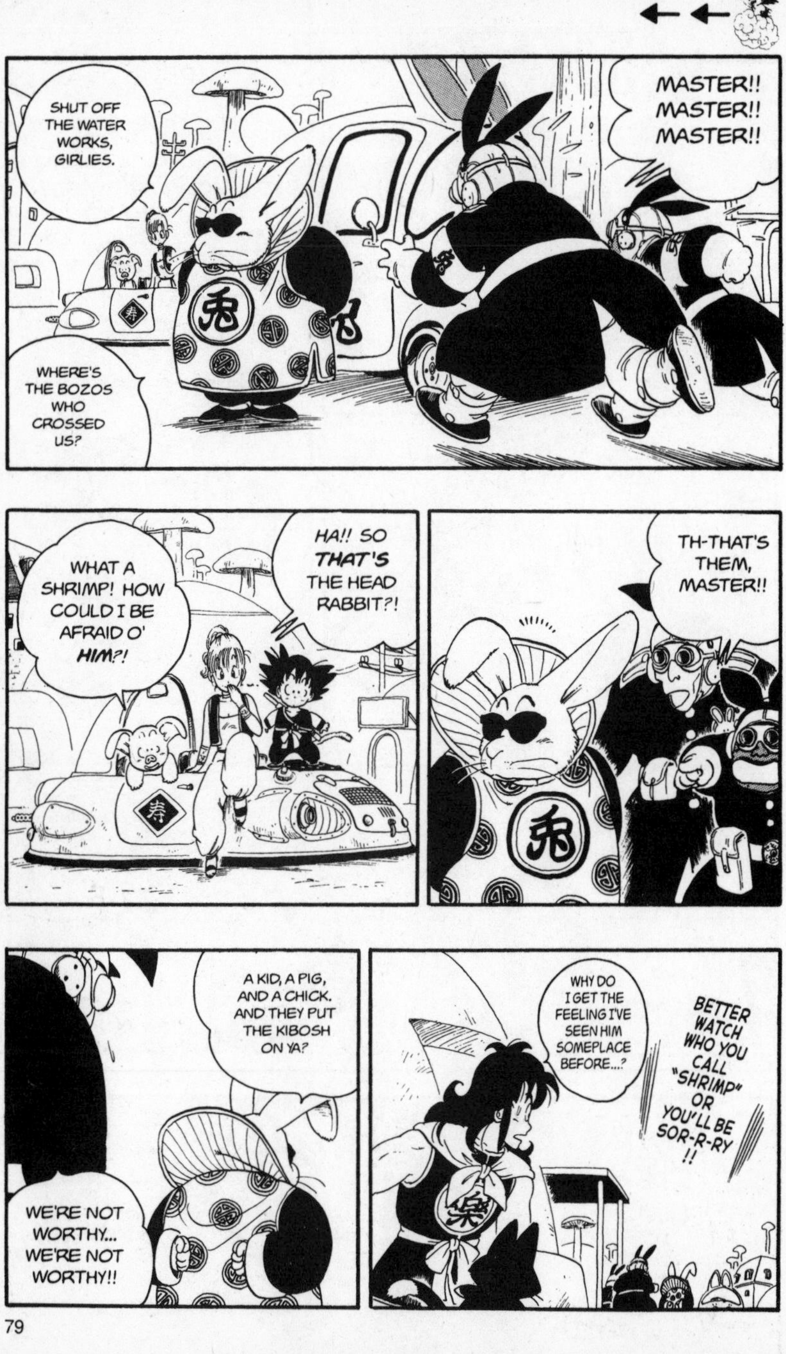
MASTER!! MASTER!! MASTER!!
SHUT OFF THE WATER WORKS, GIRLIES.
WHERE'S THE BOZOS WHO CROSSED US?
TH-THAT'S THEM, MASTER!!
HA!! SO THAT'S THE HEAD RABBIT?!
WHAT A SHRIMP! HOW COULD I BE AFRAID O' HIM?!
BETTER WATCH WHO YOU CALL "SHRIMP" OR YOU'LL BE SOR-R-RY !!
WHY DO I GET THE FEELING I'VE SEEN HIM SOMEPLACE BEFORE...?
A KID, A PIG, AND A CHICK. AND THEY PUT THE KIBOSH ON YA?
WE'RE NOT WORTHY... WE'RE NOT WORTHY!!

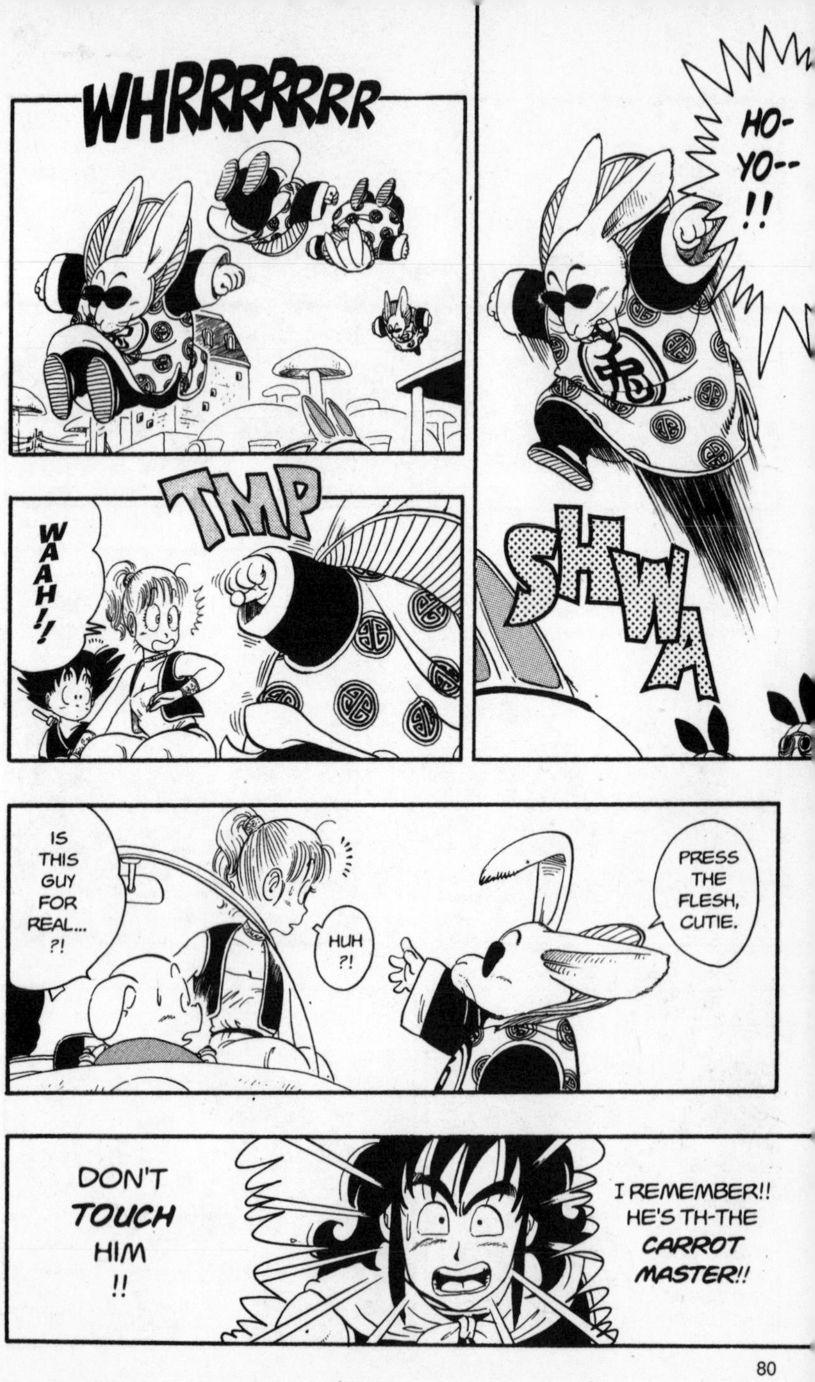
HO-YO--!!
SHWA
WHRRRRRRR
TMP
WAAH!!
PRESS THE FLESH, CUTIE.
HUH?!
IS THIS GUY FOR REAL...?!
I REMEMBER!! HE'S TH-THE CARROT MASTER!!
DON'T TOUCH HIM!!

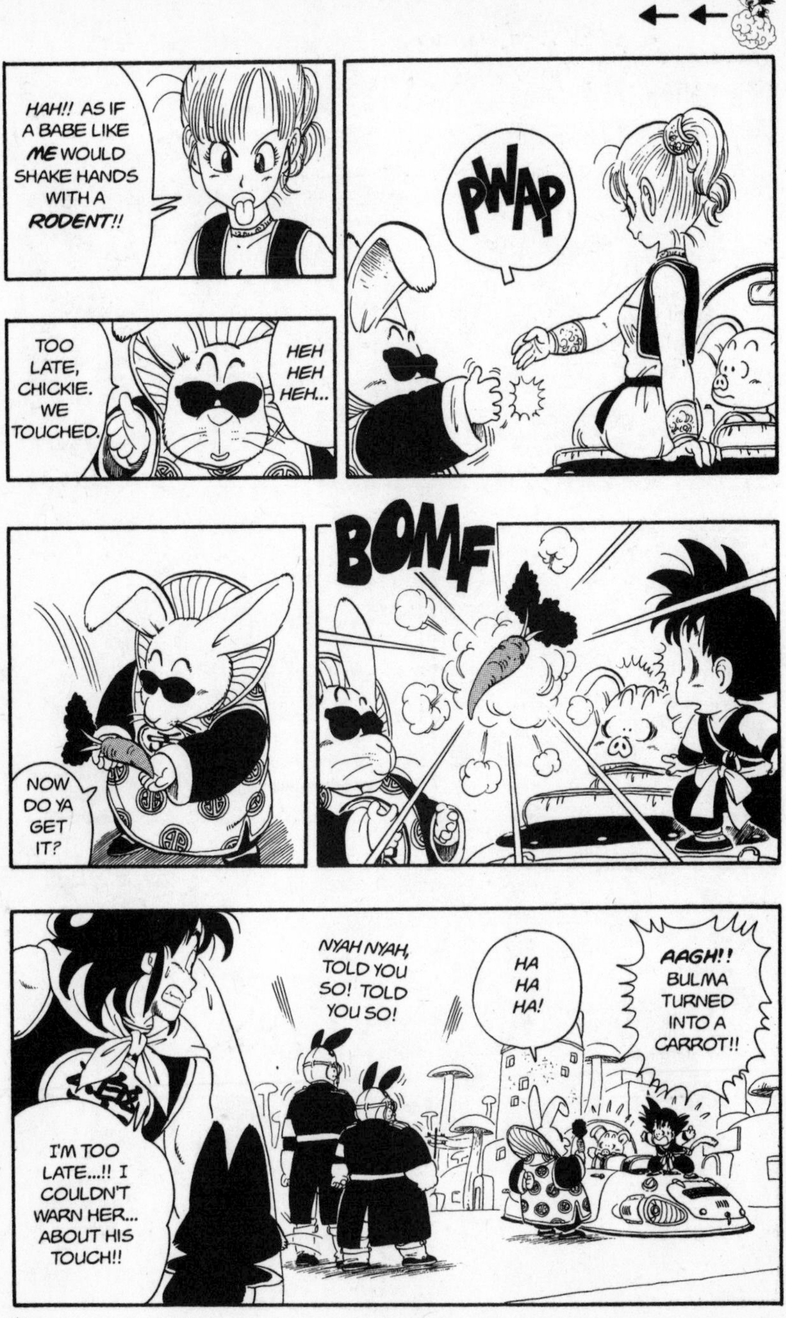
PWAP
HAH!! AS IF A BABE LIKE ME WOULD SHAKE HANDS WITH A RODENT!!
HEH HEH HEH...
TOO LATE, CHICKIE. WE TOUCHED.
BOMF
NOW DO YA GET IT?
AAGH!! BULMA TURNED INTO A CARROT!!
HA HA HA!
NYAH NYAH, TOLD YOU SO! TOLD YOU SO!
I'M TOO LATE...!! I COULDN'T WARN HER... ABOUT HIS TOUCH!!

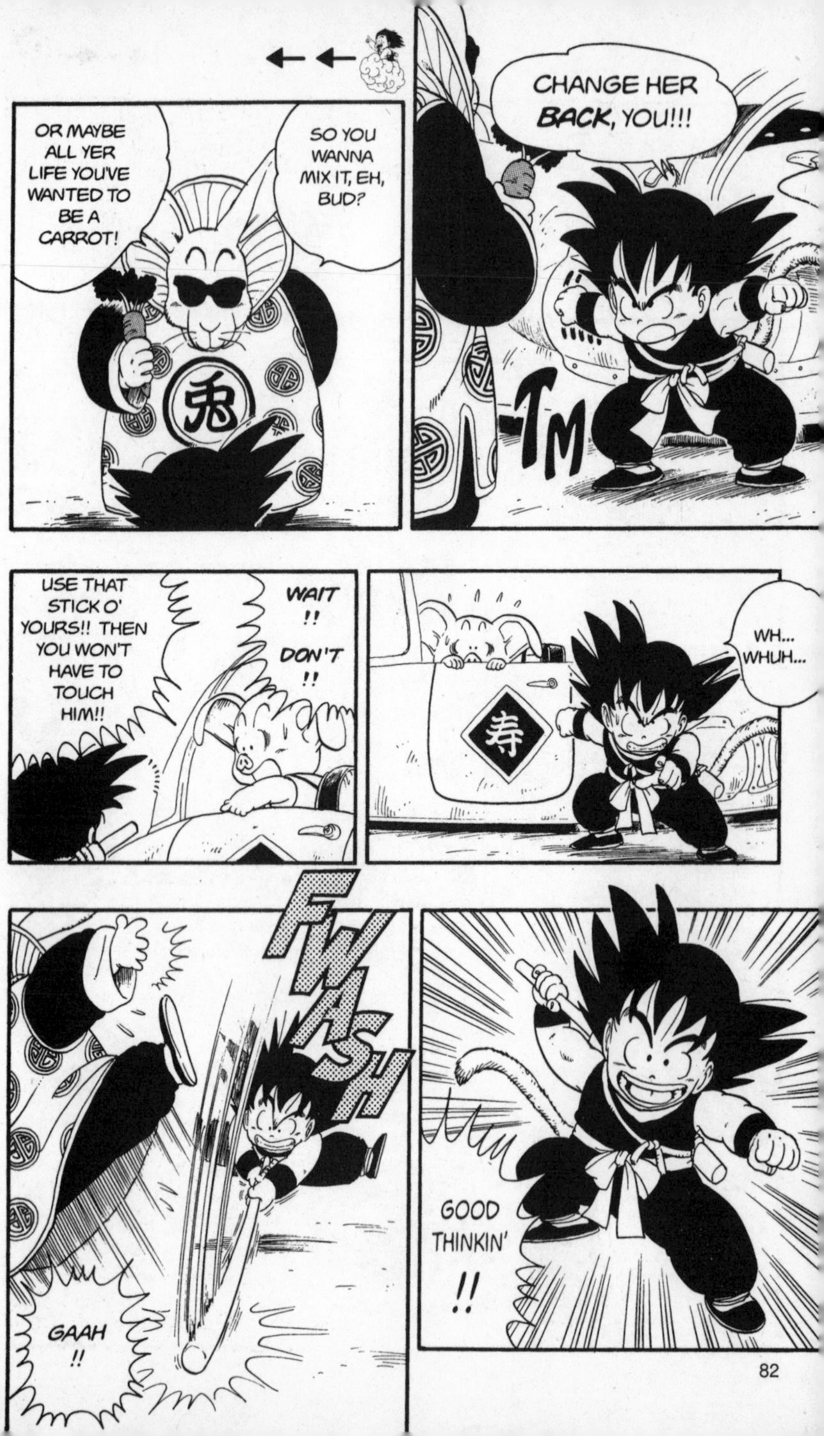
CHANGE HER BACK, YOU!!!
TM
SO YOU WANNA MIX IT, EH, BUD?
OR MAYBE ALL YER LIFE YOU'VE WANTED TO BE A CARROT!
WH... WHUH...
WAIT!! DON'T!!
USE THAT STICK O' YOURS!! THEN YOU WON'T HAVE TO TOUCH HIM!!
GOOD THINKIN' !!
FWASH
GAAH!!

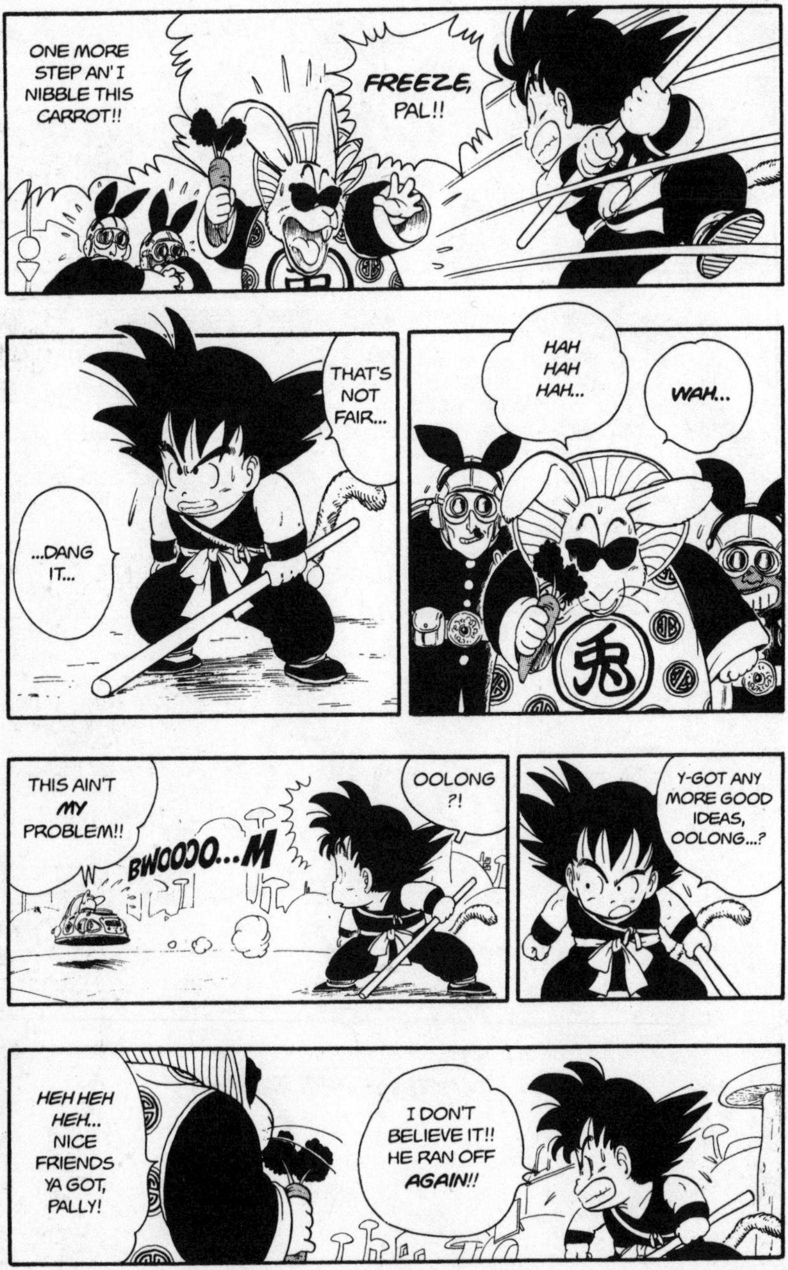
FREEZE, PAL!!
ONE MORE STEP AN' I NIBBLE THIS CARROT!!
WAH...
HAH HAH HAH...
THAT'S NOT FAIR...
...DANG IT...
Y-GOT ANY MORE GOOD IDEAS, OOLONG...?
OOLONG ?!
THIS AIN'T MY PROBLEM!!
BWOOOO...M
I DON'T BELIEVE IT!! HE RAN OFF AGAIN!!
HEH HEH HEH... NICE FRIENDS YA GOT, PALLY!

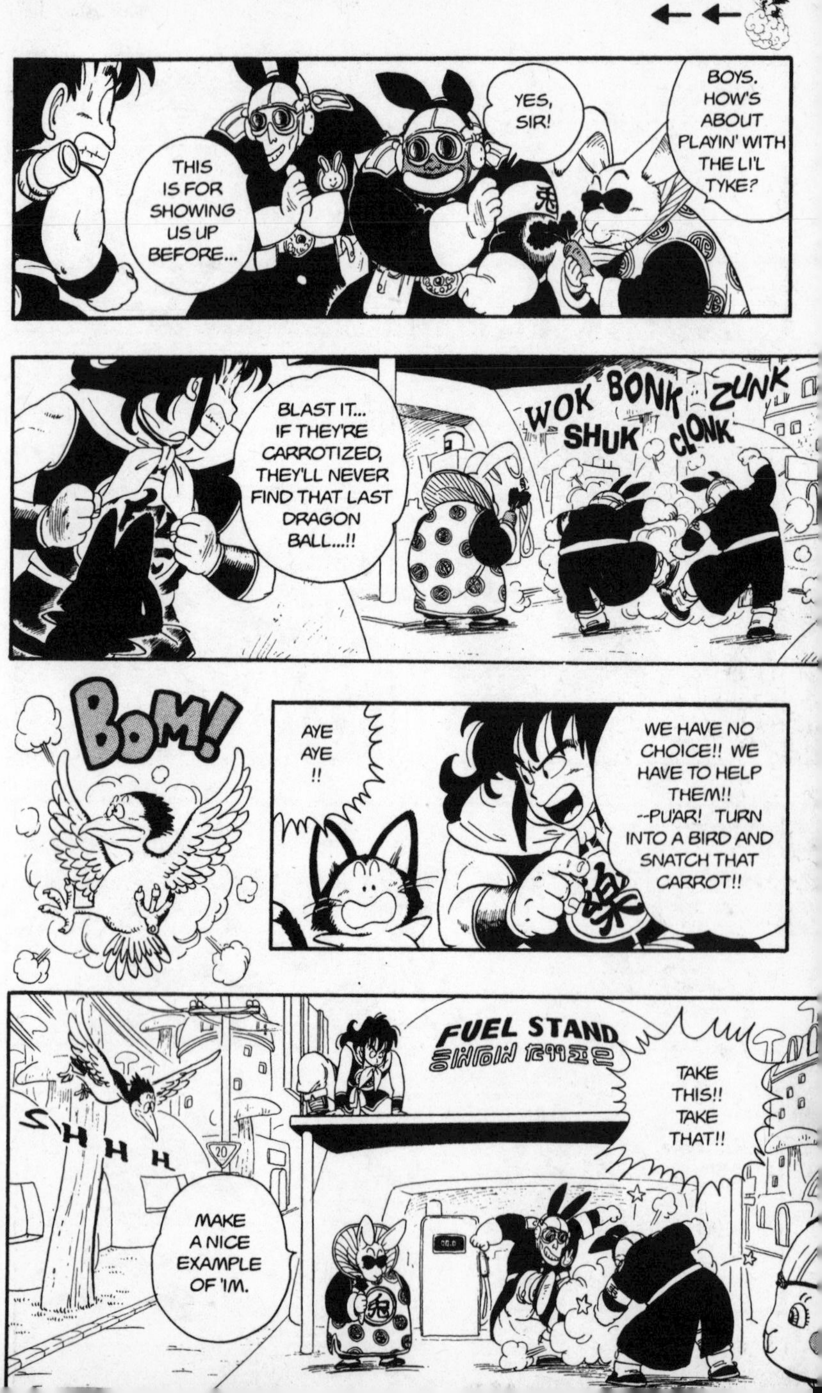
BOYS. HOW'S ABOUT PLAYIN' WITH THE LI'L TYKE?
YES, SIR!
THIS IS FOR SHOWING US UP BEFORE...
ZUNK
BONK
WOK
CLONK
SHUK
BLAST IT... IF THEY'RE CARROTIZED, THEY'LL NEVER FIND THAT LAST DRAGON BALL...!!
WE HAVE NO CHOICE!! WE HAVE TO HELP THEM!! --PU'AR! TURN INTO A BIRD AND SNATCH THAT CARROT!!
AYE AYE !!
BOM!
TAKE THIS!! TAKE THAT!!
FUEL STAND
SHHH
MAKE A NICE EXAMPLE OF 'IM.

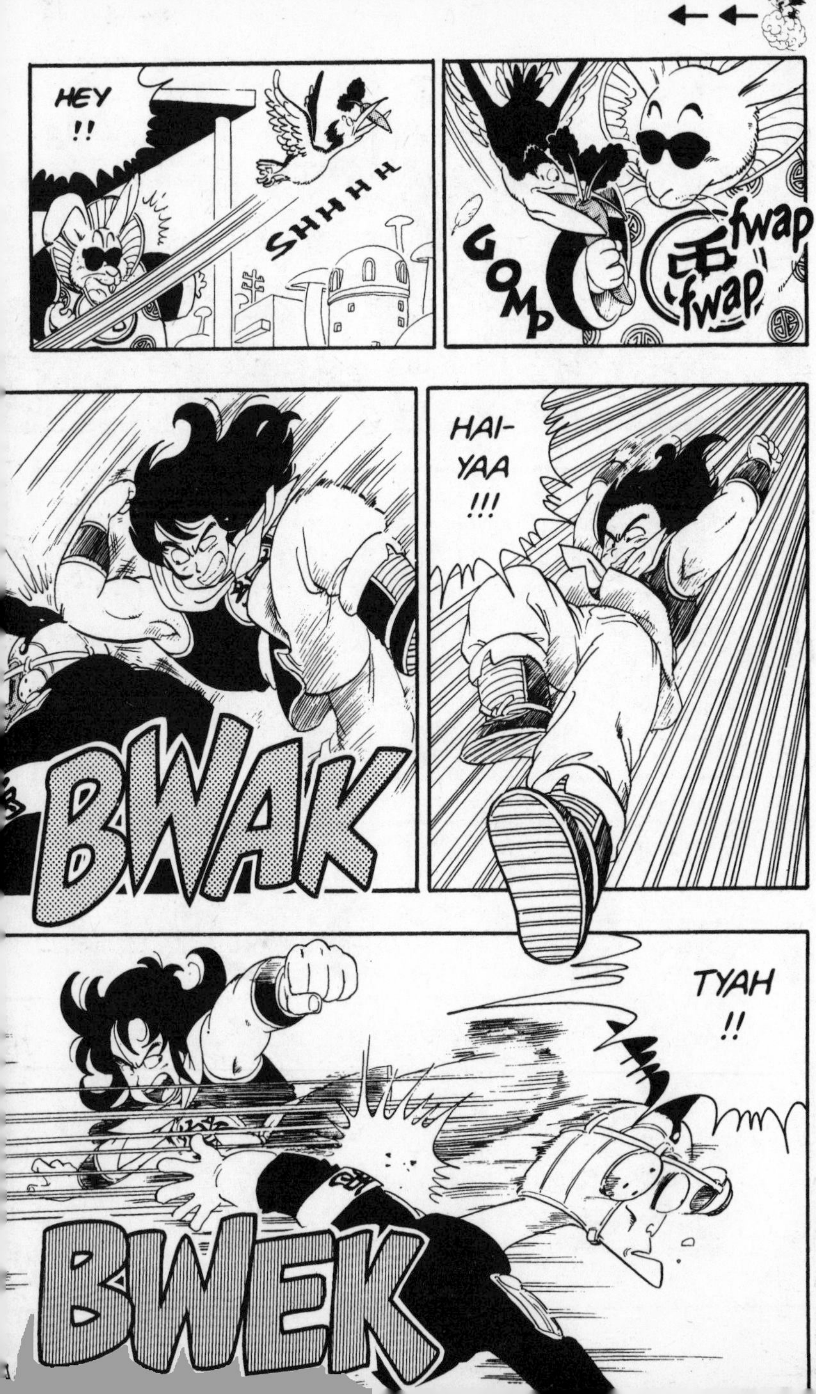
GOMP
fwap
fwap
HEY !!
SHHHH
HAI-YAA !!!
BWAK
TYAH !!
BWEK

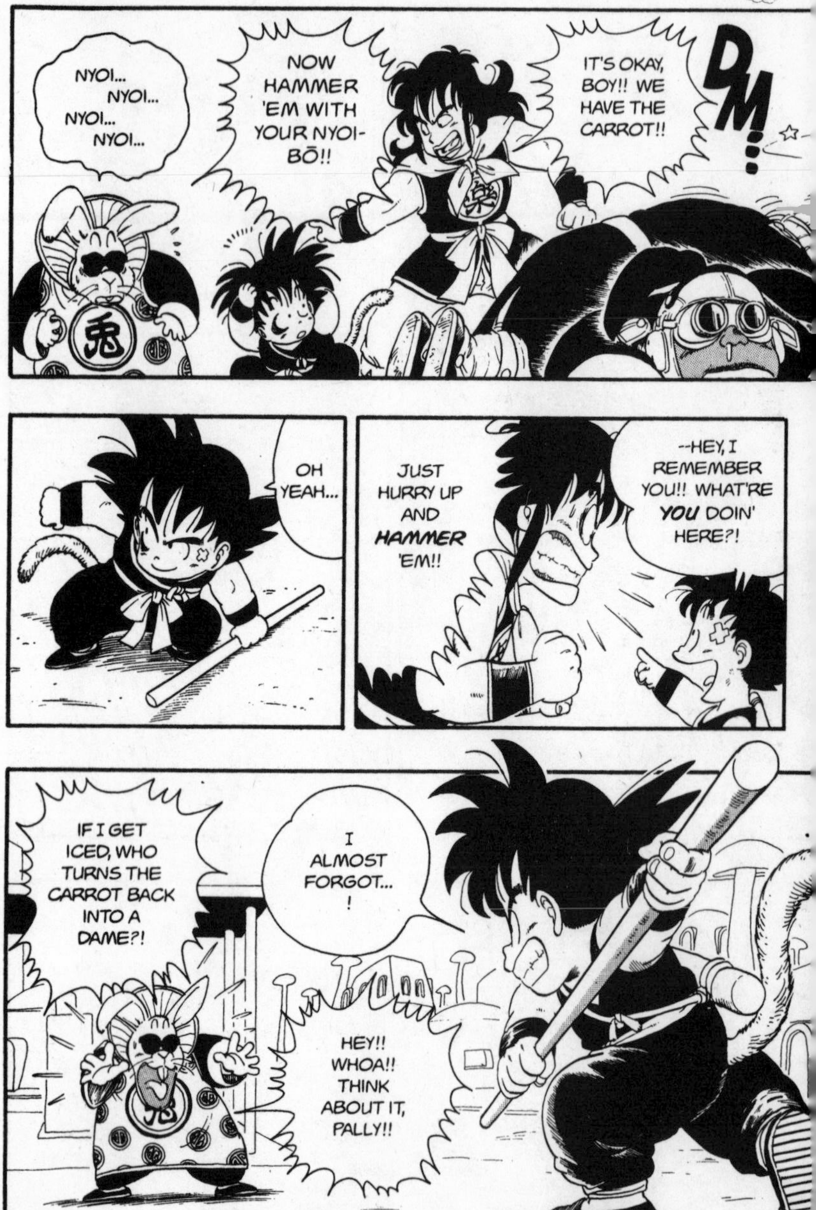
DM!!
IT'S OKAY, BOY!! WE HAVE THE CARROT!!
NOW HAMMER 'EM WITH YOUR NYOI-BŌ!!
NYOI... NYOI... NYOI... NYOI...
--HEY, I REMEMBER YOU!! WHAT'RE YOU DOIN' HERE?!
JUST HURRY UP AND HAMMER 'EM!!
OH YEAH...
I ALMOST FORGOT...!
IF I GET ICED, WHO TURNS THE CARROT BACK INTO A DAME?!
HEY!! WHOA!! THINK ABOUT IT, PALLY!!

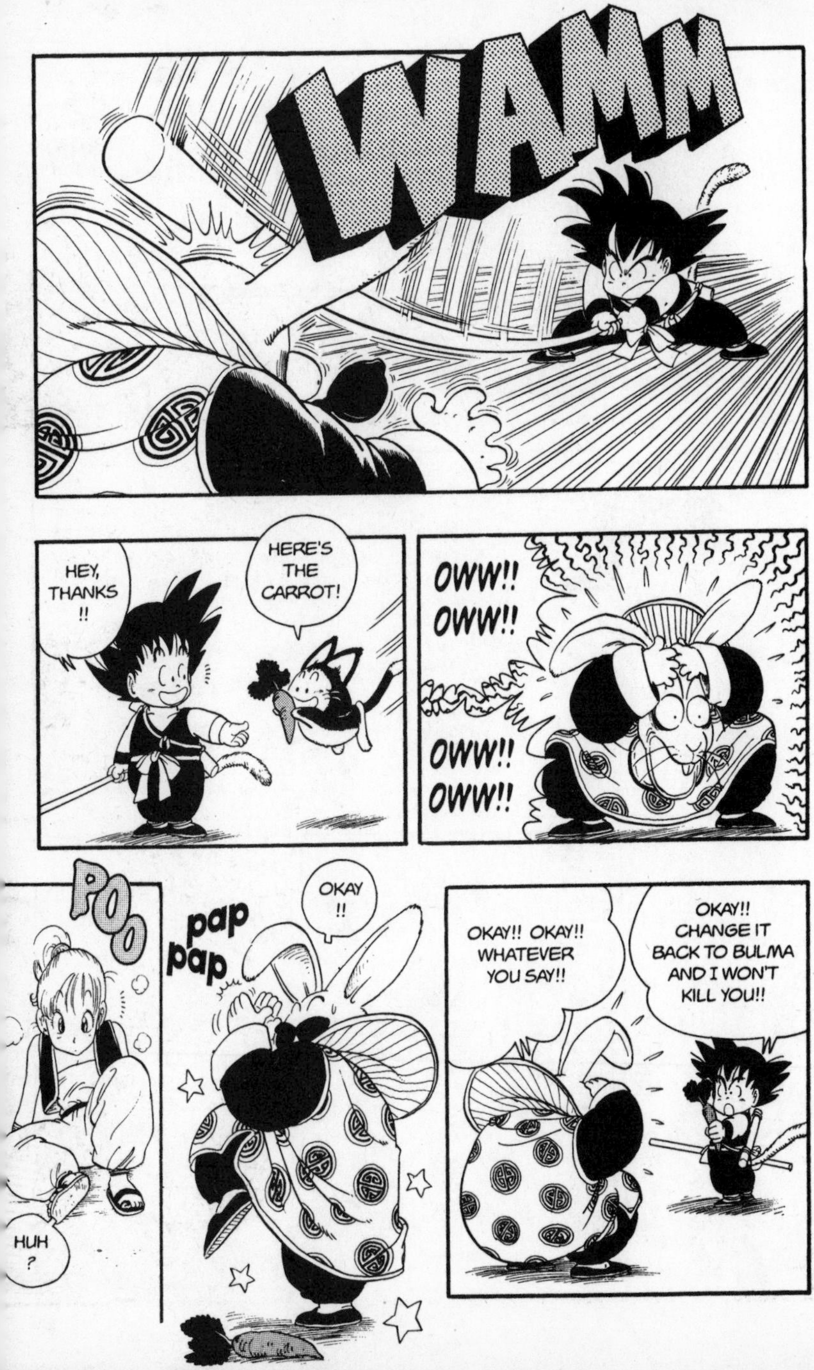
WAMM
OWW!! OWW!!
OWW!! OWW!!
HERE'S THE CARROT!
HEY, THANKS !!
OKAY!! CHANGE IT BACK TO BULMA AND I WON'T KILL YOU!!
OKAY!! OKAY!! WHATEVER YOU SAY!!
OKAY !!
pap pap
POO
HUH ?

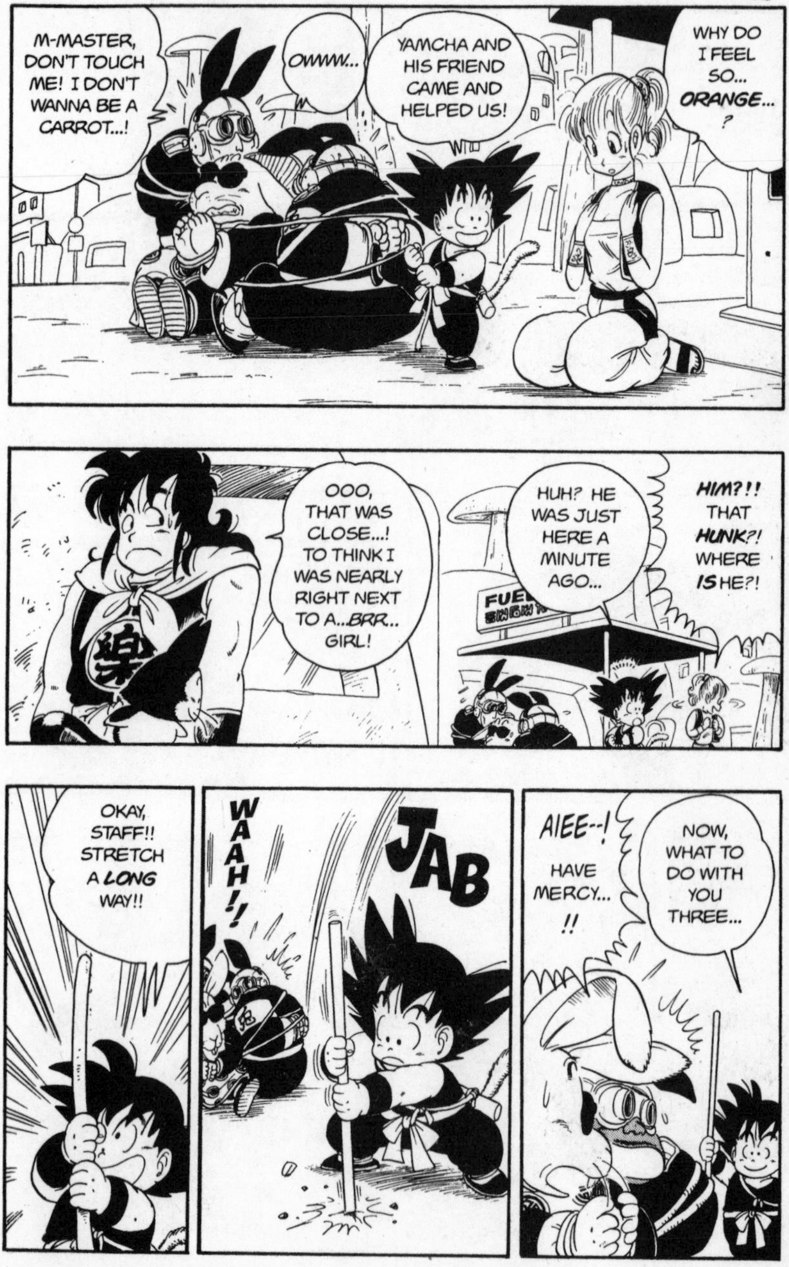
WHY DO I FEEL SO... ORANGE...?
YAMCHA AND HIS FRIEND CAME AND HELPED US!
OWWW...
M-MASTER, DON'T TOUCH ME! I DON'T WANNA BE A CARROT...!
HIM?!! THAT HUNK?! WHERE IS HE?!
HUH? HE WAS JUST HERE A MINUTE AGO...
FUEL
OOO, THAT WAS CLOSE...! TO THINK I WAS NEARLY RIGHT NEXT TO A...BRR... GIRL!
NOW, WHAT TO DO WITH YOU THREE...
AIEE--!
HAVE MERCY... !!
JAB
WAAH!!
OKAY, STAFF!! STRETCH A LONG WAY!!

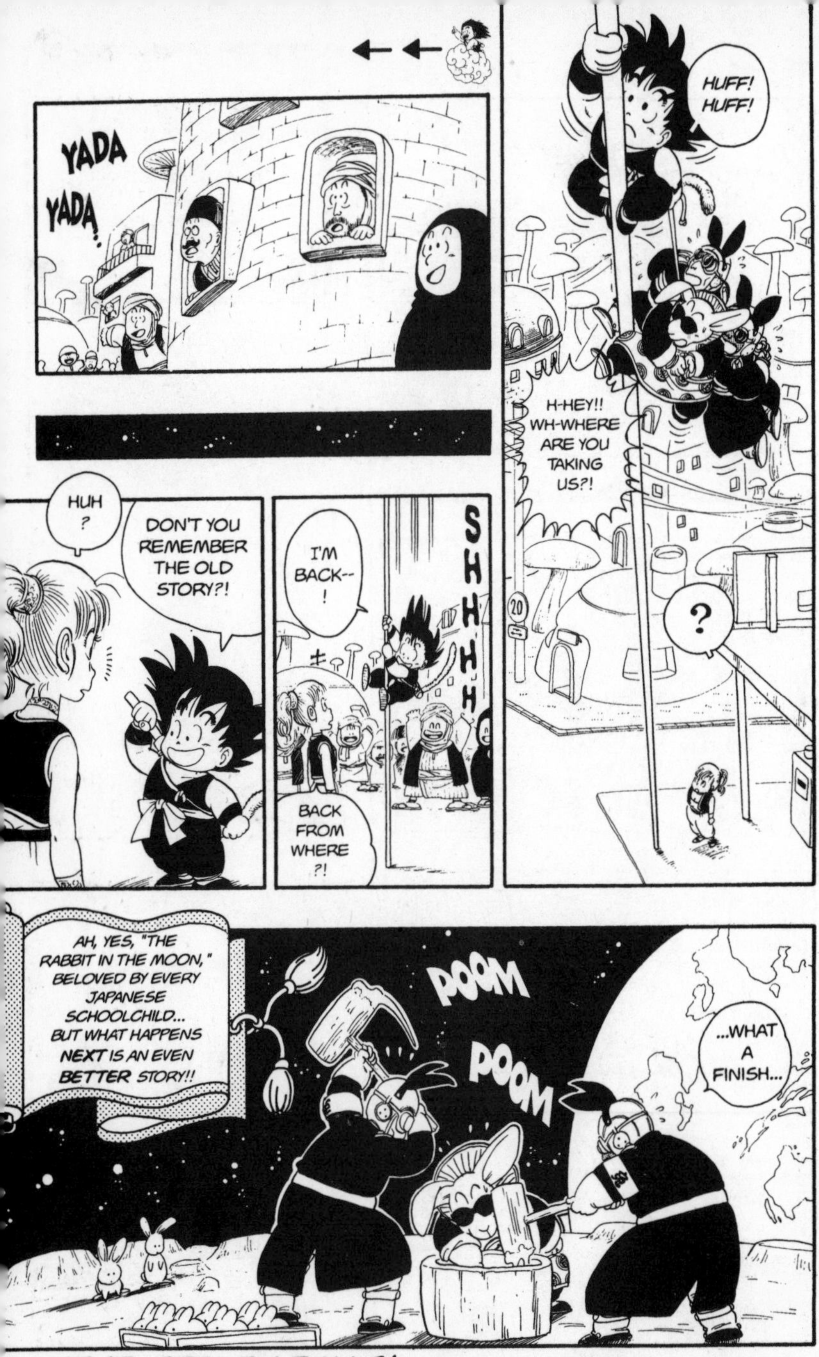
HUFF! HUFF!
H-HEY!! WH-WHERE ARE YOU TAKING US?!
?
YADA YADA
SHHHH
I'M BACK--!
BACK FROM WHERE?!
DON'T YOU REMEMBER THE OLD STORY?!
HUH?
...WHAT A FINISH...
POOM
POOM
AH, YES, "THE RABBIT IN THE MOON," BELOVED BY EVERY JAPANESE SCHOOLCHILD... BUT WHAT HAPPENS NEXT IS AN EVEN BETTER STORY!!

NEXT: STOLEN BALLS!

Tale 18 • Who's Got My Balls?!

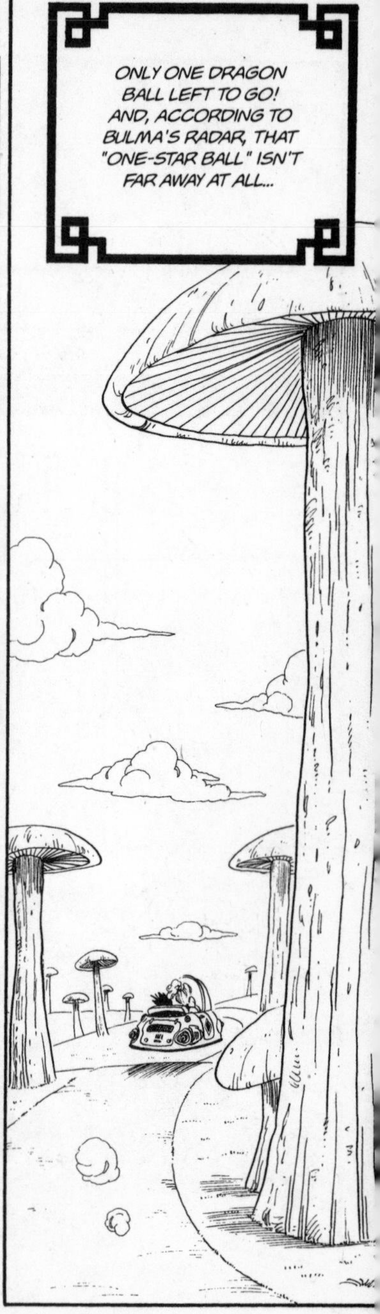
ONLY ONE DRAGON BALL LEFT TO GO! AND, ACCORDING TO BULMA'S RADAR, THAT "ONE-STAR BALL" ISN'T FAR AWAY AT ALL...

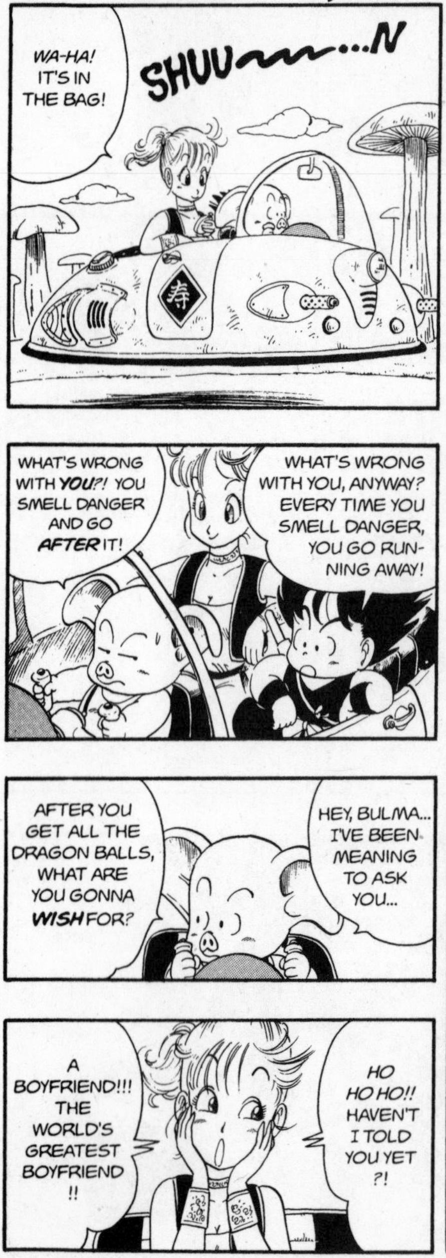
SHUU~~~...N
WA-HA! IT'S IN THE BAG!
WHAT'S WRONG WITH YOU, ANYWAY? EVERY TIME YOU SMELL DANGER, YOU GO RUN-NING AWAY!
WHAT'S WRONG WITH YOU?! YOU SMELL DANGER AND GO AFTER IT!
HEY, BULMA... I'VE BEEN MEANING TO ASK YOU...
AFTER YOU GET ALL THE DRAGON BALLS, WHAT ARE YOU GONNA WISH FOR?
HO HO HO!! HAVEN'T I TOLD YOU YET ?!
A BOYFRIEND!!! THE WORLD'S GREATEST BOYFRIEND !!

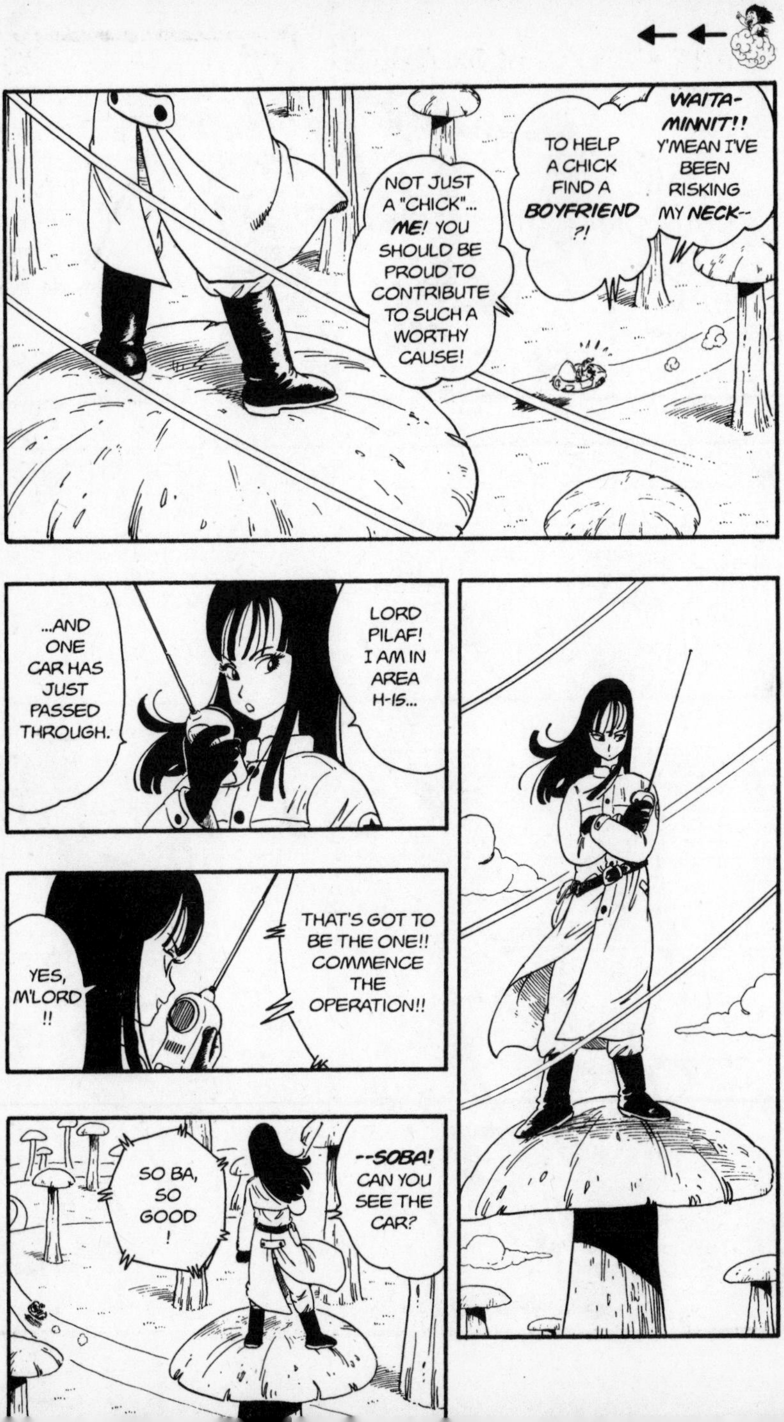
WAITA-MINNIT!! Y'MEAN I'VE BEEN RISKING MY NECK--
TO HELP A CHICK FIND A BOYFRIEND ?!
NOT JUST A "CHICK"... ME! YOU SHOULD BE PROUD TO CONTRIBUTE TO SUCH A WORTHY CAUSE!
LORD PILAF! I AM IN AREA H-15...
...AND ONE CAR HAS JUST PASSED THROUGH.
THAT'S GOT TO BE THE ONE!! COMMENCE THE OPERATION!!
YES, M'LORD !!
--SOBA! CAN YOU SEE THE CAR?
SO BA, SO GOOD !

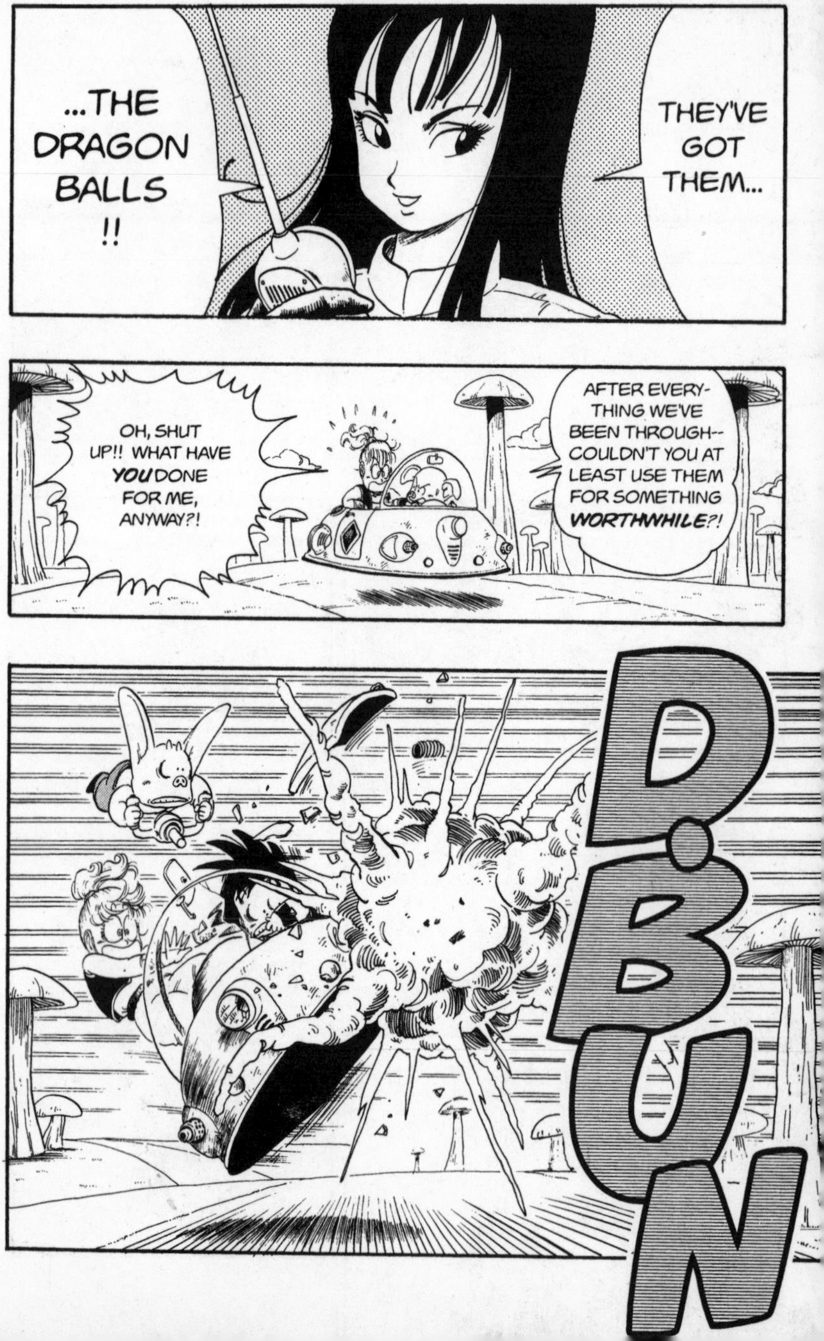
THEY'VE GOT THEM...
...THE DRAGON BALLS !!
AFTER EVERY-THING WE'VE BEEN THROUGH--COULDN'T YOU AT LEAST USE THEM FOR SOMETHING WORTHWHILE?!
OH, SHUT UP!! WHAT HAVE YOU DONE FOR ME, ANYWAY?!
DOBUN

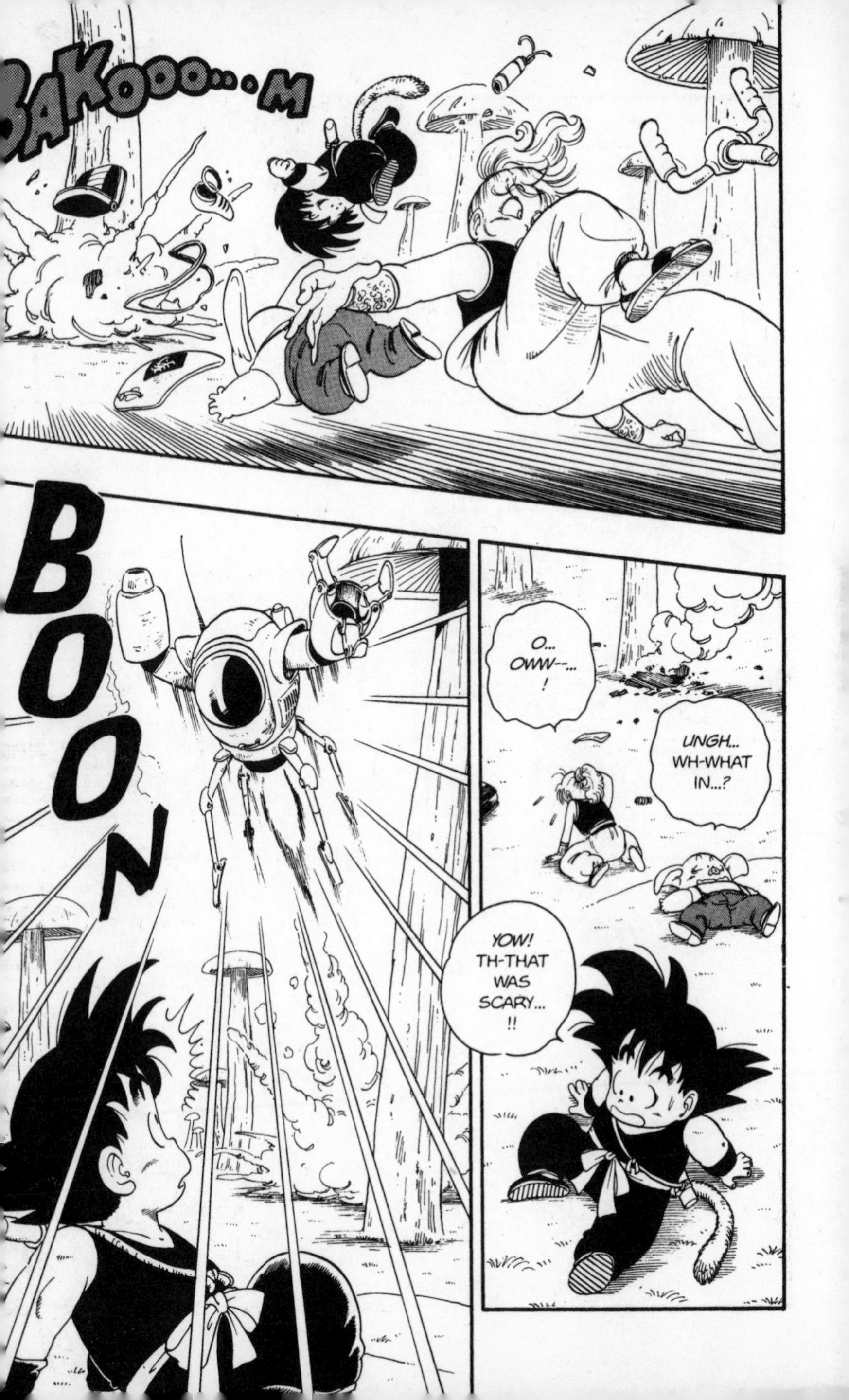
BAKOOO...M
O... OWW-... !
UNGH... WH-WHAT IN...?
YOW! TH-THAT WAS SCARY... !!
BOOON

WHAT THE... WHO THE...?!

EEEE !!

TP...

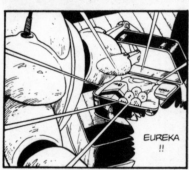

EUREKA !!

GFMP GSHMP

HUH ?!

THANKS FOR THE DRAGON BALLS... CHUMP!!

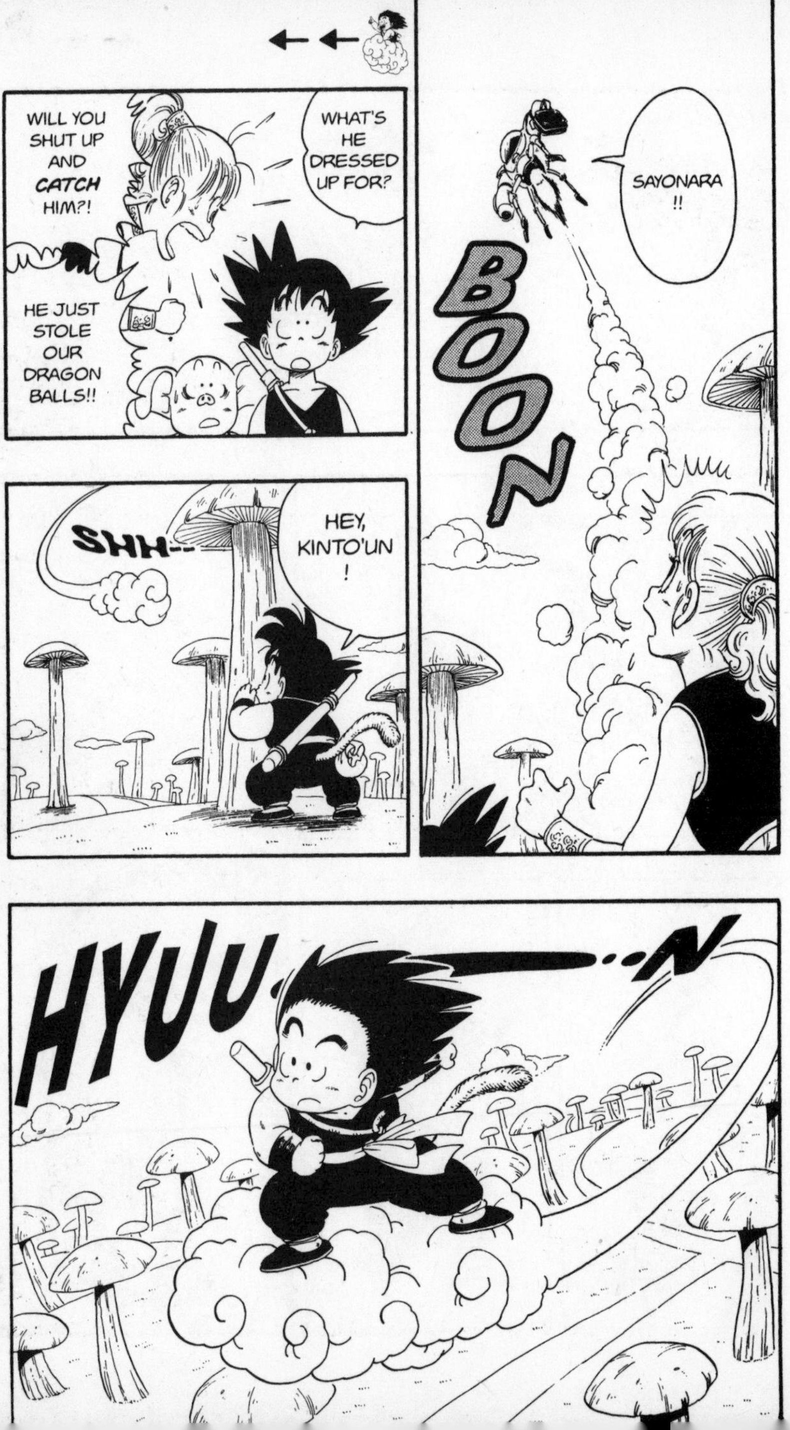
SAYONARA !!
BOOON
WHAT'S HE DRESSED UP FOR?
WILL YOU SHUT UP AND CATCH HIM?!
HE JUST STOLE OUR DRAGON BALLS!!
HEY, KINTO'UN !
SHH--
HYUU-- -N

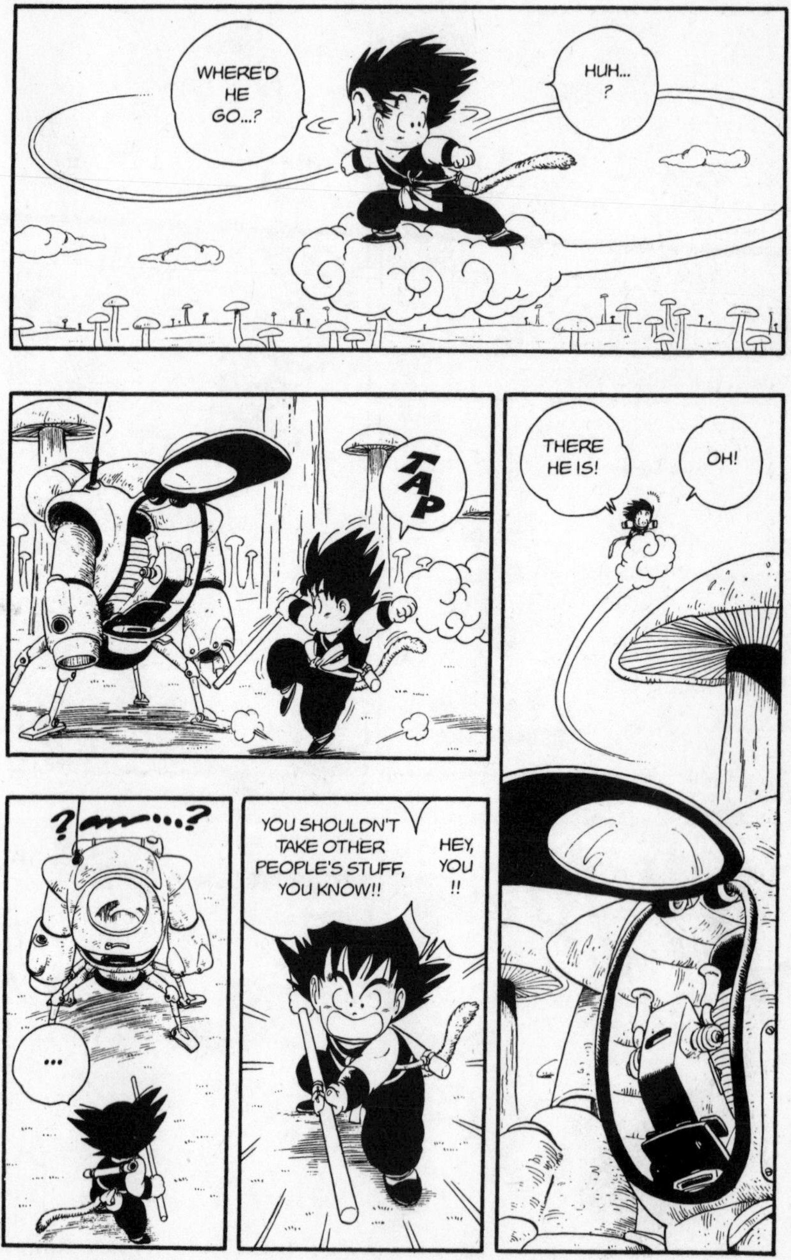
HUH... ?
WHERE'D HE GO...?
OH!
THERE HE IS!
TAP
HEY, YOU !!
YOU SHOULDN'T TAKE OTHER PEOPLE'S STUFF, YOU KNOW!!
?...?
...

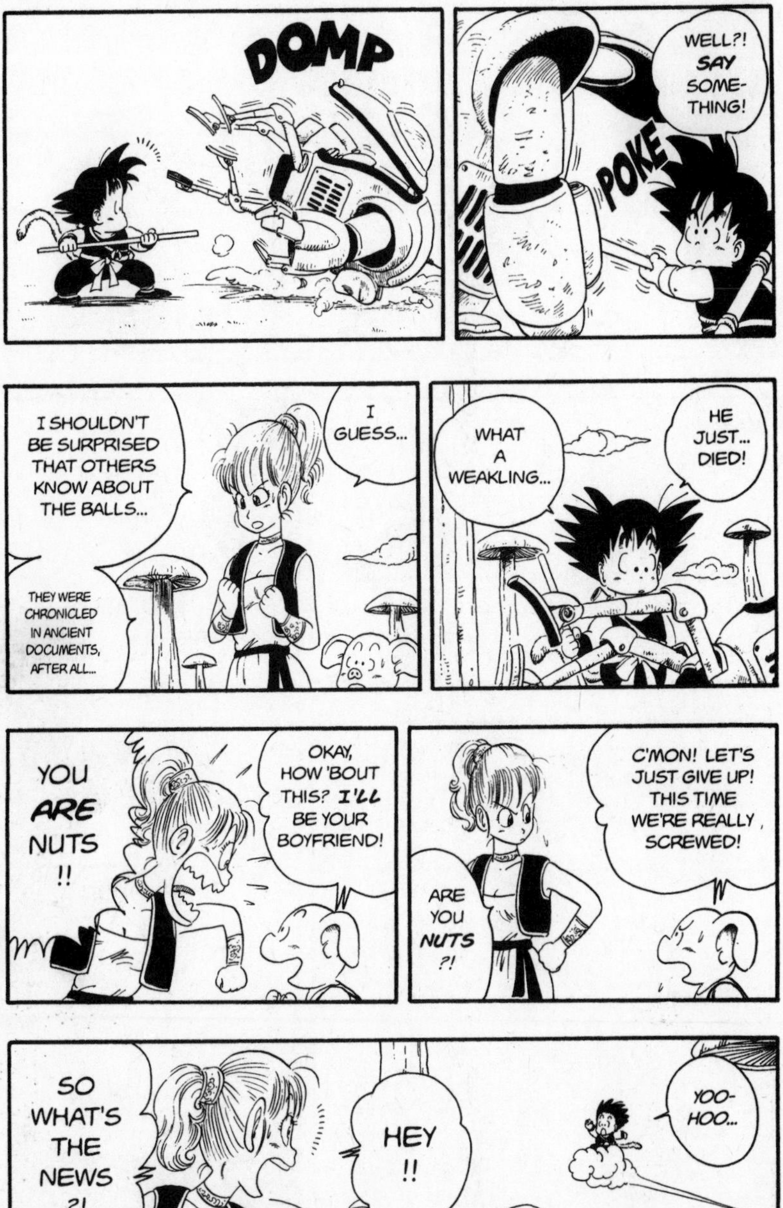
WELL?! SAY SOME-THING!
POKE
DOMP
HE JUST... DIED!
WHAT A WEAKLING...
I GUESS...
I SHOULDN'T BE SURPRISED THAT OTHERS KNOW ABOUT THE BALLS...
THEY WERE CHRONICLED IN ANCIENT DOCUMENTS, AFTER ALL...
C'MON! LET'S JUST GIVE UP! THIS TIME WE'RE REALLY SCREWED!
ARE YOU NUTS?!
OKAY, HOW 'BOUT THIS? I'LL BE YOUR BOYFRIEND!
YOU ARE NUTS!!
YOO-HOO...
HEY!!
SO WHAT'S THE NEWS?!

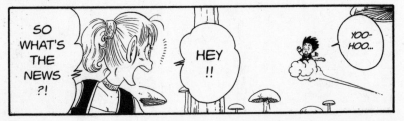

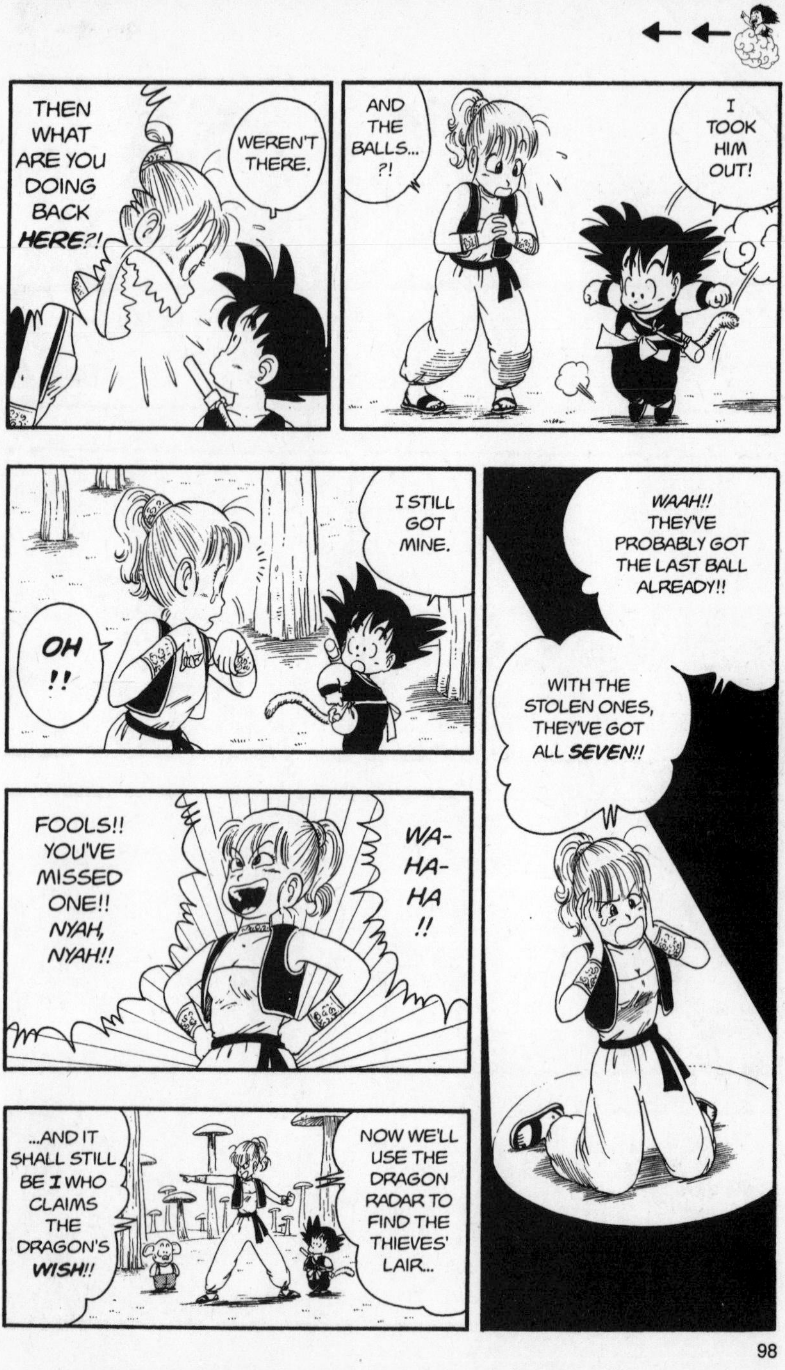
I TOOK HIM OUT!
AND THE BALLS... ?!
WEREN'T THERE.
THEN WHAT ARE YOU DOING BACK HERE?!
WAAH!! THEY'VE PROBABLY GOT THE LAST BALL ALREADY!!
WITH THE STOLEN ONES, THEY'VE GOT ALL SEVEN!!
I STILL GOT MINE.
OH !!
WA-HA-HA !!
FOOLS!! YOU'VE MISSED ONE!! NYAH, NYAH!!
NOW WE'LL USE THE DRAGON RADAR TO FIND THE THIEVES' LAIR...
...AND IT SHALL STILL BE I WHO CLAIMS THE DRAGON'S WISH!!

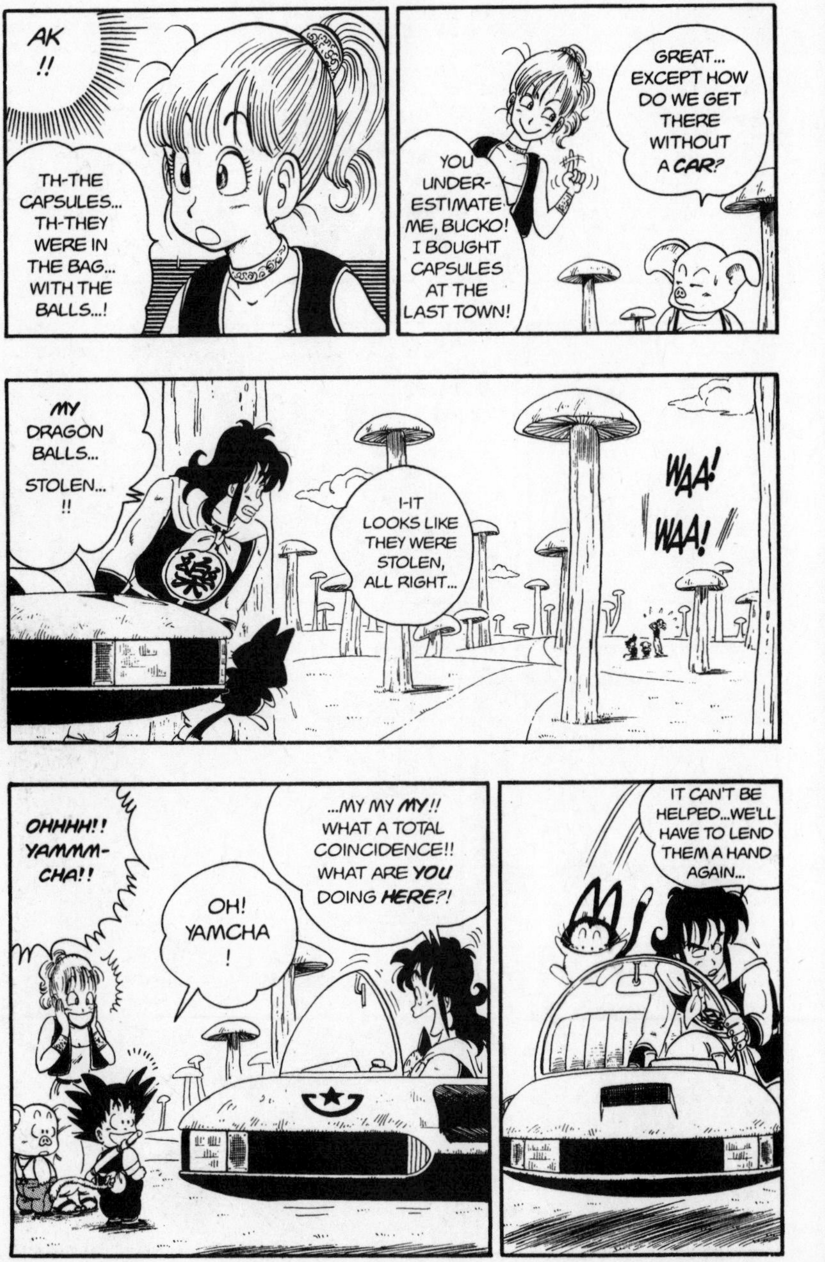
GREAT... EXCEPT HOW DO WE GET THERE WITHOUT A CAR?
YOU UNDER-ESTIMATE ME, BUCKO! I BOUGHT CAPSULES AT THE LAST TOWN!
AK !!
TH-THE CAPSULES... TH-THEY WERE IN THE BAG... WITH THE BALLS...!
WAA! WAA!
I-IT LOOKS LIKE THEY WERE STOLEN, ALL RIGHT...
MY DRAGON BALLS... STOLEN... !!
IT CAN'T BE HELPED...WE'LL HAVE TO LEND THEM A HAND AGAIN...
...MY MY MY!! WHAT A TOTAL COINCIDENCE!! WHAT ARE YOU DOING HERE?!
OH! YAMCHA !
OHHHH!! YAMMM-CHA!!

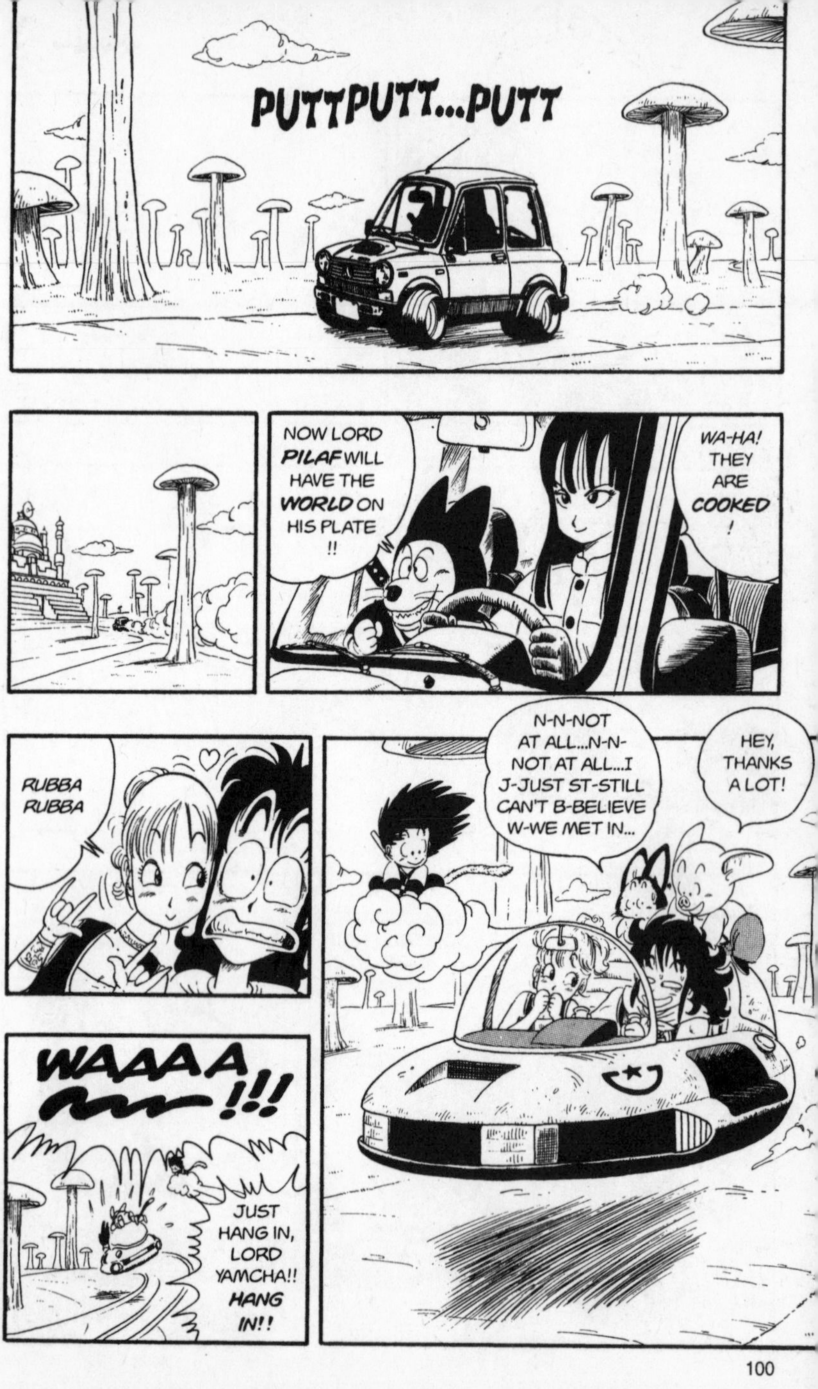
PUTTPUTT...PUTT
WA-HA! THEY ARE COOKED!
NOW LORD PILAF WILL HAVE THE WORLD ON HIS PLATE!!
HEY, THANKS A LOT!
N-N-NOT AT ALL...N-N-NOT AT ALL...I J-JUST ST-STILL CAN'T B-BELIEVE W-WE MET IN...
RUBBA RUBBA
WAAAA~!!!
JUST HANG IN, LORD YAMCHA!! HANG IN!!

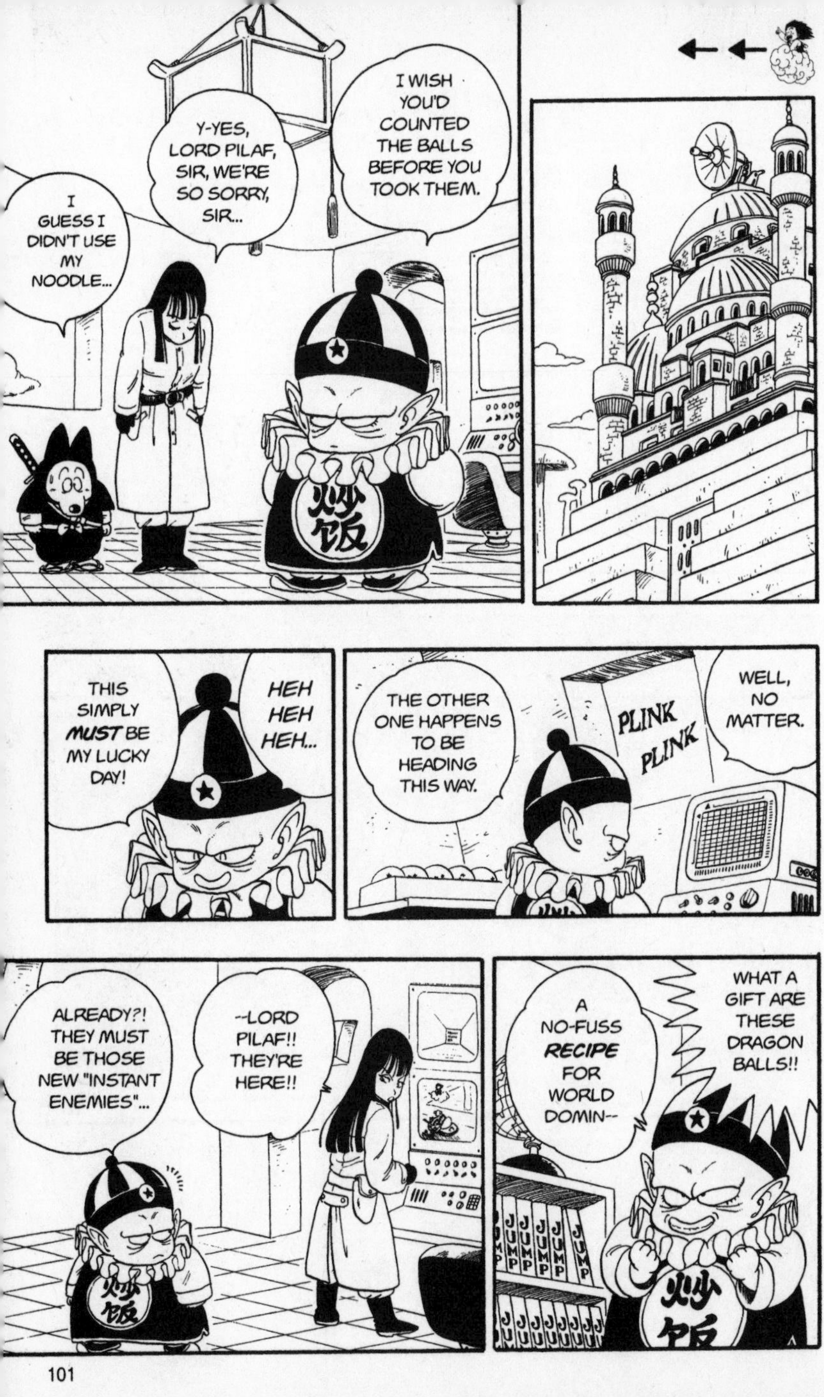
I WISH YOU'D COUNTED THE BALLS BEFORE YOU TOOK THEM.
Y-YES, LORD PILAF, SIR, WE'RE SO SORRY, SIR...
I GUESS I DIDN'T USE MY NOODLE...
WELL, NO MATTER.
PLINK PLINK
THE OTHER ONE HAPPENS TO BE HEADING THIS WAY.
HEH HEH HEH...
THIS SIMPLY MUST BE MY LUCKY DAY!
WHAT A GIFT ARE THESE DRAGON BALLS!!
A NO-FUSS RECIPE FOR WORLD DOMIN--
--LORD PILAF!! THEY'RE HERE!!
ALREADY?! THEY MUST BE THOSE NEW "INSTANT ENEMIES"...

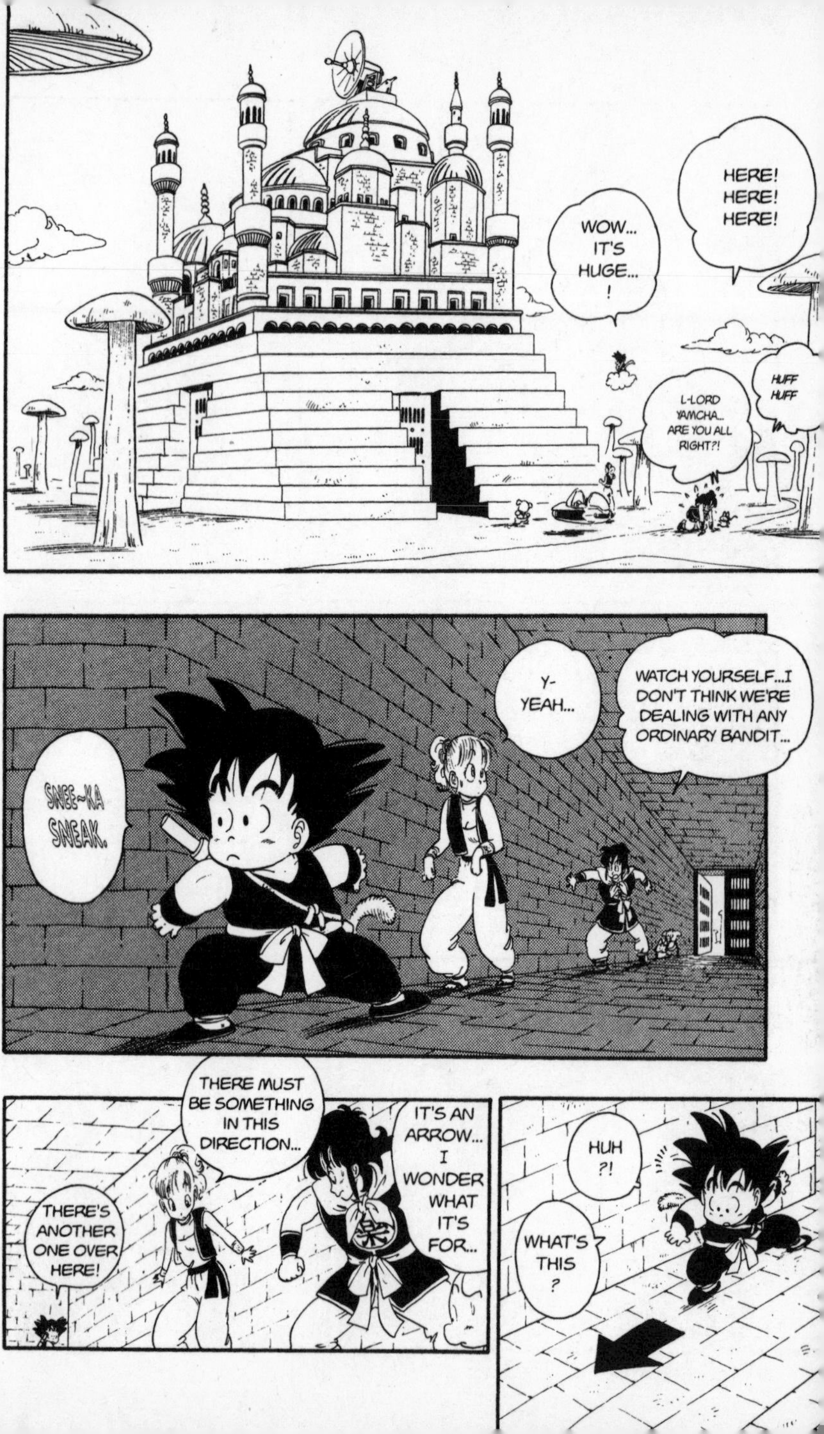
HERE! HERE! HERE!
WOW... IT'S HUGE... !
HUFF HUFF
L-LORD YAMCHA... ARE YOU ALL RIGHT?!
WATCH YOURSELF...I DON'T THINK WE'RE DEALING WITH ANY ORDINARY BANDIT...
Y- YEAH...
SNEE-KA SNEAK.
HUH ?!
WHAT'S THIS ?
IT'S AN ARROW... I WONDER WHAT IT'S FOR...
THERE MUST BE SOMETHING IN THIS DIRECTION...
THERE'S ANOTHER ONE OVER HERE!

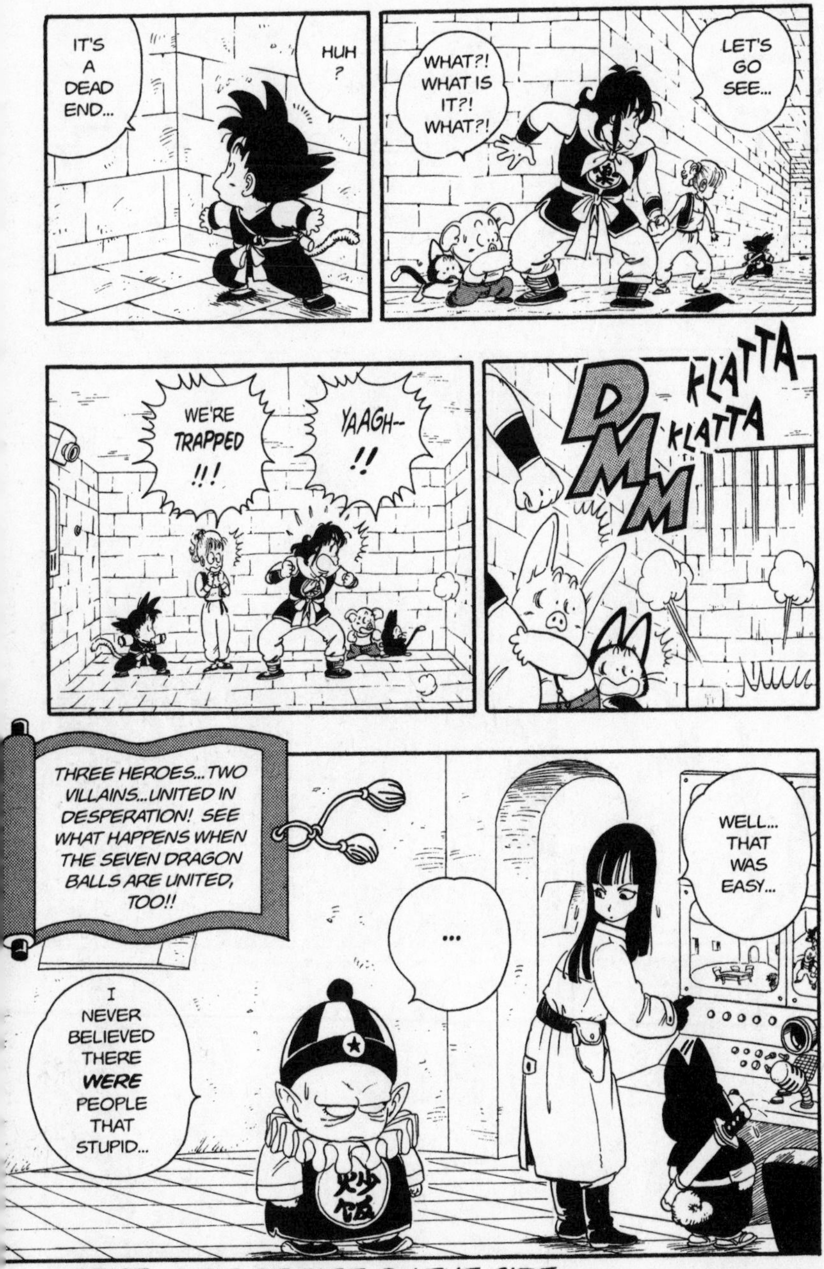
LET'S GO SEE...
WHAT?! WHAT IS IT?! WHAT?!
HUH ?
IT'S A DEAD END...
KLATTA
KLATTA
DMMM
YAAGH-- !!
WE'RE TRAPPED !!!
WELL... THAT WAS EASY...
...
THREE HEROES...TWO VILLAINS...UNITED IN DESPERATION! SEE WHAT HAPPENS WHEN THE SEVEN DRAGON BALLS ARE UNITED, TOO!!
I NEVER BELIEVED THERE WERE PEOPLE THAT STUPID...

NEXT: A BIT OF RICE ON THE SIDE

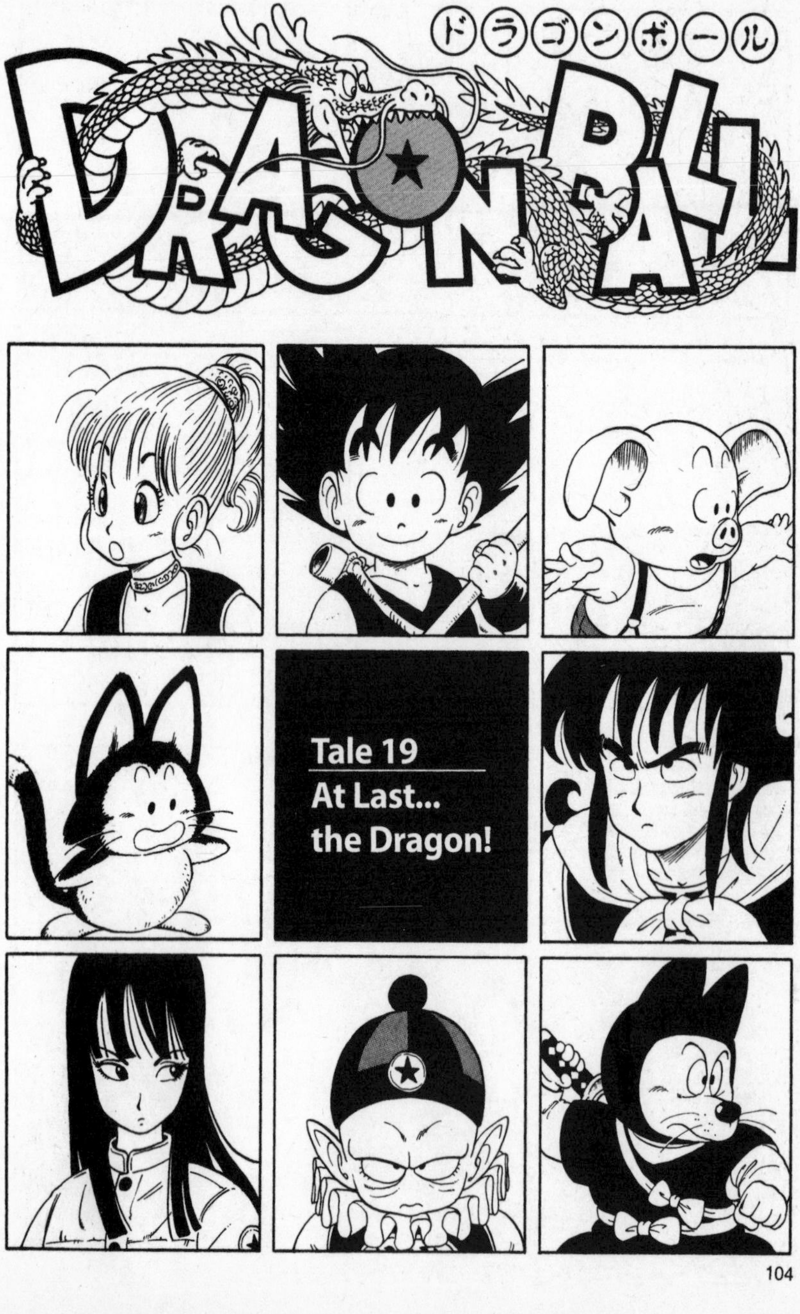
ドラゴンボール
DRAGON BALL
Tale 19
At Last...
the Dragon!

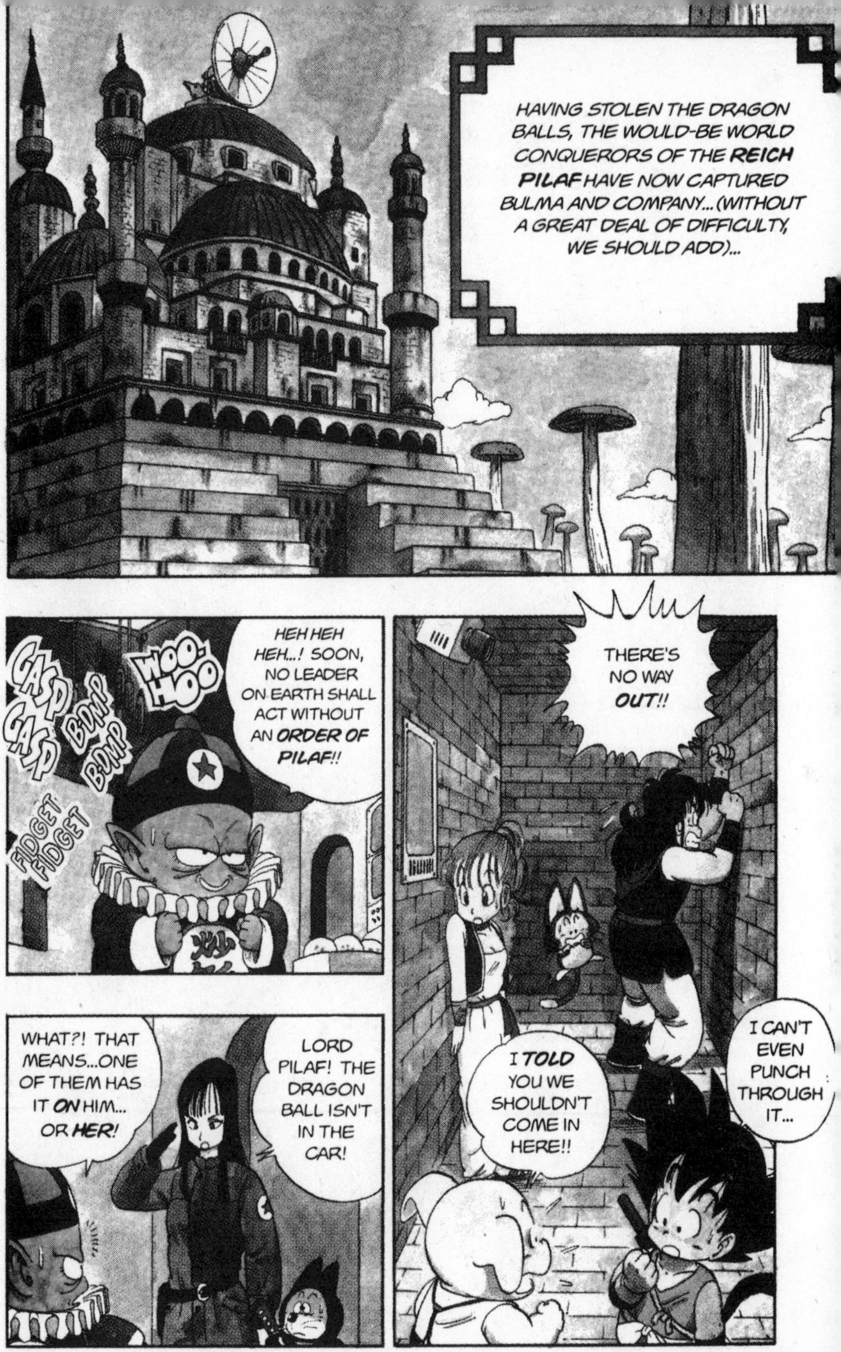
HAVING STOLEN THE DRAGON BALLS, THE WOULD-BE WORLD CONQUERORS OF THE **REICH PILAF** HAVE NOW CAPTURED BULMA AND COMPANY...(WITHOUT A GREAT DEAL OF DIFFICULTY, WE SHOULD ADD)...
THERE'S NO WAY ***OUT***!!
I CAN'T EVEN PUNCH THROUGH IT...
I ***TOLD*** YOU WE SHOULDN'T COME IN HERE!!
HEH HEH HEH...! SOON, NO LEADER ON EARTH SHALL ACT WITHOUT AN ***ORDER OF PILAF***!!
WOO-HOO
BOMP BOMP
GASP GASP
FIDGET FIDGET
LORD PILAF! THE DRAGON BALL ISN'T IN THE CAR!
WHAT?! THAT MEANS...ONE OF THEM HAS IT ***ON*** HIM... OR ***HER***!

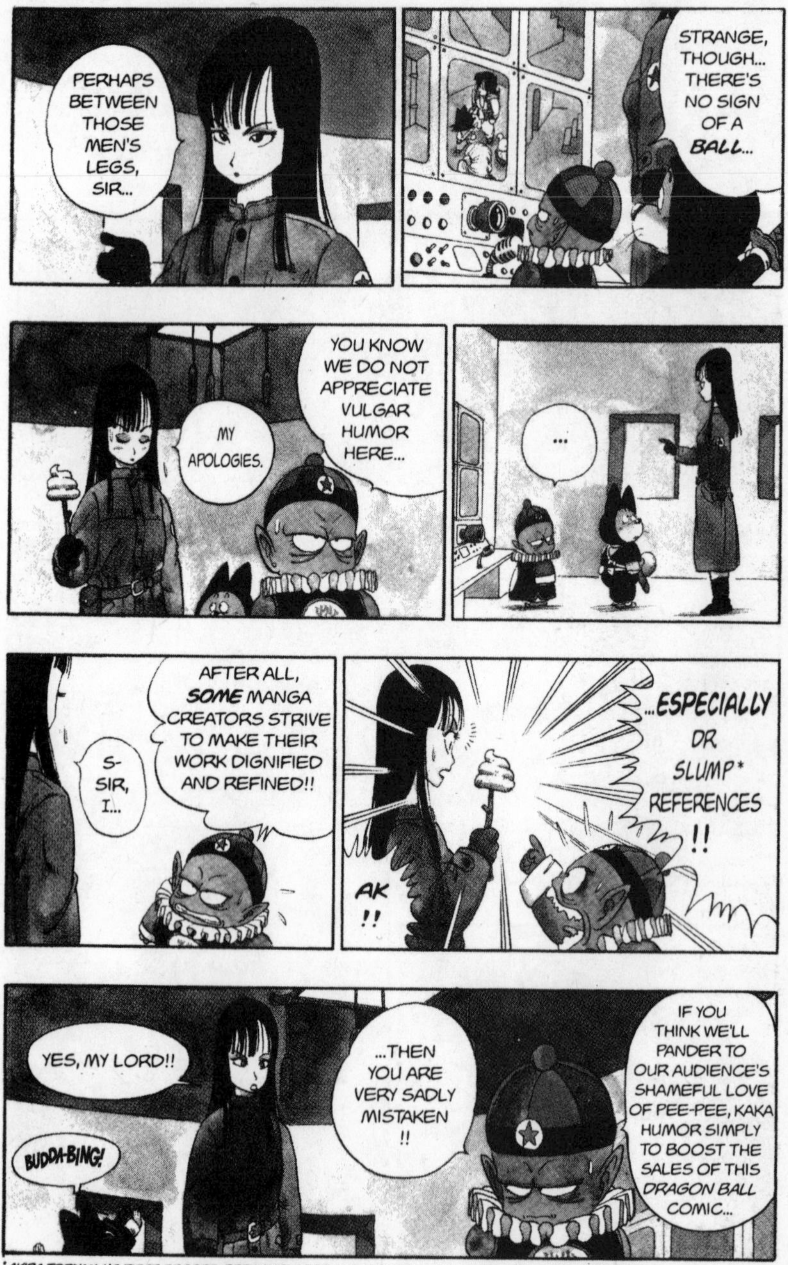

STRANGE, THOUGH... THERE'S NO SIGN OF A **BALL**...
PERHAPS BETWEEN THOSE MEN'S LEGS, SIR...
...
YOU KNOW WE DO NOT APPRECIATE VULGAR HUMOR HERE...
MY APOLOGIES.
...**ESPECIALLY DR SLUMP* REFERENCES !!**
AK !!
AFTER ALL, **SOME** MANGA CREATORS STRIVE TO MAKE THEIR WORK DIGNIFIED AND REFINED!!
S-SIR, I...
IF YOU THINK WE'LL PANDER TO OUR AUDIENCE'S SHAMEFUL LOVE OF PEE-PEE, KAKA HUMOR SIMPLY TO BOOST THE SALES OF THIS *DRAGON BALL* COMIC...
...THEN YOU ARE VERY SADLY MISTAKEN !!
YES, MY LORD!!
BUDDA-BING!

*AKIRA TORIYAMA'S FIRST RECORD-BREAKINGLY POPULAR SERIES WHICH RAN IN JAPAN FROM 1980 TO 1984.

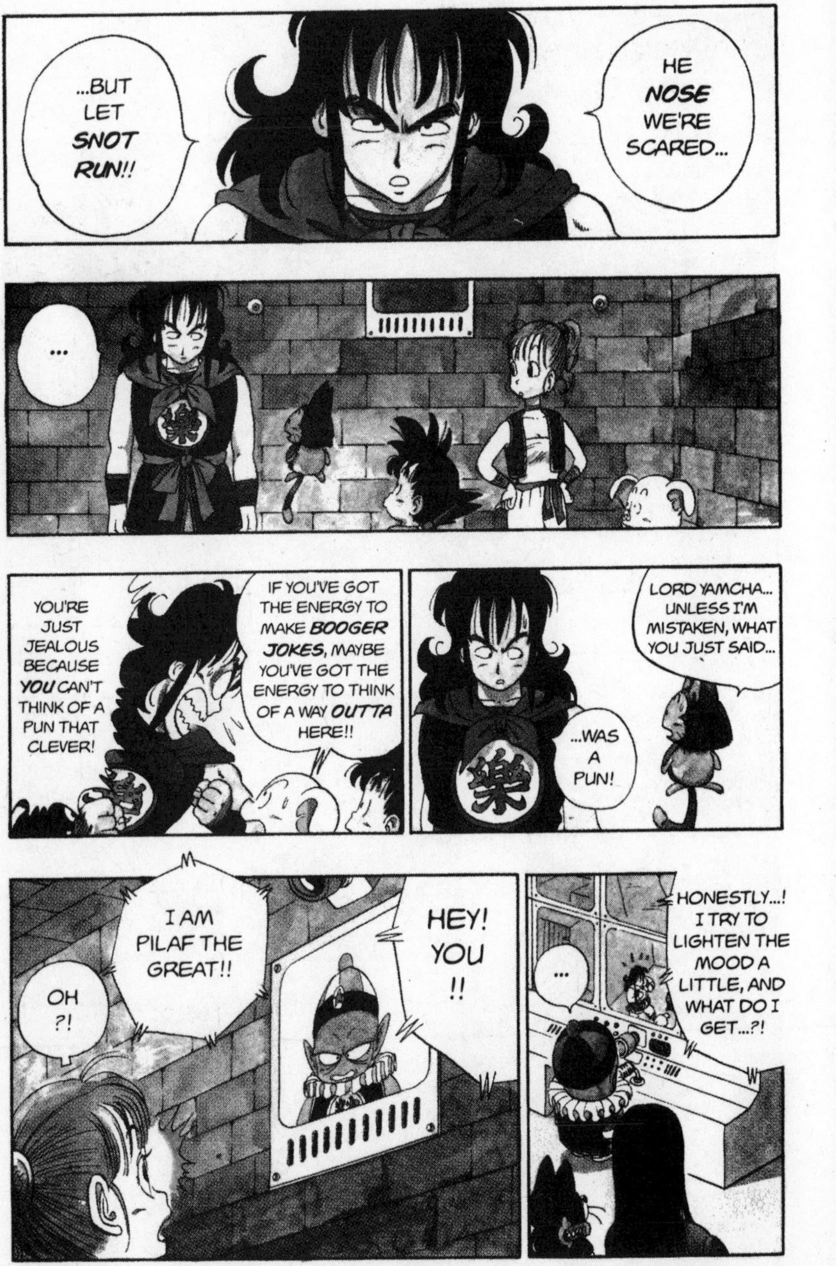
HE NOSE WE'RE SCARED...
...BUT LET SNOT RUN!!
...
LORD YAMCHA... UNLESS I'M MISTAKEN, WHAT YOU JUST SAID...
...WAS A PUN!
IF YOU'VE GOT THE ENERGY TO MAKE BOOGER JOKES, MAYBE YOU'VE GOT THE ENERGY TO THINK OF A WAY OUTTA HERE!!
YOU'RE JUST JEALOUS BECAUSE YOU CAN'T THINK OF A PUN THAT CLEVER!
HONESTLY...! I TRY TO LIGHTEN THE MOOD A LITTLE, AND WHAT DO I GET...?!
...
HEY! YOU !!
I AM PILAF THE GREAT!!
OH ?!

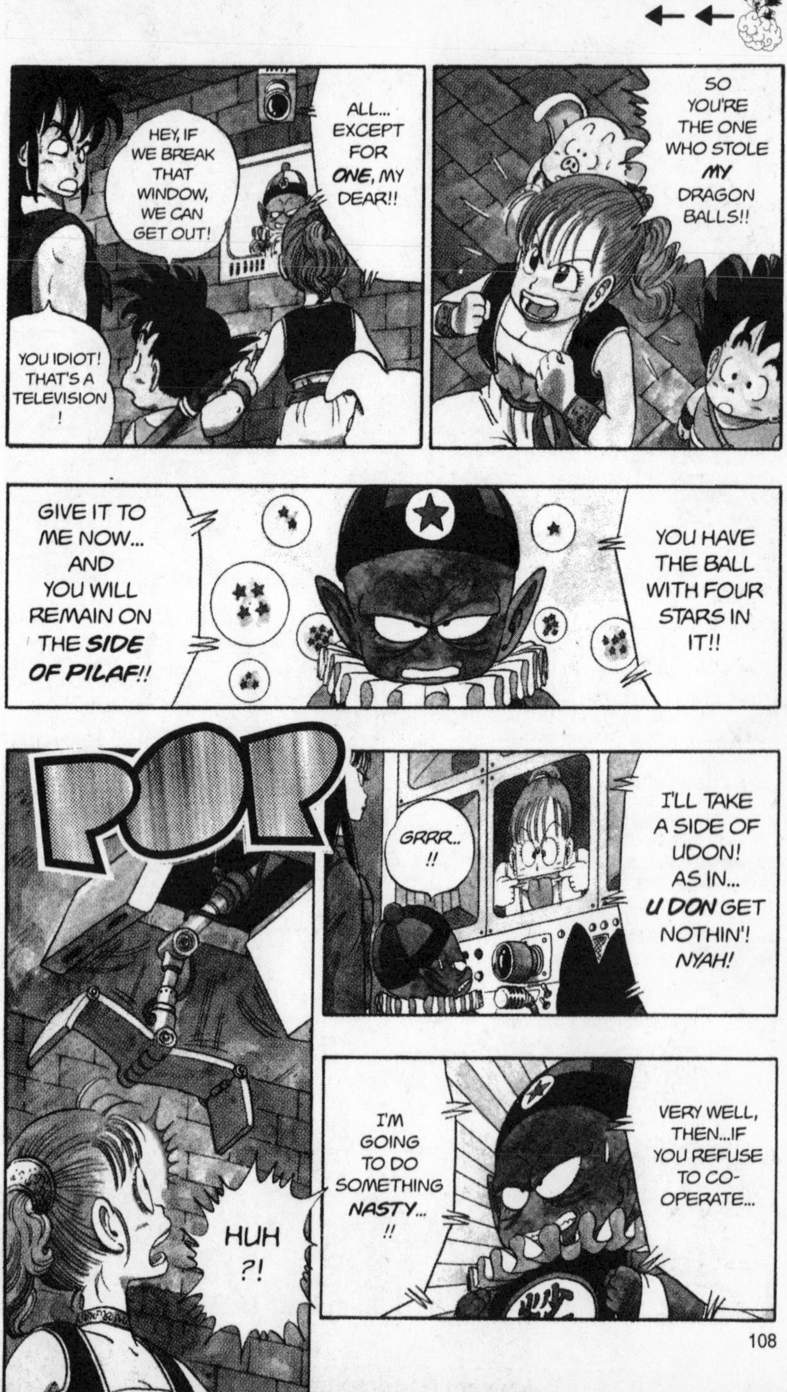

SO YOU'RE THE ONE WHO STOLE MY DRAGON BALLS!!
ALL... EXCEPT FOR ONE, MY DEAR!!
HEY, IF WE BREAK THAT WINDOW, WE CAN GET OUT!
YOU IDIOT! THAT'S A TELEVISION!
YOU HAVE THE BALL WITH FOUR STARS IN IT!!
GIVE IT TO ME NOW... AND YOU WILL REMAIN ON THE SIDE OF PILAF!!
I'LL TAKE A SIDE OF UDON! AS IN... U DON GET NOTHIN'! NYAH!
GRRR... !!
VERY WELL, THEN...IF YOU REFUSE TO CO-OPERATE...
I'M GOING TO DO SOMETHING NASTY... !!
POP
HUH ?!

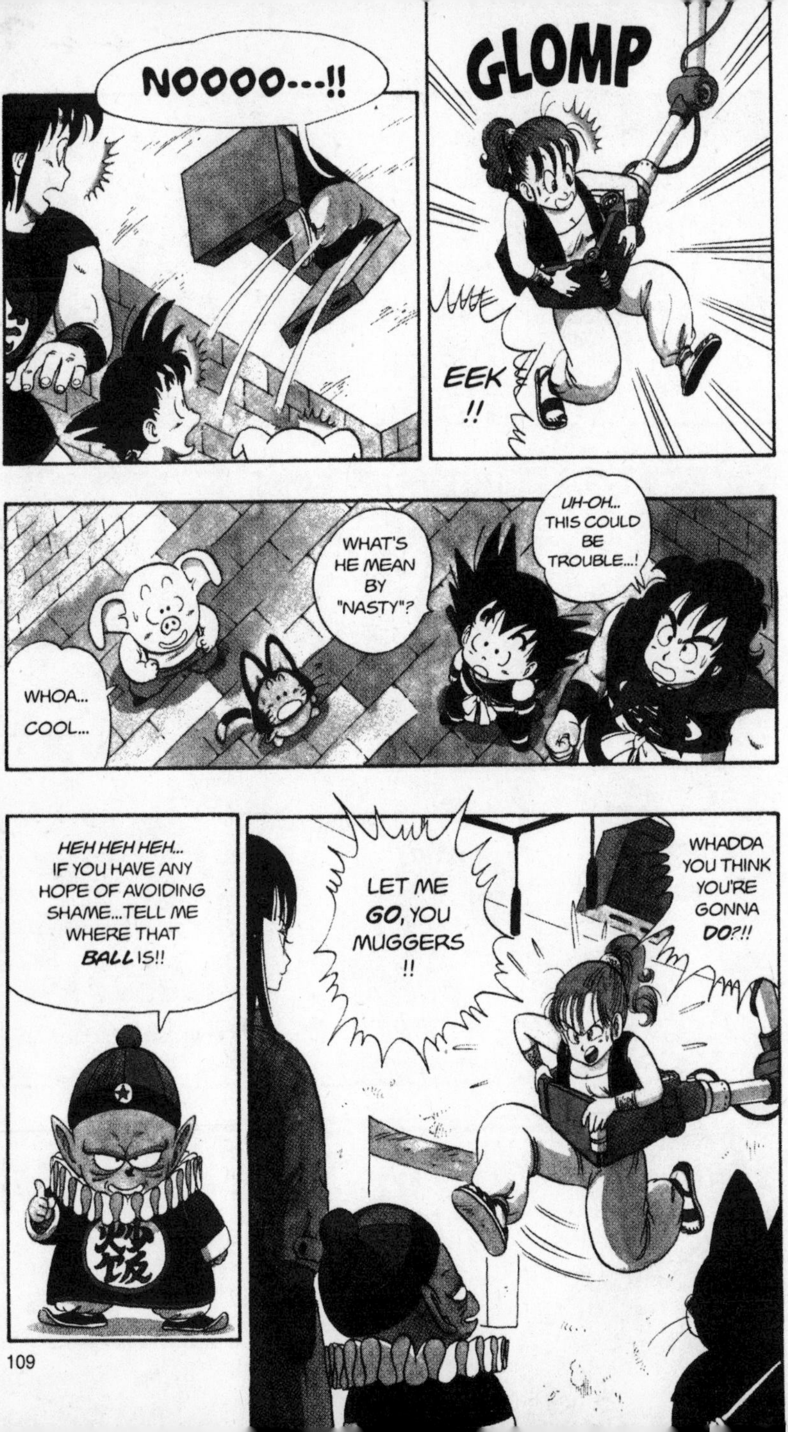
GLOMP
EEK !!
NOOOO...!!
UH-OH... THIS COULD BE TROUBLE...!
WHAT'S HE MEAN BY "NASTY"?
WHOA... COOL...
WHADDA YOU THINK YOU'RE GONNA DO?!!
LET ME GO, YOU MUGGERS !!
HEH HEH HEH... IF YOU HAVE ANY HOPE OF AVOIDING SHAME...TELL ME WHERE THAT BALL IS!!

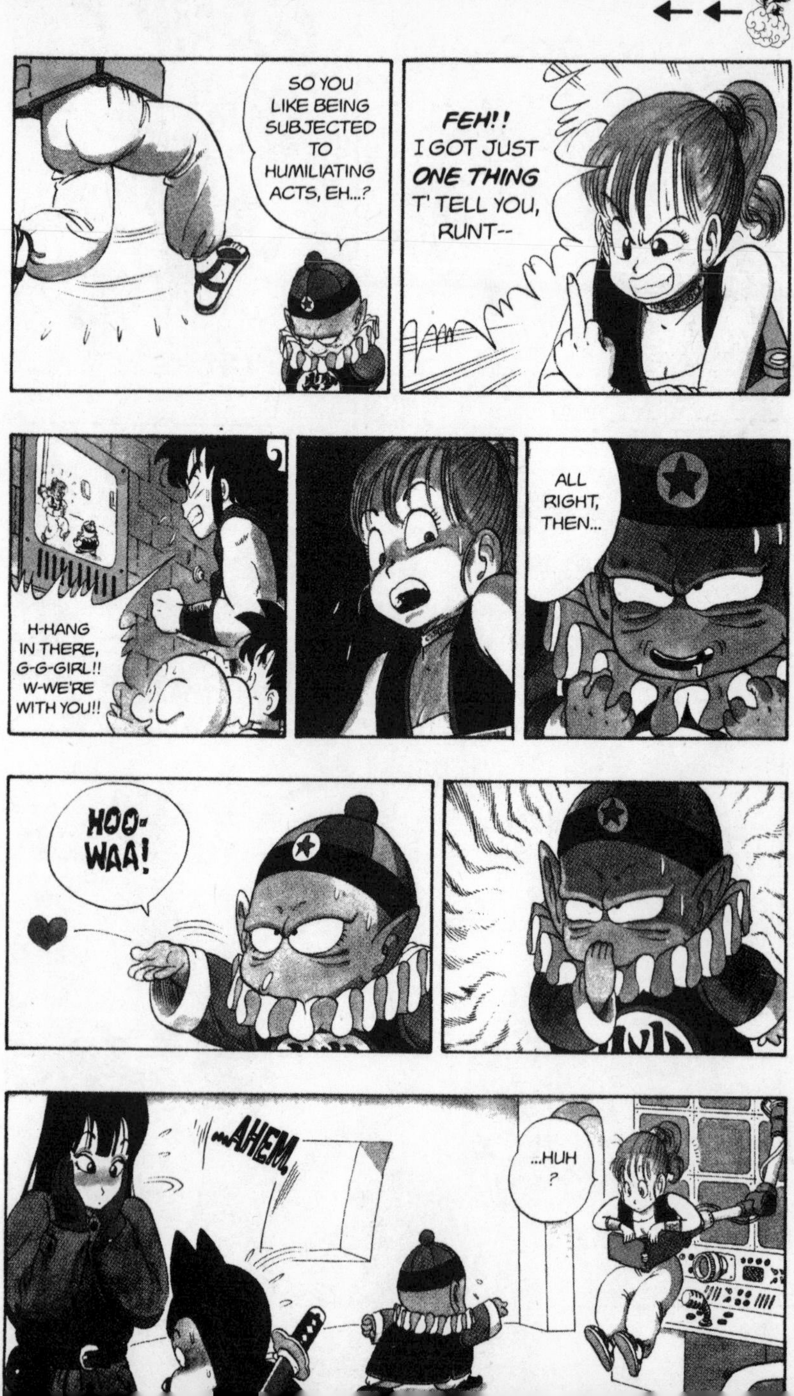
FEH!! I GOT JUST ONE THING T' TELL YOU, RUNT--
SO YOU LIKE BEING SUBJECTED TO HUMILIATING ACTS, EH...?
ALL RIGHT, THEN...
H-HANG IN THERE, G-G-GIRL!! W-WE'RE WITH YOU!!
HOO-WAA!
...HUH ?
...AHEM.

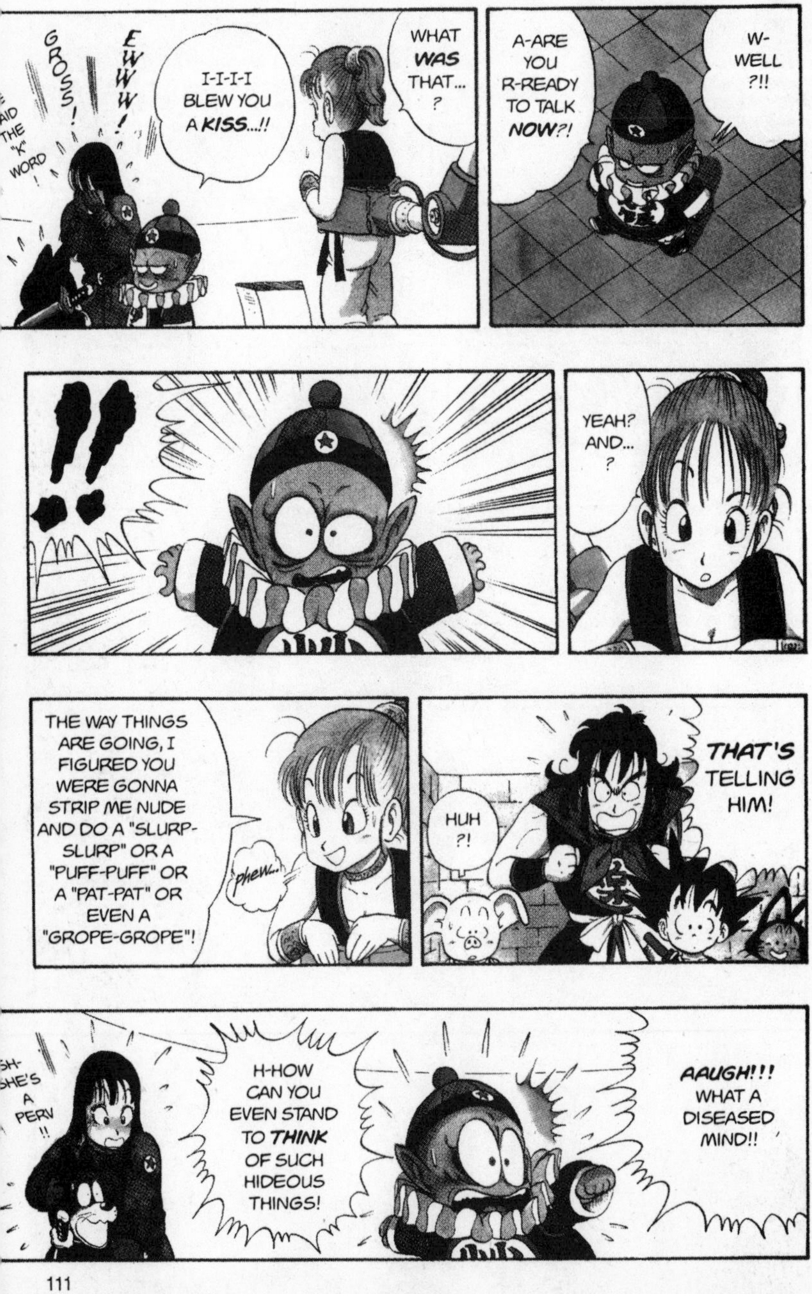
W- WELL ?!!
A-ARE YOU R-READY TO TALK NOW?!
WHAT WAS THAT... ?
I-I-I-I BLEW YOU A KISS...!!
EWWW!
GROSS!
AID THE "K" WORD !
YEAH? AND... ?
!!
THAT'S TELLING HIM!
HUH ?!
THE WAY THINGS ARE GOING, I FIGURED YOU WERE GONNA STRIP ME NUDE AND DO A "SLURP-SLURP" OR A "PUFF-PUFF" OR A "PAT-PAT" OR EVEN A "GROPE-GROPE"!
phew...
AAUGH!!! WHAT A DISEASED MIND!!
H-HOW CAN YOU EVEN STAND TO THINK OF SUCH HIDEOUS THINGS!
SH-SHE'S A PERV !!

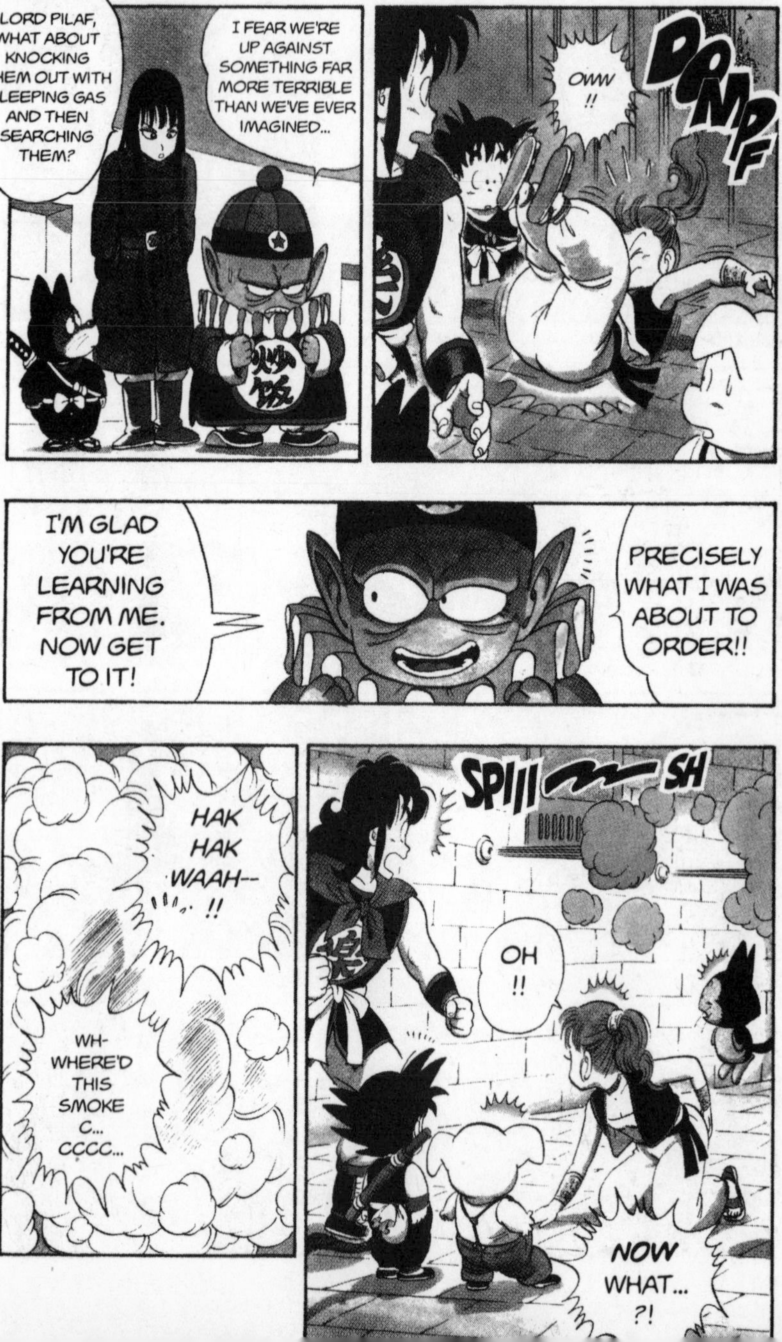
DOMPF
OWW !!
I FEAR WE'RE UP AGAINST SOMETHING FAR MORE TERRIBLE THAN WE'VE EVER IMAGINED...
LORD PILAF, WHAT ABOUT KNOCKING THEM OUT WITH SLEEPING GAS AND THEN SEARCHING THEM?
PRECISELY WHAT I WAS ABOUT TO ORDER!!
I'M GLAD YOU'RE LEARNING FROM ME. NOW GET TO IT!
SPIII—SH
OH !!
NOW WHAT... ?!
HAK HAK WAAH-- !!
WH- WHERE'D THIS SMOKE C... CCCC...

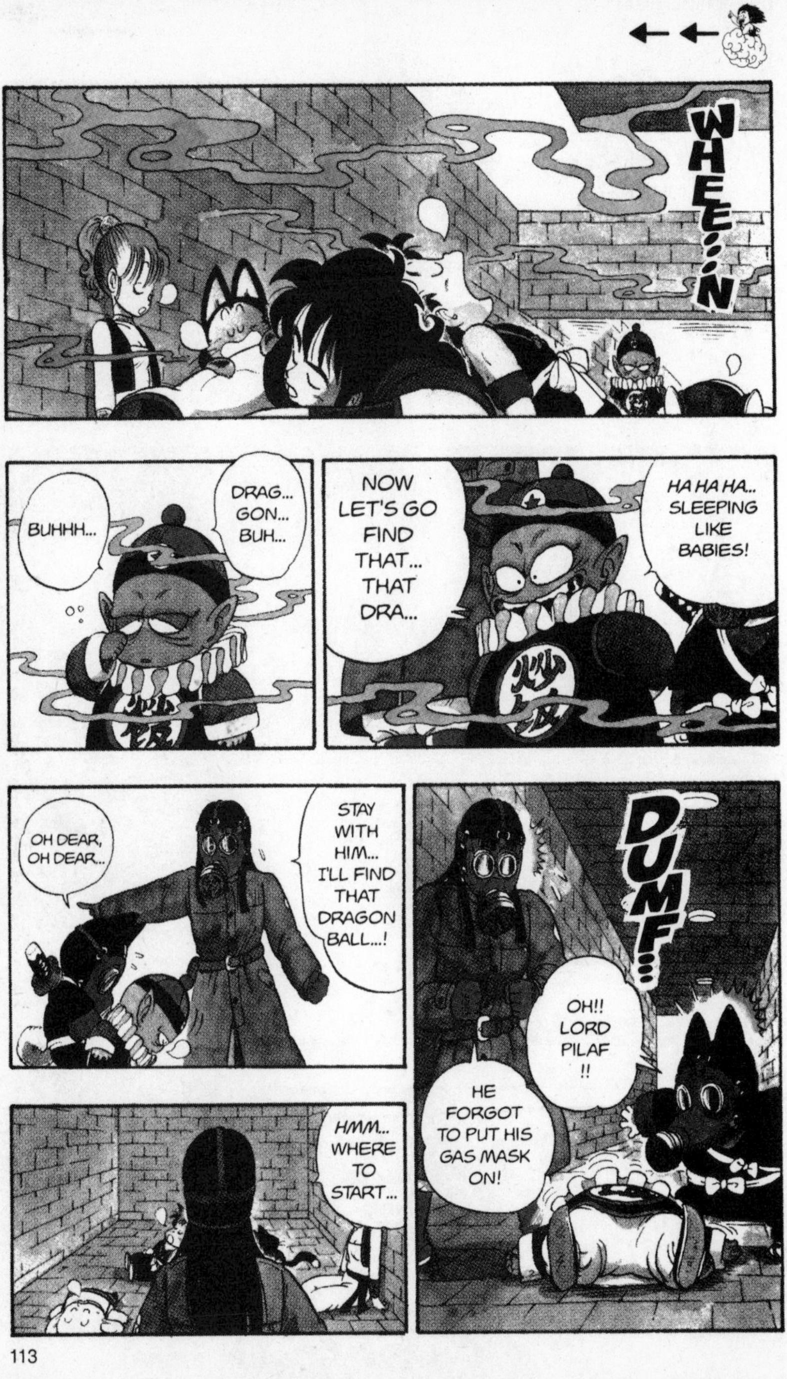
WHEE...N
HA HA HA.. SLEEPING LIKE BABIES!
NOW LET'S GO FIND THAT... THAT DRA...
DRAG... GON... BUH...
BUHHH...
DUMF...
OH!! LORD PILAF !!
HE FORGOT TO PUT HIS GAS MASK ON!
STAY WITH HIM... I'LL FIND THAT DRAGON BALL...!
OH DEAR, OH DEAR...
HMM... WHERE TO START...

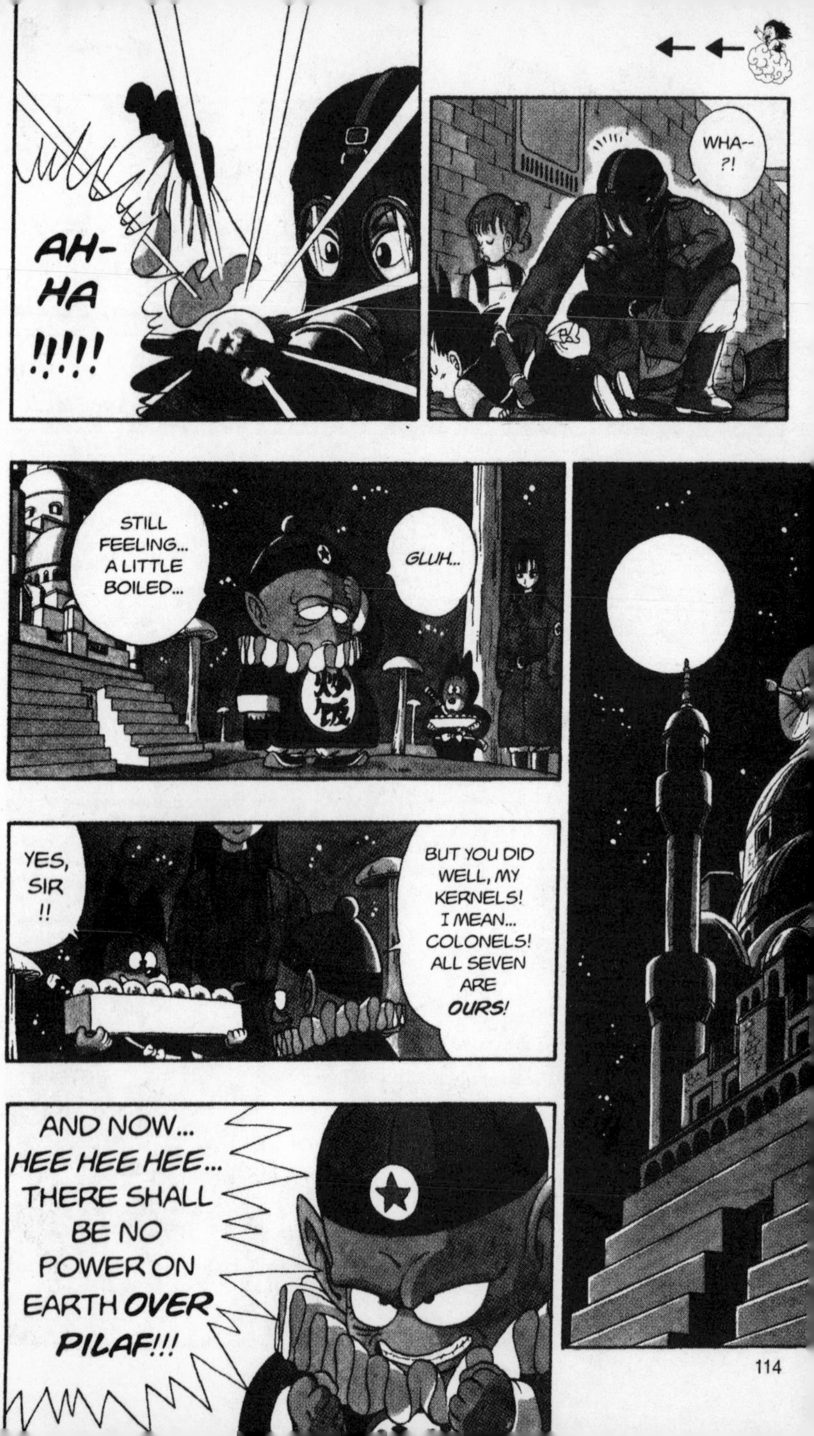
WHA-- ?!
AH-HA !!!!!
GLUH...
STILL FEELING... A LITTLE BOILED...
BUT YOU DID WELL, MY KERNELS! I MEAN... COLONELS! ALL SEVEN ARE OURS!
YES, SIR !!
AND NOW... HEE HEE HEE... THERE SHALL BE NO POWER ON EARTH OVER PILAF!!!

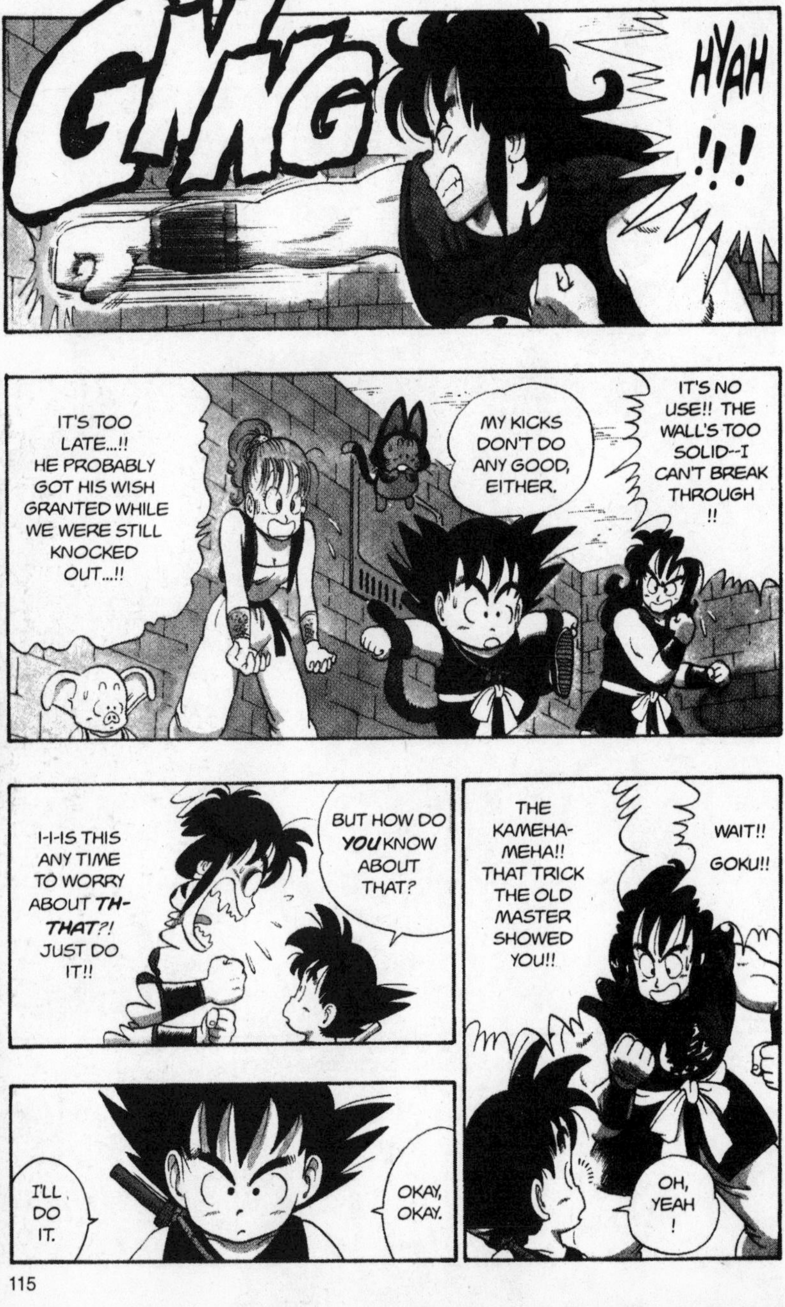
HYAH!!!
GING
IT'S NO USE!! THE WALL'S TOO SOLID--I CAN'T BREAK THROUGH!!
MY KICKS DON'T DO ANY GOOD, EITHER.
IT'S TOO LATE...!! HE PROBABLY GOT HIS WISH GRANTED WHILE WE WERE STILL KNOCKED OUT...!!
WAIT!!
GOKU!!
THE KAMEHA-MEHA!! THAT TRICK THE OLD MASTER SHOWED YOU!!
OH, YEAH!
BUT HOW DO ***YOU*** KNOW ABOUT THAT?
I-I-IS THIS ANY TIME TO WORRY ABOUT ***TH-THAT***?! JUST DO IT!!
OKAY, OKAY.
I'LL DO IT.

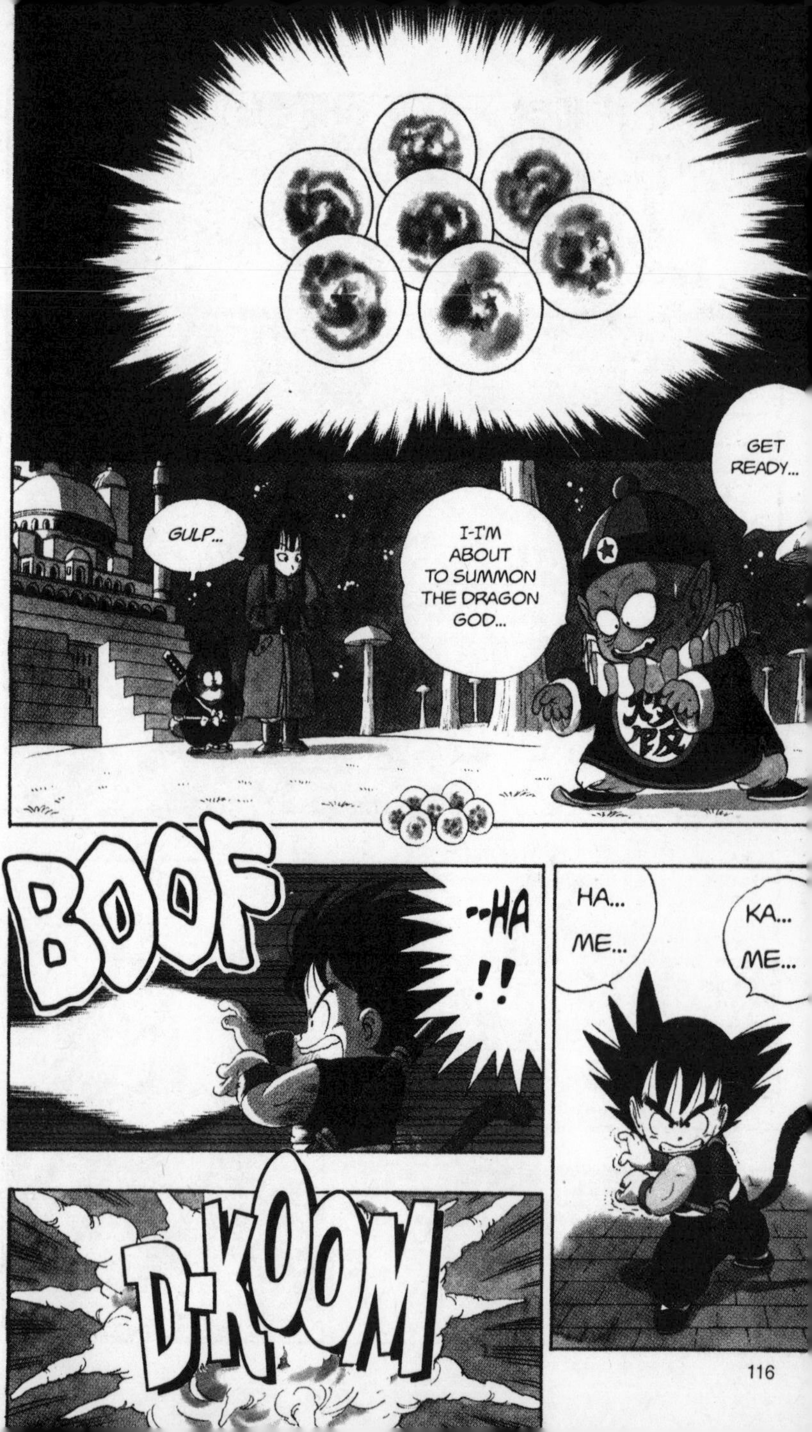
GET READY...
I-I'M ABOUT TO SUMMON THE DRAGON GOD...
GULP...
KA... ME...
HA... ME...
--HA !!
BOOF
D-KOOM

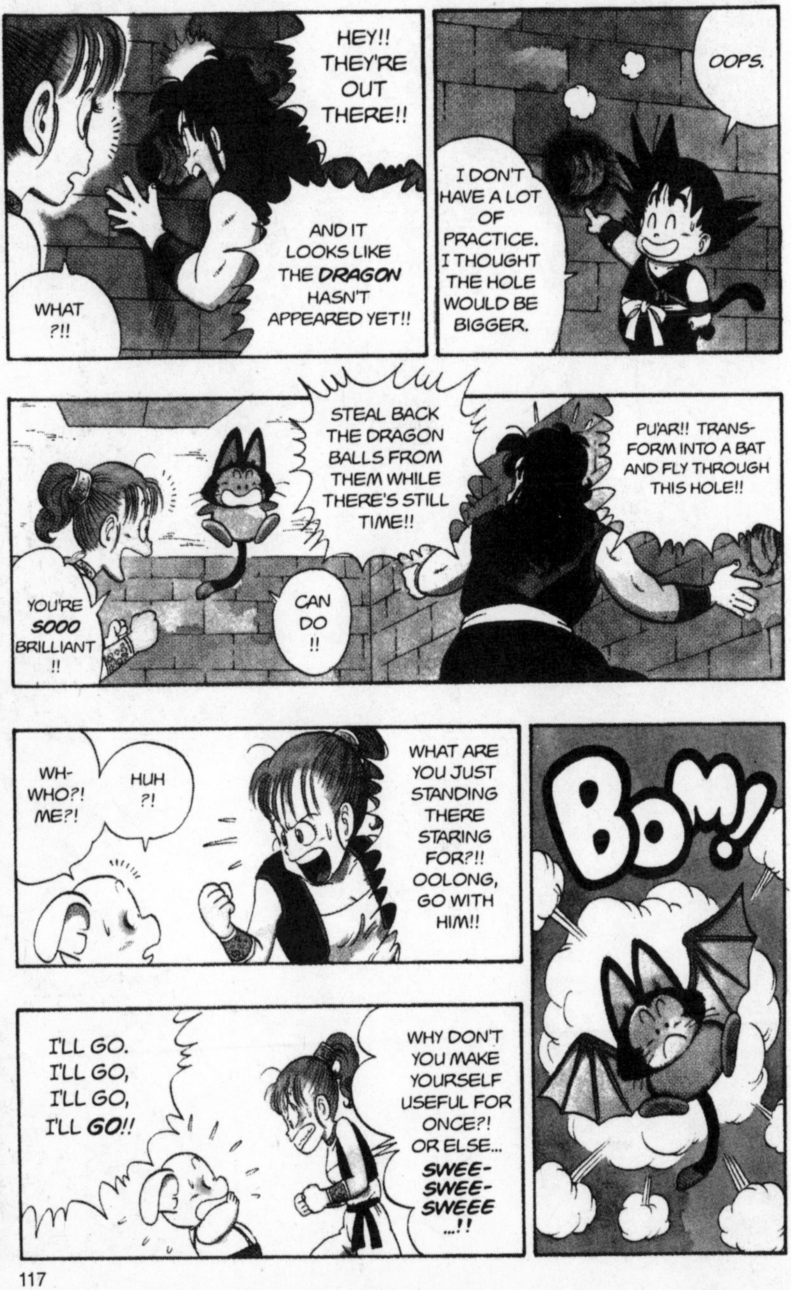
OOPS.
I DON'T HAVE A LOT OF PRACTICE. I THOUGHT THE HOLE WOULD BE BIGGER.
HEY!! THEY'RE OUT THERE!!
AND IT LOOKS LIKE THE DRAGON HASN'T APPEARED YET!!
WHAT ?!!
PU'AR!! TRANS-FORM INTO A BAT AND FLY THROUGH THIS HOLE!!
STEAL BACK THE DRAGON BALLS FROM THEM WHILE THERE'S STILL TIME!!
CAN DO !!
YOU'RE SOOO BRILLIANT !!
BOM!
WHAT ARE YOU JUST STANDING THERE STARING FOR?!! OOLONG, GO WITH HIM!!
HUH ?!
WH-WHO?! ME?!
WHY DON'T YOU MAKE YOURSELF USEFUL FOR ONCE?! OR ELSE... SWEE-SWEE-SWEEE ...!!
I'LL GO. I'LL GO, I'LL GO, I'LL GO!!

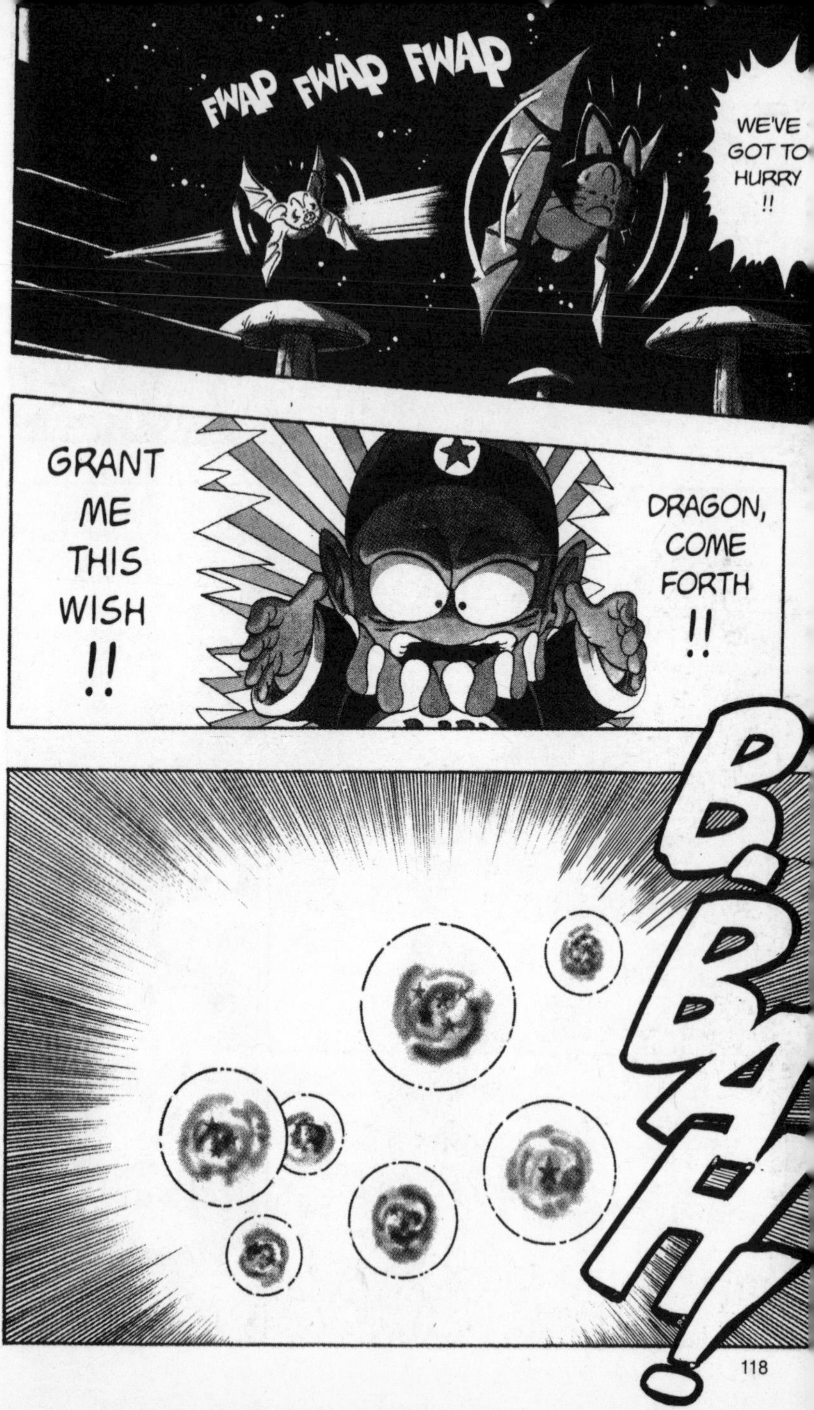
FWAP FWAP FWAP
WE'VE GOT TO HURRY!!
DRAGON, COME FORTH!!
GRANT ME THIS WISH!!
BBAHH!

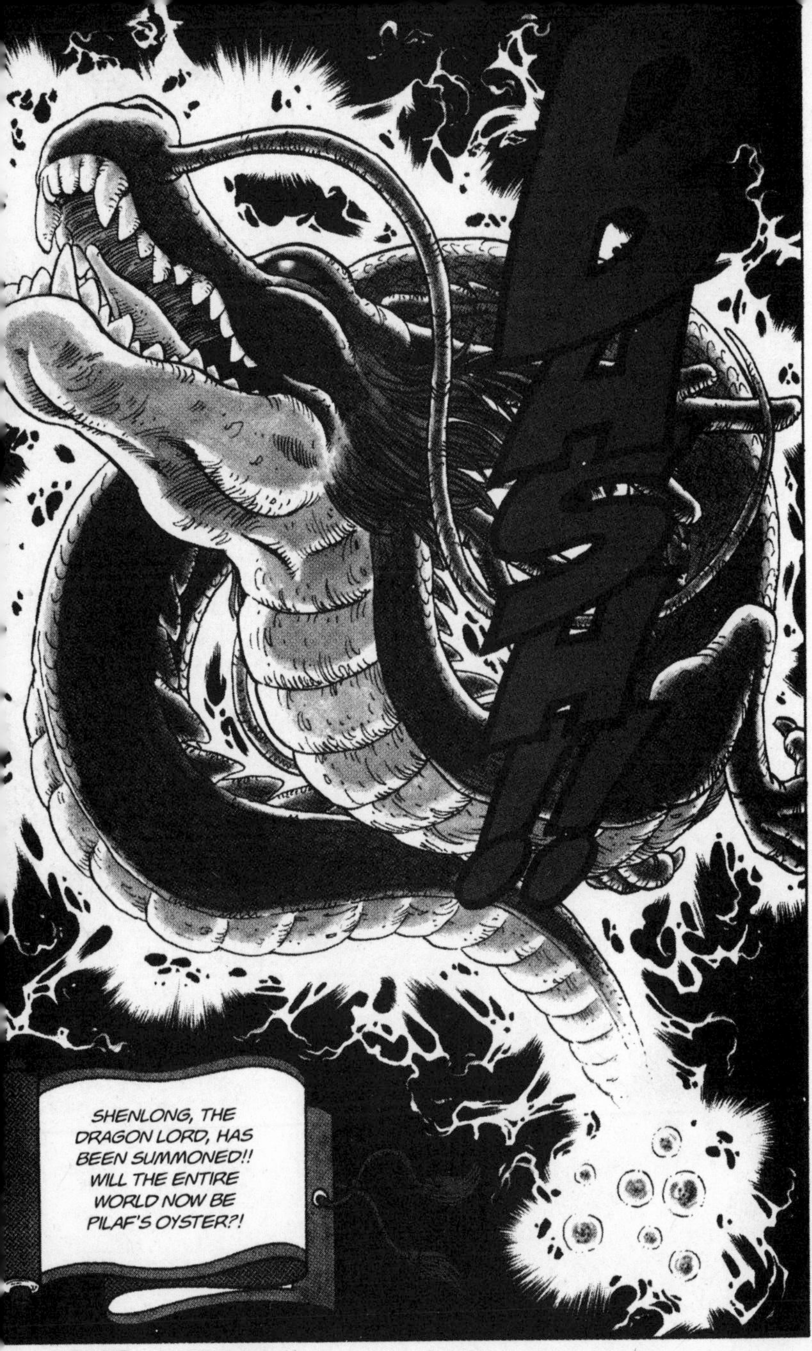
SHENLONG, THE DRAGON LORD, HAS BEEN SUMMONED!! WILL THE ENTIRE WORLD NOW BE PILAF'S OYSTER?!

NEXT: ONE WISH!

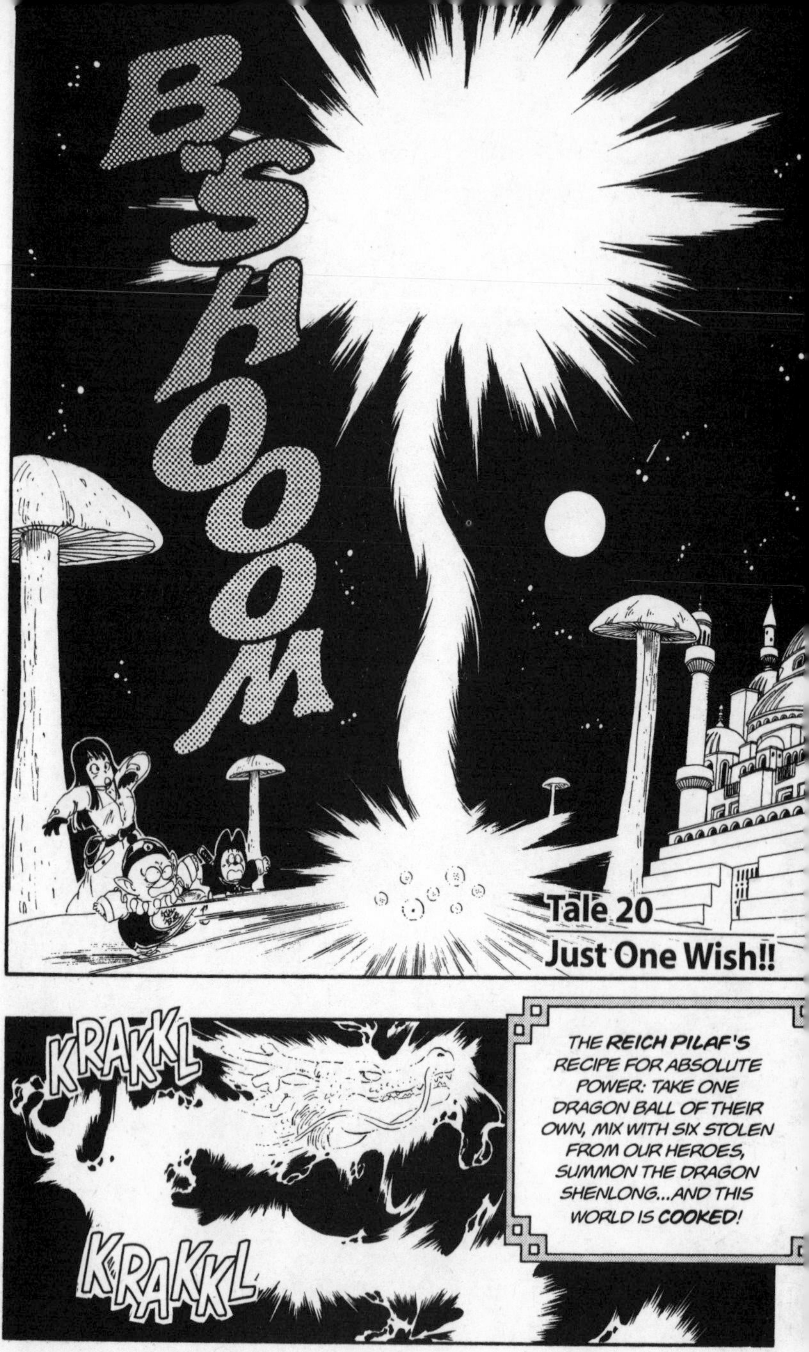
BASHOOOM
Tale 20
Just One Wish!!
THE REICH PILAF'S RECIPE FOR ABSOLUTE POWER: TAKE ONE DRAGON BALL OF THEIR OWN, MIX WITH SIX STOLEN FROM OUR HEROES, SUMMON THE DRAGON SHENLONG...AND THIS WORLD IS COOKED!
KRAKKL
KRAKKL

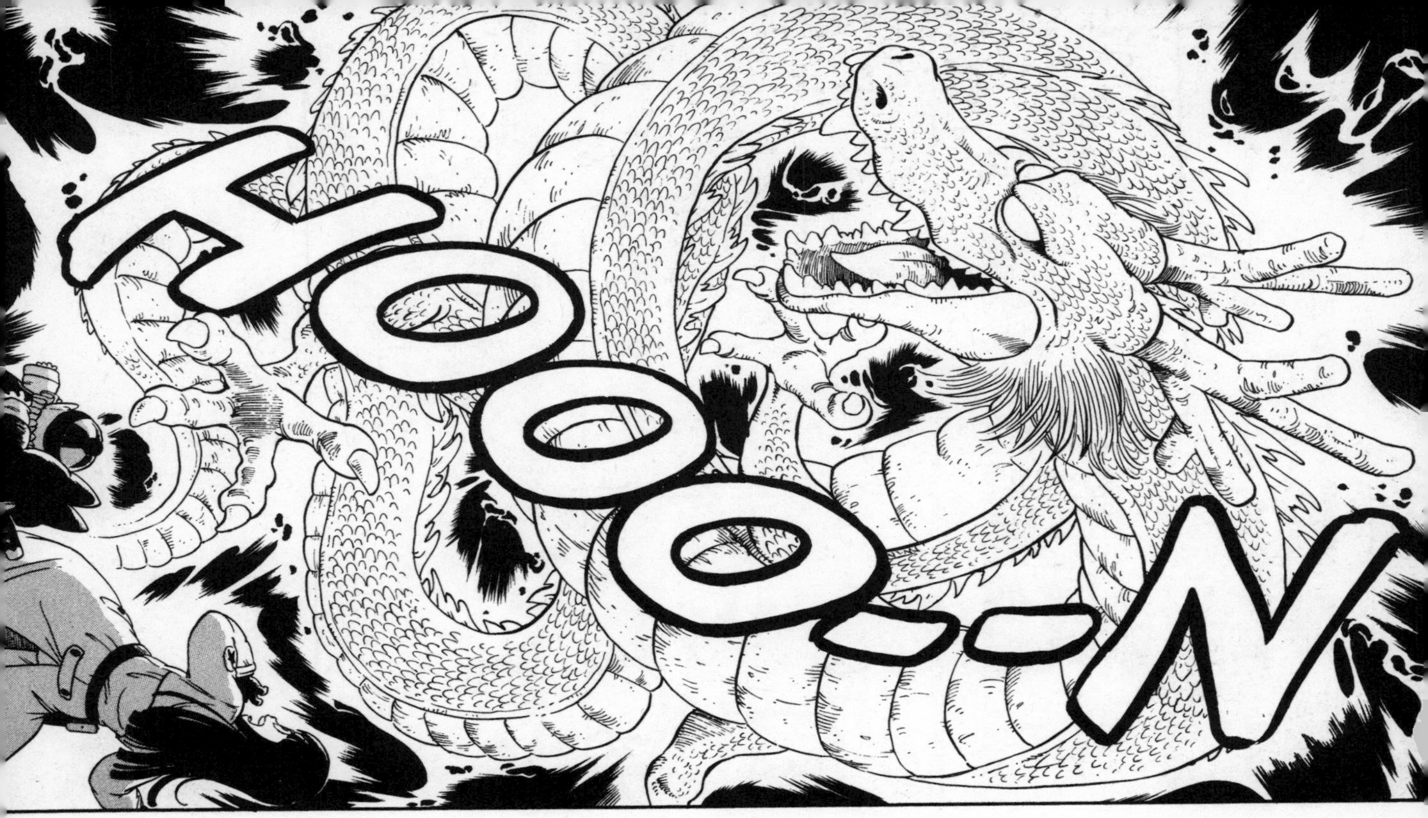
ZOOOO--N

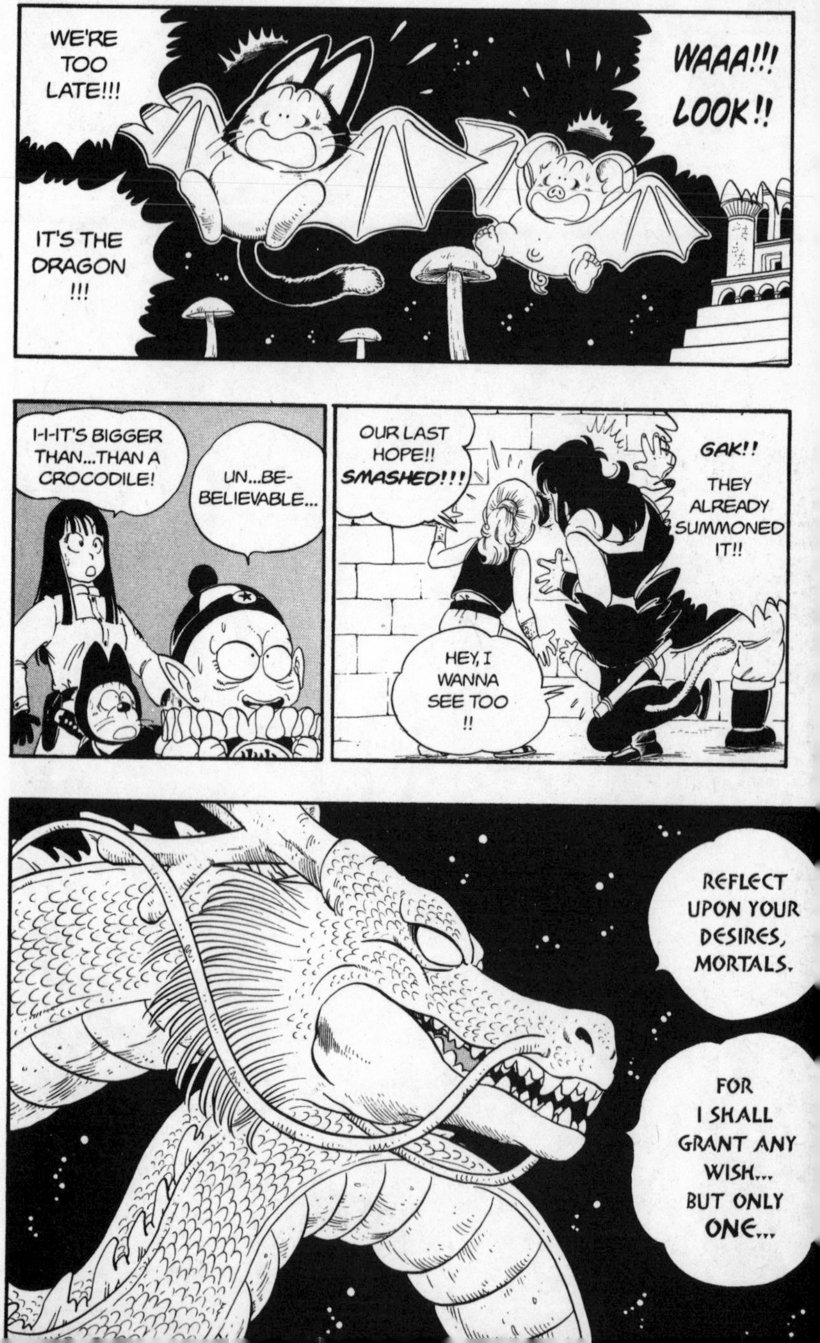
WAAA!!! LOOK!!
WE'RE TOO LATE!!!
IT'S THE DRAGON !!!
GAK!! THEY ALREADY SUMMONED IT!!
OUR LAST HOPE!! SMASHED!!!
HEY, I WANNA SEE TOO !!
UN...BE-BELIEVABLE...
I-I-IT'S BIGGER THAN...THAN A CROCODILE!
REFLECT UPON YOUR DESIRES, MORTALS.
FOR I SHALL GRANT ANY WISH... BUT ONLY ONE...

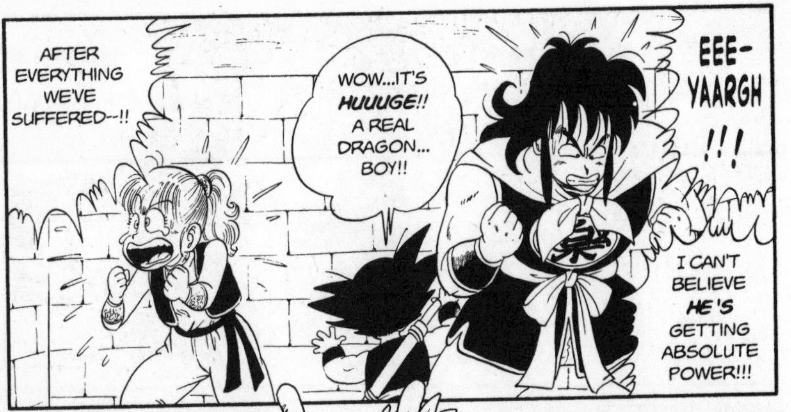
EEE-YAARGH!!!
I CAN'T BELIEVE HE'S GETTING ABSOLUTE POWER!!!
WOW...IT'S HUUUGE!! A REAL DRAGON... BOY!!
AFTER EVERYTHING WE'VE SUFFERED--!!

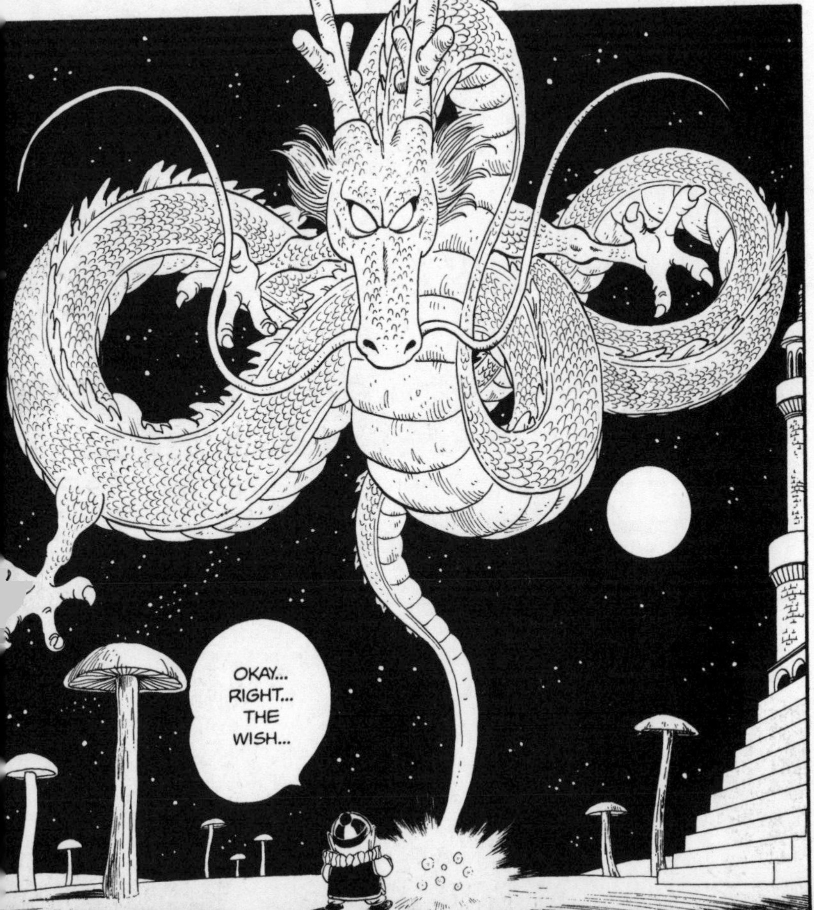
OKAY... RIGHT... THE WISH...

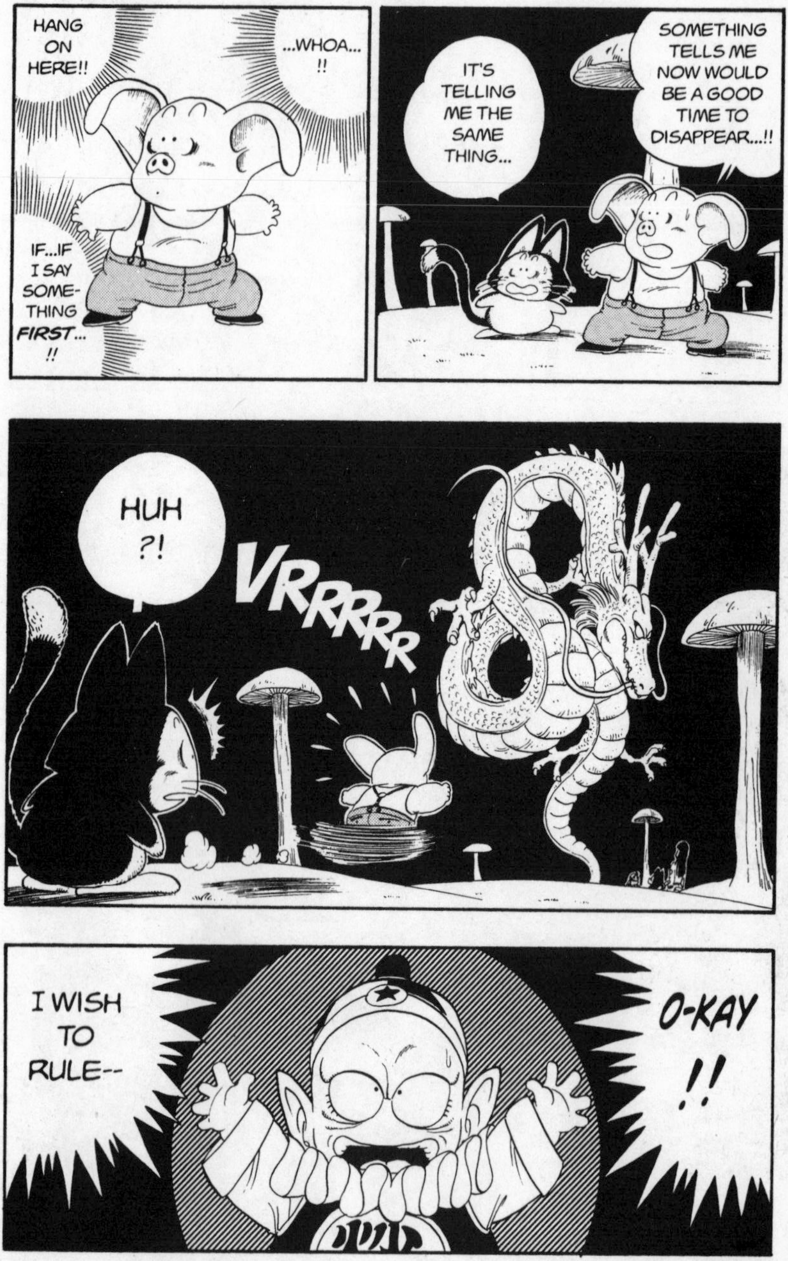
SOMETHING TELLS ME NOW WOULD BE A GOOD TIME TO DISAPPEAR...!!
IT'S TELLING ME THE SAME THING...
...WHOA... !!
HANG ON HERE!!
IF...IF I SAY SOME-THING FIRST... !!
HUH ?!
VRRRRR
O-KAY !!
I WISH TO RULE--

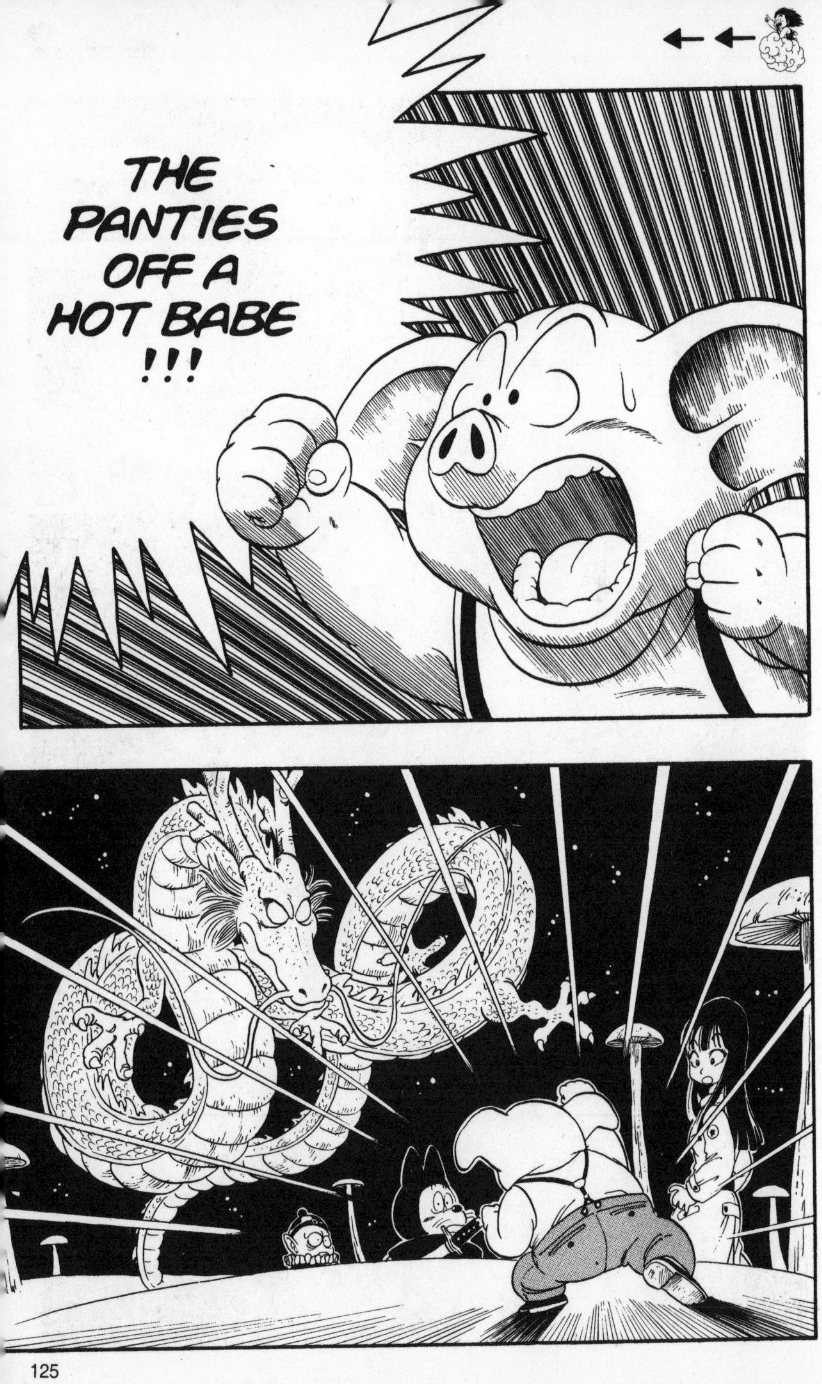
THE PANTIES OFF A HOT BABE !!!

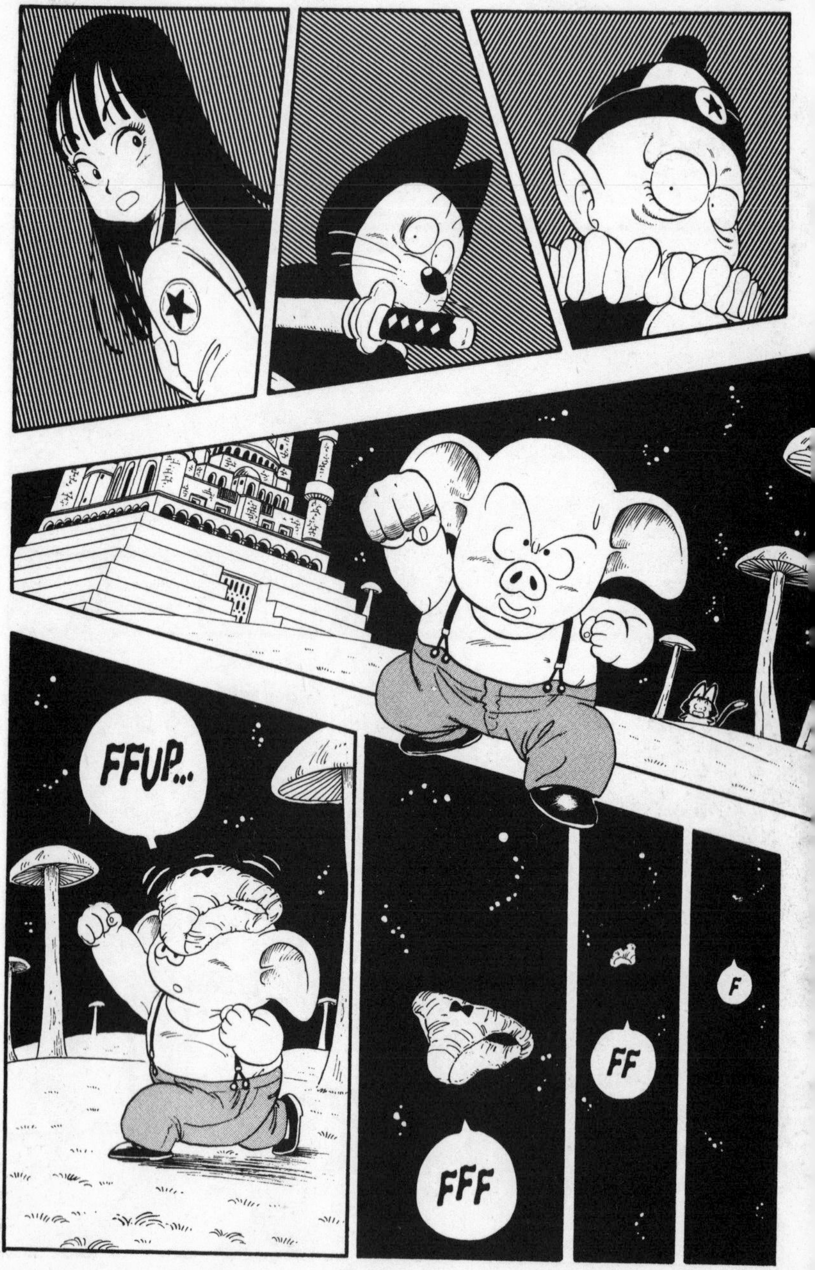
F
FF
FFF
FFUP...

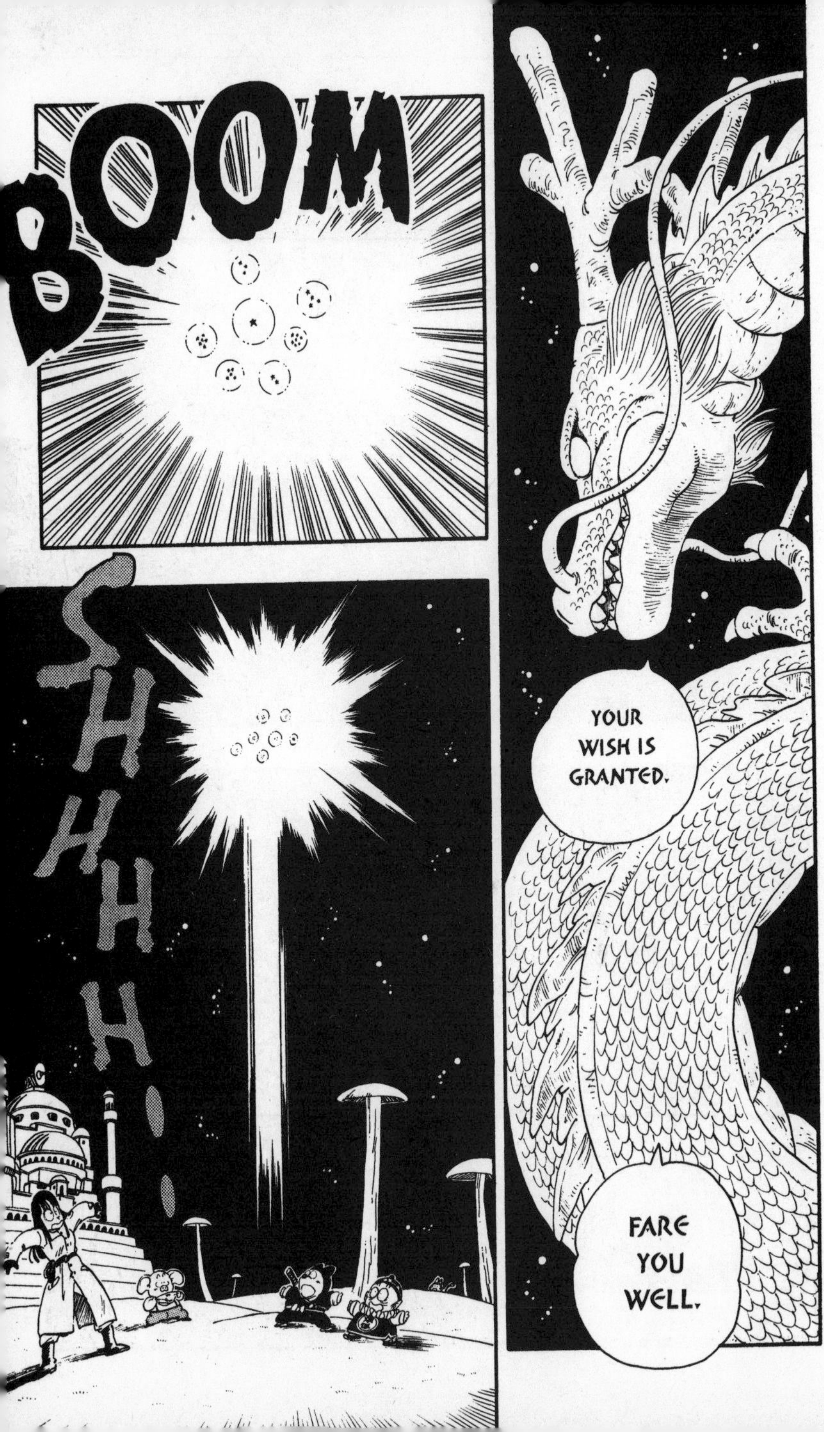
YOUR WISH IS GRANTED.
FARE YOU WELL.
BOOM
SHHHH!

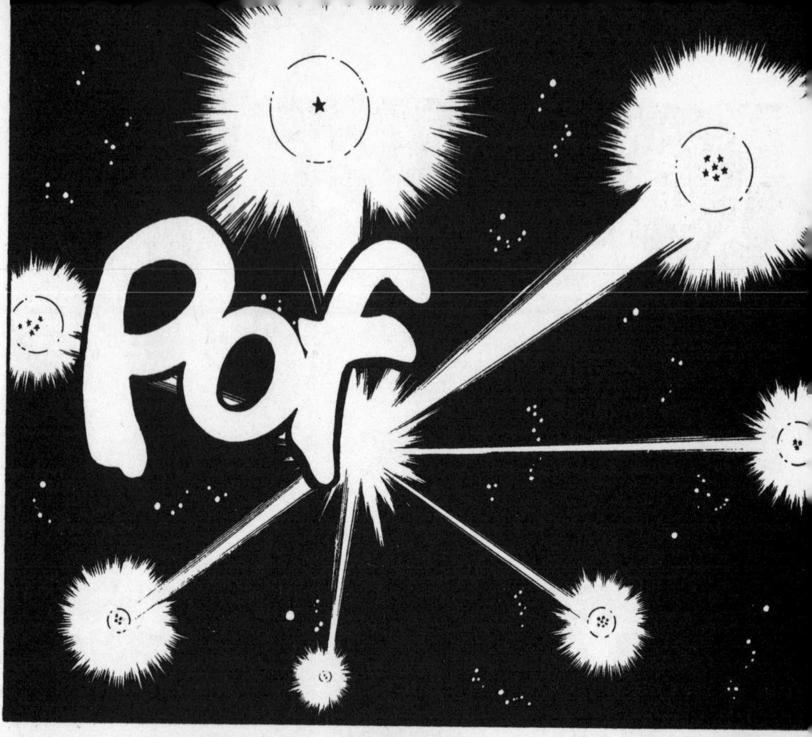
POF

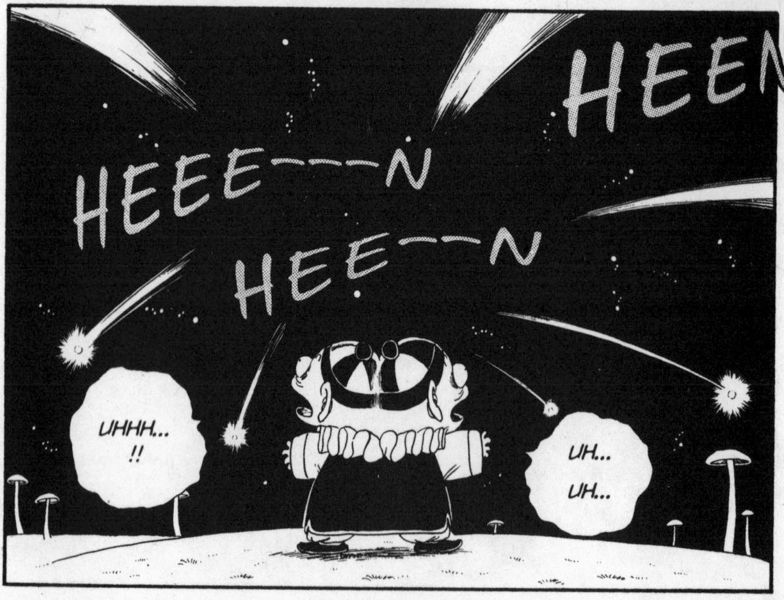
HEEN
HEEE---N
HEE---N
UH... UH...
UHHH... !!

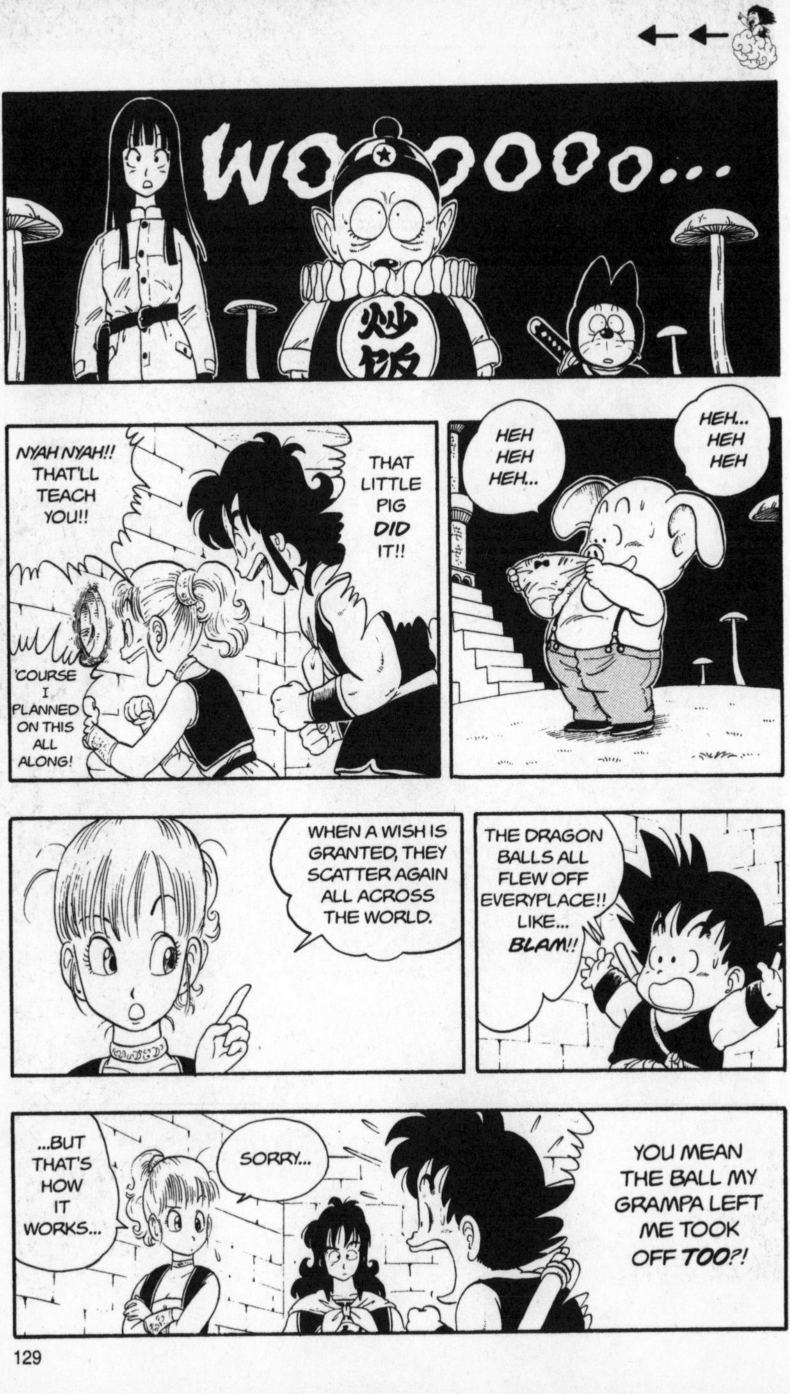
WOOOOOO...
HEH... HEH HEH
HEH HEH HEH...
THAT LITTLE PIG DID IT!!
NYAH NYAH!! THAT'LL TEACH YOU!!
'COURSE I PLANNED ON THIS ALL ALONG!
THE DRAGON BALLS ALL FLEW OFF EVERYPLACE!! LIKE... BLAM!!
WHEN A WISH IS GRANTED, THEY SCATTER AGAIN ALL ACROSS THE WORLD.
YOU MEAN THE BALL MY GRAMPA LEFT ME TOOK OFF TOO?!
SORRY...
...BUT THAT'S HOW IT WORKS...

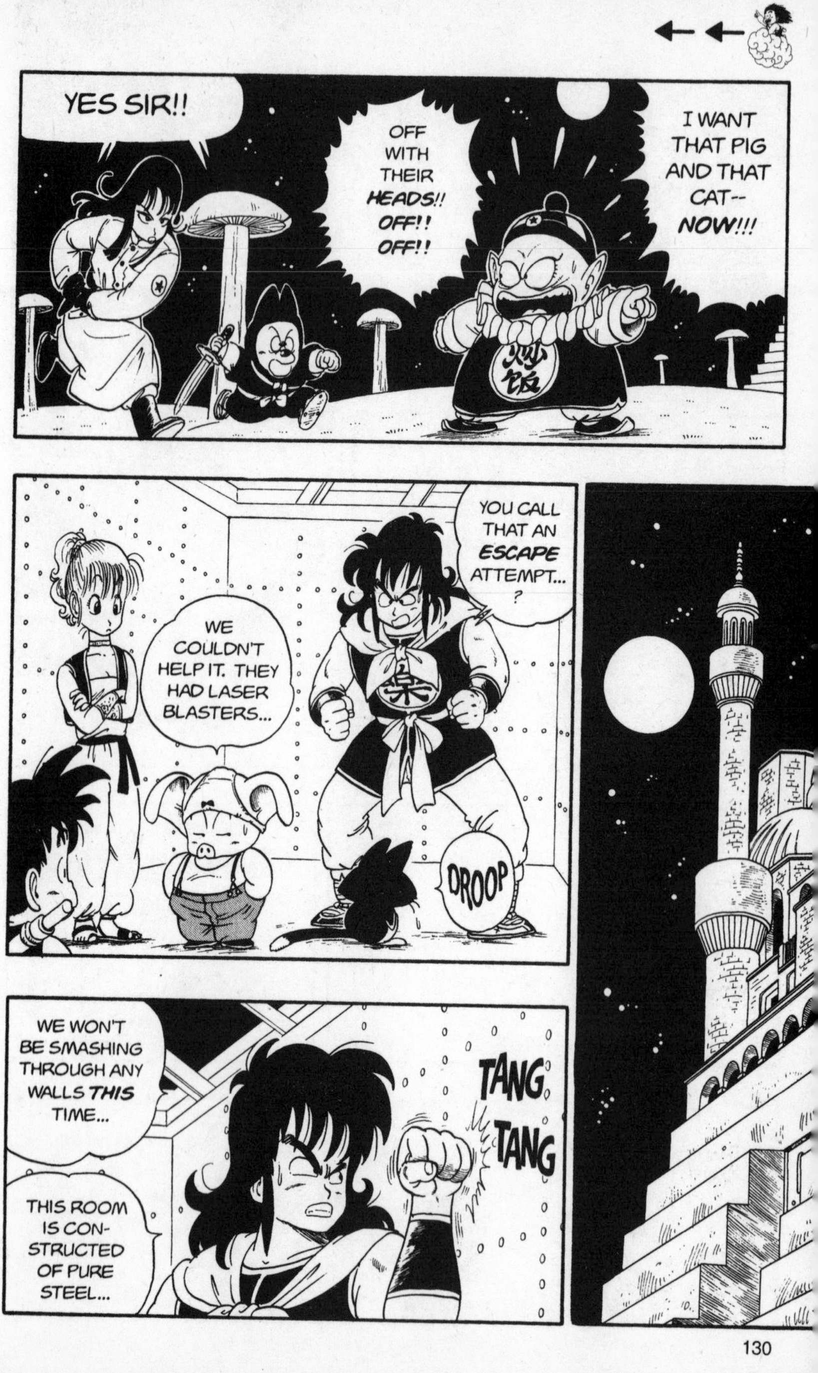

I WANT THAT PIG AND THAT CAT-- NOW!!!
OFF WITH THEIR HEADS!! OFF!! OFF!!
YES SIR!!
YOU CALL THAT AN ESCAPE ATTEMPT... ?
WE COULDN'T HELP IT. THEY HAD LASER BLASTERS...
DROOP
TANG
TANG
WE WON'T BE SMASHING THROUGH ANY WALLS THIS TIME...
THIS ROOM IS CON-STRUCTED OF PURE STEEL...

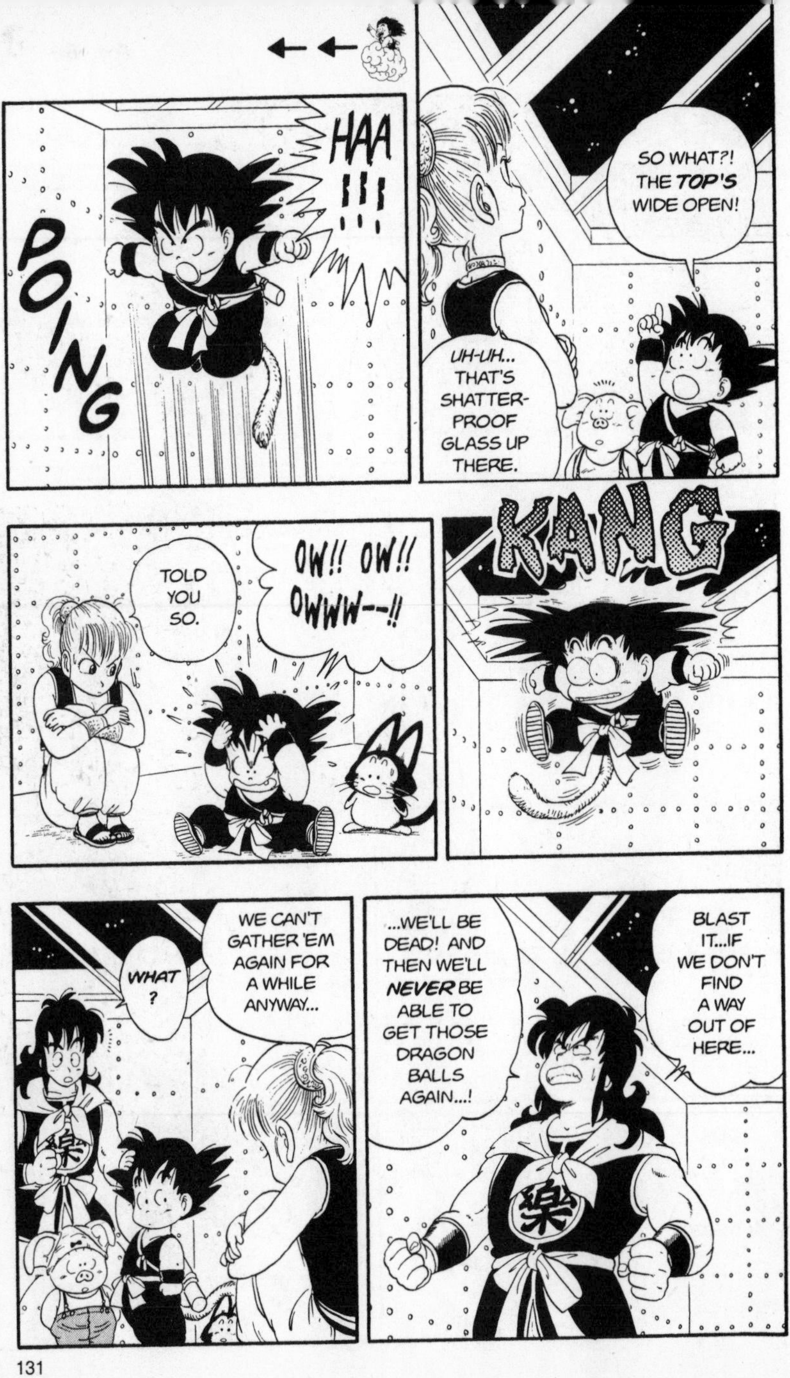
SO WHAT?! THE TOP'S WIDE OPEN!
UH-UH... THAT'S SHATTER-PROOF GLASS UP THERE.
HAA!!!
POING
KANG
OW!! OW!! OWWW--!!
TOLD YOU SO.
BLAST IT...IF WE DON'T FIND A WAY OUT OF HERE...
...WE'LL BE DEAD! AND THEN WE'LL NEVER BE ABLE TO GET THOSE DRAGON BALLS AGAIN...!
WE CAN'T GATHER 'EM AGAIN FOR A WHILE ANYWAY...
WHAT?

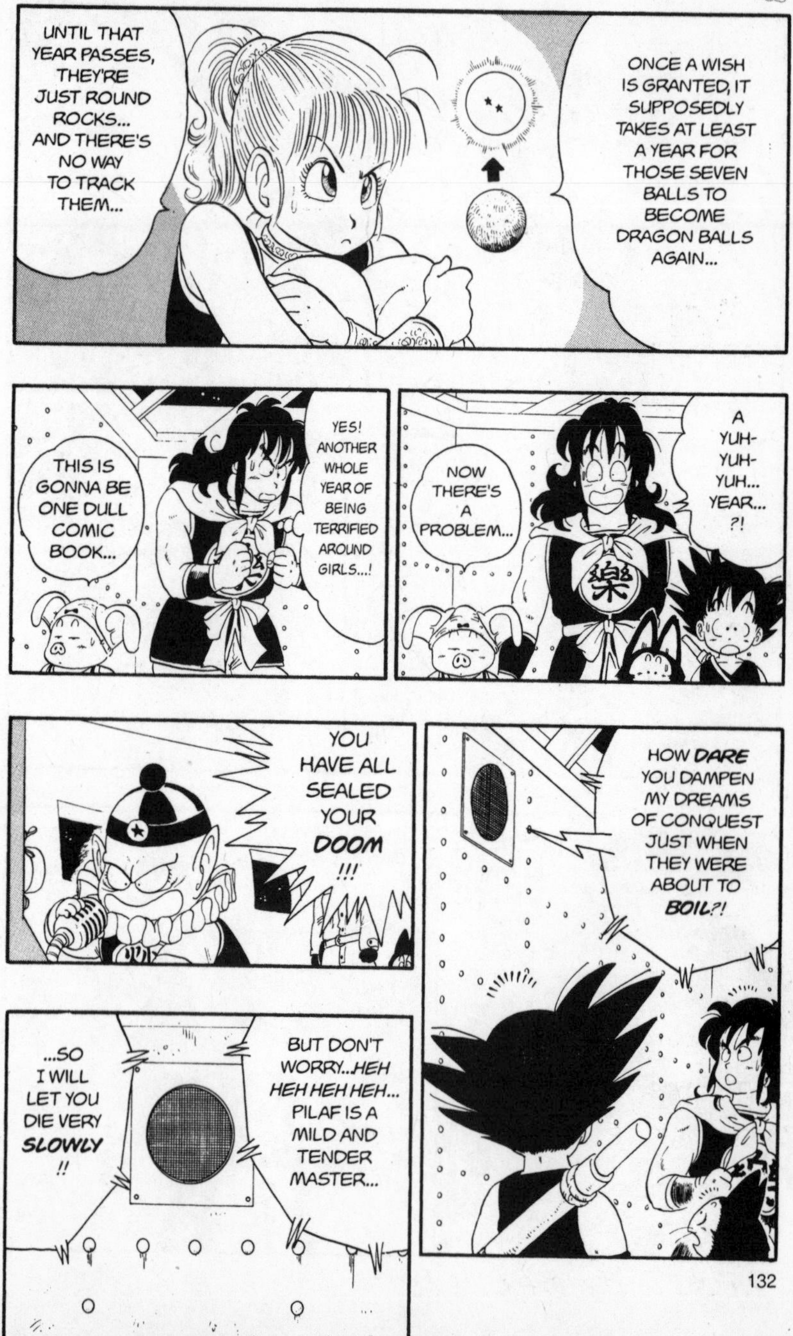
ONCE A WISH IS GRANTED, IT SUPPOSEDLY TAKES AT LEAST A YEAR FOR THOSE SEVEN BALLS TO BECOME DRAGON BALLS AGAIN...
UNTIL THAT YEAR PASSES, THEY'RE JUST ROUND ROCKS... AND THERE'S NO WAY TO TRACK THEM...
A YUH-YUH-YUH... YEAR...?!
NOW THERE'S A PROBLEM...
YES! ANOTHER WHOLE YEAR OF BEING TERRIFIED AROUND GIRLS...!
THIS IS GONNA BE ONE DULL COMIC BOOK...
HOW DARE YOU DAMPEN MY DREAMS OF CONQUEST JUST WHEN THEY WERE ABOUT TO BOIL?!
YOU HAVE ALL SEALED YOUR DOOM!!!
BUT DON'T WORRY...HEH HEH HEH HEH... PILAF IS A MILD AND TENDER MASTER...
...SO I WILL LET YOU DIE VERY SLOWLY!!

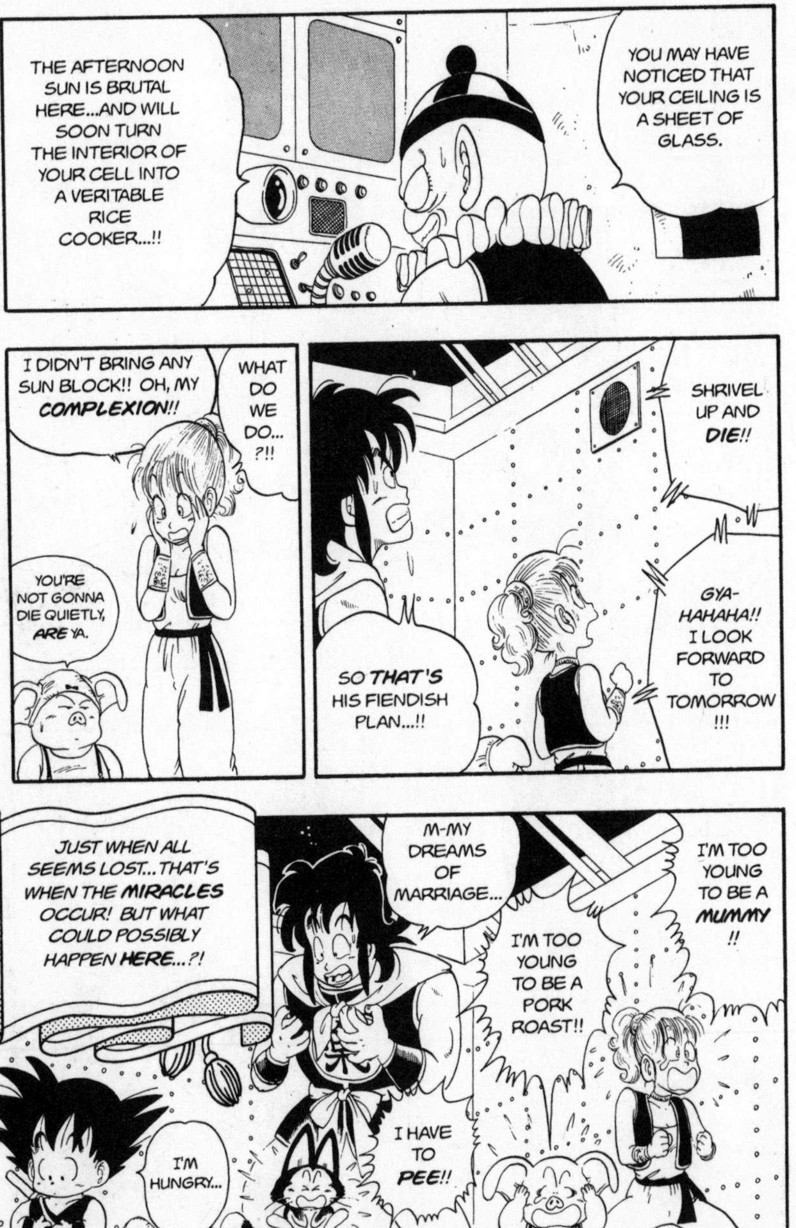

YOU MAY HAVE NOTICED THAT YOUR CEILING IS A SHEET OF GLASS.
THE AFTERNOON SUN IS BRUTAL HERE...AND WILL SOON TURN THE INTERIOR OF YOUR CELL INTO A VERITABLE RICE COOKER...!!
SHRIVEL UP AND DIE!!
GYA-HAHAHA!! I LOOK FORWARD TO TOMORROW!!!
SO THAT'S HIS FIENDISH PLAN...!!
WHAT DO WE DO...?!!
I DIDN'T BRING ANY SUN BLOCK!! OH, MY COMPLEXION!!
YOU'RE NOT GONNA DIE QUIETLY, ARE YA.
I'M TOO YOUNG TO BE A MUMMY!!
M-MY DREAMS OF MARRIAGE...
I'M TOO YOUNG TO BE A PORK ROAST!!
JUST WHEN ALL SEEMS LOST...THAT'S WHEN THE MIRACLES OCCUR! BUT WHAT COULD POSSIBLY HAPPEN HERE...?!
I HAVE TO PEE!!
I'M HUNGRY...

NEXT: My APE is UP!

Tale 21
Full Moon

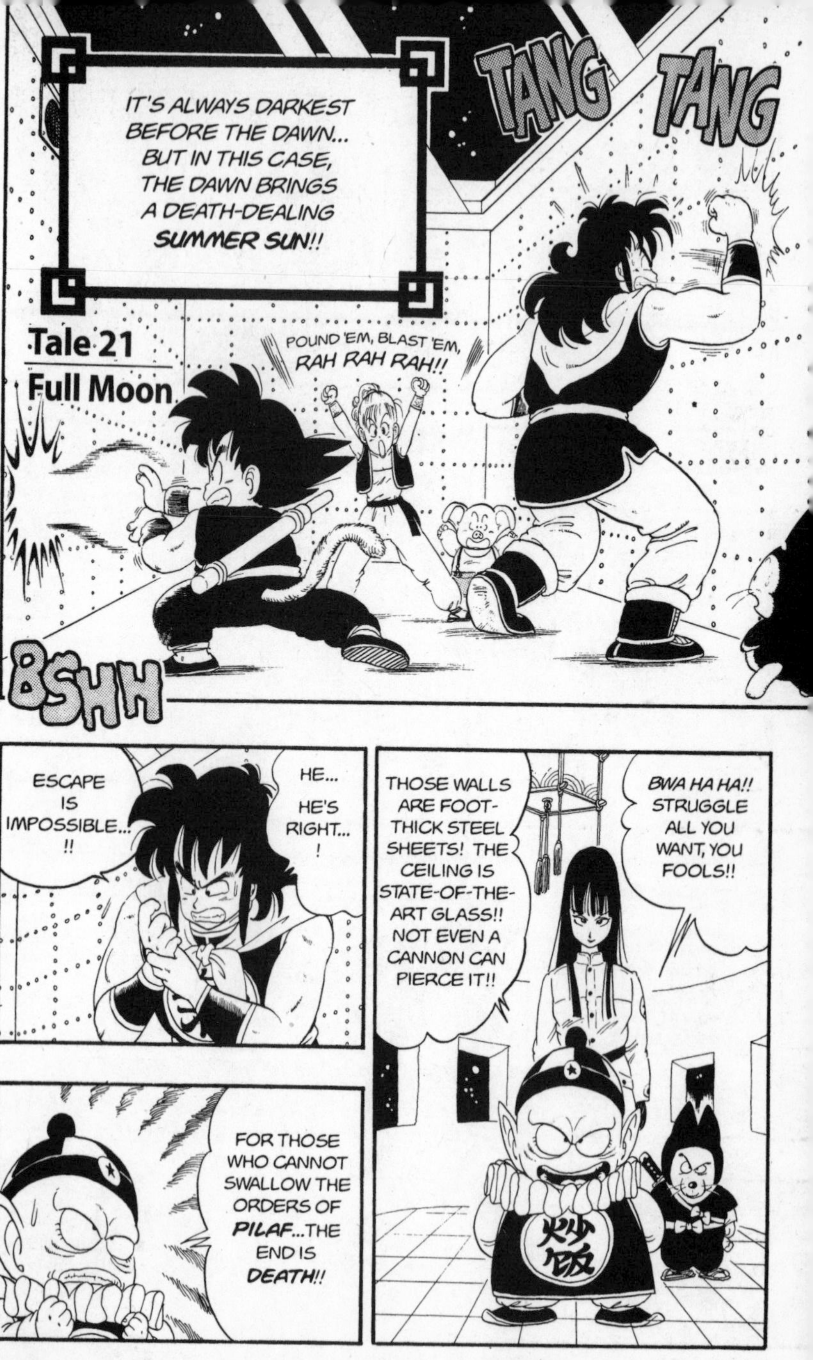

TANG TANG
IT'S ALWAYS DARKEST BEFORE THE DAWN... BUT IN THIS CASE, THE DAWN BRINGS A DEATH-DEALING SUMMER SUN!!
POUND 'EM, BLAST 'EM, RAH RAH RAH!!
BSHH
BWA HA HA!! STRUGGLE ALL YOU WANT, YOU FOOLS!!
THOSE WALLS ARE FOOT-THICK STEEL SHEETS! THE CEILING IS STATE-OF-THE-ART GLASS!! NOT EVEN A CANNON CAN PIERCE IT!!
HE... HE'S RIGHT...!
ESCAPE IS IMPOSSIBLE...!!
FOR THOSE WHO CANNOT SWALLOW THE ORDERS OF PILAF...THE END IS DEATH!!

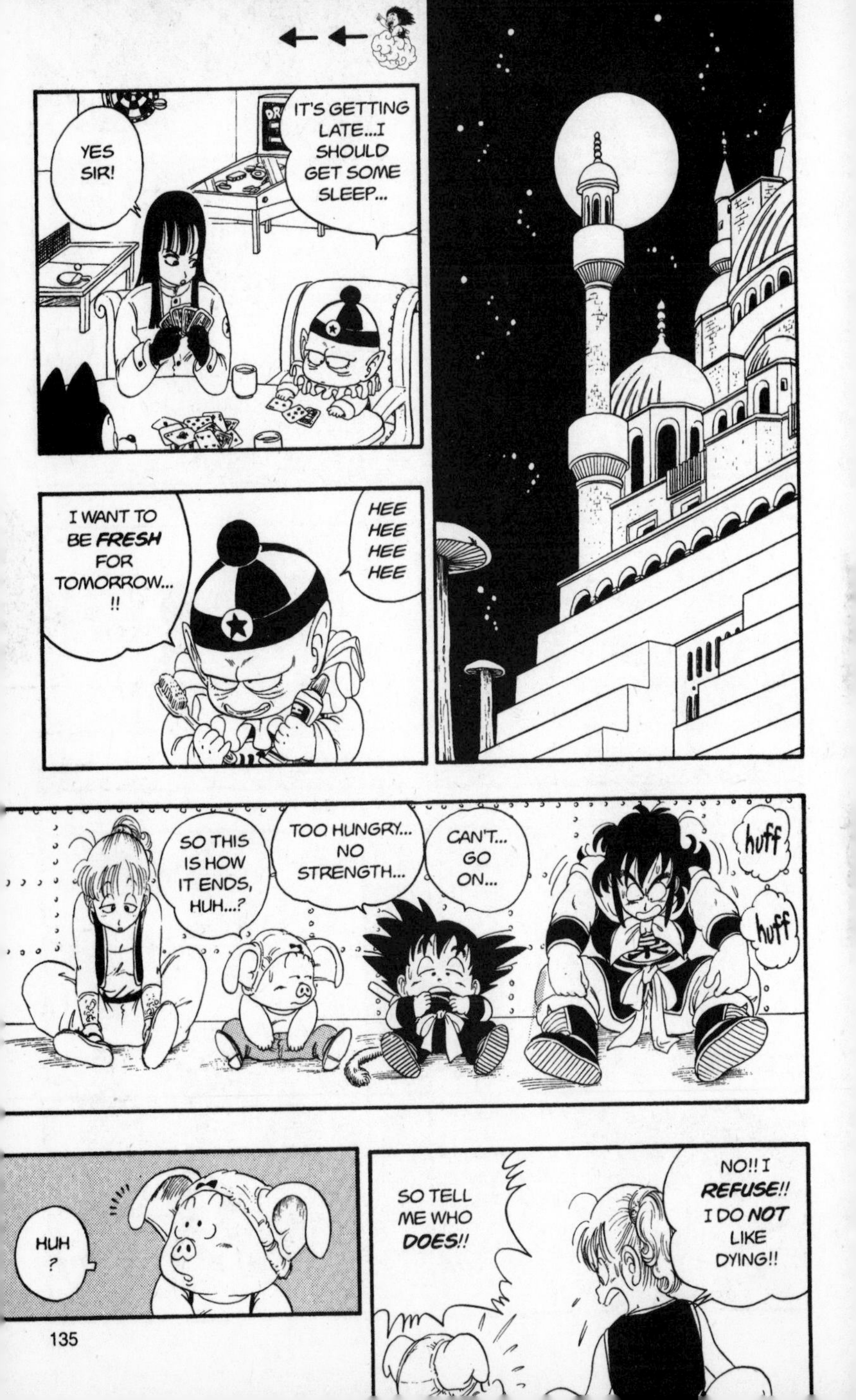
IT'S GETTING LATE...I SHOULD GET SOME SLEEP...
YES SIR!
HEE HEE HEE HEE
I WANT TO BE **FRESH** FOR TOMORROW... !!
huff
huff
CAN'T... GO ON...
TOO HUNGRY... NO STRENGTH...
SO THIS IS HOW IT ENDS, HUH...?
NO!! I **REFUSE!!** I DO **NOT** LIKE DYING!!
SO TELL ME WHO **DOES!!**
HUH ?

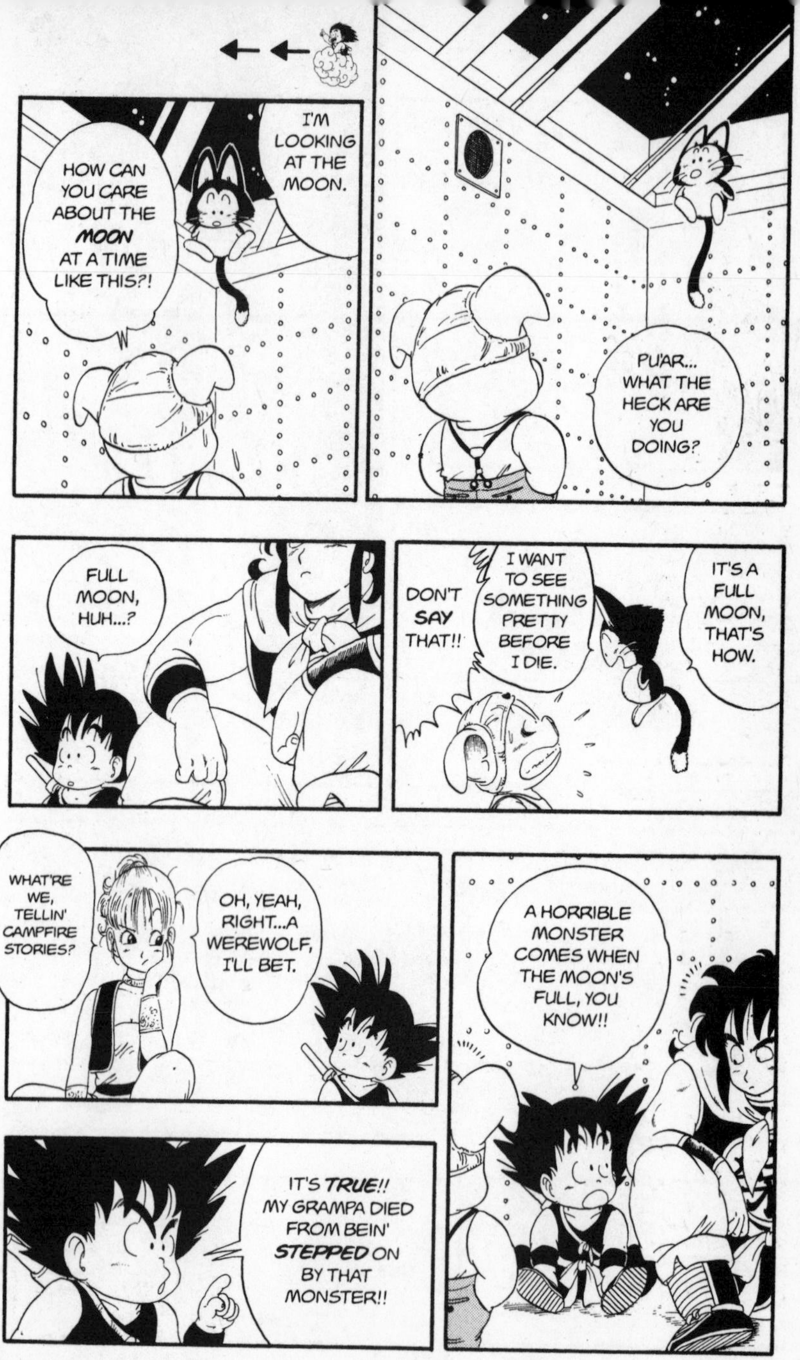
PU'AR... WHAT THE HECK ARE YOU DOING?
I'M LOOKING AT THE MOON.
HOW CAN YOU CARE ABOUT THE **MOON** AT A TIME LIKE THIS?!
IT'S A FULL MOON, THAT'S HOW.
I WANT TO SEE SOMETHING PRETTY BEFORE I DIE.
DON'T **SAY** THAT!!
FULL MOON, HUH...?
A HORRIBLE MONSTER COMES WHEN THE MOON'S FULL, YOU KNOW!!
OH, YEAH, RIGHT...A WEREWOLF, I'LL BET.
WHAT'RE WE, TELLIN' CAMPFIRE STORIES?
IT'S ***TRUE!!*** MY GRAMPA DIED FROM BEIN' ***STEPPED*** ON BY THAT MONSTER!!

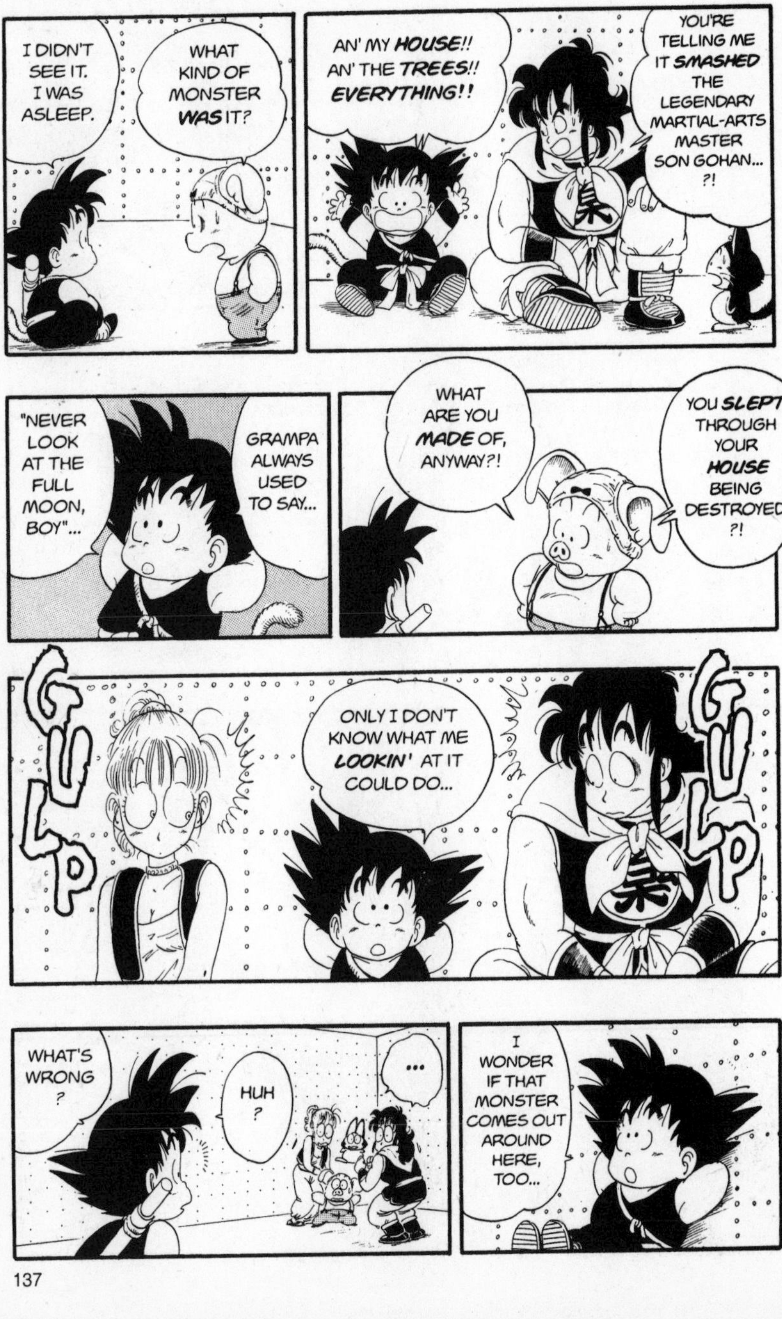
YOU'RE TELLING ME IT SMASHED THE LEGENDARY MARTIAL-ARTS MASTER SON GOHAN... ?!
AN' MY HOUSE!! AN' THE TREES!! EVERYTHING!!
WHAT KIND OF MONSTER WAS IT?
I DIDN'T SEE IT. I WAS ASLEEP.
YOU SLEPT THROUGH YOUR HOUSE BEING DESTROYED ?!
WHAT ARE YOU MADE OF, ANYWAY?!
GRAMPA ALWAYS USED TO SAY...
"NEVER LOOK AT THE FULL MOON, BOY"...
GULP
ONLY I DON'T KNOW WHAT ME LOOKIN' AT IT COULD DO...
GULP
I WONDER IF THAT MONSTER COMES OUT AROUND HERE, TOO...
...
HUH ?
WHAT'S WRONG ?

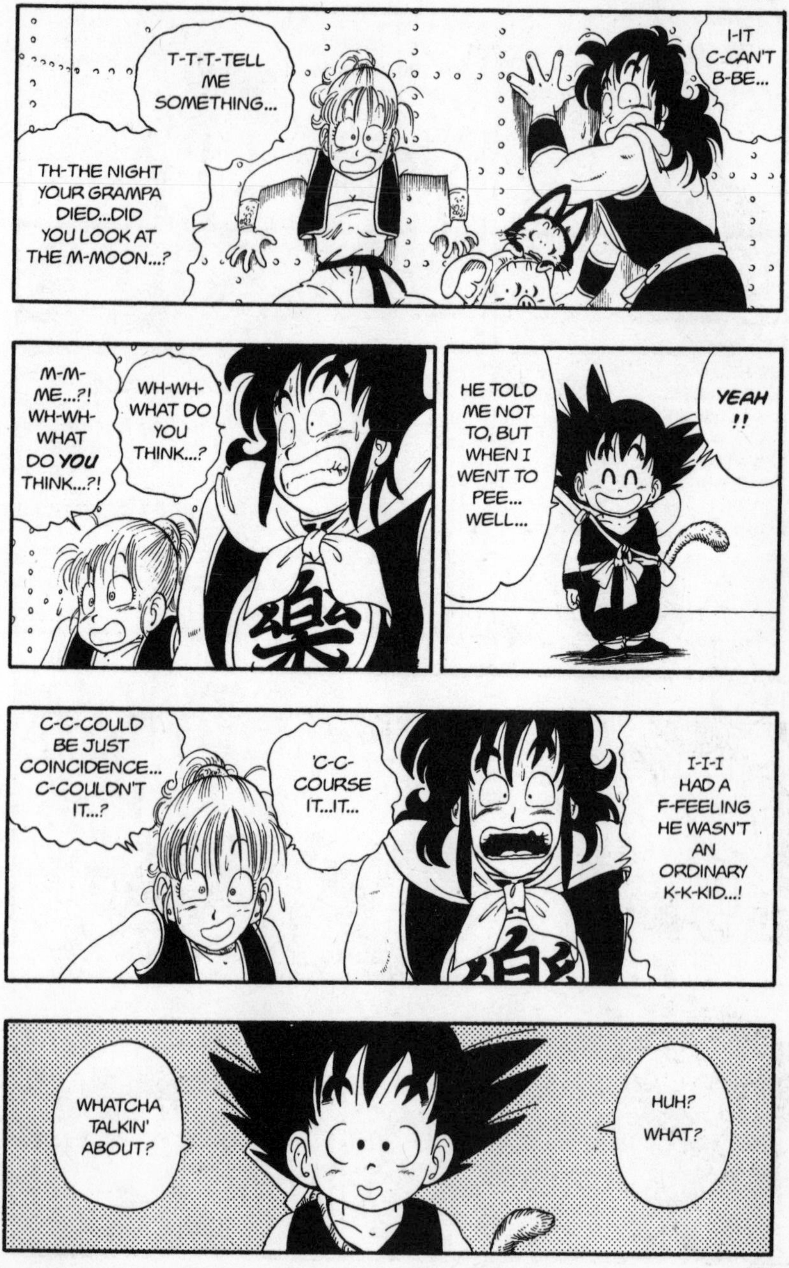
I-IT C-CAN'T B-BE...
T-T-T-TELL ME SOMETHING...
TH-THE NIGHT YOUR GRAMPA DIED...DID YOU LOOK AT THE M-MOON...?
YEAH !!
HE TOLD ME NOT TO, BUT WHEN I WENT TO PEE... WELL...
WH-WH-WHAT DO YOU THINK...?
M-M-ME...?! WH-WH-WHAT DO ***YOU*** THINK...?!
I-I-I HAD A F-FEELING HE WASN'T AN ORDINARY K-K-KID...!
'C-C-COURSE IT...IT...
C-C-COULD BE JUST COINCIDENCE... C-COULDN'T IT...?
HUH? WHAT?
WHATCHA TALKIN' ABOUT?

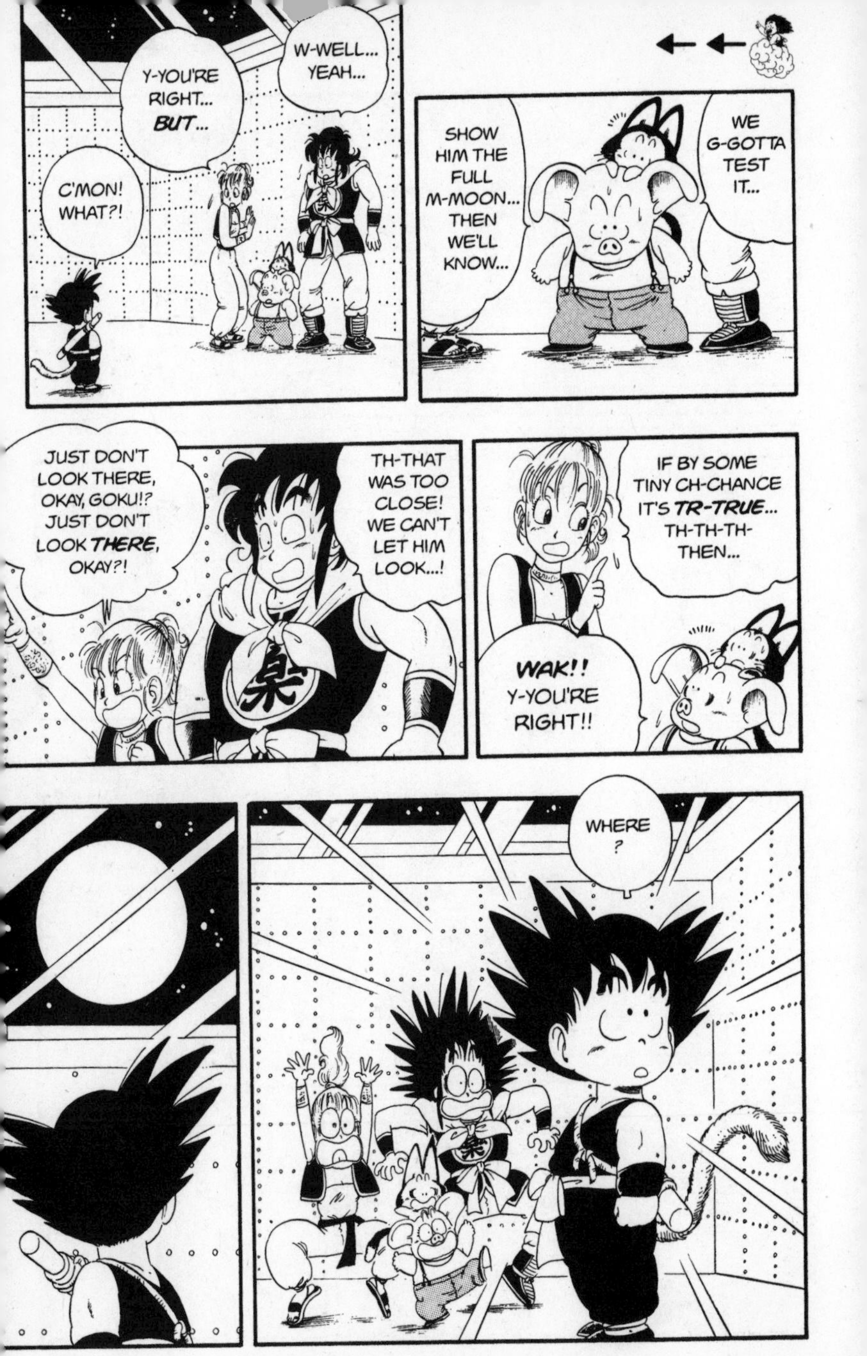
WE G-GOTTA TEST IT...
SHOW HIM THE FULL M-MOON... THEN WE'LL KNOW...
W-WELL... YEAH...
Y-YOU'RE RIGHT... BUT...
C'MON! WHAT?!
IF BY SOME TINY CH-CHANCE IT'S TR-TRUE... TH-TH-TH-THEN...
WAK!! Y-YOU'RE RIGHT!!
TH-THAT WAS TOO CLOSE! WE CAN'T LET HIM LOOK...!
JUST DON'T LOOK THERE, OKAY, GOKU!? JUST DON'T LOOK THERE, OKAY?!
WHERE ?

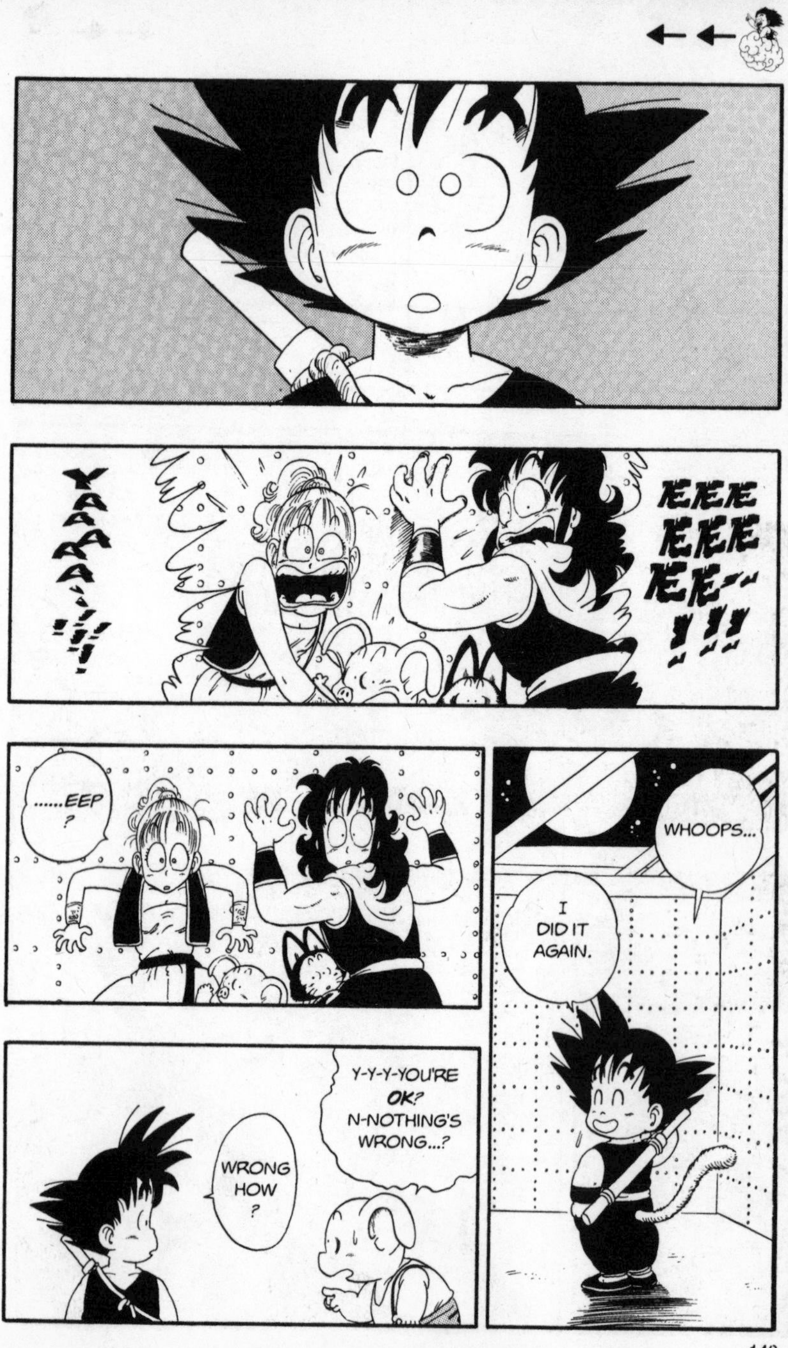
EEEEEEEE--!!!
YAAAAA--!!!
WHOOPS...
I DID IT AGAIN.
......EEP?
Y-Y-Y-YOU'RE OK? N-NOTHING'S WRONG...?
WRONG HOW?

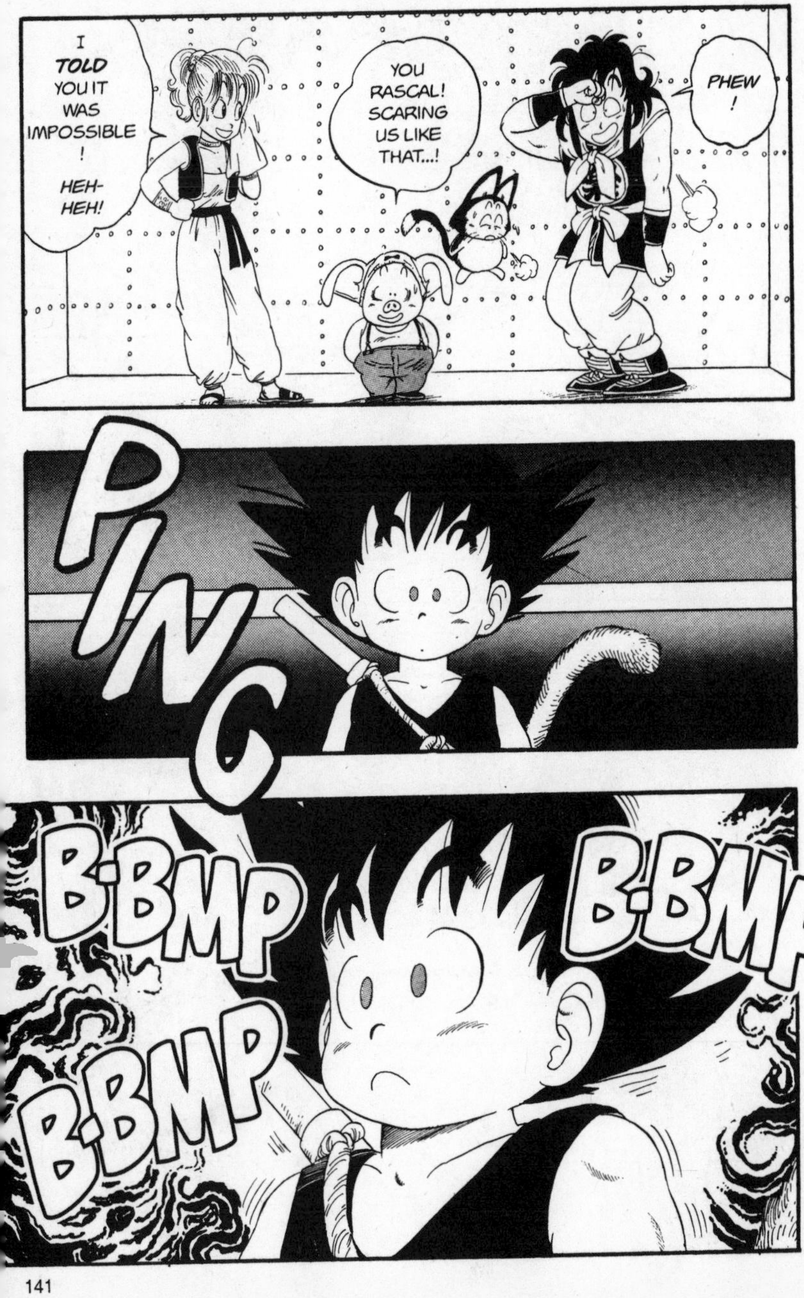
PHEW!
YOU RASCAL! SCARING US LIKE THAT...!
I TOLD YOU IT WAS IMPOSSIBLE! HEH-HEH!
PING
B-BMP
B-BMP
B-BMP

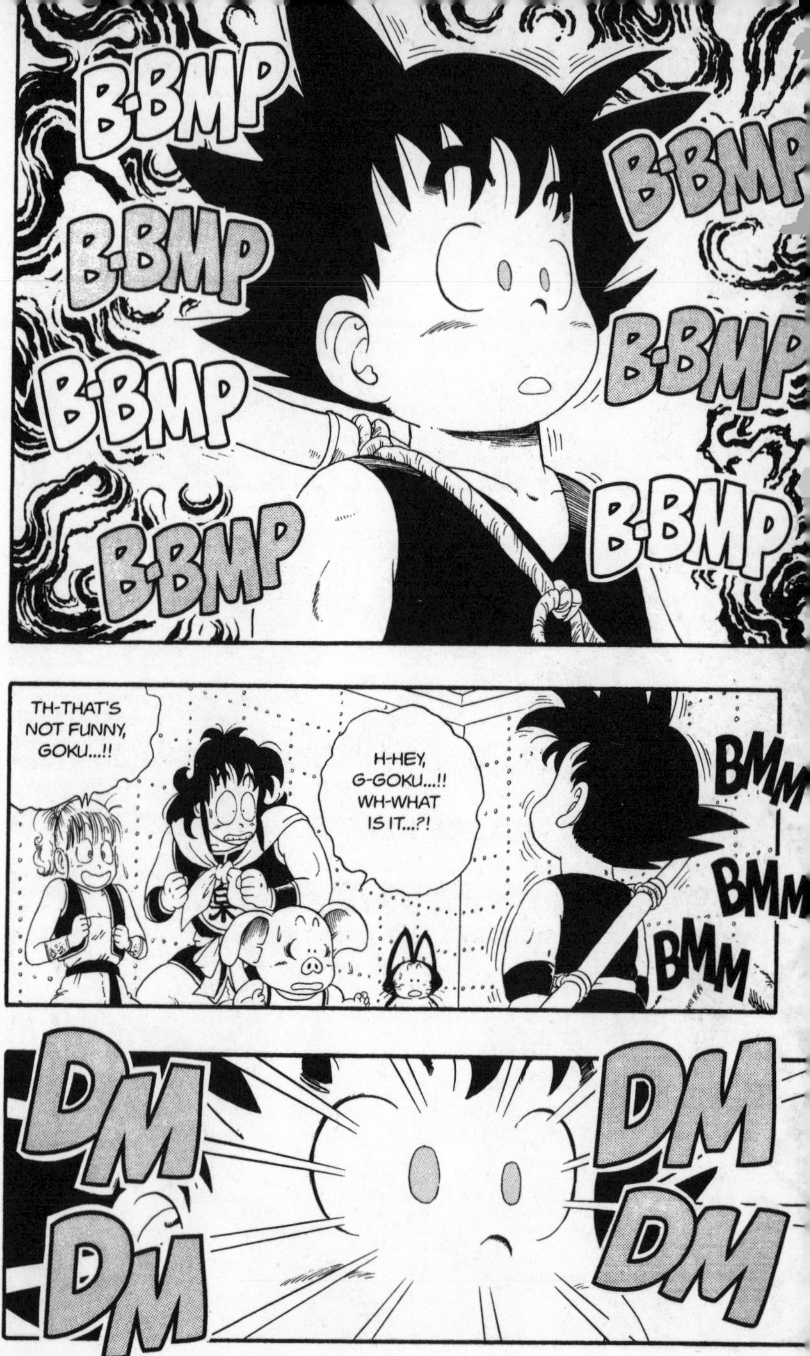
B-BMP
B-BMP
B-BMP
B-BMP
B-BMP
B-BMP
B-BMP
BMM
BMM
BMM
H-HEY, G-GOKU...!! WH-WHAT IS IT...?!
TH-THAT'S NOT FUNNY, GOKU...!!
DM
DM
DM
DM

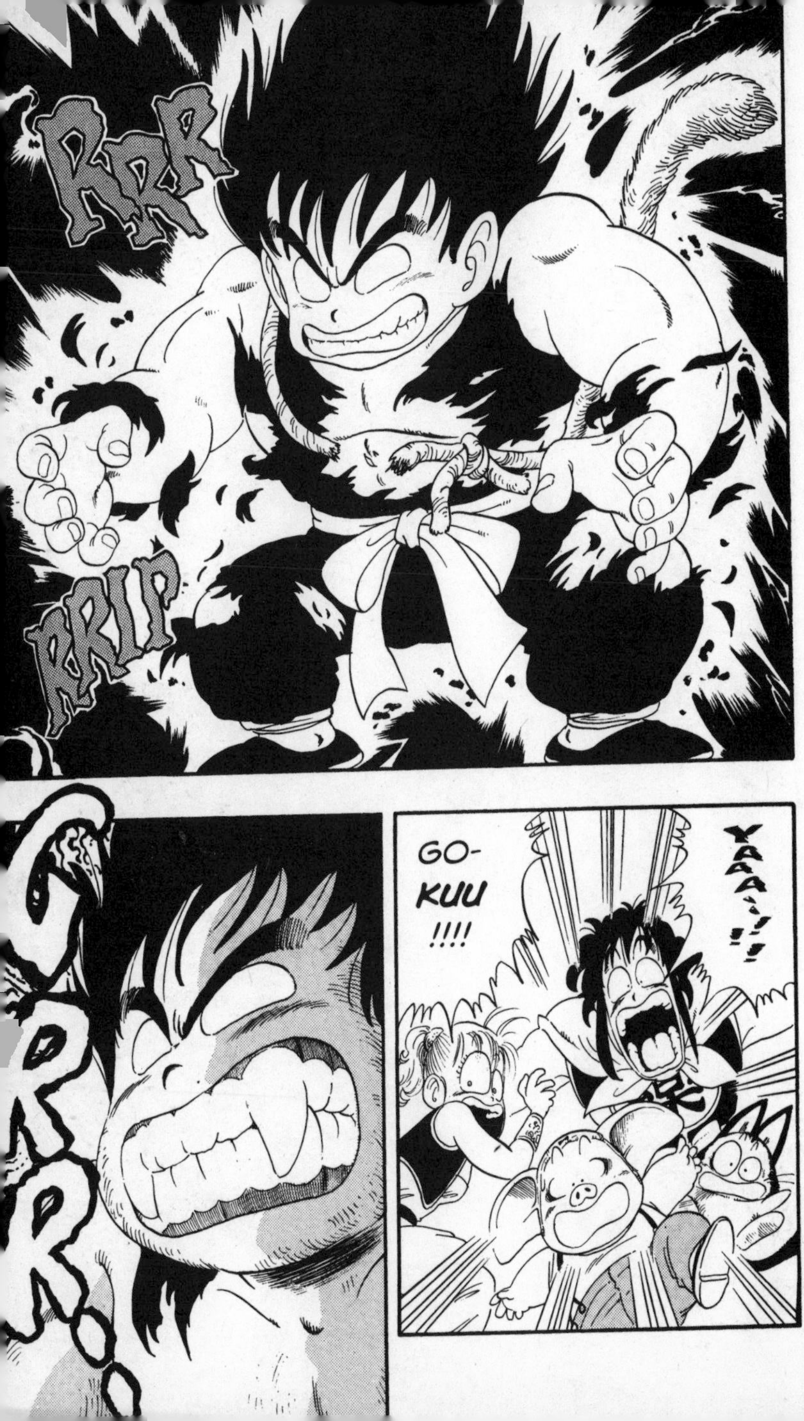
RRR
RRIP
GO-KUU !!!!
YAAA!!

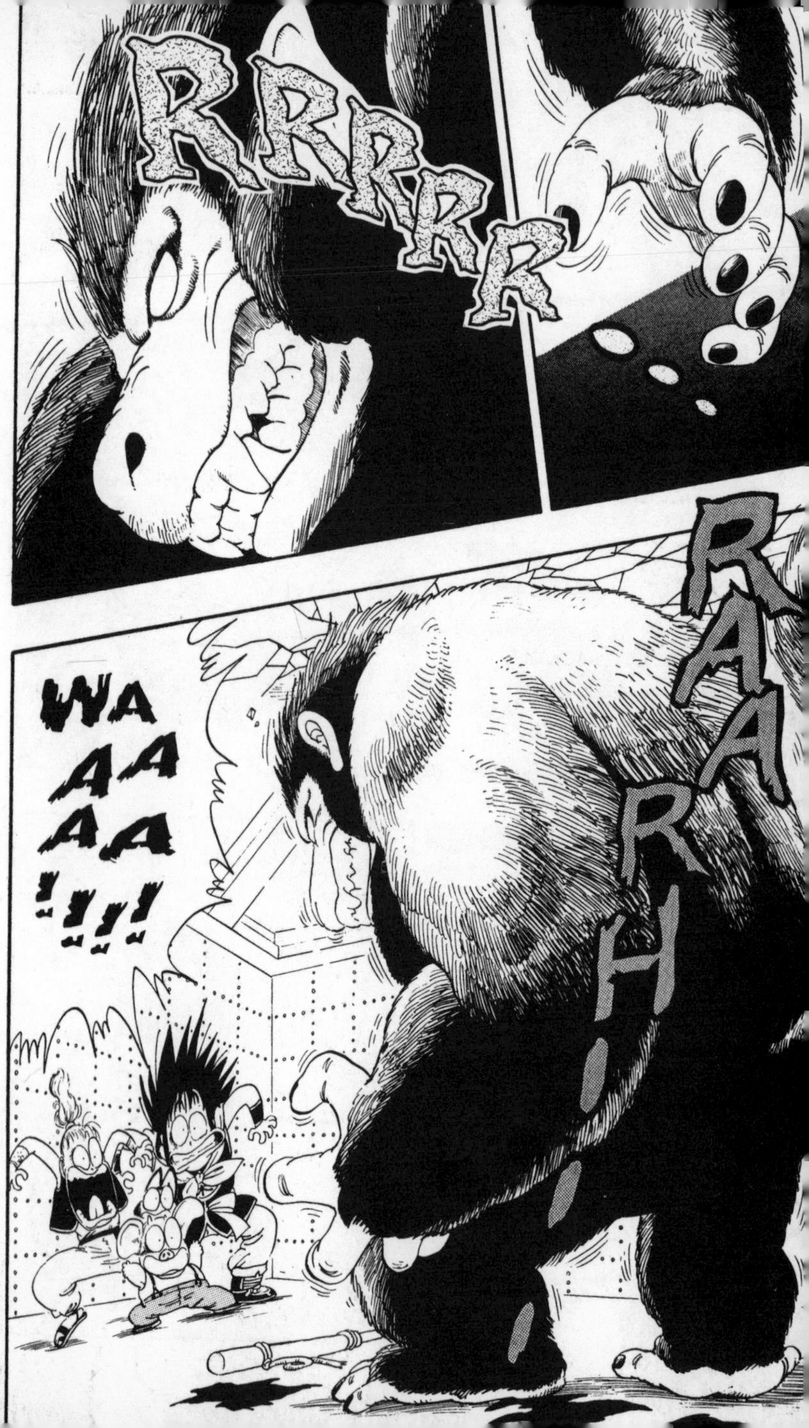
RRRRRR
RAARH!!
WAAAAA!!!!

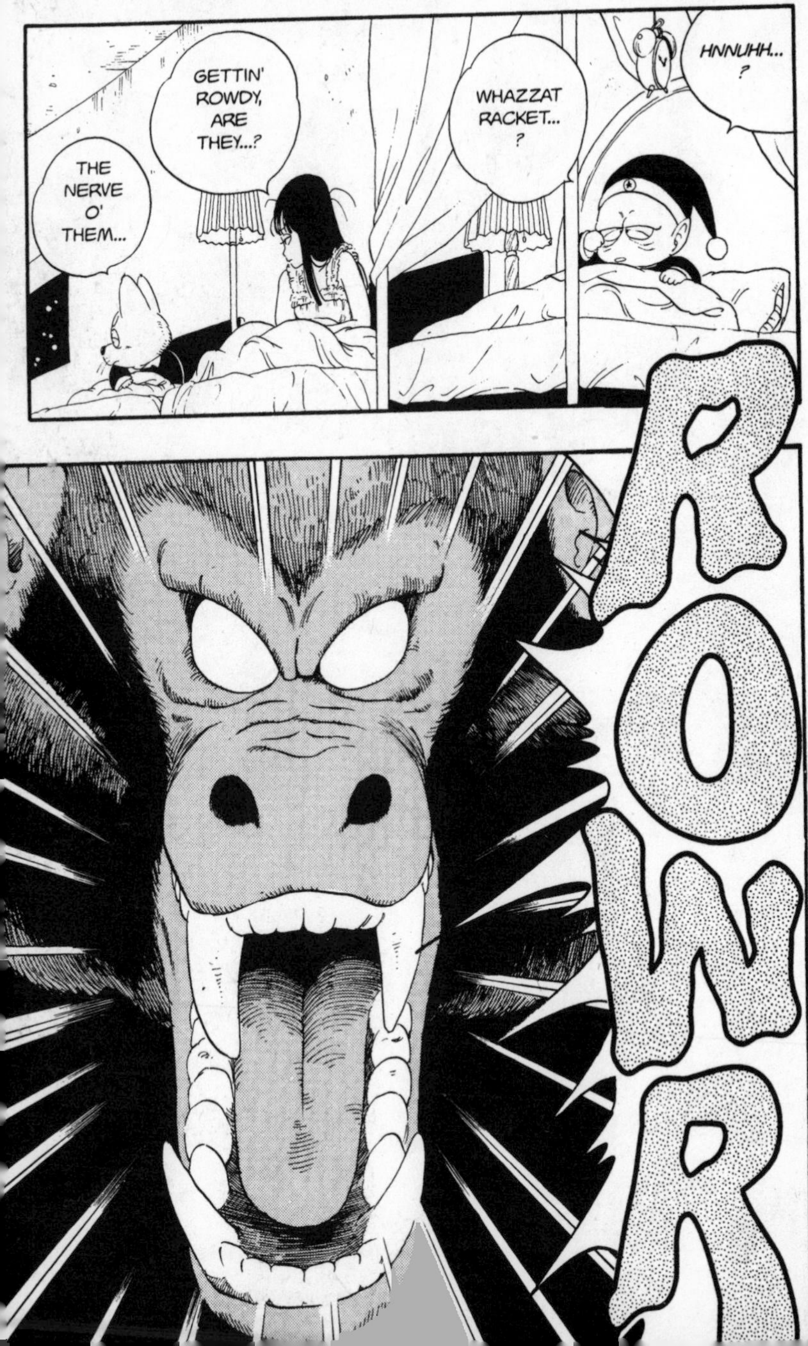
HNNUHH... ?
WHAZZAT RACKET... ?
GETTIN' ROWDY, ARE THEY...?
THE NERVE O' THEM...
ROWR

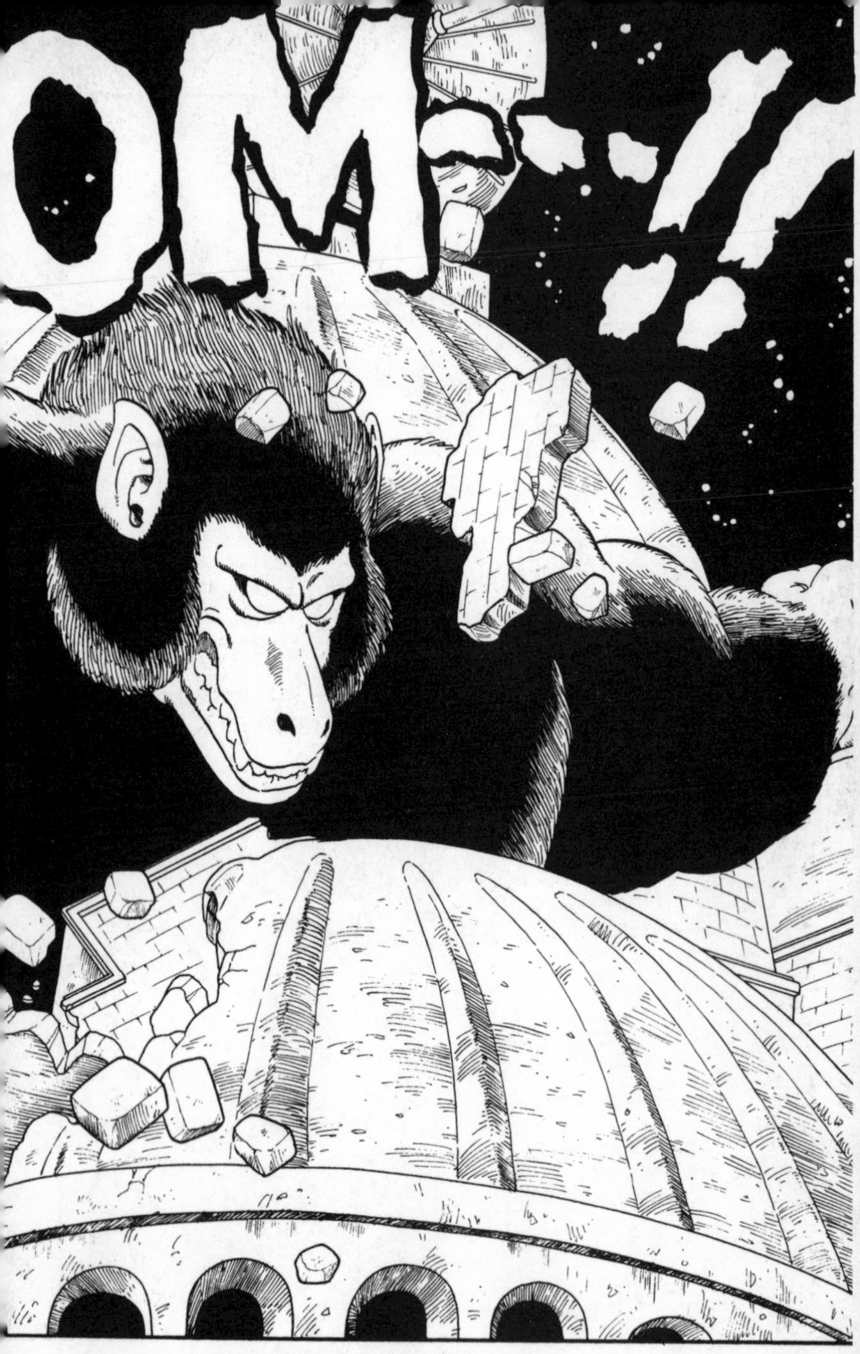
OM!!

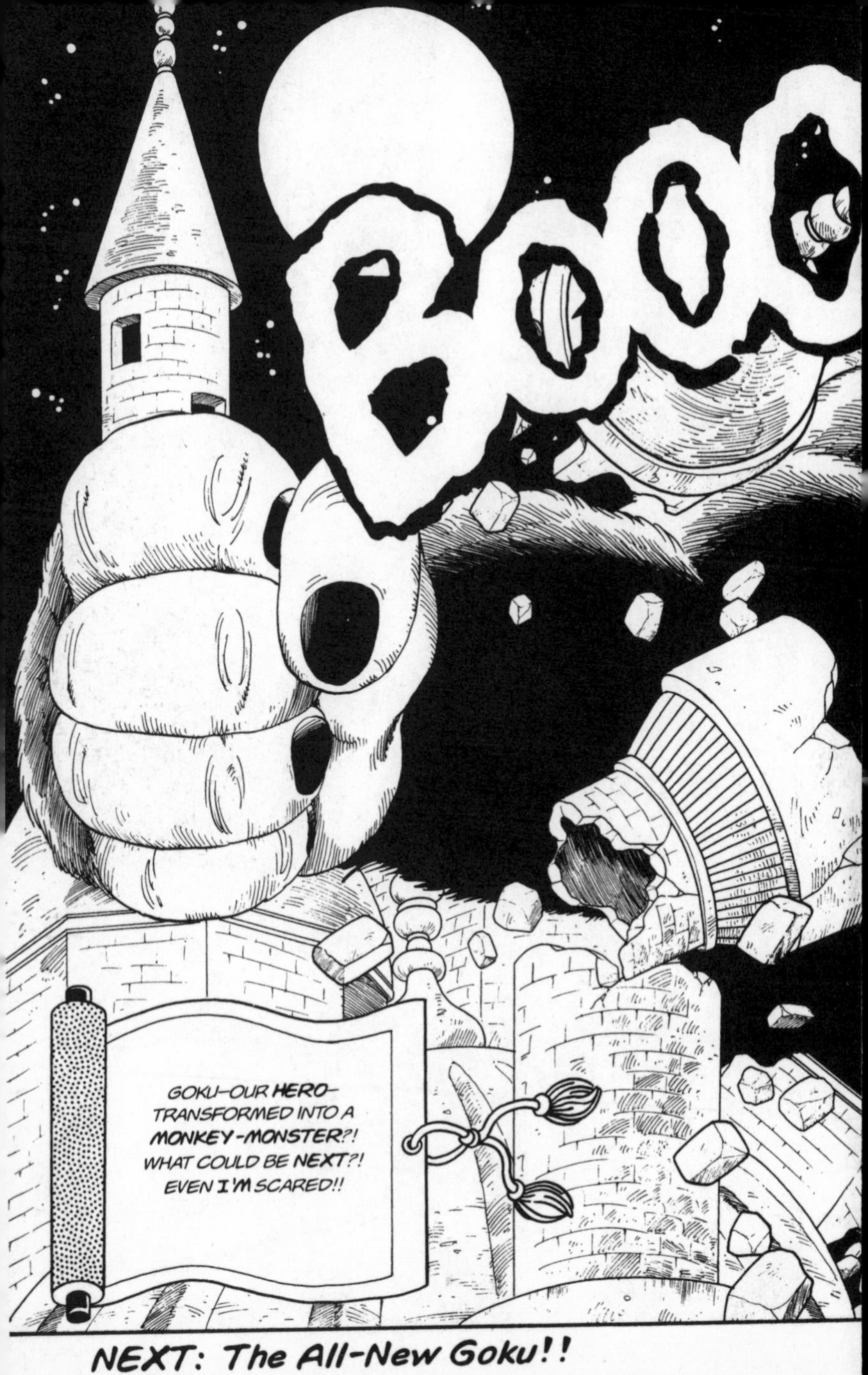
GOKU—OUR HERO—
TRANSFORMED INTO A
MONKEY-MONSTER?!
WHAT COULD BE NEXT?!
EVEN I'M SCARED!!

NEXT: The All-New Goku!!

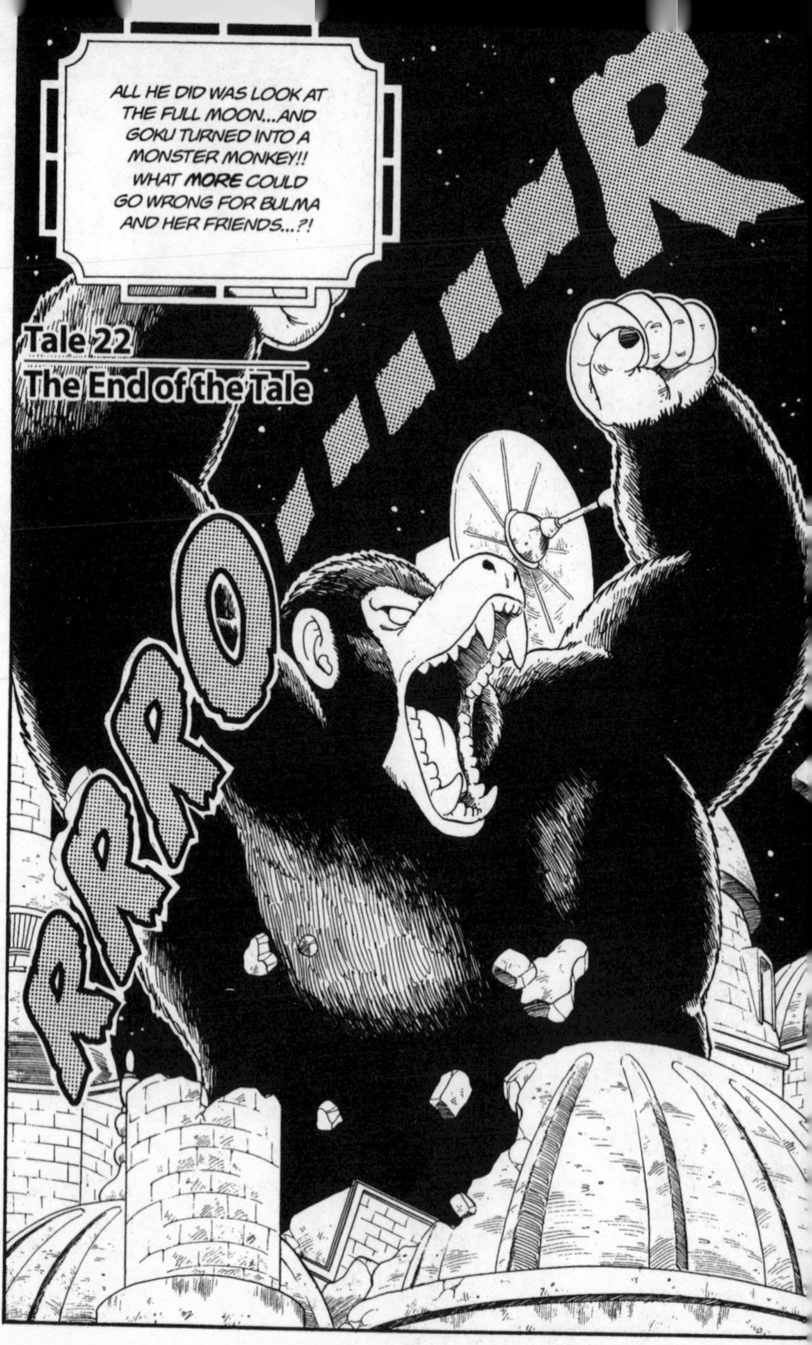
ALL HE DID WAS LOOK AT THE FULL MOON...AND GOKU TURNED INTO A MONSTER MONKEY!! WHAT MORE COULD GO WRONG FOR BULMA AND HER FRIENDS...?!
Tale 22
The End of the Tale
RRRROOAAAR

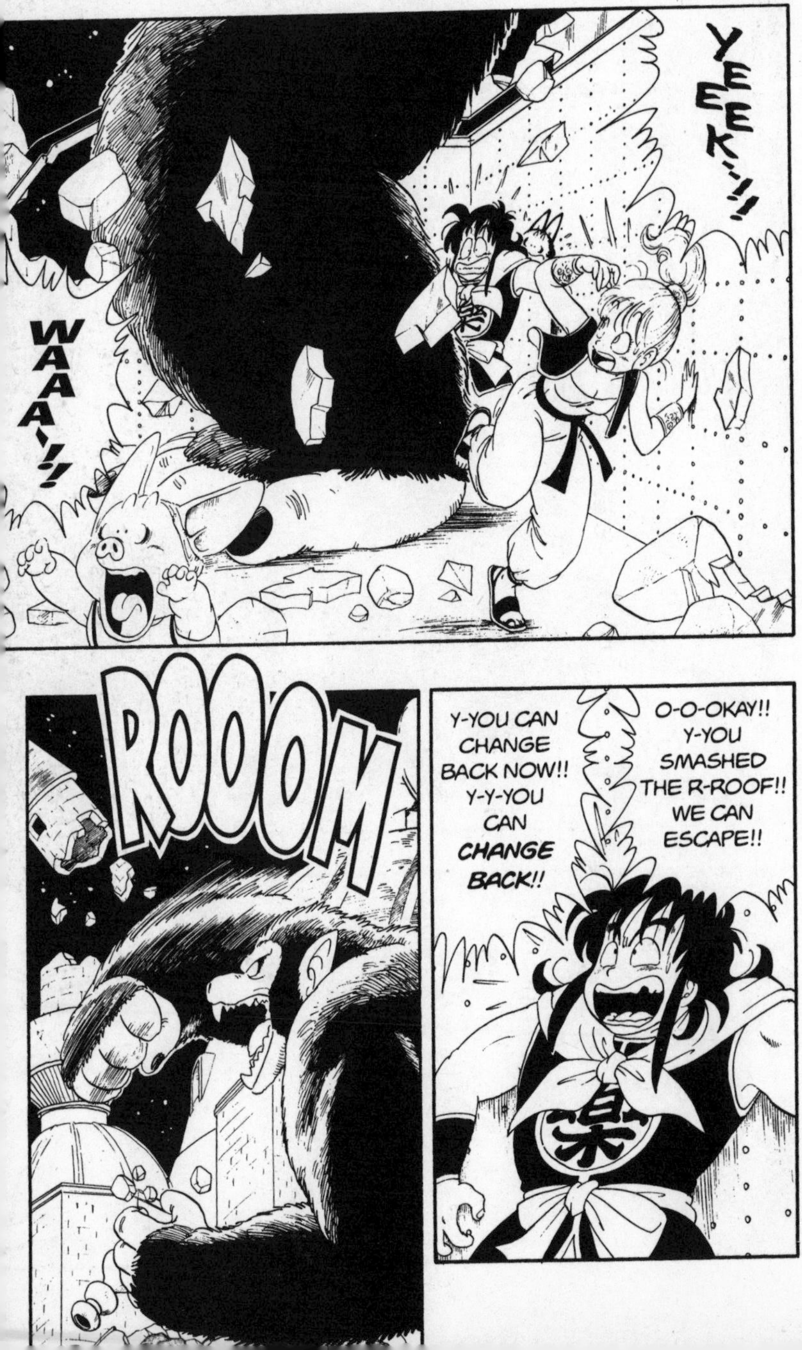
YEEEK~!!
WAAAA~!!
O-O-OKAY!! Y-YOU SMASHED THE R-ROOF!! WE CAN ESCAPE!!
Y-YOU CAN CHANGE BACK NOW!! Y-Y-YOU CAN **CHANGE BACK!!**
ROOOM

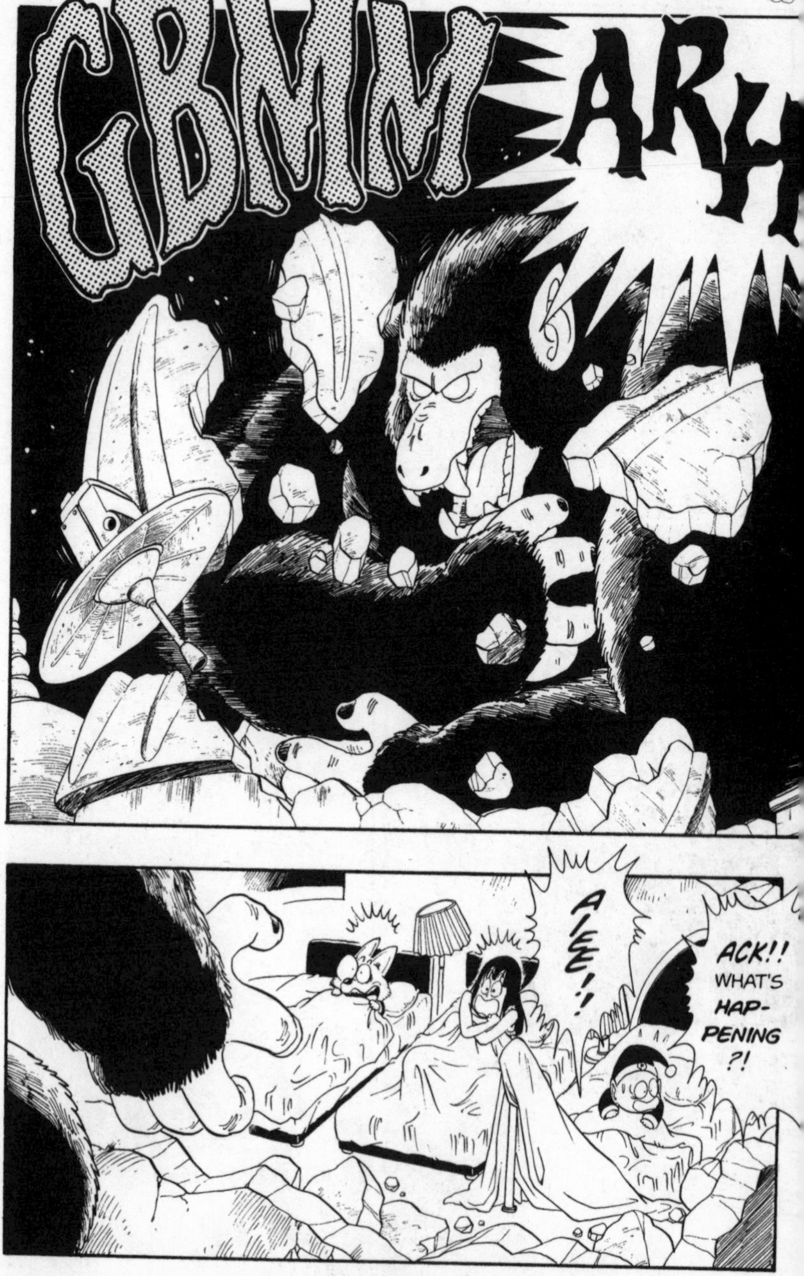
GBMM
ARH
ACK!! WHAT'S HAP-PENING ?!
AIEE!!

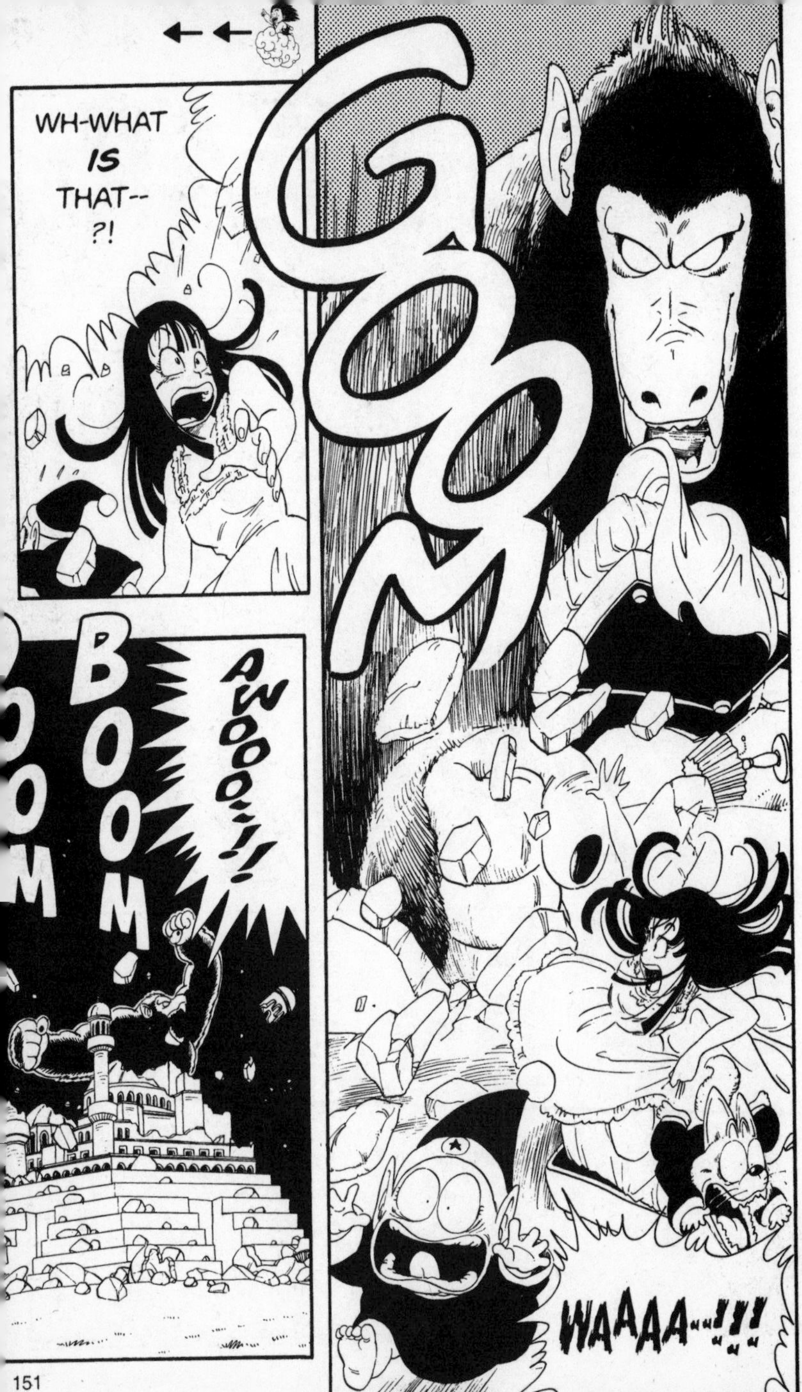
←←
WH-WHAT IS THAT--?!
BOOM
BOOM
AWOOO~!!
GOOM
WAAAA--!!!

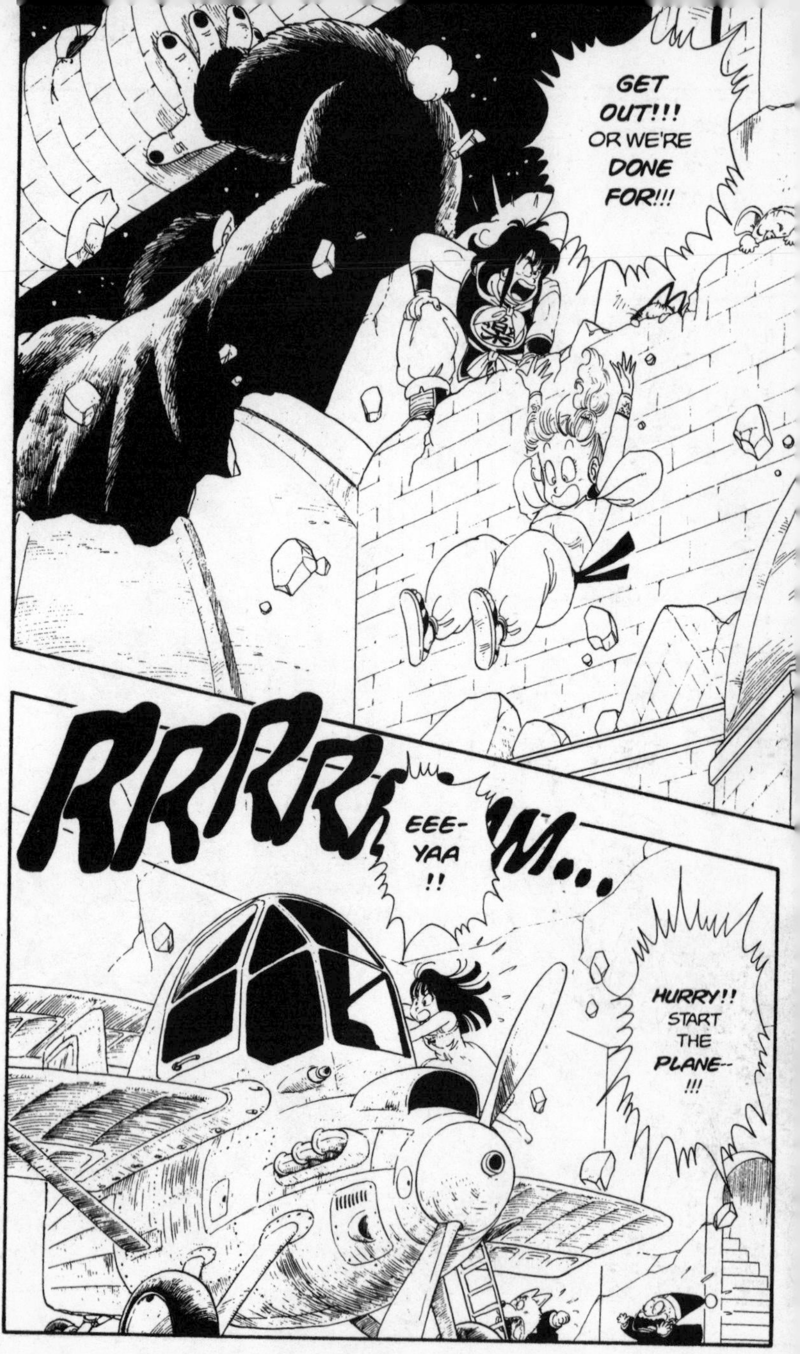
GET OUT!!! OR WE'RE DONE FOR!!!
HURRY!! START THE PLANE--!!!
EEE-YAA!!
RRRRRM...

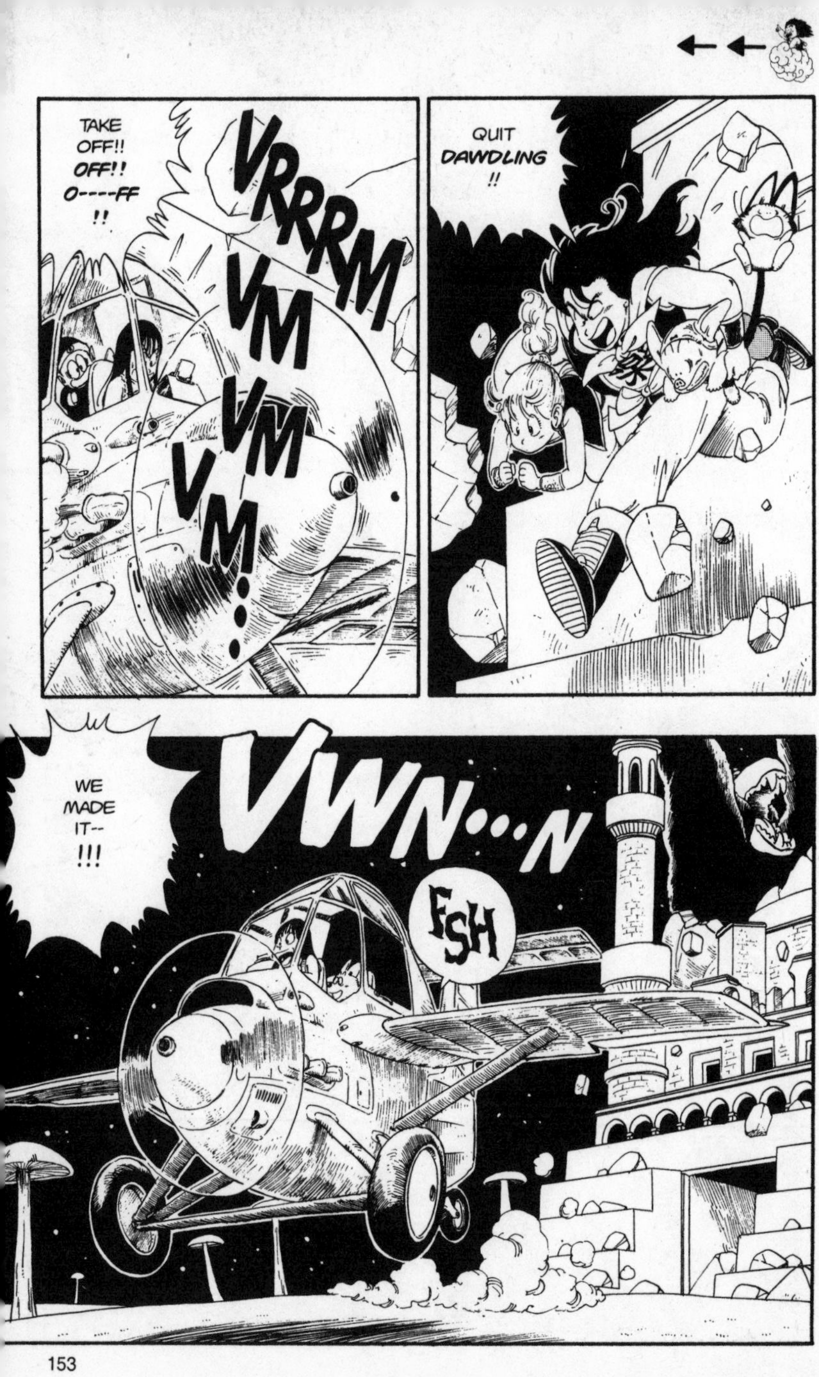
QUIT DAWDLING !!
TAKE OFF!! OFF!! O----FF !!
VRRRM VM VM VM...
WE MADE IT-- !!!
VWN...N
FSH

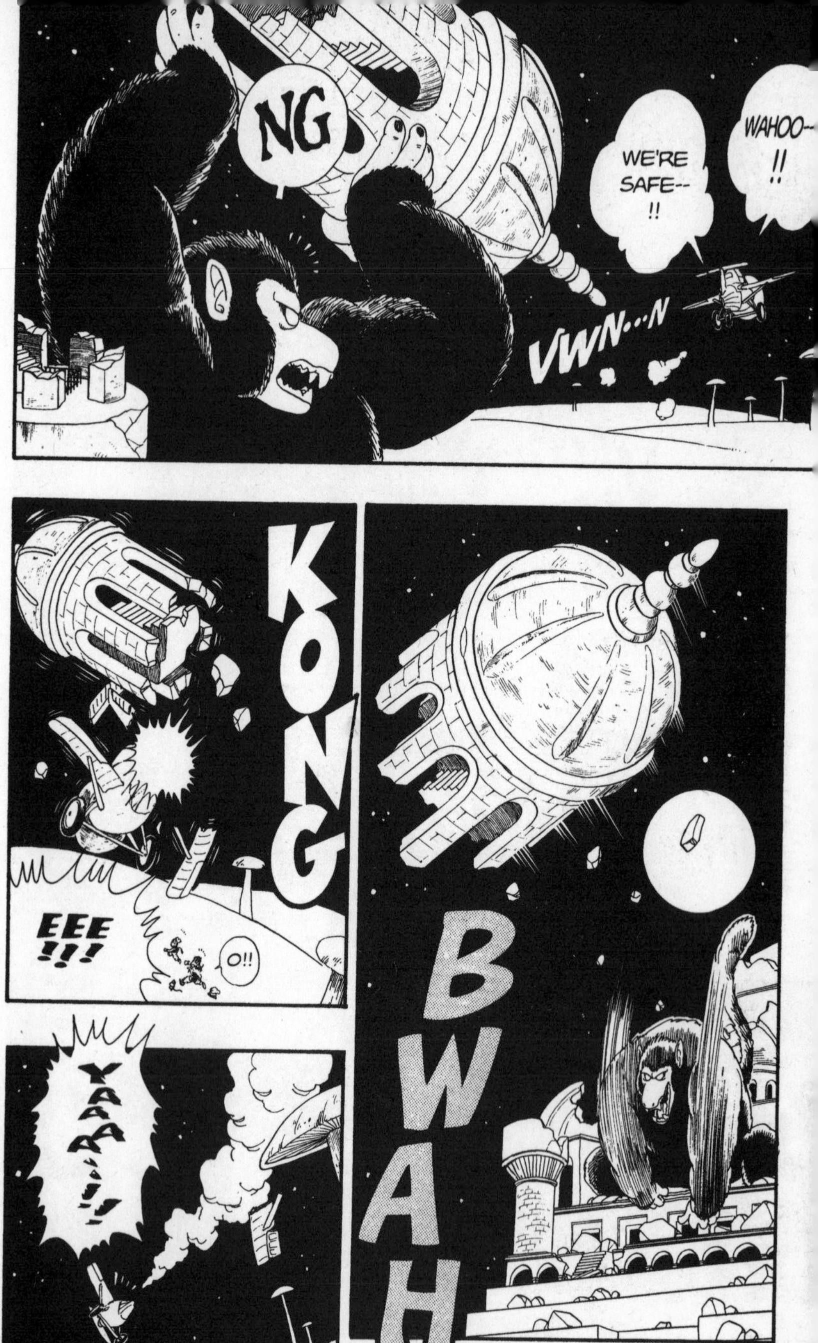
WAHOO--!!
WE'RE SAFE--!!
NG
VWN...N
BWAH
KONG
EEE!!!
O!!
YAAA...!!!

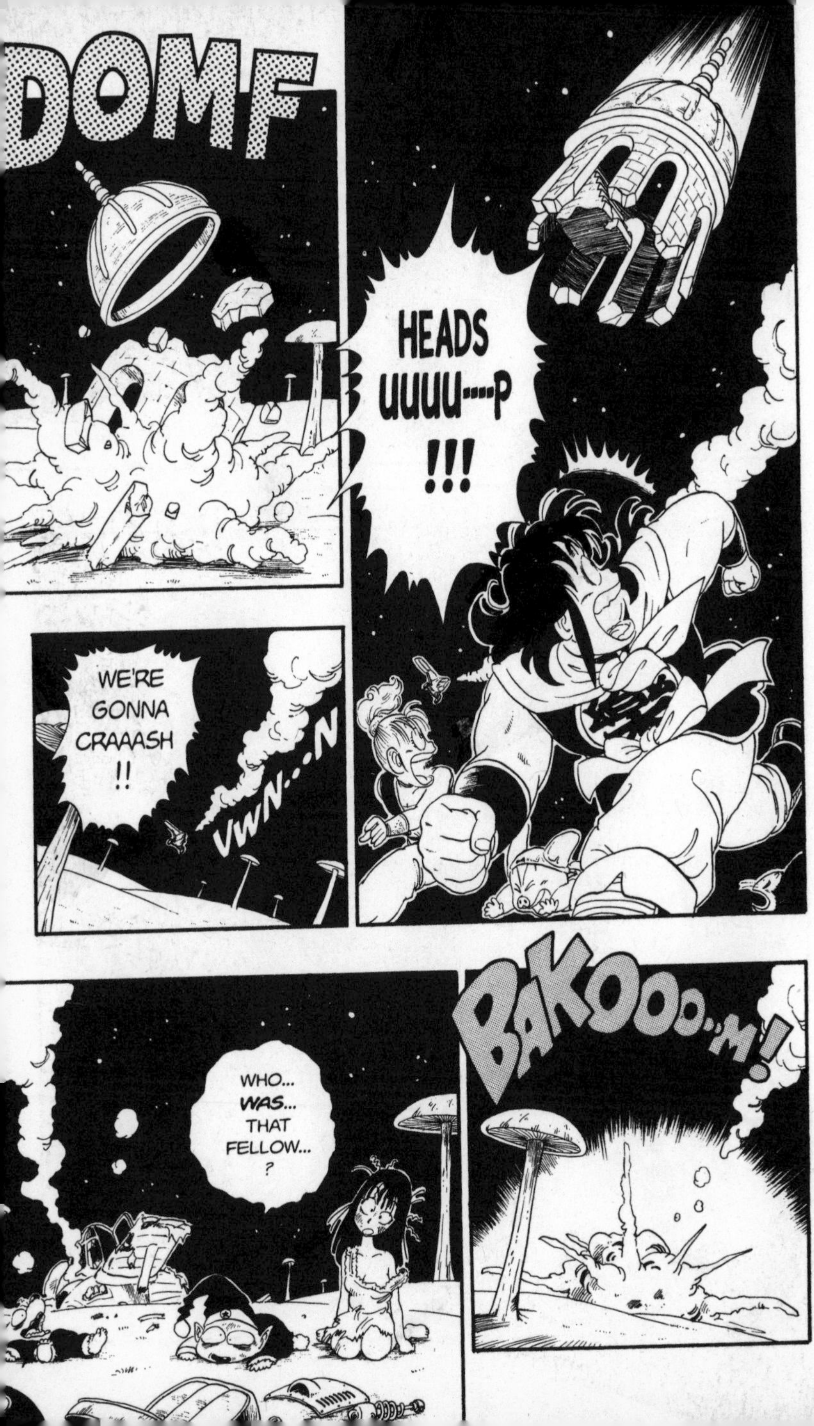
HEADS UUUU----P !!!
DOMF
WE'RE GONNA CRAAASH !!
VWN...N
BAKOOO..M!
WHO... WAS... THAT FELLOW... ?

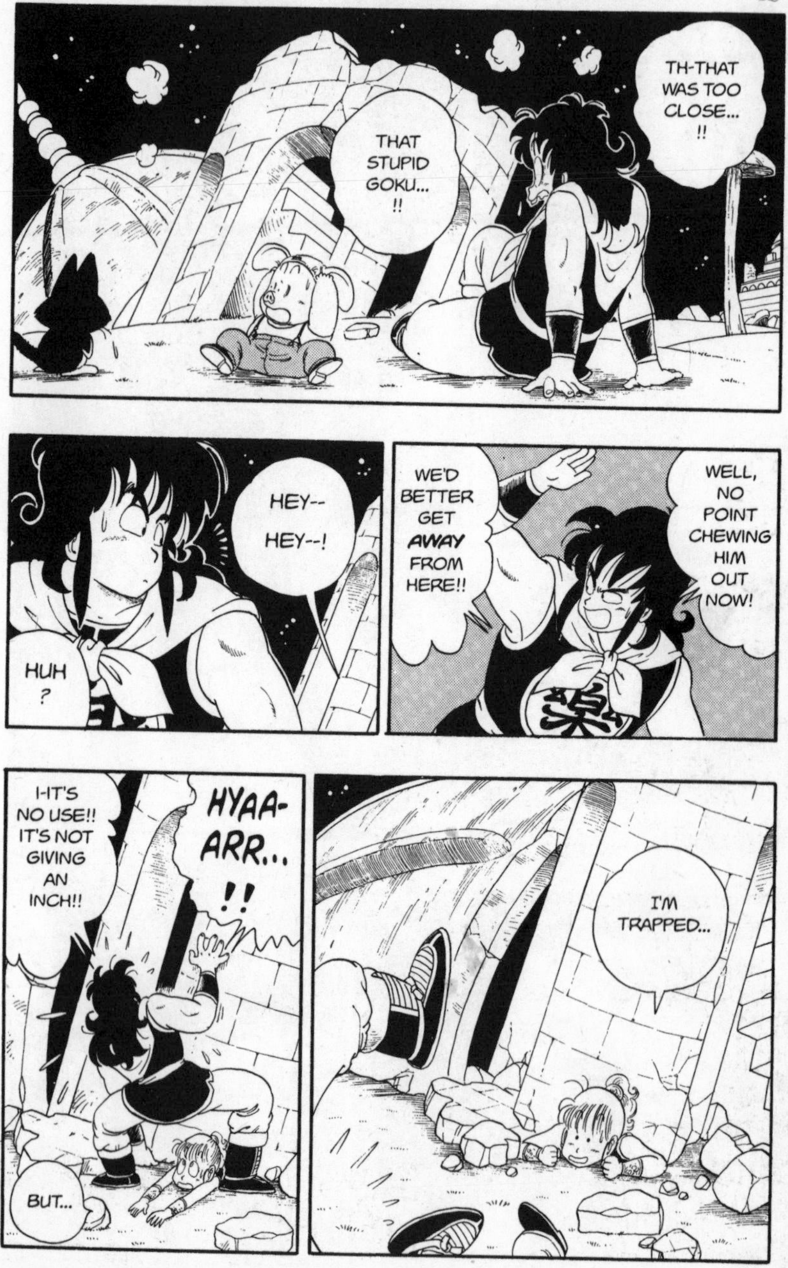
TH-THAT WAS TOO CLOSE... !!
THAT STUPID GOKU... !!
WELL, NO POINT CHEWING HIM OUT NOW!
WE'D BETTER GET AWAY FROM HERE!!
HEY-- HEY--!
HUH ?
I'M TRAPPED...
HYAA-ARR... !!
I-IT'S NO USE!! IT'S NOT GIVING AN INCH!!
BUT...

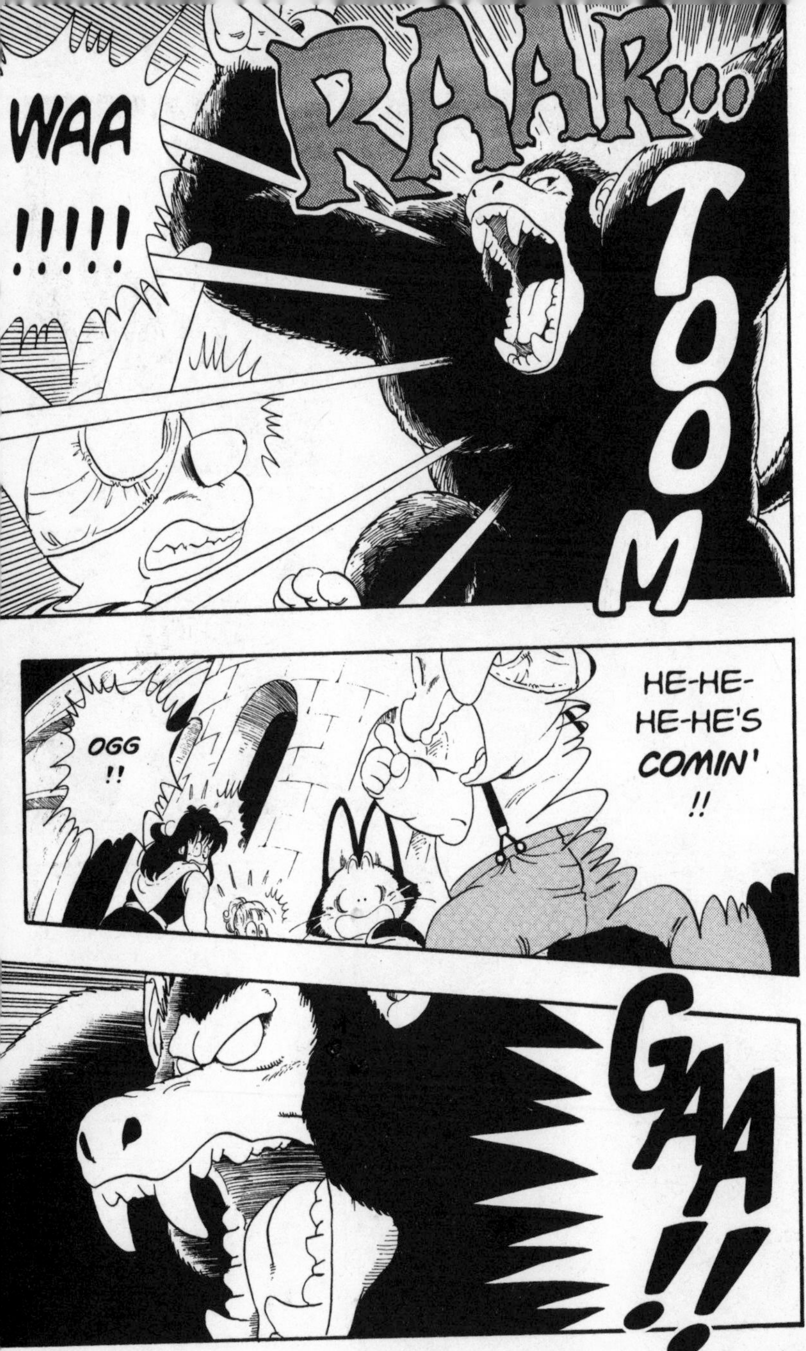
RAAR...
TOOM
WAA!!!!!
HE-HE-HE-HE'S COMIN'!!
OGG!!
GAA!!

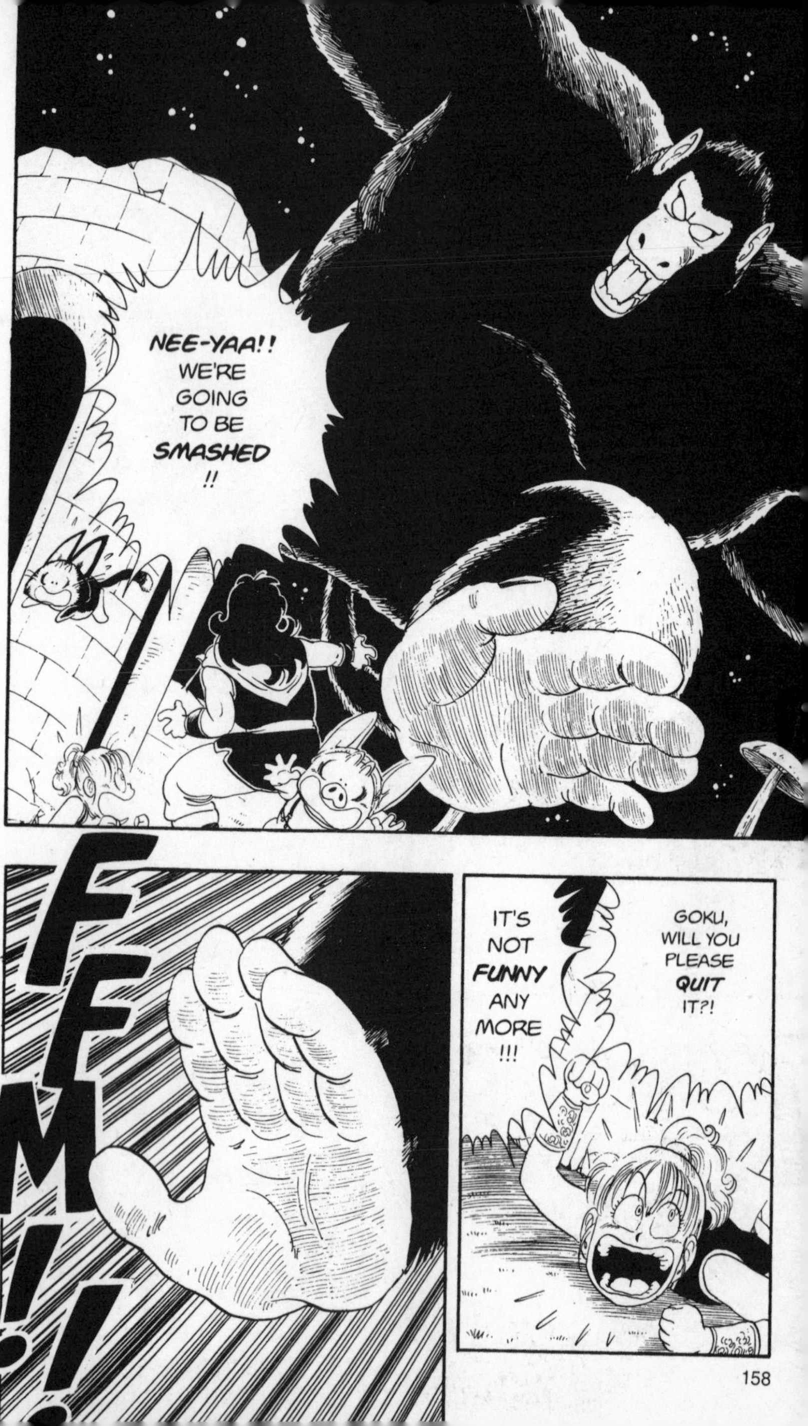
NEE-YAA!! WE'RE GOING TO BE SMASHED !!
GOKU, WILL YOU PLEASE QUIT IT?!
IT'S NOT FUNNY ANY MORE !!!
FFMM!!!

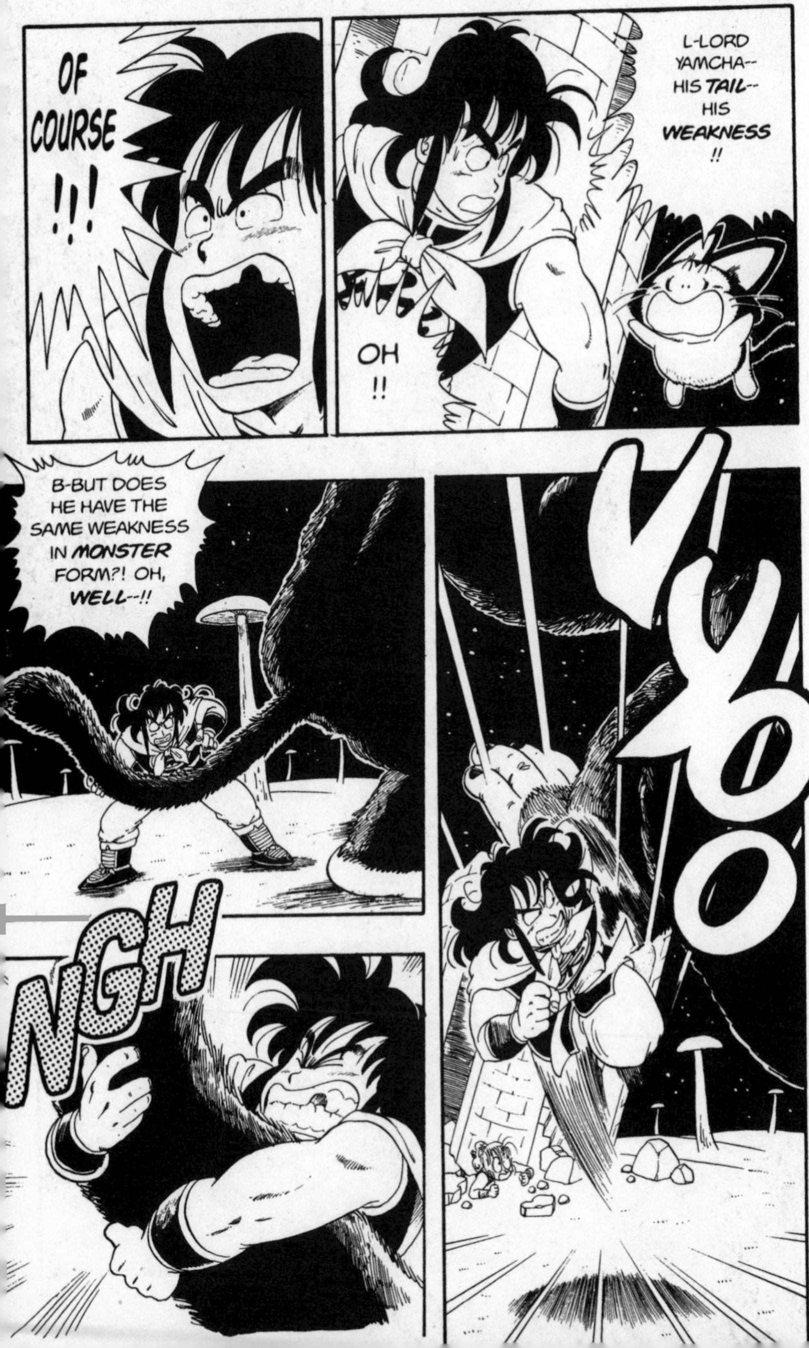
L-LORD YAMCHA-- HIS **TAIL**-- HIS **WEAKNESS** !!
OH !!
OF COURSE !!!
B-BUT DOES HE HAVE THE SAME WEAKNESS IN **MONSTER** FORM?! OH, **WELL**--!!
NGH

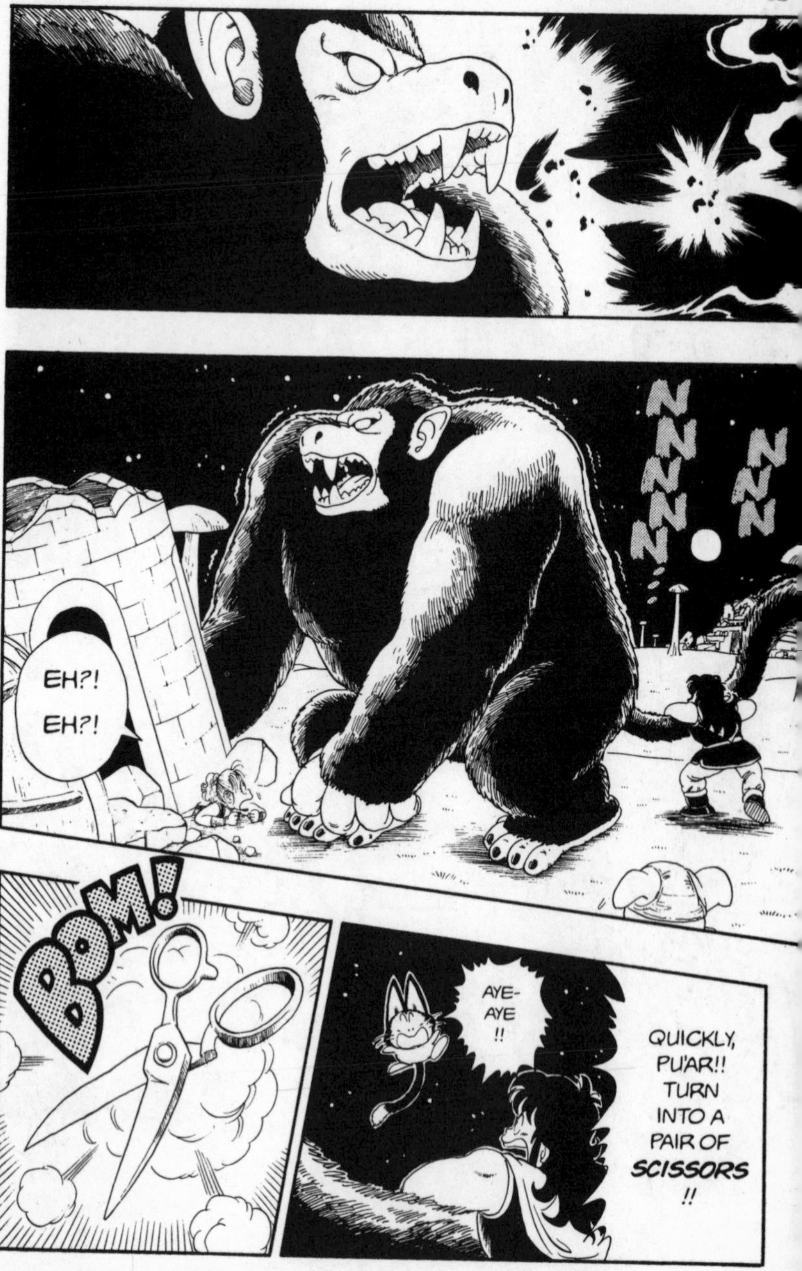
NNN
NNNNN
EH?!
EH?!
QUICKLY, PU'AR!! TURN INTO A PAIR OF SCISSORS !!
AYE-AYE !!
BOM!

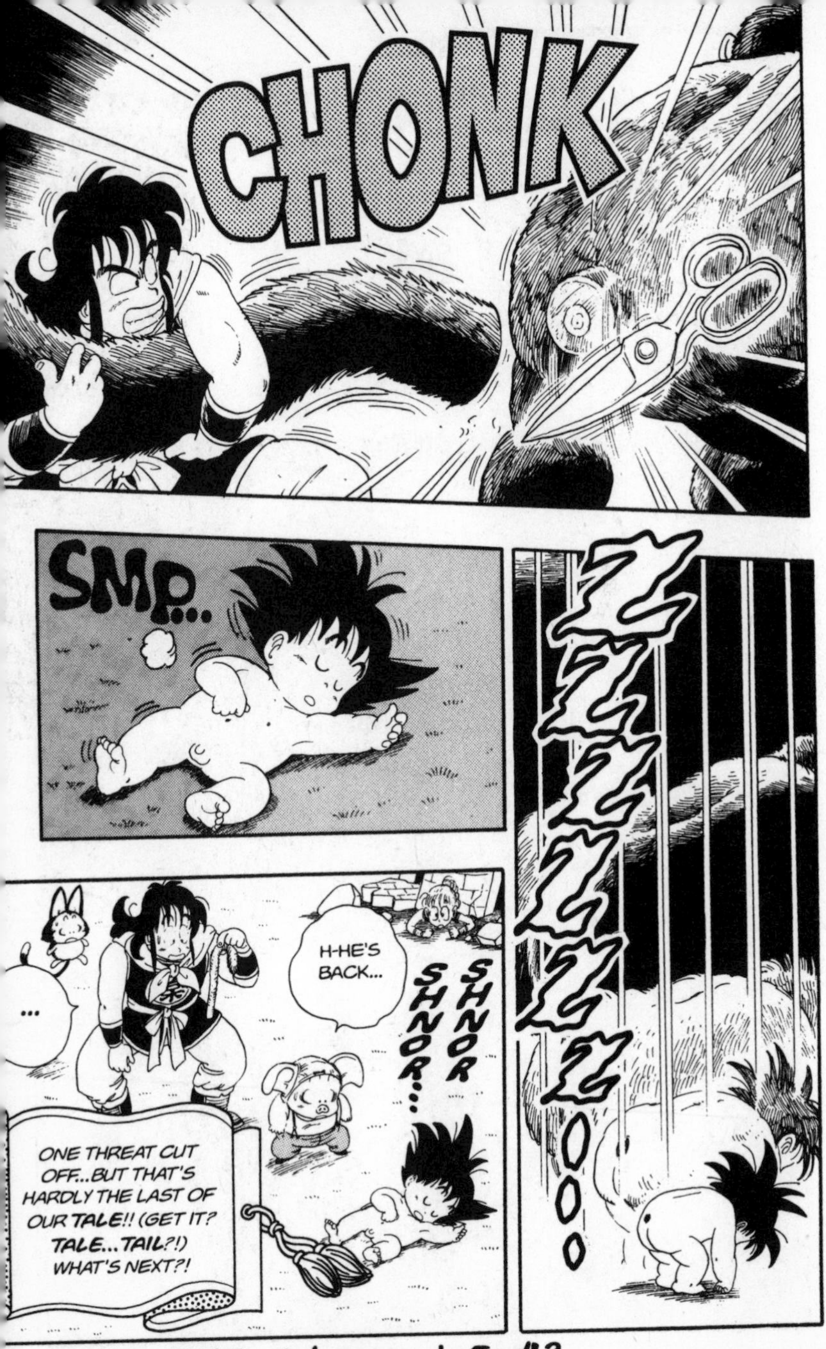
CHONK
ZZZZZZ...
SMP...
SHNOR SHNOR...
H-HE'S BACK...
...
ONE THREAT CUT OFF...BUT THAT'S HARDLY THE LAST OF OUR TALE!! (GET IT? TALE...TAIL?!) WHAT'S NEXT?!

NEXT TIME: Adventure's End!?

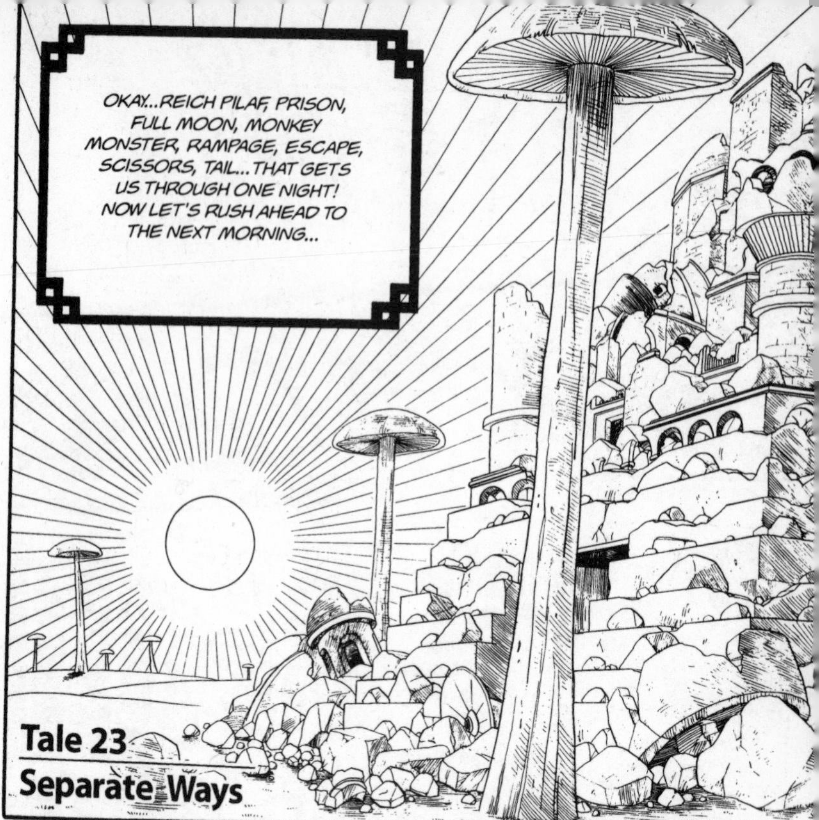
OKAY...REICH PILAF, PRISON, FULL MOON, MONKEY MONSTER, RAMPAGE, ESCAPE, SCISSORS, TAIL...THAT GETS US THROUGH ONE NIGHT! NOW LET'S RUSH AHEAD TO THE NEXT MORNING...
Tale 23
Separate Ways

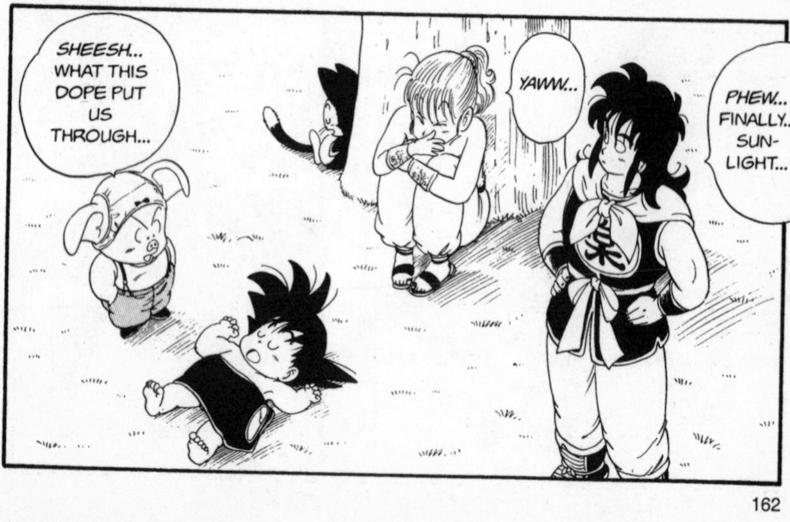
PHEW... FINALLY... SUN-LIGHT...
YAWN...
SHEESH... WHAT THIS DOPE PUT US THROUGH...

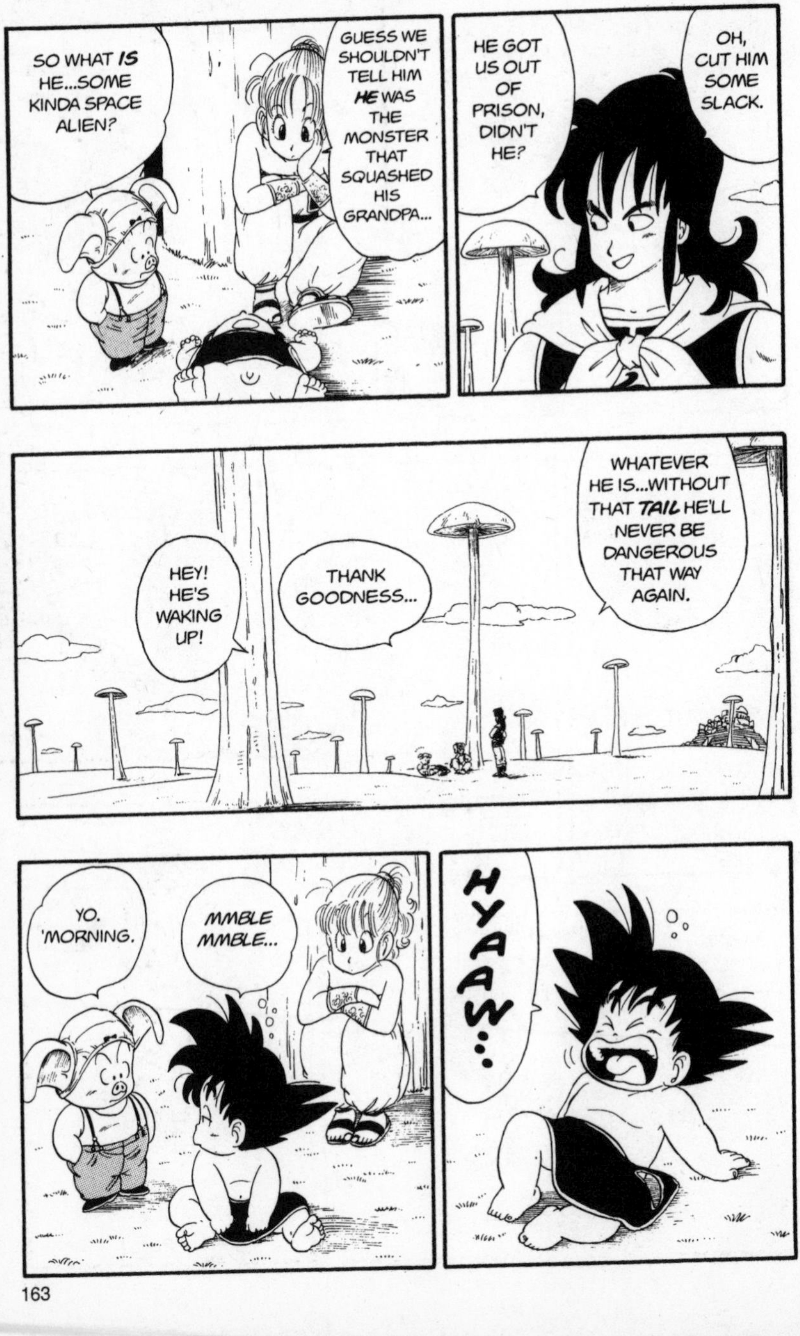
OH, CUT HIM SOME SLACK.
HE GOT US OUT OF PRISON, DIDN'T HE?
GUESS WE SHOULDN'T TELL HIM HE WAS THE MONSTER THAT SQUASHED HIS GRANDPA...
SO WHAT IS HE...SOME KINDA SPACE ALIEN?
WHATEVER HE IS...WITHOUT THAT TAIL HE'LL NEVER BE DANGEROUS THAT WAY AGAIN.
THANK GOODNESS...
HEY! HE'S WAKING UP!
HYAAW...
MMBLE MMBLE...
YO. 'MORNING.

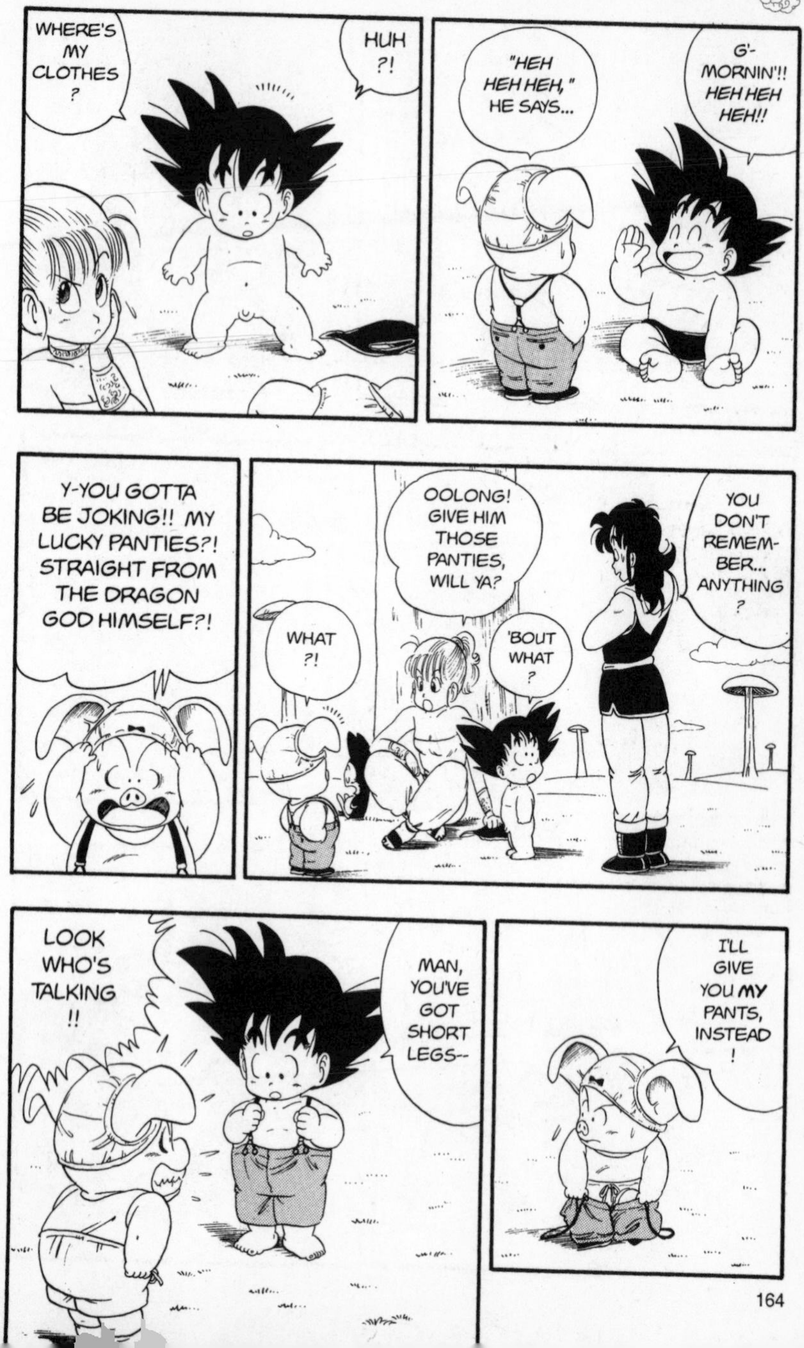
G'-MORNIN'!! HEH HEH HEH!!
"HEH HEH HEH," HE SAYS...
HUH ?!
WHERE'S MY CLOTHES ?
YOU DON'T REMEM-BER... ANYTHING ?
OOLONG! GIVE HIM THOSE PANTIES, WILL YA?
'BOUT WHAT ?
WHAT ?!
Y-YOU GOTTA BE JOKING!! MY LUCKY PANTIES?! STRAIGHT FROM THE DRAGON GOD HIMSELF?!
I'LL GIVE YOU **MY** PANTS, INSTEAD !
MAN, YOU'VE GOT SHORT LEGS--
LOOK WHO'S TALKING !!

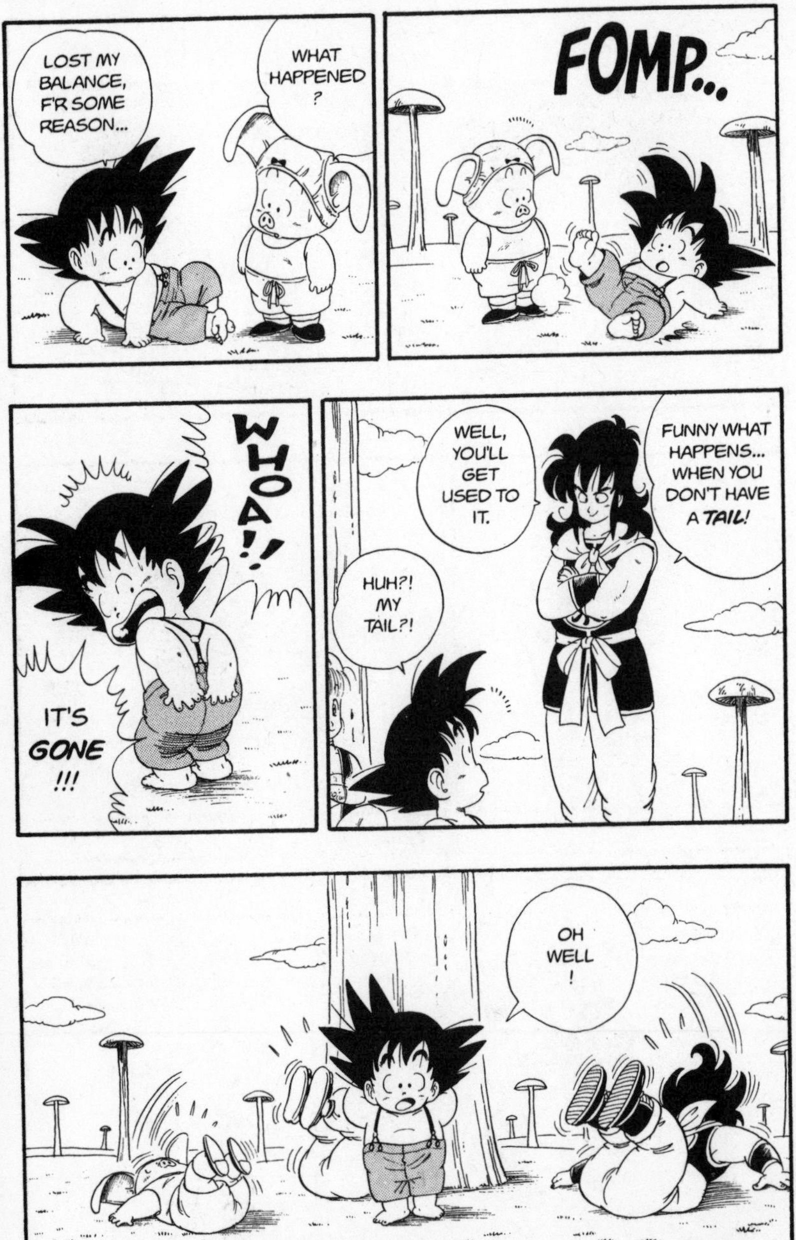
FOMP...
WHAT HAPPENED ?
LOST MY BALANCE, F'R SOME REASON...
FUNNY WHAT HAPPENS... WHEN YOU DON'T HAVE A TAIL!
WELL, YOU'LL GET USED TO IT.
HUH?! MY TAIL?!
WHOA!!
IT'S GONE !!!
OH WELL !

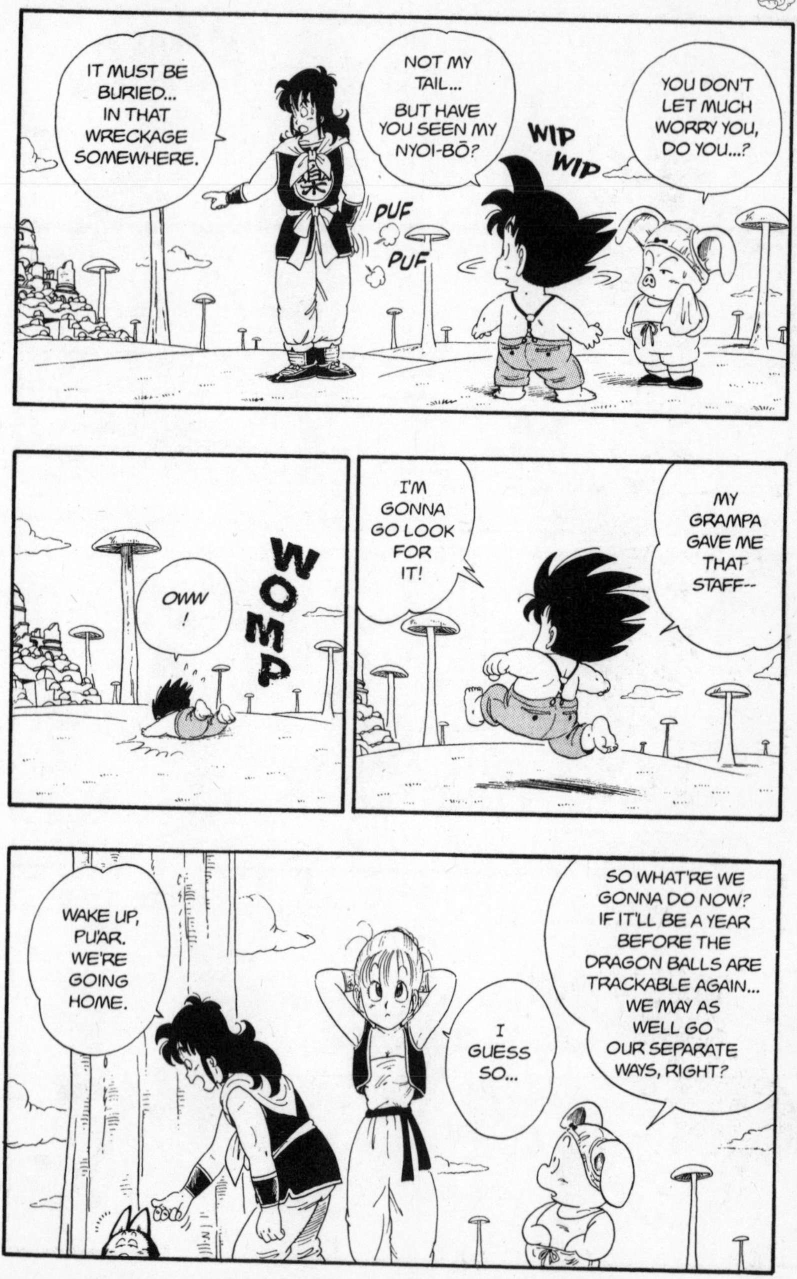
YOU DON'T LET MUCH WORRY YOU, DO YOU...?
WIP WIP
NOT MY TAIL... BUT HAVE YOU SEEN MY NYOI-BŌ?
PUF PUF
IT MUST BE BURIED... IN THAT WRECKAGE SOMEWHERE.
MY GRAMPA GAVE ME THAT STAFF--
I'M GONNA GO LOOK FOR IT!
WOMP
OWW!
SO WHAT'RE WE GONNA DO NOW? IF IT'LL BE A YEAR BEFORE THE DRAGON BALLS ARE TRACKABLE AGAIN... WE MAY AS WELL GO OUR SEPARATE WAYS, RIGHT?
I GUESS SO...
WAKE UP, PU'AR. WE'RE GOING HOME.

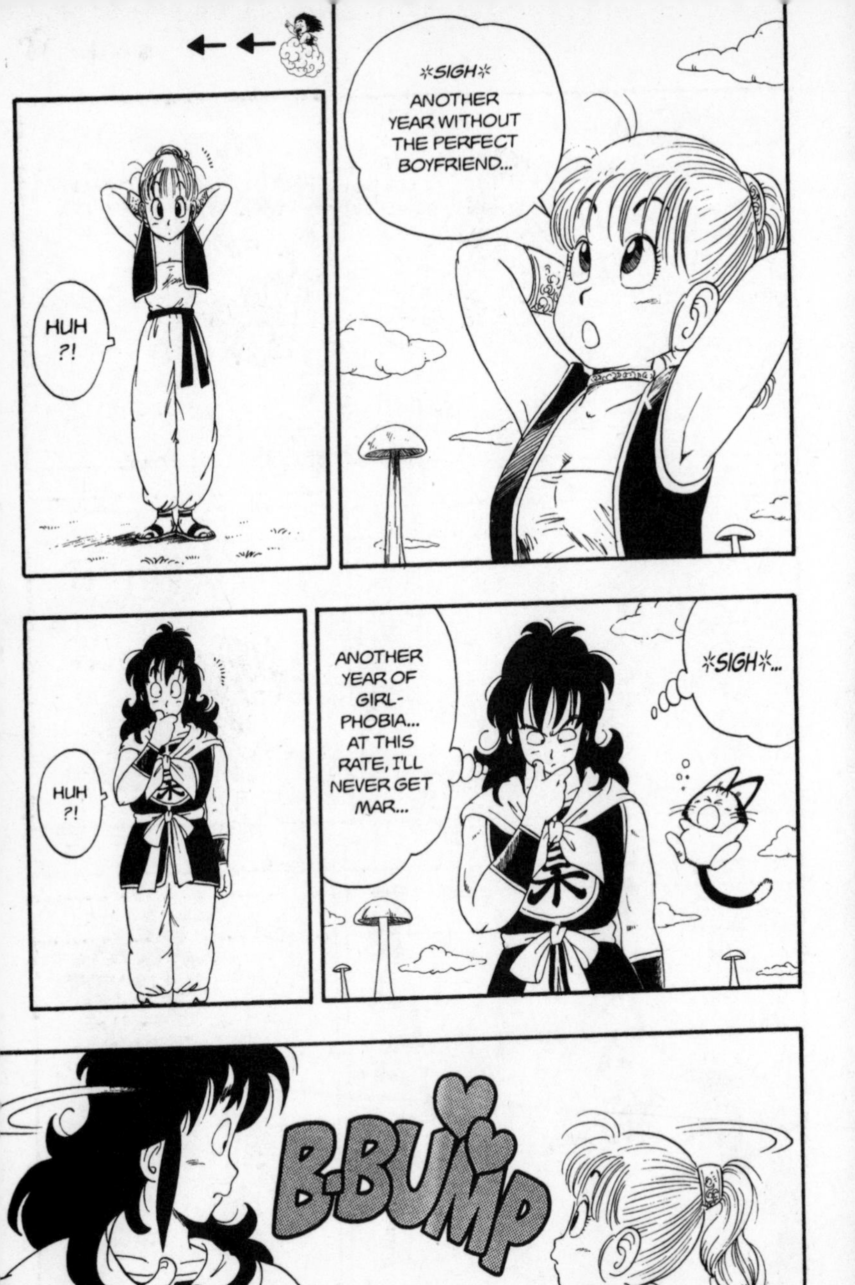
SIGH ANOTHER YEAR WITHOUT THE PERFECT BOYFRIEND...
HUH ?!
SIGH...
ANOTHER YEAR OF GIRL-PHOBIA... AT THIS RATE, I'LL NEVER GET MAR...
HUH ?!
B-BUMP

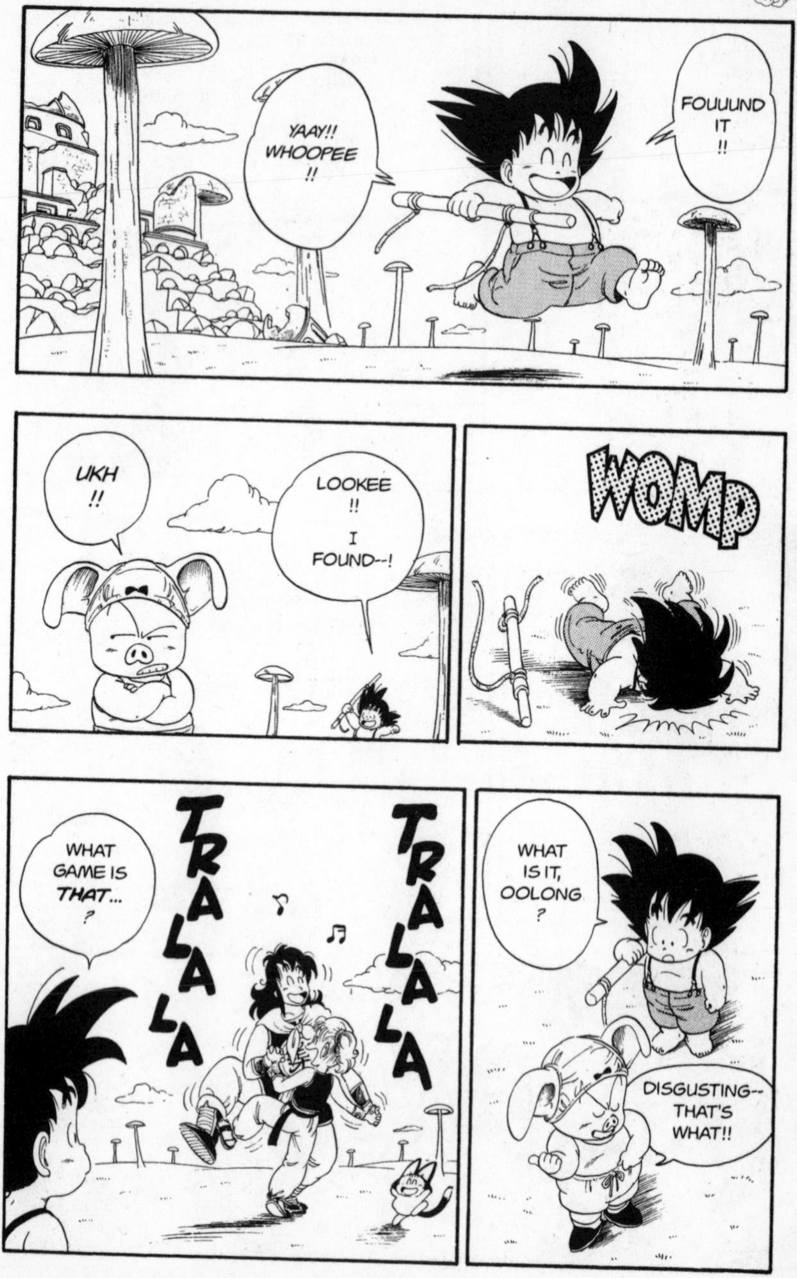
FOUUUND IT !!
YAAY!! WHOOPEE !!
WOMP
LOOKEE !! I FOUND--!
UKH !!
WHAT IS IT, OOLONG ?
DISGUSTING-- THAT'S WHAT!!
TRA LA LA
WHAT GAME IS THAT... ?
TRA LA LA

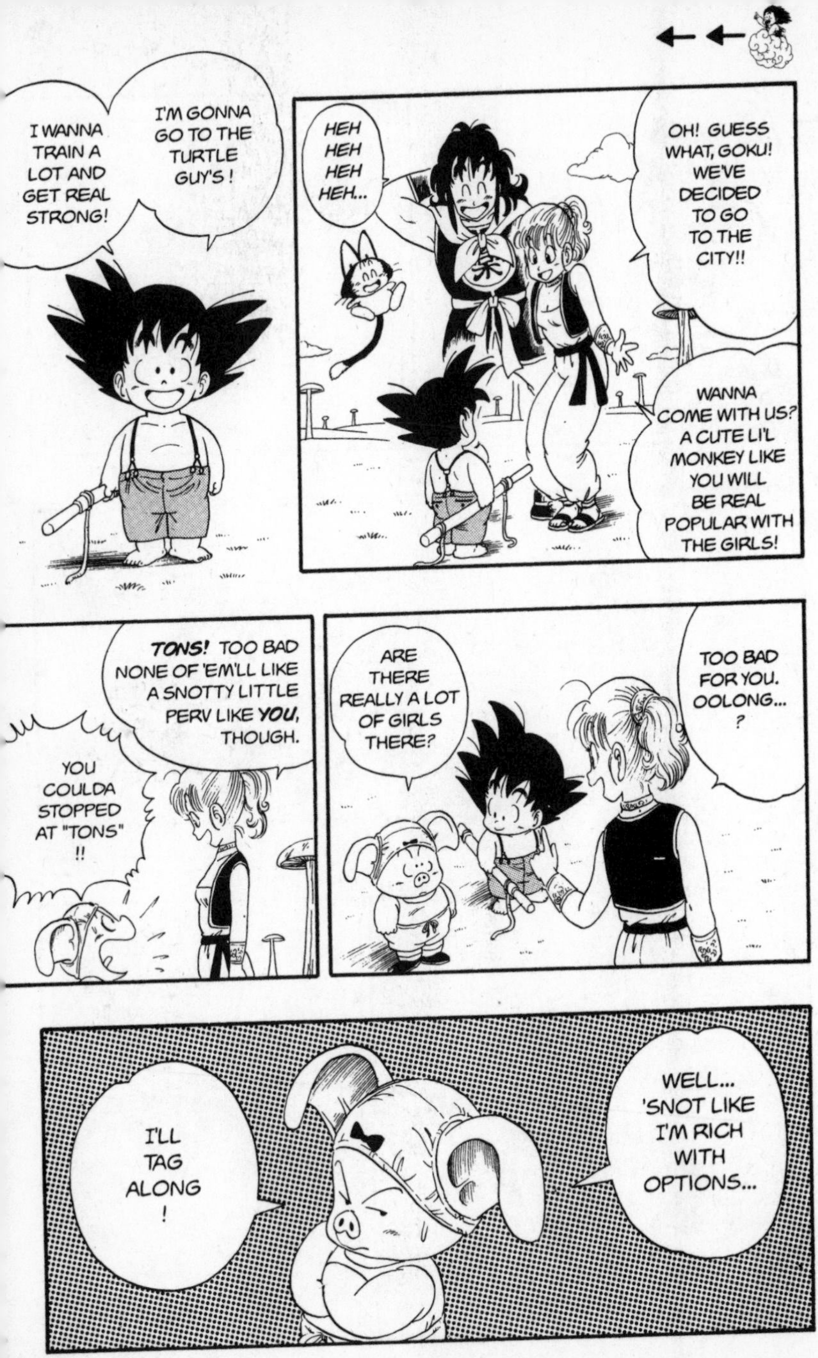
OH! GUESS WHAT, GOKU! WE'VE DECIDED TO GO TO THE CITY!!
HEH HEH HEH HEH...
WANNA COME WITH US? A CUTE LI'L MONKEY LIKE YOU WILL BE REAL POPULAR WITH THE GIRLS!
I'M GONNA GO TO THE TURTLE GUY'S!
I WANNA TRAIN A LOT AND GET REAL STRONG!
TOO BAD FOR YOU. OOLONG... ?
ARE THERE REALLY A LOT OF GIRLS THERE?
TONS! TOO BAD NONE OF 'EM'LL LIKE A SNOTTY LITTLE PERV LIKE YOU, THOUGH.
YOU COULDA STOPPED AT "TONS" !!
WELL... 'SNOT LIKE I'M RICH WITH OPTIONS...
I'LL TAG ALONG !

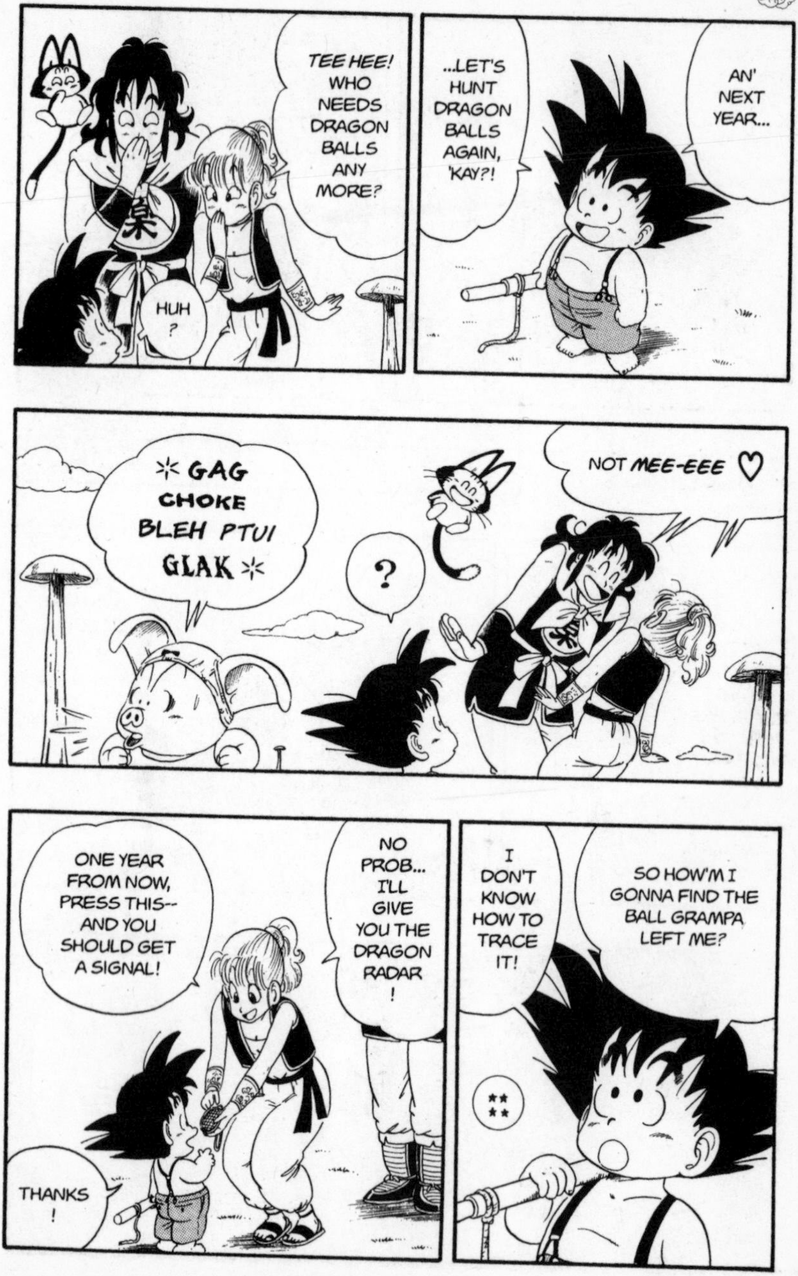
AN' NEXT YEAR...
...LET'S HUNT DRAGON BALLS AGAIN, 'KAY?!
TEE HEE! WHO NEEDS DRAGON BALLS ANY MORE?
HUH ?
NOT MEE-EEE ♡
?
GAG CHOKE BLEH PTUI GLAK
SO HOW'M I GONNA FIND THE BALL GRAMPA LEFT ME?
I DON'T KNOW HOW TO TRACE IT!
NO PROB... I'LL GIVE YOU THE DRAGON RADAR !
ONE YEAR FROM NOW, PRESS THIS-- AND YOU SHOULD GET A SIGNAL!
THANKS !

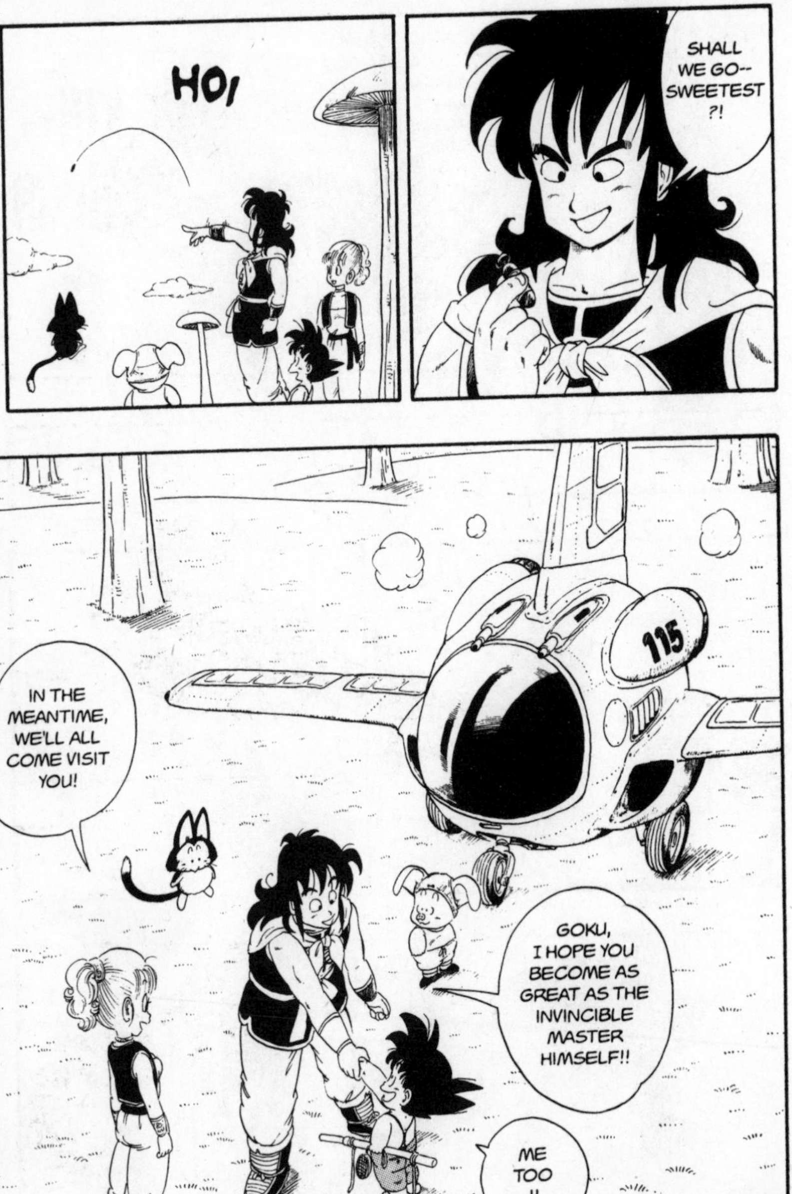
SHALL WE GO-- SWEETEST ?!
HOI
GOKU, I HOPE YOU BECOME AS GREAT AS THE INVINCIBLE MASTER HIMSELF!!
IN THE MEANTIME, WE'LL ALL COME VISIT YOU!
ME TOO !!

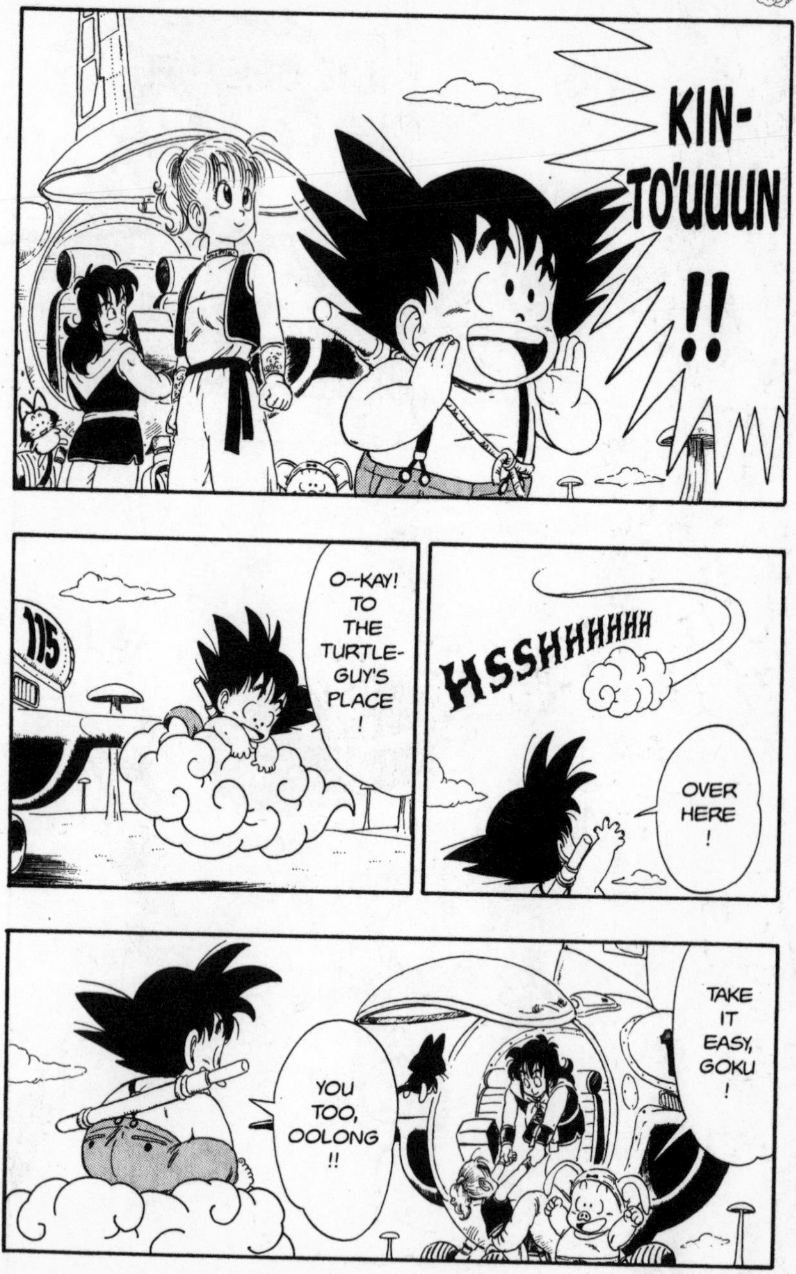
KIN-TO'UUUN!!
HSSHHHHHH
OVER HERE!
O--KAY! TO THE TURTLE-GUY'S PLACE!
TAKE IT EASY, GOKU!
YOU TOO, OOLONG!!

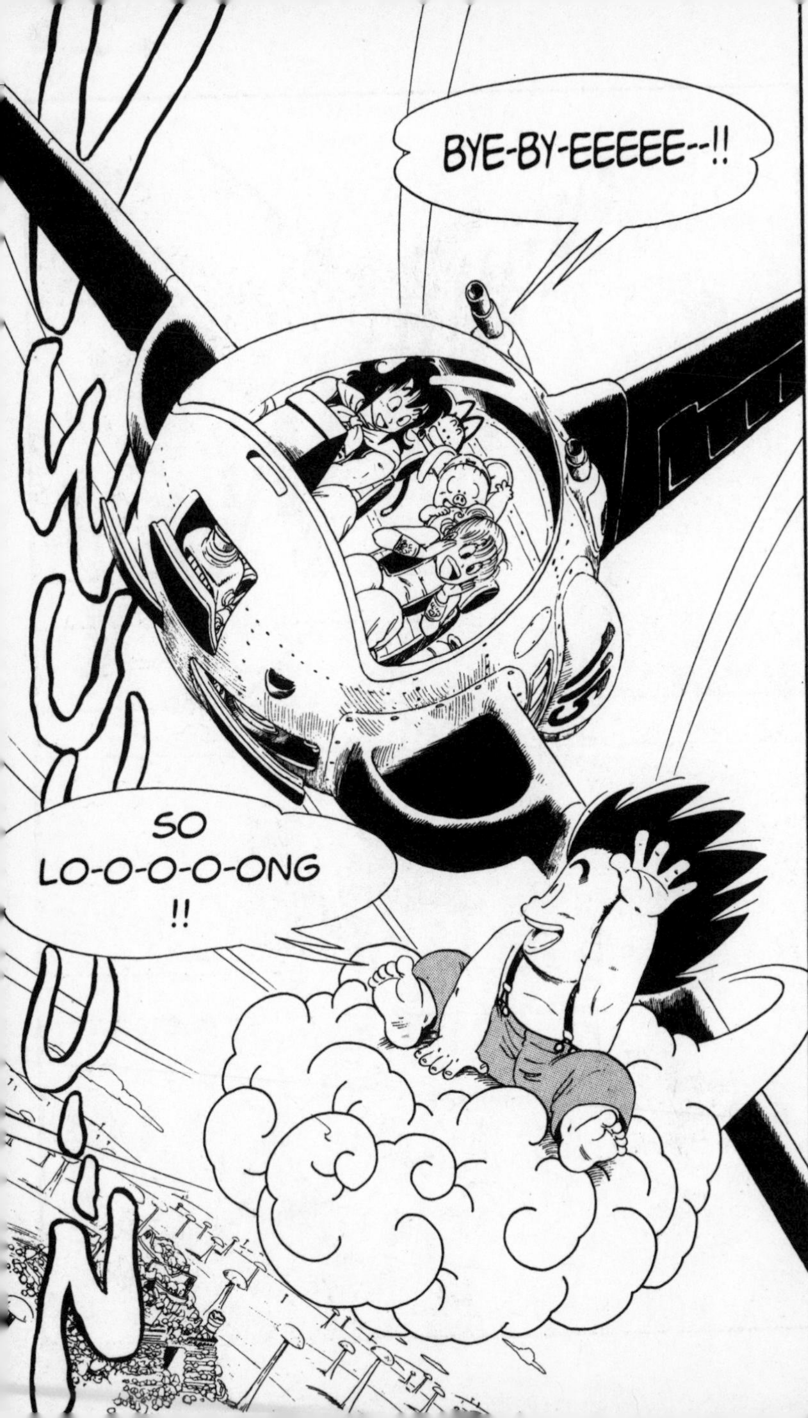
BYE-BY-EEEEE--!!
SO LO-O-O-O-ONG !!

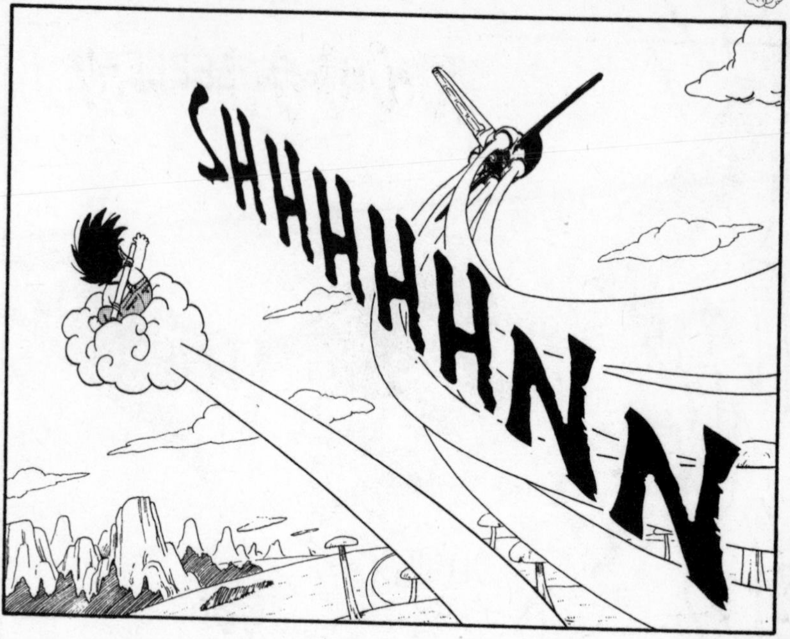
SHHHHHNN

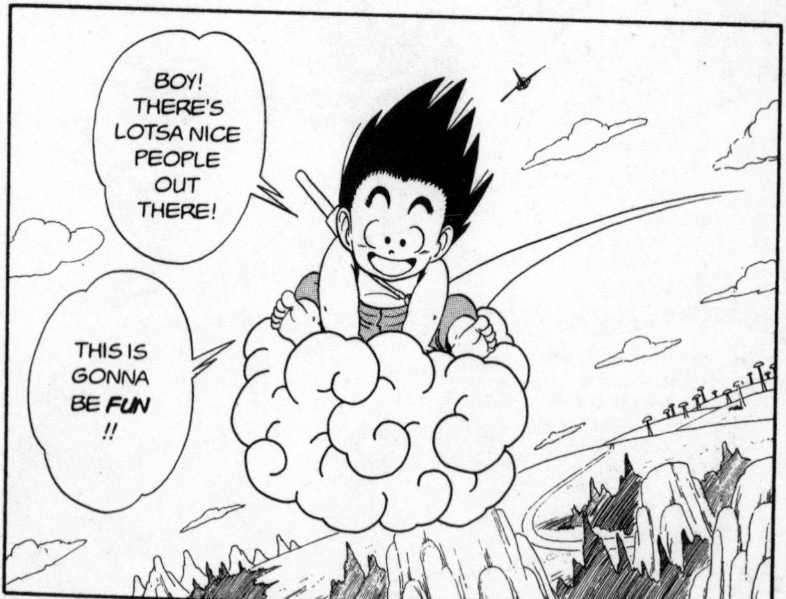
BOY! THERE'S LOTSA NICE PEOPLE OUT THERE!
THIS IS GONNA BE **FUN** !!

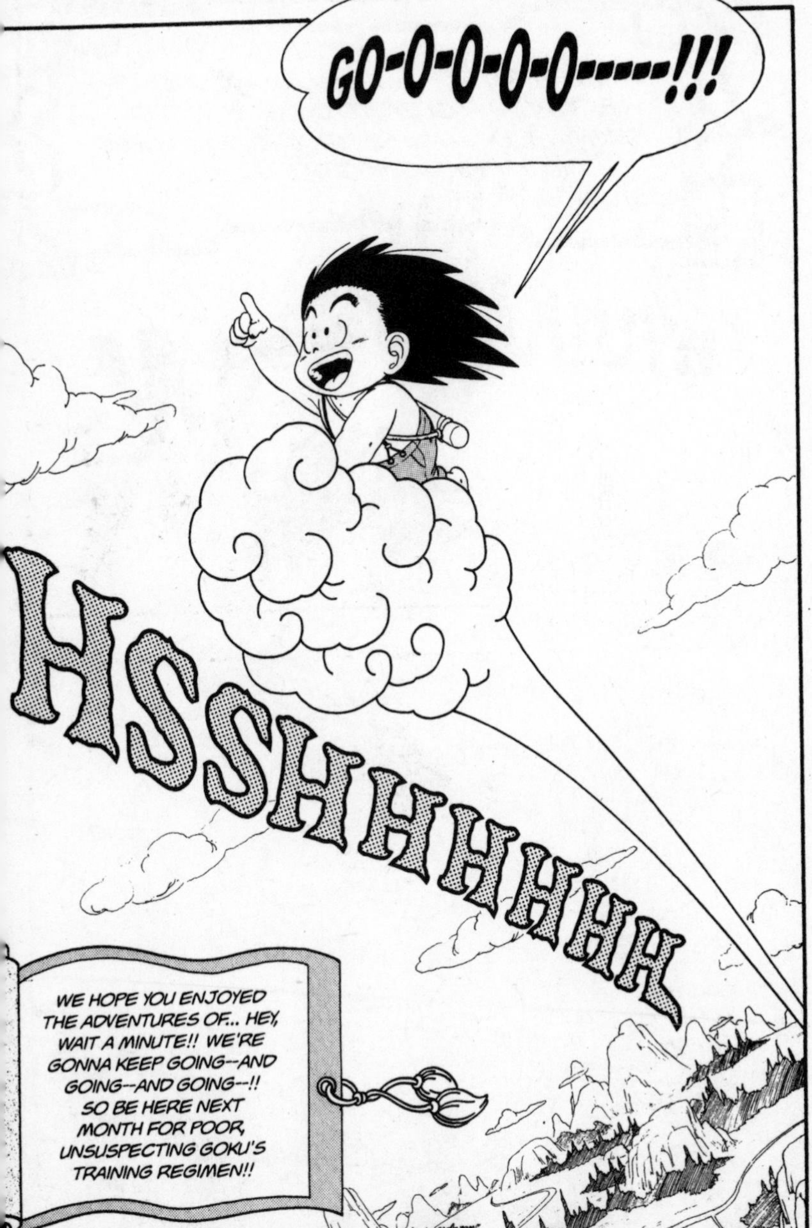
GO-O-O-O-O-----!!!
HSSHHHHHH
WE HOPE YOU ENJOYED THE ADVENTURES OF... HEY, WAIT A MINUTE!! WE'RE GONNA KEEP GOING--AND GOING--AND GOING--!! SO BE HERE NEXT MONTH FOR POOR, UNSUSPECTING GOKU'S TRAINING REGIMEN!!

Next: The Price of Power

Tale 24 • The High Price of Education

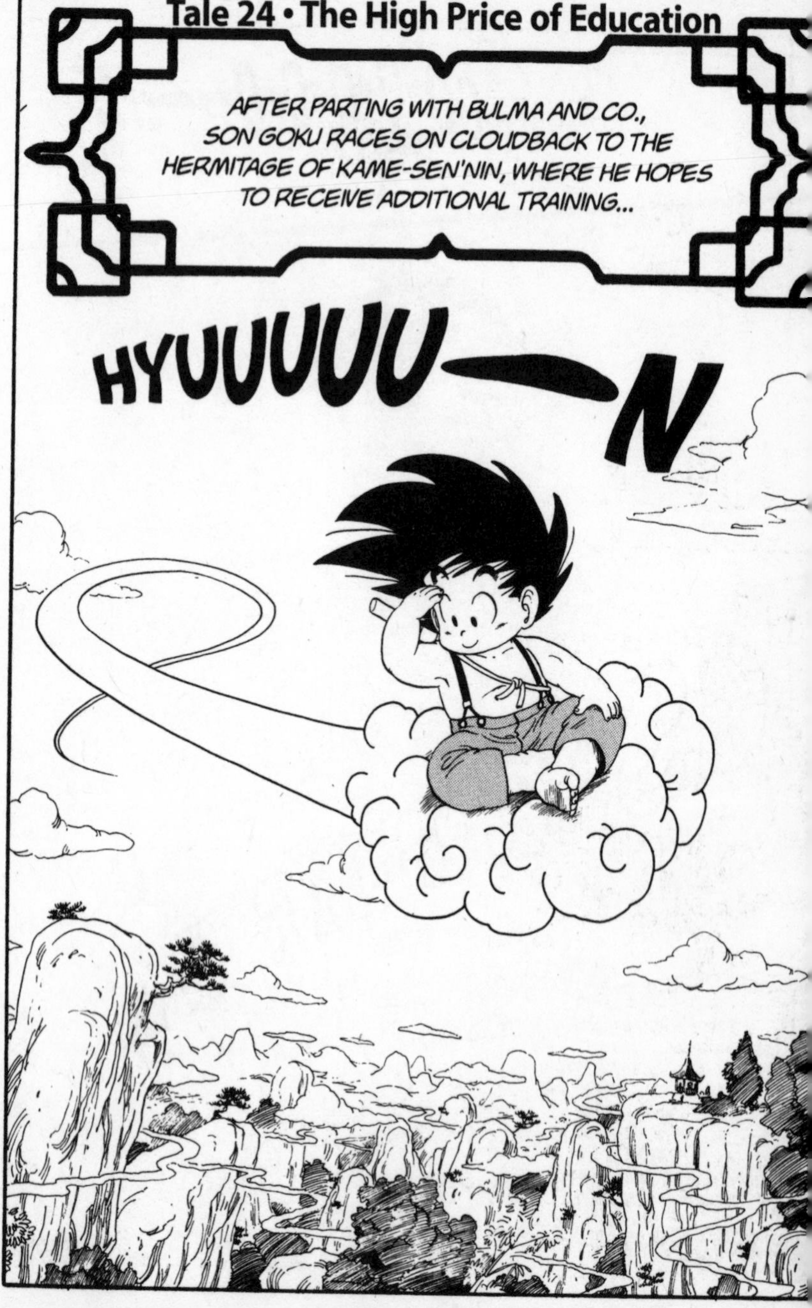
AFTER PARTING WITH BULMA AND CO., SON GOKU RACES ON CLOUDBACK TO THE HERMITAGE OF KAME-SEN'NIN, WHERE HE HOPES TO RECEIVE ADDITIONAL TRAINING...
HYUUUUU—N

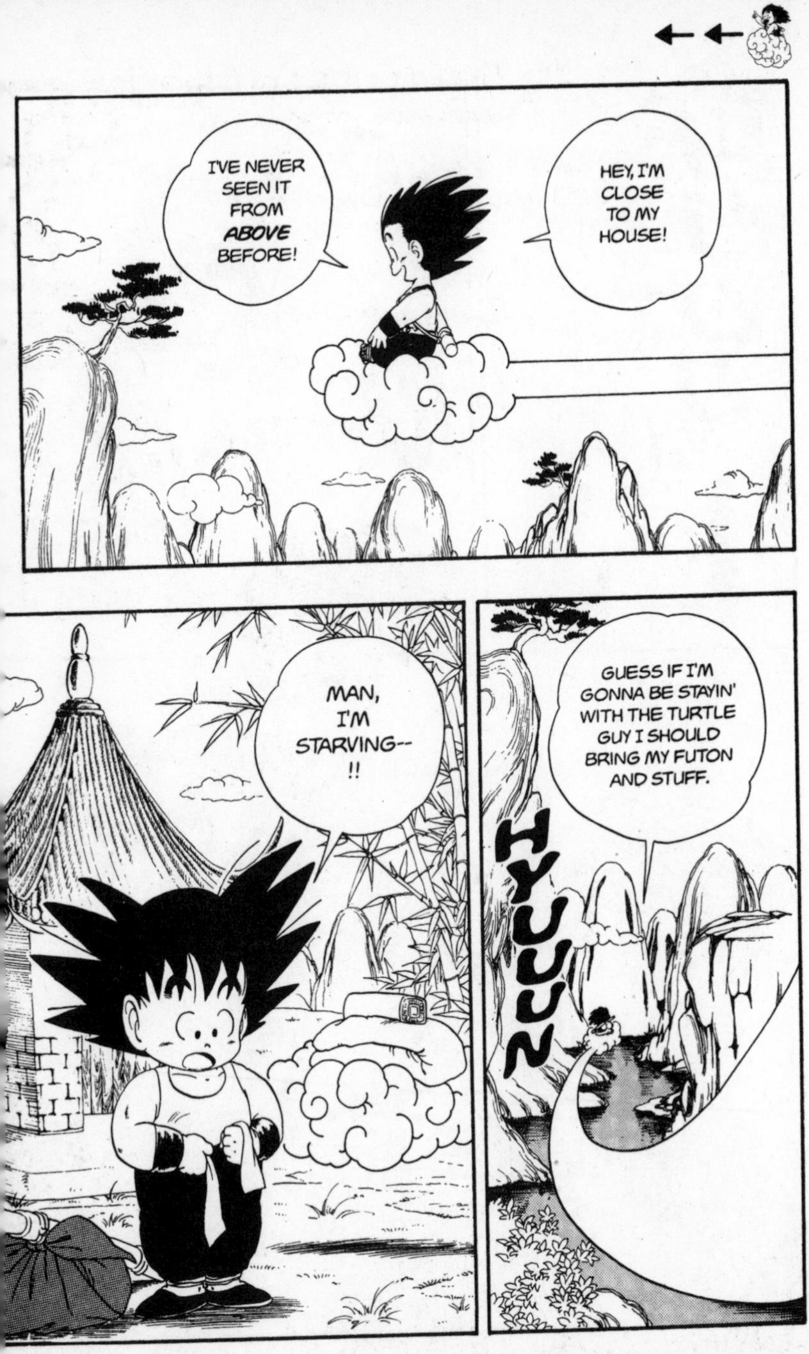
HEY, I'M CLOSE TO MY HOUSE!
I'VE NEVER SEEN IT FROM **ABOVE** BEFORE!
GUESS IF I'M GONNA BE STAYIN' WITH THE TURTLE GUY I SHOULD BRING MY FUTON AND STUFF.
HYUUUN
MAN, I'M STARVING-- !!

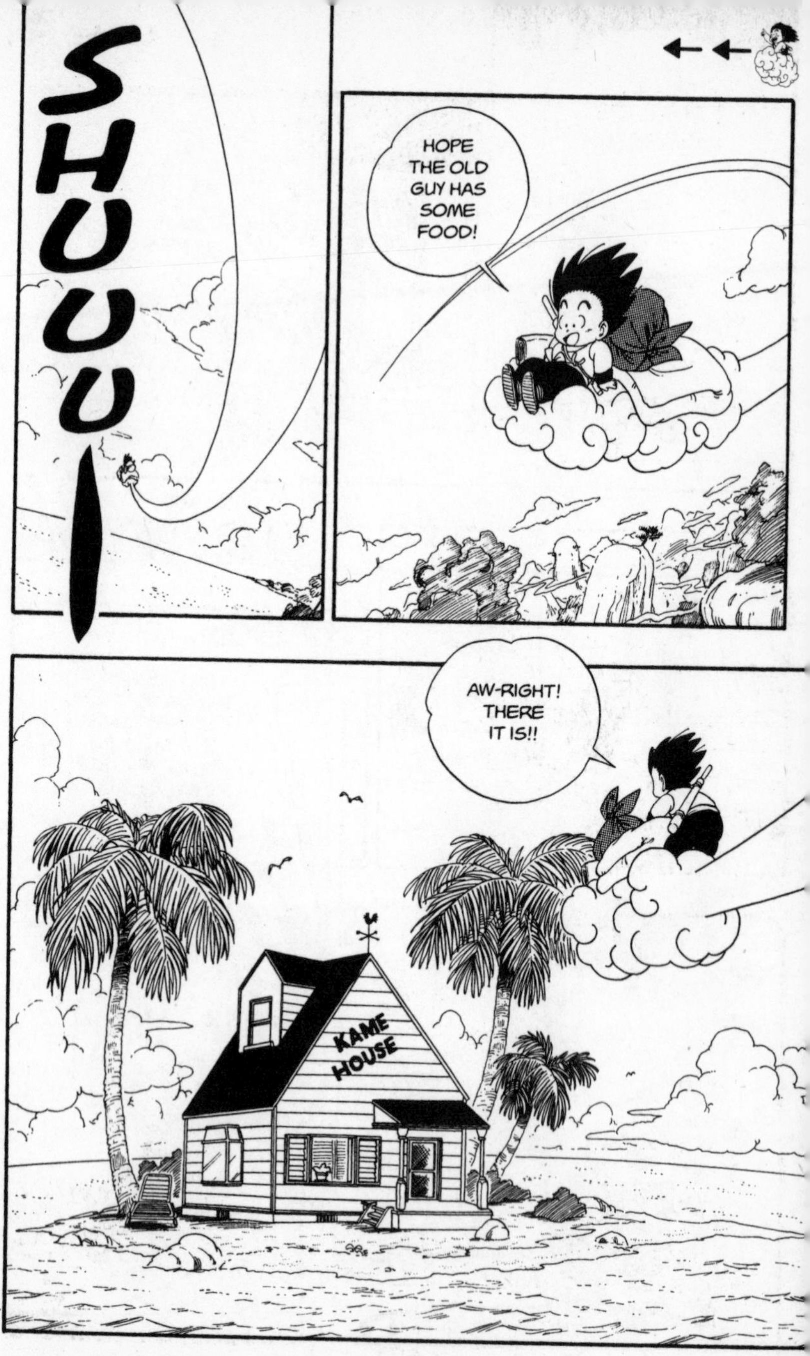
HOPE THE OLD GUY HAS SOME FOOD!
SHUUU
AW-RIGHT! THERE IT IS!!
KAME HOUSE

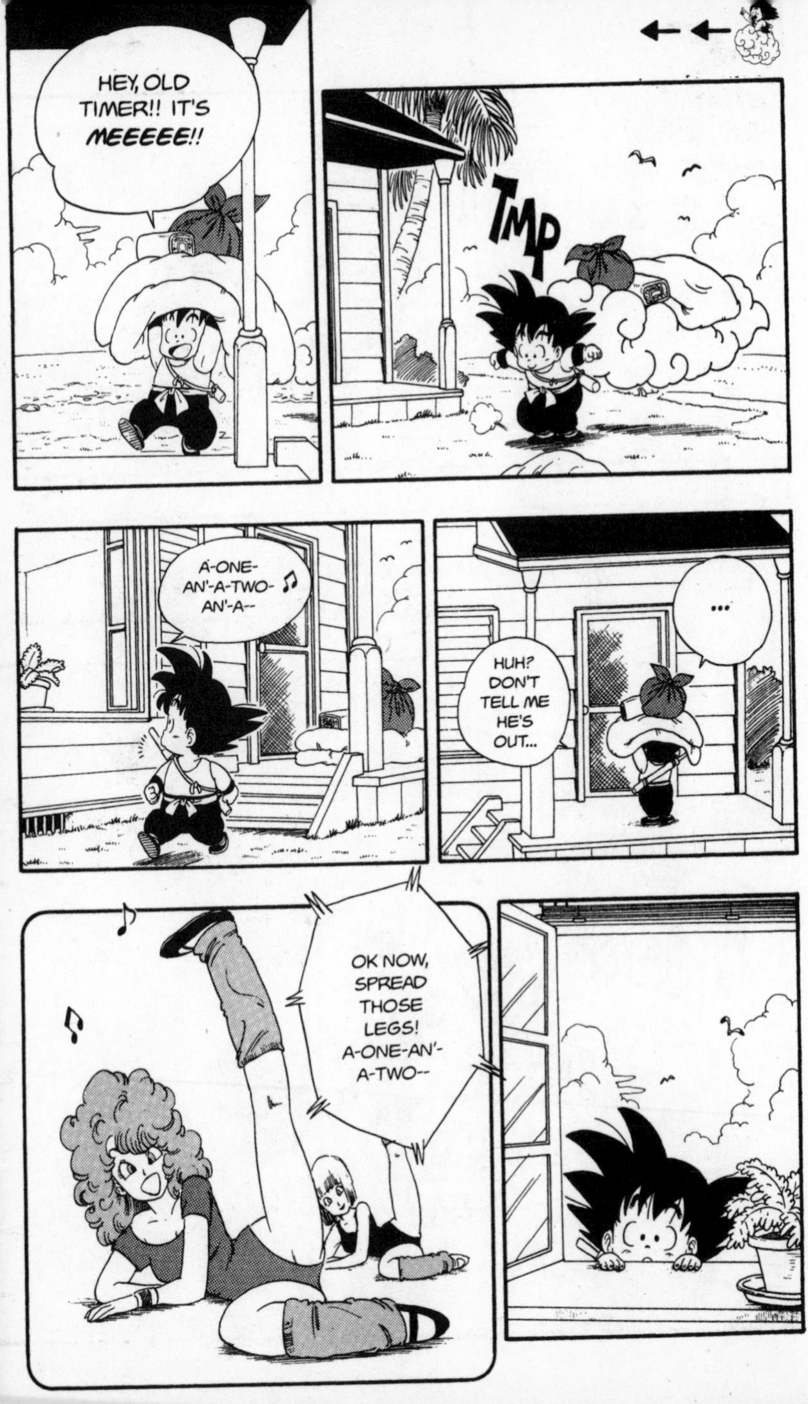
TMP
HEY, OLD TIMER!! IT'S MEEEEE!!
...
HUH? DON'T TELL ME HE'S OUT...
A-ONE-AN'-A-TWO-AN'-A--
OK NOW, SPREAD THOSE LEGS! A-ONE-AN'-A-TWO--

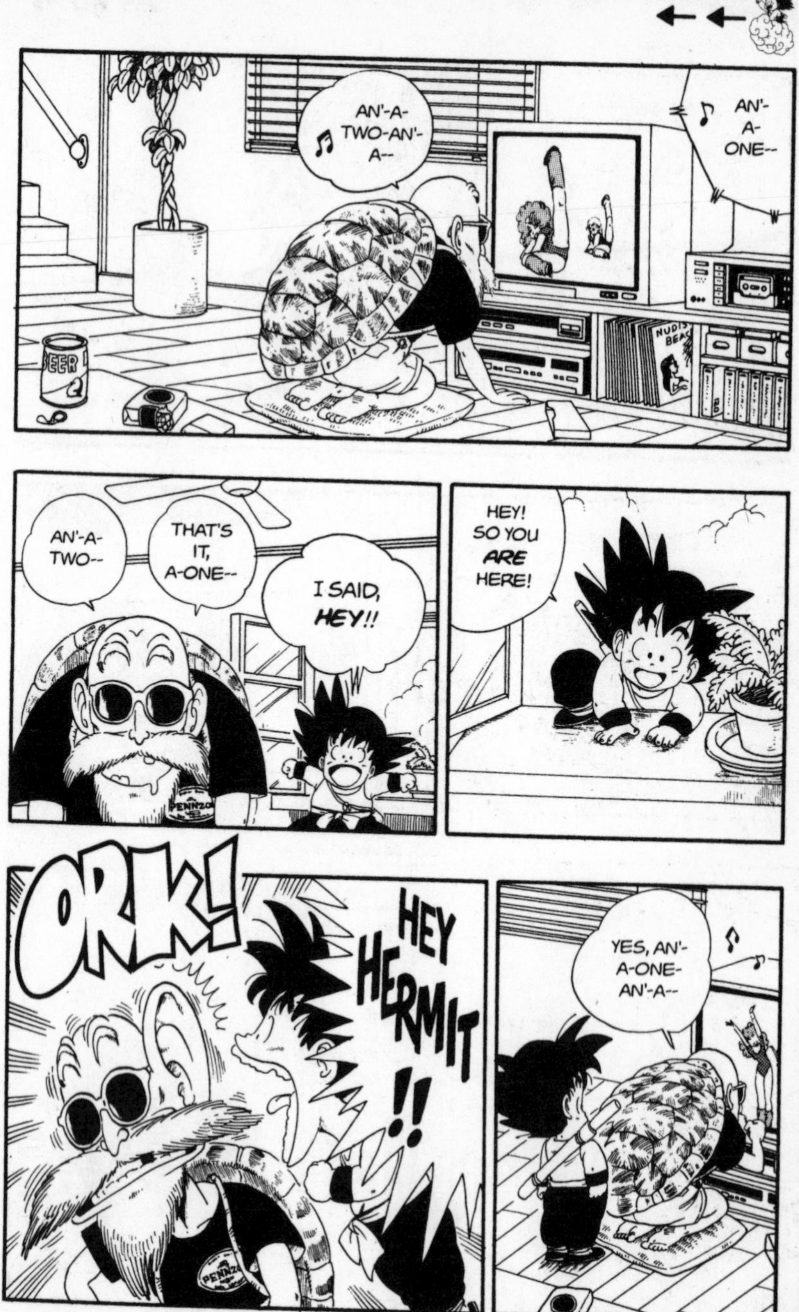
AN'-A-ONE--
AN'-A-TWO-AN'-A--
HEY! SO YOU ARE HERE!
THAT'S IT, A-ONE--
AN'-A-TWO--
I SAID, HEY!!
YES, AN'-A-ONE-AN'-A--
HEY HERMIT!!
ORK!

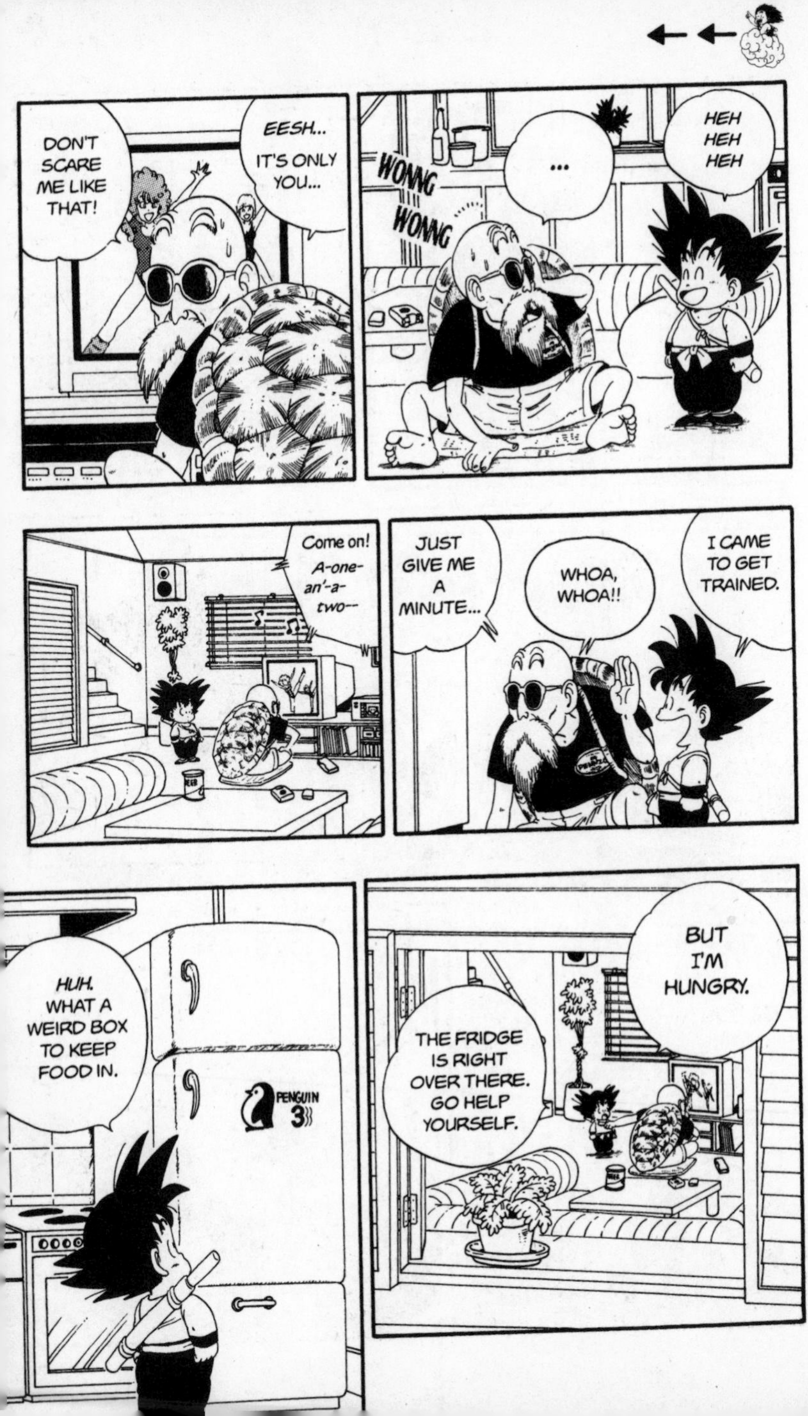
HEH HEH HEH
...
WONNG WONNG
EESH... IT'S ONLY YOU...
DON'T SCARE ME LIKE THAT!
I CAME TO GET TRAINED.
WHOA, WHOA!!
JUST GIVE ME A MINUTE...
Come on! A-one-an'-a-two--
BUT I'M HUNGRY.
THE FRIDGE IS RIGHT OVER THERE. GO HELP YOURSELF.
HUH. WHAT A WEIRD BOX TO KEEP FOOD IN.
PENGUIN 3

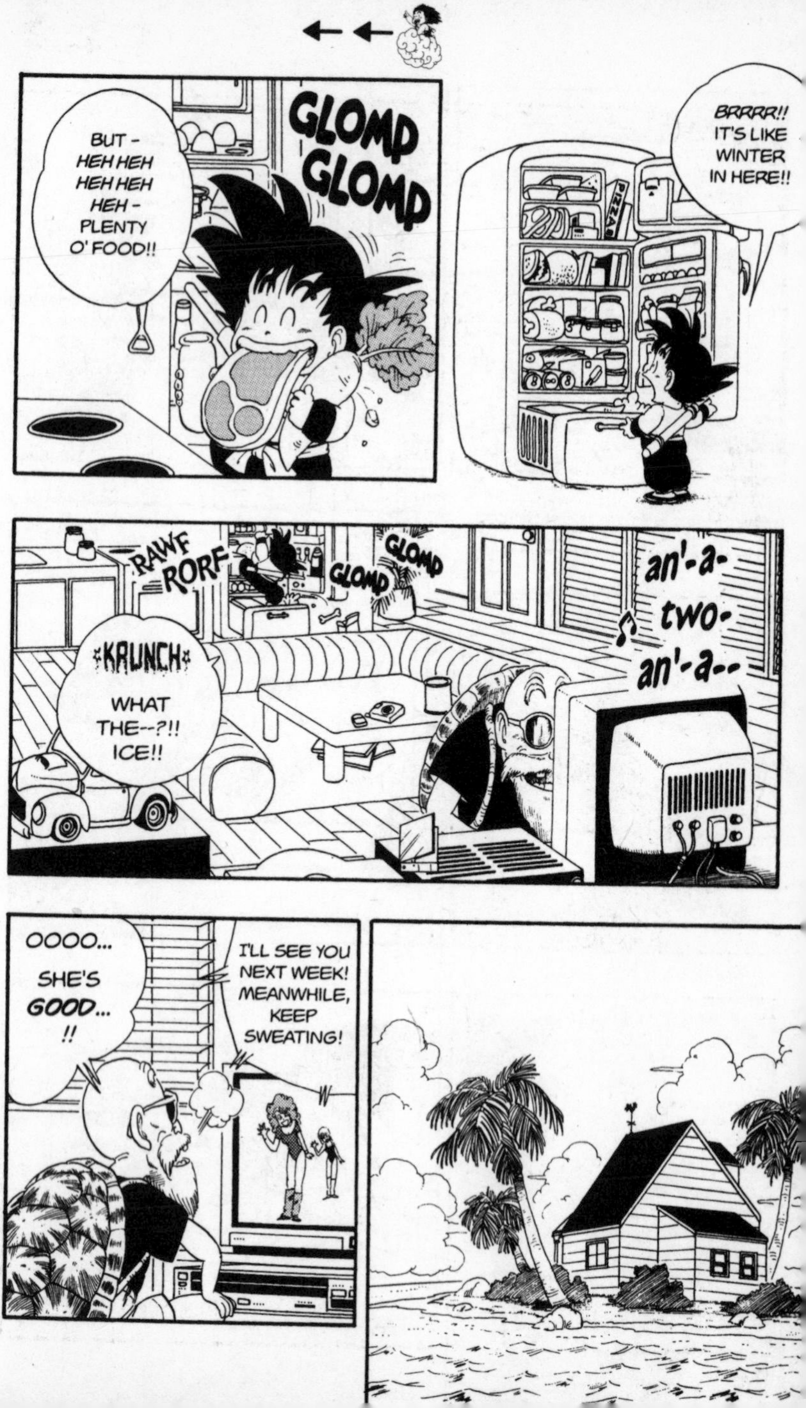
BRRRR!! IT'S LIKE WINTER IN HERE!!
GLOMP GLOMP
BUT - HEH HEH HEH HEH HEH - PLENTY O' FOOD!!
an'-a- two- an'-a--
GLOMP
GLOMP
RAWF RORF
KRUNCH
WHAT THE--?!! ICE!!
I'LL SEE YOU NEXT WEEK! MEANWHILE, KEEP SWEATING!
OOOO... SHE'S GOOD... !!

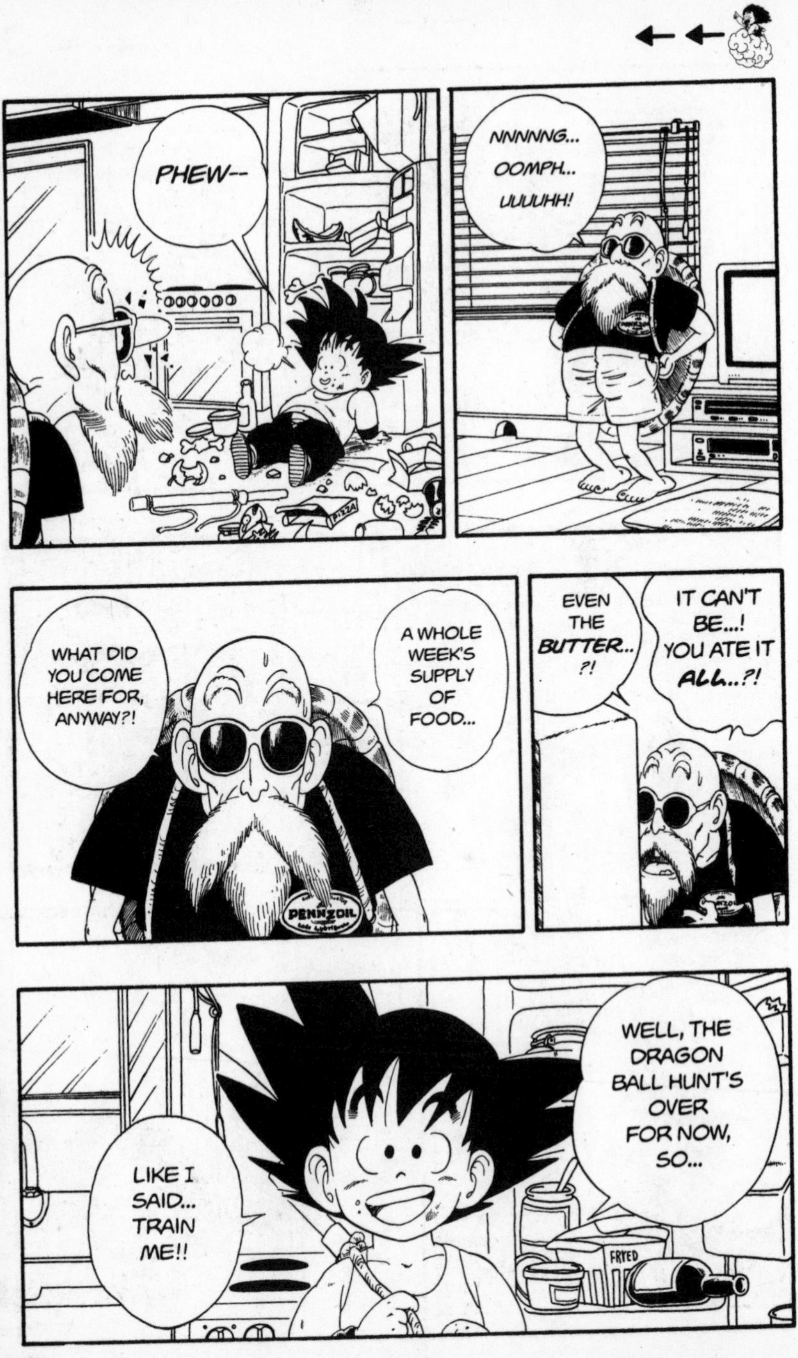
NNNNNG... OOMPH... UUUUHH!
PHEW--
PIZZA
IT CAN'T BE...! YOU ATE IT ALL...?!
EVEN THE BUTTER...?!
A WHOLE WEEK'S SUPPLY OF FOOD...
WHAT DID YOU COME HERE FOR, ANYWAY?!
PENNZOIL
WELL, THE DRAGON BALL HUNT'S OVER FOR NOW, SO...
LIKE I SAID... TRAIN ME!!
FRYED

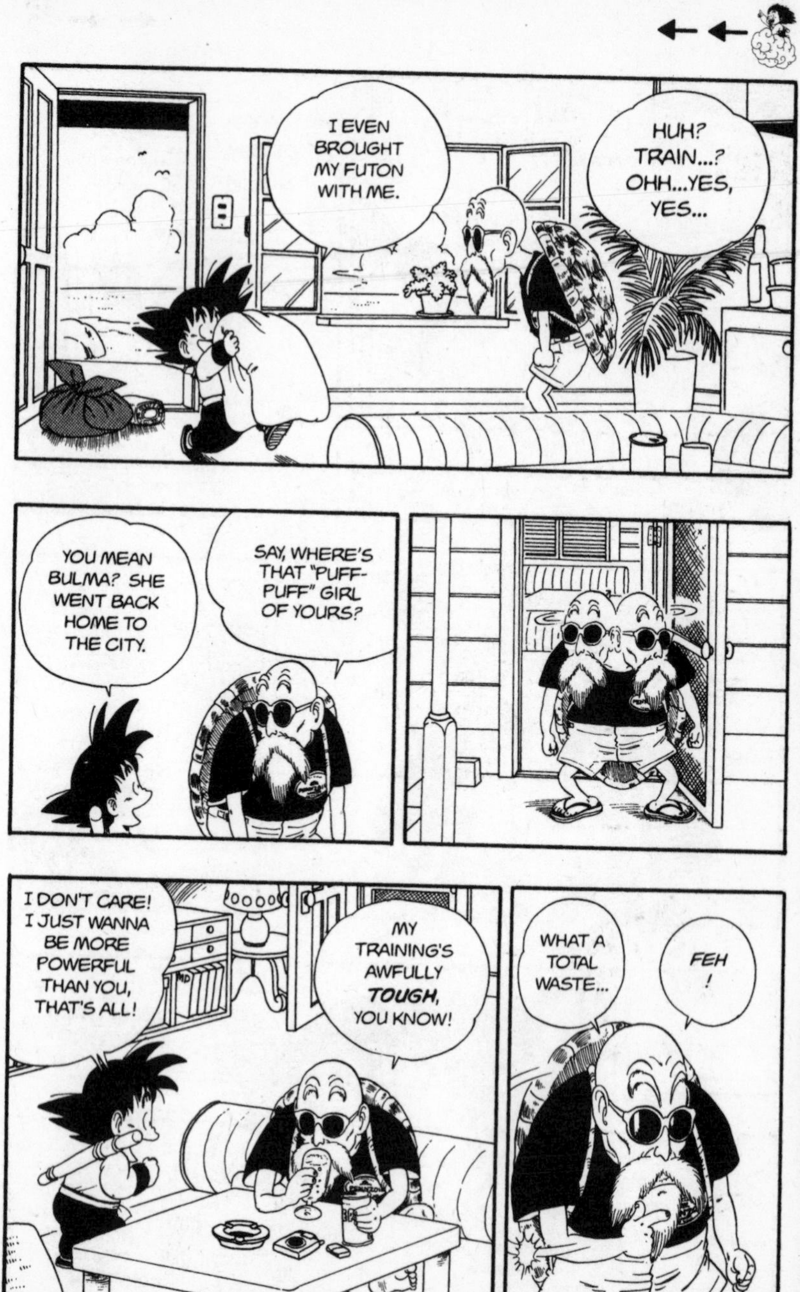
HUH? TRAIN...? OHH...YES, YES...
I EVEN BROUGHT MY FUTON WITH ME.
SAY, WHERE'S THAT "PUFF-PUFF" GIRL OF YOURS?
YOU MEAN BULMA? SHE WENT BACK HOME TO THE CITY.
FEH!
WHAT A TOTAL WASTE...
MY TRAINING'S AWFULLY **TOUGH**, YOU KNOW!
I DON'T CARE! I JUST WANNA BE MORE POWERFUL THAN YOU, THAT'S ALL!

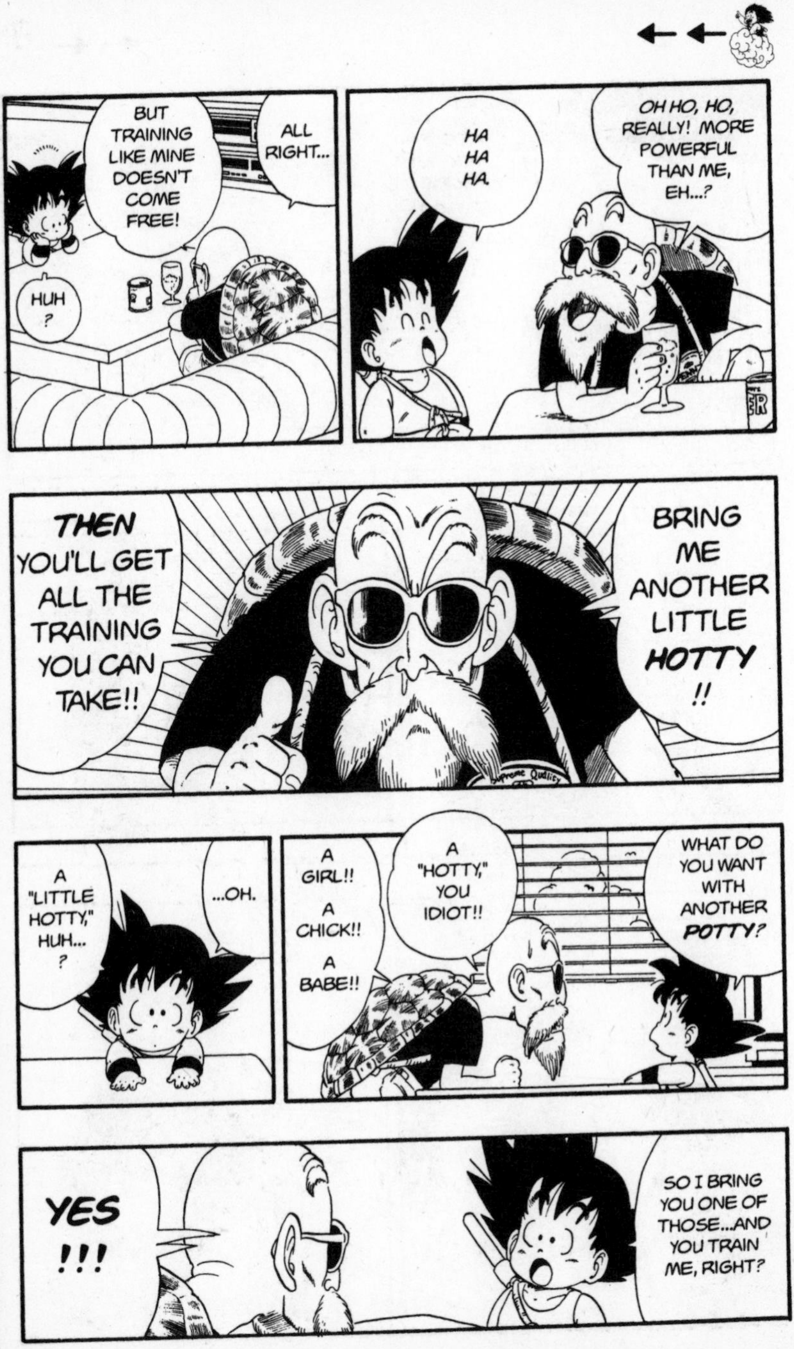
OH HO, HO, REALLY! MORE POWERFUL THAN ME, EH...?
HA HA HA.
ALL RIGHT...
BUT TRAINING LIKE MINE DOESN'T COME FREE!
HUH ?
BRING ME ANOTHER LITTLE HOTTY !!
THEN YOU'LL GET ALL THE TRAINING YOU CAN TAKE!!
WHAT DO YOU WANT WITH ANOTHER POTTY?
A "HOTTY," YOU IDIOT!!
A GIRL!! A CHICK!! A BABE!!
...OH.
A "LITTLE HOTTY," HUH... ?
SO I BRING YOU ONE OF THOSE...AND YOU TRAIN ME, RIGHT?
YES !!!

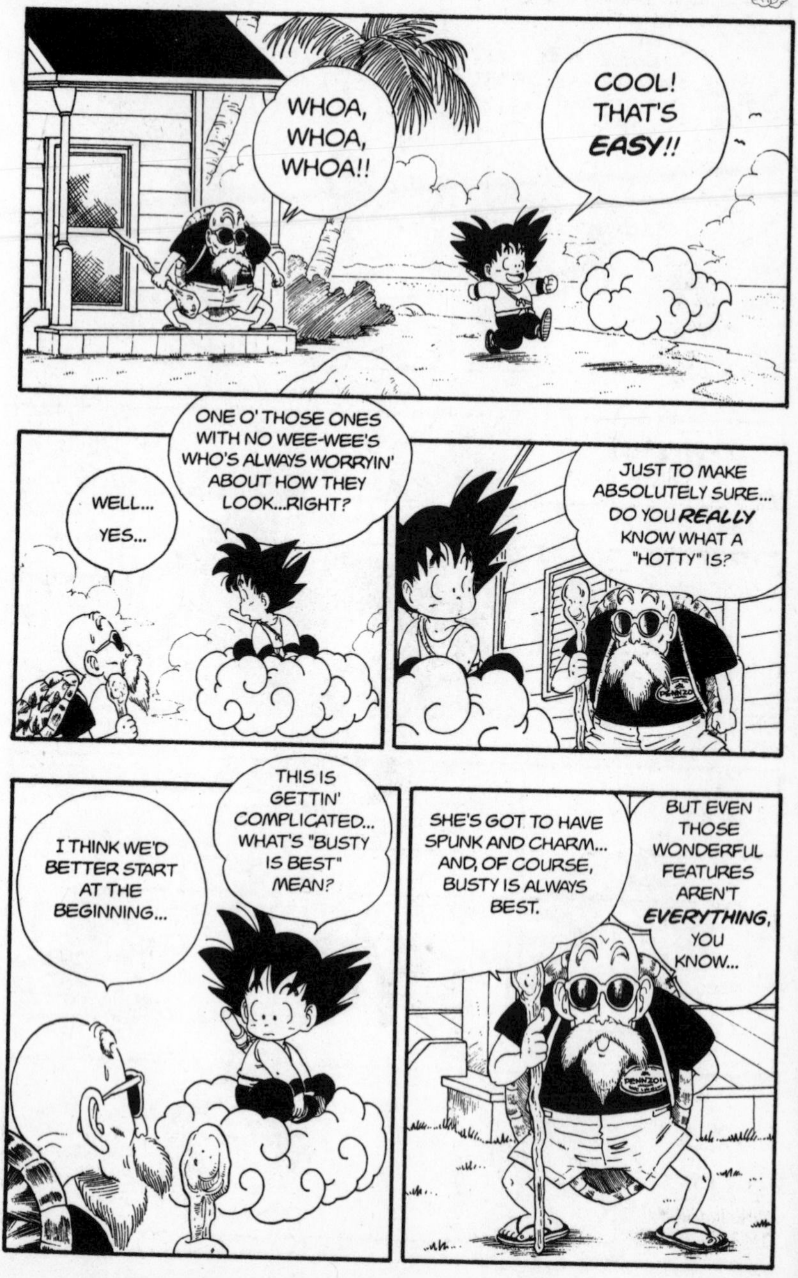
COOL! THAT'S EASY!!
WHOA, WHOA, WHOA!!
JUST TO MAKE ABSOLUTELY SURE... DO YOU REALLY KNOW WHAT A "HOTTY" IS?
ONE O' THOSE ONES WITH NO WEE-WEE'S WHO'S ALWAYS WORRYIN' ABOUT HOW THEY LOOK...RIGHT?
WELL... YES...
BUT EVEN THOSE WONDERFUL FEATURES AREN'T EVERYTHING, YOU KNOW...
SHE'S GOT TO HAVE SPUNK AND CHARM... AND, OF COURSE, BUSTY IS ALWAYS BEST.
THIS IS GETTIN' COMPLICATED... WHAT'S "BUSTY IS BEST" MEAN?
I THINK WE'D BETTER START AT THE BEGINNING...

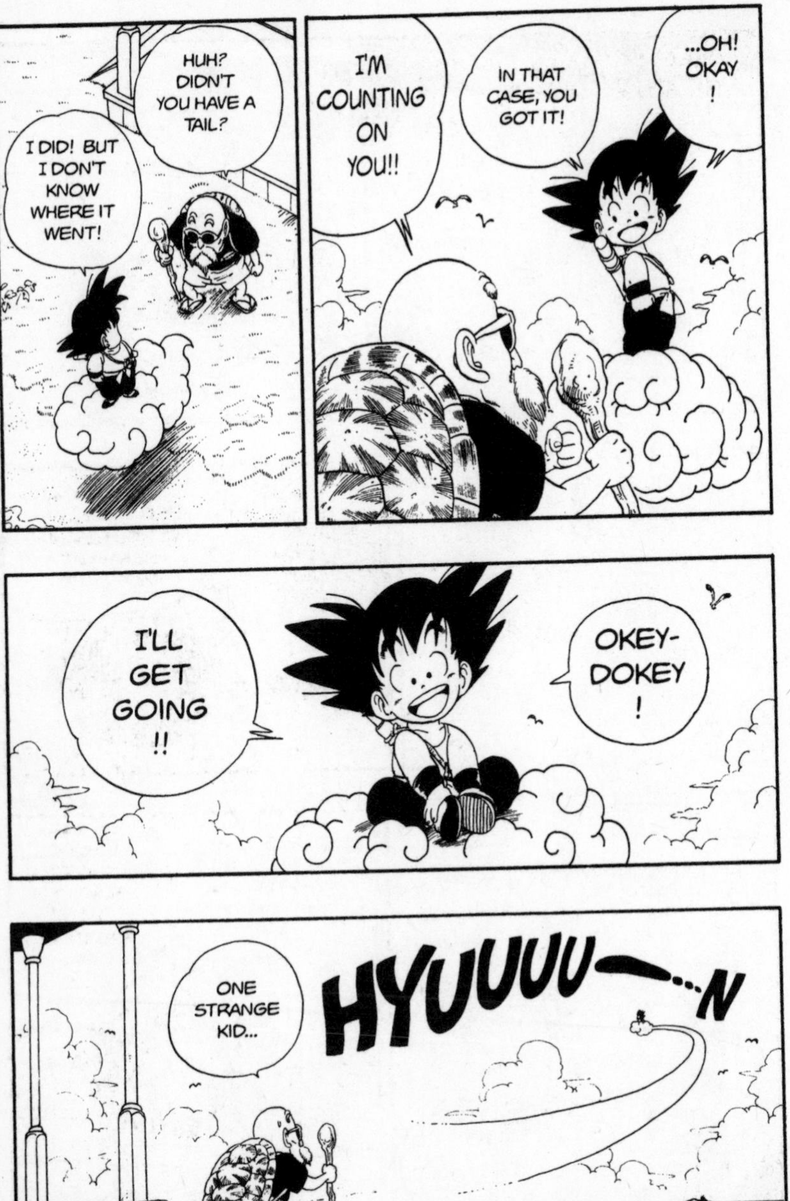
...OH! OKAY!
IN THAT CASE, YOU GOT IT!
I'M COUNTING ON YOU!!
HUH? DIDN'T YOU HAVE A TAIL?
I DID! BUT I DON'T KNOW WHERE IT WENT!
OKEY-DOKEY!
I'LL GET GOING!!
HYUUUU—...N
ONE STRANGE KID...

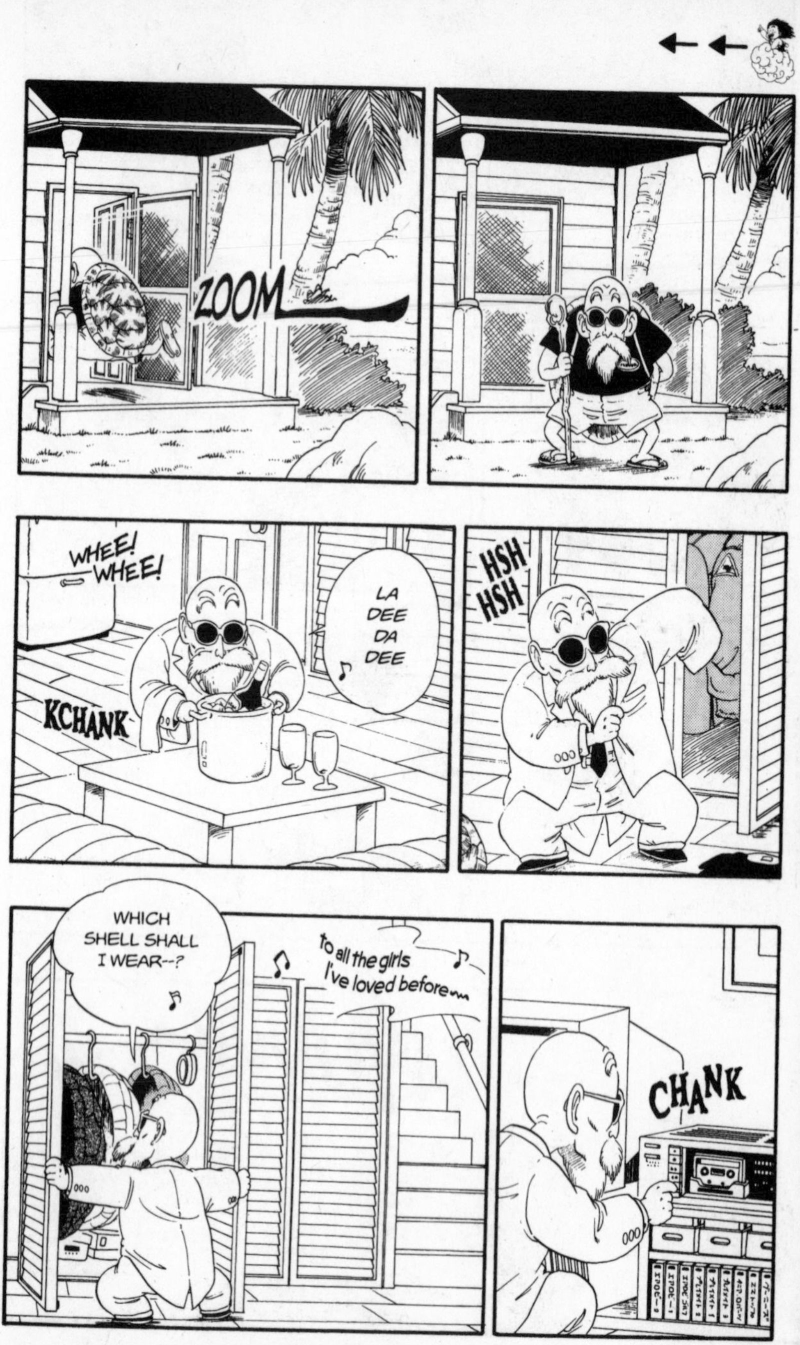
ZOOM
HSH HSH
WHEE! WHEE!
LA DEE DA DEE
KCHANK
CHANK
to all the girls I've loved before...
WHICH SHELL SHALL I WEAR--?

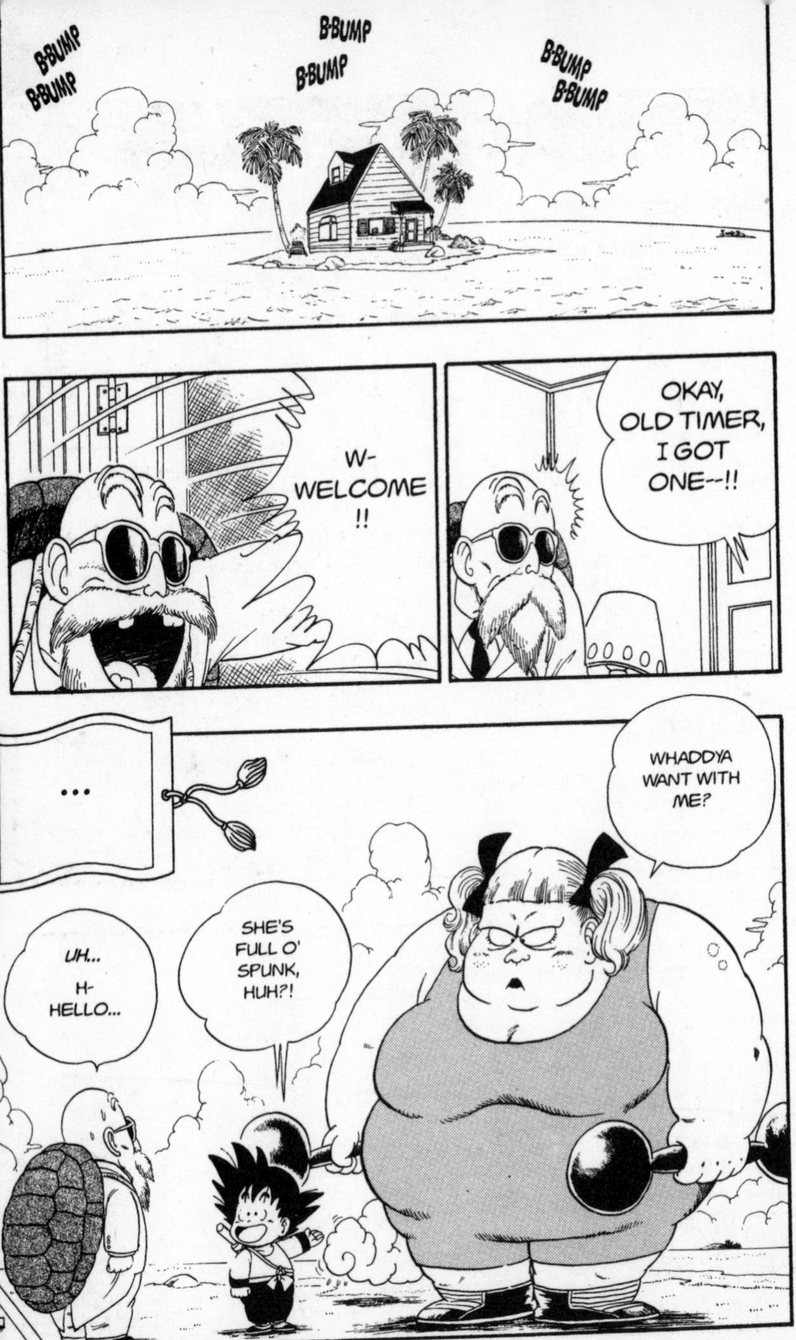
B-BUMP B-BUMP
B-BUMP B-BUMP
B-BUMP B-BUMP
OKAY, OLD TIMER, I GOT ONE--!!
W- WELCOME !!
WHADDYA WANT WITH ME?
...
SHE'S FULL O' SPUNK, HUH?!
UH... H- HELLO...

NEXT: Cue Ball, Corner Pocket

Akira Toriyama's "ASK ME ANYTHING" Corner!

That's right! These are actual questions asked by Japanese readers and answered by Akira Toriyama in the original **Dragon Ball** Vols. 1-6! (Sorry, Toriyama is too busy to do these sessions nowadays.)

Q. Hi. You always make excellent manga and I get a good laugh out of them. Your characters have wonderful personalities; if I'm feeling down, they always make me feel better. Please keep making such great characters! (Especially the cute girls.)

Yuji Chiba
Saitama Prefecture

A. Well, thank you very much. I'm pleased to hear your comments. I'll keep working hard on my manga.

Q. Hello Akira Toriyama-*sensei*. I'm a third-year middle school student [equivalent of an American high school freshman—Ed.]. Every week I read **Dragon Ball** in **Weekly Shonen Jump** [the Japanese manga magazine where **Dragon Ball** was first printed—Ed.], because your drawings are great and your jokes are always funny. I think that's why you've got so many readers. Goku is nice and always cool, and Kame-Sen'nin is always a pervert. I'm always telling everyone at school to buy **Weekly Shonen Jump**. Please take care of your health and keep up the funny gags.

Kazuhiko Sato
Miyagi Prefecture

A. Thanks for your support. By the way,

when you tell people to buy my manga, please recommend **Shonen Jump**.

Q. Hello. My friend Dai-chan and I were walking past this house and a big dog and a little dog started chasing after us. I felt like crying, and we both ran. I was scared, I can't forget about what happened. Have you ever experienced anything like this?

Hidemori Okano
Ibaraki Prefecture

A. When I was young, I too was chased by a dog. But dogs seem to like chasing things that run away from them, so next time you see one, it may be better if you walk calmly past it. If you make friends with dogs, they can be really loveable. (I know this letter has nothing to do with **Dragon Ball**.)

Q. I hope you are doing well. Every week I buy **Jump** to read **Dragon Ball**. I especially like Kame-Sen'nin. Please have him play a bigger role in the series. Bye.

Taisuke Fujiwara
Saitama Prefecture

A. Hmmm…Kame-Sen'nin, it seems you have a fan.

Kame-Sen'nin: Of course! There's nobody better when it comes to martial arts! So, Taisuke Fujiwara, eh?…Hey, wait a minute! That's a guy's name! I'd rather have female fans. Girls, send me fan mail!

Q. Hello. I'm writing you for the first time
CONTINUED ON PAGE 191

because I have a favor to ask. When is the first **Dragon Ball** graphic novel going to come out? Please let me know!

Kaoru Okino
Hiroshima Prefecture

A. It's out! The one you're reading right now is Vol. 2.

Q. Hello *sensei*. Please allow me to ask you some questions:

(1) How long does it take for you to create one chapter of **Dragon Ball**?
(2) Do you draw the backgrounds yourself?
(3) How many assistants do you have?
(4) Does your assistant live at your house?

Hajime Higaki
Mie Prefecture

A. (1) It takes me about five days to think of the story and draw it all. I draw one chapter a week. (2) I draw the backgrounds if it's the first time they show up, otherwise it's mostly my assistant that draws them. If there's a lot of scenery to draw then I'll also draw some of it. (3) I have one assistant named Matsuyama. If things get really busy his wife also helps out. (4) He commutes. He doesn't have to draw every day. Having him come two days a week is sufficient.

Q. I really like **Dragon Ball**. I store my graphic novels in plastic bags and always wash my hands before reading them. That's how much I like **Dragon Ball**. Please keep up the good work and come out with the next volume soon. Thank you.

Kazuo Takahashi
Tokyo

A. You're a good boy! A very good boy! Yes, you're good…but that sure sounds like a hassle…

Q. Hello Toriyama-*sensei*. Are you hand-some?

Eriko Hirano
Hyogo Prefecture

A. Yes!!!

Q. Shen Long, mighty dragon god! Please answer my wish and allow my letter to be printed in Toriyama's "Ask Me Anything" Corner.

Isami Gunbara
Kagoshima Prefecture

A. It has been printed. The power of the Dragon Balls is incredible, isn't it? (By the way, this won't work for anyone else who tries this.)

Q. Hello Toriyama-*sensei*. I always enjoy reading **Dragon Ball**. By the way, when will Vol. 19 of **Dr. Slump** come out? I'm looking forward to reading it.

Kenichi Yatsuka
Shizuoka Prefecture

A. Uh…**Dr. Slump** ended with Vol. 18. No matter how long you wait, even if you become an old man, Vol. 19 won't be coming out…

Q. I have all the **Jumps** with **Dr. Slump** and **Dragon Ball**. I also have Vols. 1-4 of Masakazu Katsura's **Wingman**. I am a great fan of both you and Katsura-*sensei*. But if I had to choose, I think you are cooler and more contemporary.

Sakura Yoshino
Kanagawa Prefecture

A. You are a good girl! A very good girl! I'm sure you'll grow up to be a great woman.

Q. Hello *sensei*. I bought **Dragon Ball** Vol. 1. The drawings and the story are so cute that even a girl like me loves it.

CONTINUED ON PAGE 192

Ikumi Akita
Gifu Prefecture

A. Thank you! I hope that more girls like you become fans.

Q. I have all of your comics. I read **Shonen Jump** every week. Here is my question for you: is Kame-Sen'nin based on Shibui ("Cool Old Guy") Kami-sama [not the same character as Kami-sama in **Dragon Ball**—Ed.] from **Dr. Slump** Vol. 17? They look just the same, except that Kame-Sen'nin has sunglasses.

Katsuya Miyoshi
Hyogo Prefecture

A. Wow, you're sharp! You are correct!! I just put sunglasses on Shibui Kami-sama. I really liked that old guy, so I wanted to use him in **Dragon Ball**.

Q. I have four questions for Akira Toriyama-*sensei*:
　　　(1) Were you good at drawing manga even when you were in elementary school?
　　　(2) You draw a lot of naughty stuff in your comics. Is this naughty of you?
　　　(3) Do you own a video game console?
　　　(4) Please continue to draw great manga.

Masahiro Kojima
Osaka Prefecture

A. (1) I was okay. (2) Yes! (3) I do own one, but it can distract me from working so I don't play that often. But when I do play, I'm really good at it! (4) Thank you for your words of encouragement.

Q. Ummm…I have a question. It doesn't have anything to do with **Dragon Ball**. When will Vol. 2 of **Toriyama Akira Marusaku Gekijô** ("Akira Toriyama's Insert-Adjective-Here Theatre") come out? You didn't forget about it, did you?

Takuya Miyamoto
Osaka Prefecture

A. Unfortunately, I am about 45 pages short of completing Vol. 2 of the Theatre book. As of now there are no plans to release it. I think it may come out after I finish the 45 pages. [Unfortunately **Toriyama Akira Marusaku Gekijô** is only available in Japan—Ed.]

Q. Toriyama-*sensei*, hello. Goodbye.

Satoshi Sasaki
Hiroshima Prefecture

A. Thank you.

Q. I really love **Dragon Ball**. I especially like Yamcha (go Yamcha, go!). I hope you continue to create more and more manga. I will be a fan of **Dragon Ball** until I die.

Mika Noma
Ehime Prefecture

A. Please support my work until you die! A lot of people give up halfway…

Q. I loan out my **Dragon Ball** comics for 100 yen for three days. Am I bad for doing this? (But everyone keeps borrowing them…)

Koji Asano
Aiichi Prefecture

A. Yes you're bad! You make money but I don't get anything!!

Q. I really like **Dragon Ball**. It's so much fun I can't stand it. I can't believe how happy I am that your manga exists.

Seiji Hayashi
Kyoto Prefecture

A. Hmm…if you like it that much, it makes me really happy as well.

CONTINUED ON PAGE 193

Q. Since Son Goku and Kuririn both trained with Kame-Sen'nin, please have "Goku vs. Kuririn" be the final match at the *Tenka'ichi Budôkai*!

Masayuki Katsumata • Osaka Prefecture

A. That's a very intriguing idea, but unfortunately it's too late for this tournament. The final match has already been set as Son Goku vs. Jackie Chun. But I think if there ever was a Goku vs. Kuririn match, Goku would win overwhelmingly.

Q. I always get a thrill reading **Dragon Ball**. I like **Dragon Ball** so much that my friends think I'm weird. I have almost all of the toys, I've bought all of the comics, and I record the TV show every week.

Yoko Yoshida
Shizuoka Prefecture

A. Wonderful! I hereby grant you a first *dan* black belt in Toriyama School Shorinji Kempo (Shaolin kung fu). You are my greatest student! Please continue to support my work.

Q. Just so you know, I really like Oolong tea and Pu'ar tea. By the way, on page 18 of volume 1, Son Goku says to Bulma, "I never saw another human before!" Wasn't Goku's "grandpa" (the guy who raised him) a human?

Yasuhiro Kubo
Nara Prefecture

A. W-Well…if you put it that way…yes. Oops…I made a mistake. Sorry, I apologize. You're also very smart to realize that I got the name "Pu'ar" from the name of the Chinese tea.

Q. Hello Toriyama-*sensei*. I have a question. If you had one whole day of uninterrupted free time, what would you do?

Naohiro Yonemoto
Tokushima Prefecture

A. Occasionally I do have a day of free time. [For **Dragon Ball**, Akira Toriyama drew an average of 15 pages every week for about 10 years—Ed.] I usually end up sleeping late and when I wake up I may go to the supermarket with my wife, or ride my bike, or see a movie, or work on a plastic model, or watch TV, or…I pretty much just putter away the day.

Q. Help! I'm running out of air! Please get some air and send it to me by *kame-hameha*. Bye.

Takeshi Mayumi
Mie Prefecture

A. Huh…? W-What are you talking about? I assume that you didn't write this letter while you were drowning… Uh… please continue to support my work.

Q. Okay, I've figured it out… **Dragon Ball** is based on the old Chinese legend **Saiyûki** ("Journey to the West"). Even the characters are the same: Bulma is Sanzô Hôshi, Oolong is Hakkai, Yamcha is Sagojo, and Shen Long is Sanzô Hôshi's horse. Even the order that they appear is the same. Am I wrong? I am a girl in my third year of middle school. [In Japan, junior high is always three years, and high school is always three years, so this is the same as being a 9th grader or a high school freshman—Ed.] I am afraid of the high school entrance exams!

Masae O'ouchi
Ibaraki Prefecture

A. It's true, in the beginning I set out to create a modern day version of **Saiyûki**. But soon it became difficult to remain true to the original, so I started ignoring it. So even though they have the same name, please consider my Son Goku and the monkey king Son Goku to be two different characters. However, I did get the Ox King story from **Saiyûki**. Good luck on your entrance exams!

CONTINUED ON PAGE 194

Q. At my house we have volumes 1-24 of the **Kinnikuman** ("Muscleman") manga and one **Kinnikuman** video.

Naoki Koyama
Okayama Prefecture

A. Umm… I'm sorry, Naoki. **Kinnikuman** is drawn by a person named Yudetamago…If you'd like, please take a look at **Dragon Ball**. Ha ha…ha…

Q. Hello. I really like **Dragon Ball**. I really like you too. I have a question for you. **Dr. Slump** lasted for 18 volumes. How long will **Dragon Ball** continue for?

Eiji Harada
Okayama Prefecture

A. Hmm…maybe for ten volumes or so. I think I'd like to make it short and sweet. But then again, there are lots of things I want to include in the story so I don't really know.

Q. This is the first time I've written to a manga artist. Do you think that the technique I thought up is good for **Dragon Ball**? [see below]

Tsuyoshi Maezawa
Hokkaido Prefecture

A. Wow! This technique is most certainly impressive. I may be able to use it in the manga. Thank you for your assistance!

Waterfall of Flames Technique

Q. I always look at your manga and use them as a reference to draw my own manga. I really respect you. I have all of your manga including **Dr. Slump**, **Dragon Ball**, **Hetappi Manga Kenkyujō** ("Lousy Manga Laboratory"), and **Toriyama Akira Marusaku Gekijō**. I keep them to use as reference material. In particular, **Hetappi Manga Kenkyujō** greatly influenced the way I draw manga.

Takeya Nakamura
Okinawa Prefecture

A. Thank you. You've complimented me so much I'm a bit embarrassed. Please keep up the hard work on drawing your own manga.

Q. I love **Dragon Ball**. I really like Bulma. Please continue to draw your great manga.

Mami Sato
Ibaraki Prefecture

A. Surprisingly, there are a great number of girls that say they like Bulma. Perhaps it's because her personality is a bit like a boy's. Personally, I don't really like harsh, selfish girls like Bulma.

Q. I was really happy to see Kuririn appear in the manga. (Although he hasn't made an appearance in a while.) Kuririn looks exactly like my daughter who is about to turn one year old.

Akina Deura (my daughter)
Shizuoka Prefecture

A. Thank you. So, your daughter looks exactly like Kuririn…I don't know how to respond to that. But I'm sure your daughter is very cute. By the way, does she have a nose?

Q. On the spines of the **Dragon Ball** graphic novels, so far you've drawn a Dragon Ball with one star for every volume of the series. What will you do if the series goes over seven volumes?

CONTINUED ON PAGE 195

Tatsuhira Koike
Saitama Prefecture

A. You're right! The spines with the drawings of the dragon and the Dragon Balls will end after the seventh volume. I am wondering myself what to do from the eighth volume on.

Q. I like Pu'ar. I told my brother that Pu'ar is a cat and he told me that Pu'ar is a mouse. Who is right?

Nobukatsu Sekigawa
Kanagawa Prefecture

A. Actually, Pu'ar is neither a cat nor a mouse, but I draw him a little bit like a cat.

Q. Over New Year's break, I made a stamp using your characters [see below]. Nine months from now, I am planning on using the dragon from **Dragon Ball** to make my New Year's greeting cards.

Kimio Nagasaki
Shizuoka Prefecture

A. This is a great stamp! I imagine it took quite a lot of work. I am really impressed. I look forward to seeing your dragon cards, please send me one when you're finished.

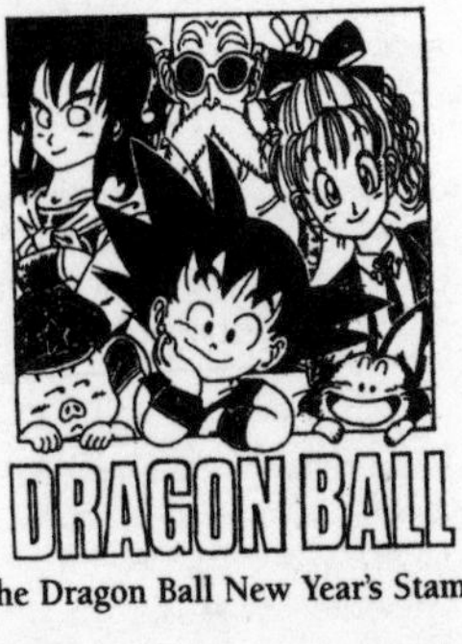
DRAGON BALL

The Dragon Ball New Year's Stamp

Q. The caricature that you draw of yourself in the comics looks like a dirty old man, so I thought that you probably looked like a dirty old man yourself. But I saw your photograph in **Shonen Jump** and you looked very handsome.

Yasuhiro Ando
Aichi Prefecture

A. Ha ha ha! You think so? You're right! I *do* look good! You're a great guy! Unfortunately, I just can't get too excited about a *guy* complimenting me like this…

Q. What are those six marks on Kuririn's face? Is it a scar? Please tell me.

Yasuto Tamagawa
Osaka Prefecture

A. Ah! You noticed it! The marks on Kuririn's forehead are incense burns. Sometimes you see these scars on Chinese monks in the movies. I thought I should add them because Kuririn's face is so plain.

Q. Often in the last page of your comic in **Shonen Jump** [the "free talk" page, where the artist answers letters from readers and talks about upcoming projects—Ed.], you write about how you have pet birds. I would like to become a manga artist, and I also love animals. I would love to draw manga and have a lot of pets.

Koki Yasuda
Osaka Prefecture

A. I think it's a great thing to be an animal lover, although if you are going to have pets you should be responsible for them. In my household we have a bird, a cat, and a dog. Actually, if I could, I would love to also have a goat and a chicken.

Akira Toriyama's "Ask Me Anything!" Corner will return in a later volume of the ***Dragon Ball*** *graphic novels!* •

Dr. SLUMP

SJ

by Akira Toriyama, the creator of *Dragon Ball* and *Dragon Ball Z*

Manga series on sale now!

When goofy inventor Senbei Norimaki creates a precocious robot named Arale, his masterpiece turns out to be more than he bargained for!

Dr. SLUMP

SHONEN JUMP GRAPHIC NOVEL

Story & Art by **Akira Toriyama**

volume 1

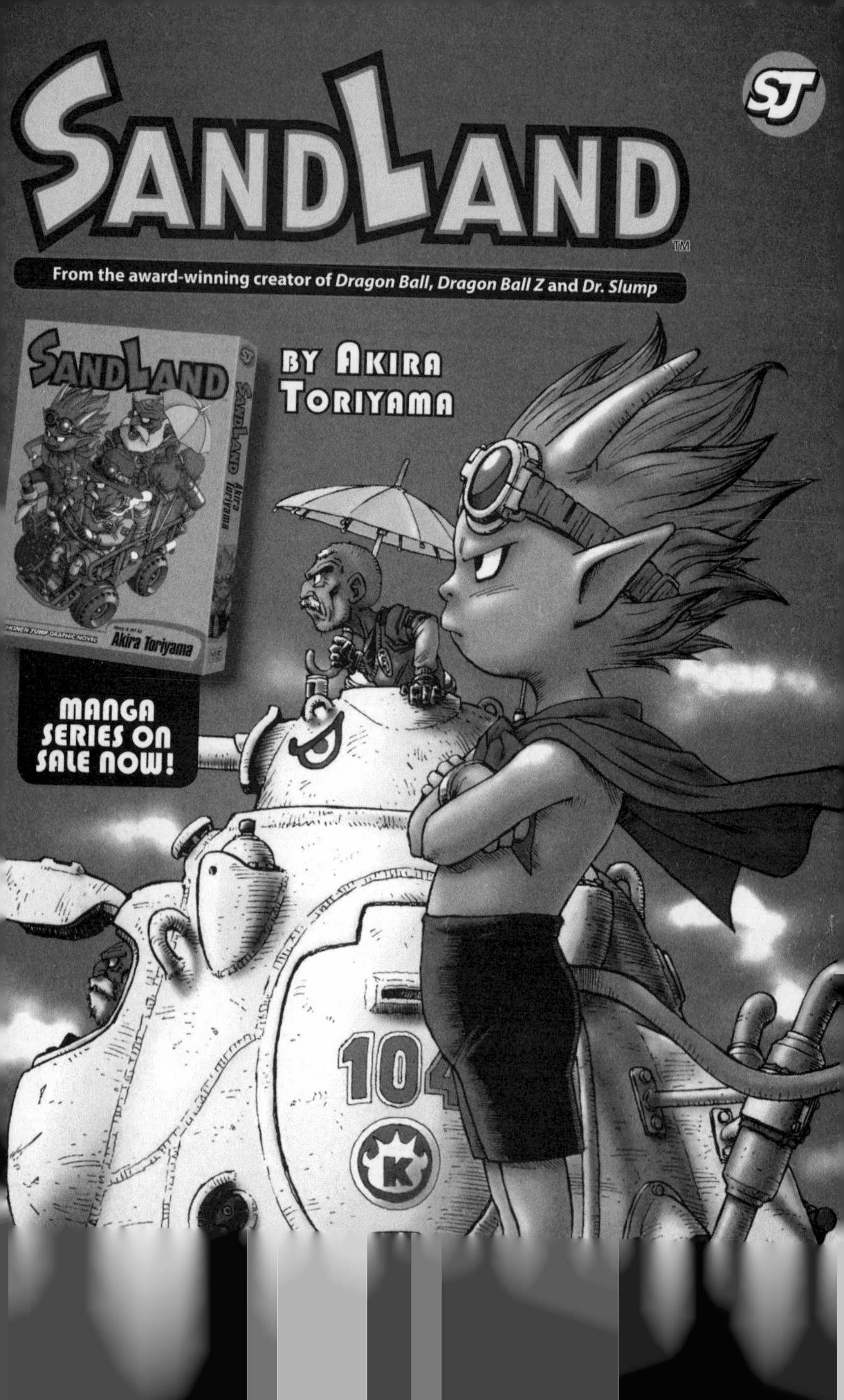
SJ
SANDLAND™
From the award-winning creator of Dragon Ball, Dragon Ball Z and Dr. Slump
BY AKIRA TORIYAMA
SANDLAND
Akira Toriyama
MANGA SERIES ON SALE NOW!
104
K

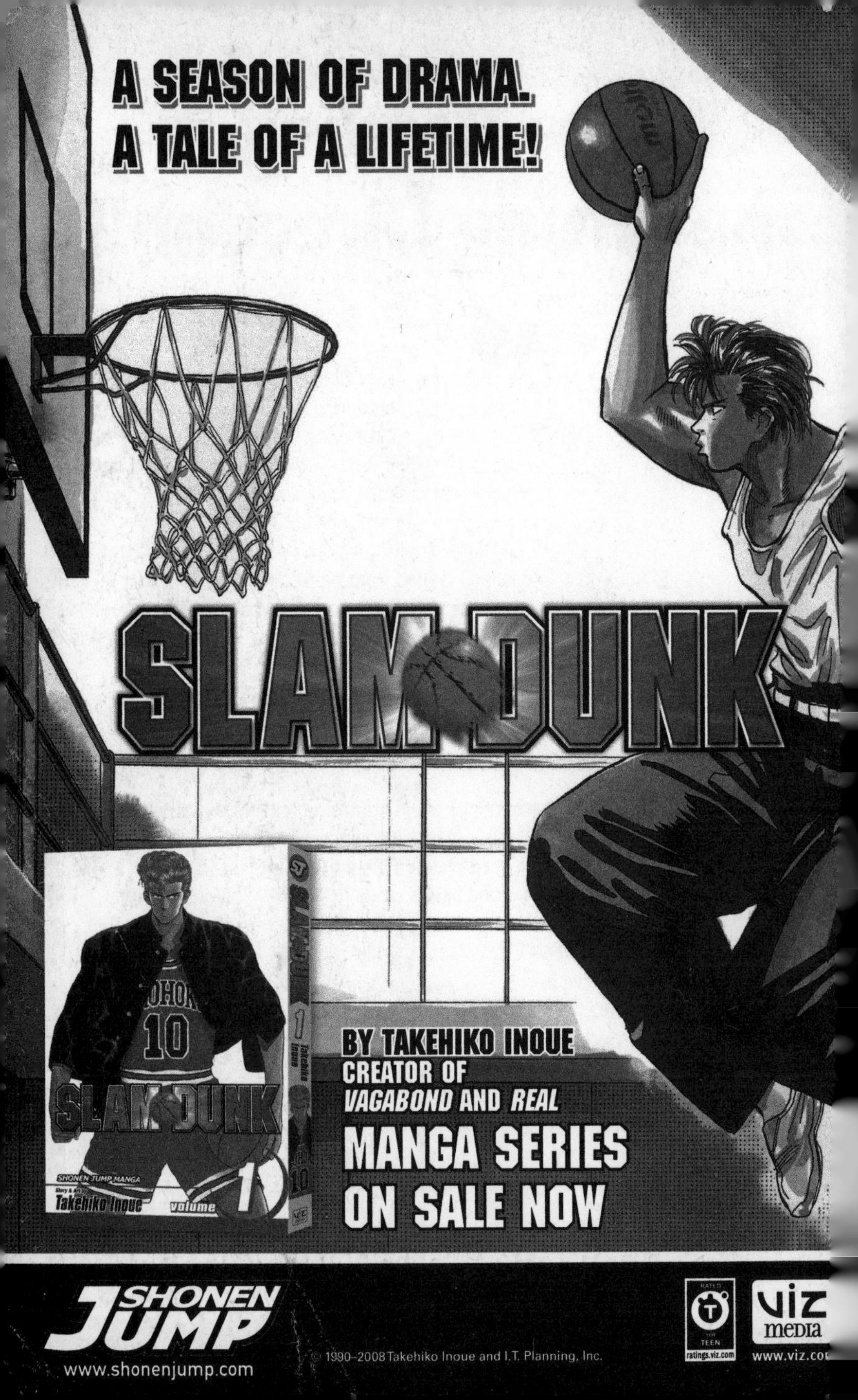
A SEASON OF DRAMA.
A TALE OF A LIFETIME!
SLAM DUNK
SHONEN JUMP MANGA
Story & Art by
Takehiko Inoue
volume 1
BY TAKEHIKO INOUE
CREATOR OF
VAGABOND AND REAL
MANGA SERIES
ON SALE NOW
SHONEN JUMP
www.shonenjump.com
© 1990–2008 Takehiko Inoue and I.T. Planning, Inc.
RATED T TEEN
ratings.viz.com
viz media
www.viz.co

You're Reading in the Wrong Direction!!

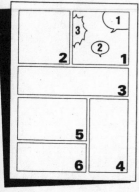

Whoops! Guess what? You're starting at the wrong end of the comic!

...It's true! In keeping with the original Japanese format, Akira Toriyama's world-famous **Dragon Ball** series is meant to be read from right to left, starting in the upper-right corner.

Unlike English, which is read from left to right, Japanese is read from right to left, meaning that action, sound effects and word-balloon order are completely reversed...something which can make readers unfamiliar with Japanese feel pretty backwards themselves. For this reason, manga or Japanese comics published in the U.S. in English have traditionally been published "flopped"—that is, printed in exact reverse order, as though seen from the other side of a mirror.

By flopping pages, U.S. publishers can avoid confusing readers, but the compromise is not without its downside. For one thing, a character in a flopped manga series who once wore in the original Japanese version a T-shirt emblazoned with "M A Y" (as in "the merry month of") now wears one which reads "Y A M"! Additionally, many manga creators in Japan are themselves unhappy with the process, as some feel the mirror-imaging of their art reveals otherwise unnoticeable flaws or skews in perspective.

In recognition of the importance and popularity of **Dragon Ball**, we are proud to bring it to you in the original unflopped format.

For now, though, turn to the other side of the book and let the adventure begin...!

—Editor